GERMAN FOREIGN POLICY
FROM
BISMARCK TO ADENAUER

TITLES OF RELATED INTEREST

GERMAN FOREIGN POLICY FROM BISMARCK TO ADENAUER

The limits of statecraft

KLAUS HILDEBRAND

Translated by Louise Willmot

London
UNWIN HYMAN
Boston   Sydney   Wellington

Published by the Academic Division of
Unwin Hyman Ltd
15/17 Broadwick Street, London W1V 1FP, UK

Unwin Hyman Inc.,
8 Winchester Place, Winchester, Mass. 01890, USA

Allen & Unwin (Australia) Ltd,
8 Napier Street, North Sydney, NSW 2060, Australia

Allen & Unwin (New Zealand) Ltd in association with the
Port Nicholson Press Ltd,
Compusales Building, 75 Ghuznee Street, Wellington 1, New Zealand

First published in 1989

British Library Cataloguing in Publication Data

Hildebrand, Klaus
    German foreign policy from Bismarck to
    Adenauer : the limits of statecraft.
    1.West Germany. Foreign relations, history
    I. Title
    327.43

ISBN 0-04-445070-2

Library of Congress Cataloging-in-Publication Data

Hildebrand, Klaus.
    [Staatskunst oder Systemzwang. English]
    German foreign policy from Bismarck to Adenauer : the limits of
statecraft / Klaus Hildebrand ; translated by Louise Willmot.
        p.   cm.
    Translation of: Staatskunst oder Systemzwang.
    Bibliography: p.
    Includes index.
    ISBN 0-04-445070-2
    1. Germany—Foreign relations—1871. 2. Germany (West)—Foreign
relations. 3. Bismarck, Otto, Fürst von, 1815–1898. 4. Adenauer,
Konrad, 1876–1967. I. Title.
DD221.H5713 1989
327.43′09′034--dc20   89-5693
                                                            CIP

Typeset in 10 on 12 point Garamond and printed in Great Britain by
The University Press, Cambridge.

Contents

Acknowledgements

Chapter 1, 'Great Britain and the foundation of the German Reich', first appeared as 'Grossbritannien und die deutsche Reichsgründung', in *Europa und die Reichsgründung. Preussen-Deutschland in der Sicht der grossen europäischen Mächte 1860–1880. Beiheft 6 der Historischen Zeitschrift*, ed. E. Kolb, (Munich: 1980), published by Oldenbourg-Verlag GmbH of Postfach 801 360, 8000 Munich 80. Chapter 2, 'Lord Clarendon, Bismarck and the problem of European disarmament, 1870. Possibilities and limitations in British-Prussian relations on the eve of the Franco-Prussian War', first appeared as 'Lord Clarendon, Bismarck und das Problem der europäischen Abrüstung. Möglichkeiten und Grenzen im britisch-preussichen Verhältnis am Vorabend des deutsch-französischen Krieges', in *Studien zur Geschichte Englands und der deutsch-britischen Beziehungen. Festschrift für Paul Kluke*, ed. L. Kettenacker, M. Schlenke, H. Seier (Munich: 1981), published by Wilhelm Fink Verlag of Nikolaistrasse 2, 8000 Munich 40. Chapter 3, 'Between alliance and antagonism. The problem of bilateral normality in British-German relations in the nineteenth century (1870–1914)', first appeared as 'Zwischen Allianz und Antagonismus. Das Problem bilateraler Normalität in den britisch-deutschen Beziehungen des 19.Jahrhunderts (1870–1914)', in *Weltpolitik, Europagedanke, Regionalismus. Festschrift für Heinz Gollwitzer zum 65.Geburtstag*, ed. H. Dollinger. H. Gründer, A. Hanschmidt (Aschendorff/Münster: 1982), published by Verlag Aschendorff GmbH & Co. of Soester Strasse 13, Postfach 1124, 4400 Münster. Chapter 4, 'The crisis of July 1914: The European security dilemma. Observations on the outbreak of the First World War', first appeared as 'Julikrise 1914: Das europäische Sicherheitsdilemma. Betrachtungen über den Ausbruch des Ersten Weltkrieges', in *Geschichte in Wissenschaft und Unterricht* 36 (1985), pp. 469–502 published by Klett-Verlag of Postfach 809, 7000 Stuttgart 1.

Chapter 5, 'Hitler's policy towards France until 1936', first appeared as 'Die Frankreichpolitik Hitlers bis 1936', in *Francia* 5 (1977). pp. 591–625, published by Artemis-Verlag of Matius-Strasse 8, 8000 Munich 40. Chapter 6, 'War in peace and peace in war. On the problem of legitimacy in the history of the international order, 1931–41', was published as 'Krieg im Frieden und Frieden im Krieg. über das Problem der Legitimität in der Geschichte der Staatengesellschaft 1931–41', in *Historische Zeitschrift*

(198⁻) published by Oldenbourg-Verlag GmbH of Postfach 801 360, 8000 Munich 80. Chapter 7, 'The German Resistance and its proposals for the political future of Eastern Europe', first appeared as 'Die ostpolitischen Vorstellungen im deutschen Widerstand', in *Geschichte in Wissenschaft und Unterricht* 29 (1978), pp. 213–41, published by Klett-Verlag, Postfach 809, ⁻000 Stuttgart 1.

Chapter 8, 'The provisional state and "eternal France". Franco-German relations, 1963–9', first appeared as 'Der provisorische Staat und das ewige Frankreich. Die deutsch-französischen Beziehungen 1963–1969', in *Historische Zeitschrift* 240 (1985), pp. 283–311, published by Oldenbourg-Verlag GmbH of Postfach 801 360, 8000 Munich 80. Chapter 9, 'Adenauer and Soviet Russia, 1963–7. The foreign policy ideas of the retired Federal Chancellor', first appeared as 'Adenauer und Sowjetrussland 1963–1967. Zur aussenpolitischen Konzeption des Kanzlers ohne Amt', in *Politik und Konfession. Festschrift für Konrad Repgen zum 60.Geburtstag*, ed. D. Albrecht, H. G. Hockerts, P. Mikat, R. Morsey (Berlin: 1963), published by Verlag Duncker & Humblot of Dietrich-Schäfter Weg, Postfach 410329, 1000 Berlin 41. Chapter 10, 'The German *Eigenweg*. On the problem of normality in the modern history of Germany and Europe', first appeared as 'Der deutsche Eigenweg. über ein Grundproblem der europäischen und deutschen Geschichte im 19. und 20.Jahrhundert', and was published in *Festschrift für Karl-Dietrich Bracher*, ed. M. Funke, H.-A. Jacobsen, H.-H. Knütter, H.-P. Schwarz (1987).

Introduction

Tackling the problem of Germany's role in the history of world politics in the nineteenth and twentieth centuries is one of the most interesting tasks of historiography. Furthermore, the relationship between Britain and Germany is of central significance in understanding this role. In the first section of this book, dealing with the history of the international order between German unification in 1871 and the outbreak of the First World War in 1914, the issue is investigated in three ways. One chapter describes British-Prussian negotiations over military disarmament in Europe in the period immediately before the Franco-Prussian War of 1870–1. Another provides detailed examination of the British attitude towards German unification, an event of profound significance in modern European history. In this context, particular attention is devoted to an issue which had an enormous impact on the future development of international relations – the compatibility of the new German Reich with the existing European order of states. The problem is then examined in greater depth in the following chapter, which traces the history of Anglo-German relations until the outbreak of the First World War. Finally, and widening the scope beyond the relationship between Britain and Germany, a further chapter is devoted to an investigation of the security dilemma which haunted all the European powers during the years before the First World War and in the crisis of July 1914, and which culminated in what George F. Kennan has described as 'the great seminal catastrophe of this century'.

The conflict of the nations between 1914 and 1918 had a revolutionary effect on the existing international and social order. It was followed by a wholly understandable desire to eliminate the evils of continual war once and for all, and to establish a stable and lasting peace. However, it rapidly became clear that the course being taken by the world which had developed in the postwar years was the opposite of what had been intended. The 'totalization' of conflict, in which war was waged by peoples and societies rather than by cabinets and states as in earlier times, introduced an age of wars and revolution.

Hitler's Germany was the special representative and most radical protagonist of this new era. The dictator's foreign policy towards France, the nation which embodied the status quo established in the Paris peace agreements of 1919–20, is the theme of the chapter which opens the second section of this book. The next deals with the condition and development of the system of states in the years between 1931, when Japan began its conquest of Manchuria, and 1941, when the United States of America entered the war. During this period the international order was characterized by a complex mixture of peace and war. and the destruction of that order is analysed from a universal point of view. The section is concluded by a detailed investigation of the proposals of the German Resistance for the political future of eastern Europe. This chapter also offers an opportunity for the analysis of Hitler's own political and radical goals, to be achieved at the expense of the Soviet Union and east central Europe. At the centre of the analysis there is a description of the unmistakable similarities and the fundamental differences between national socialism and conservatism, between the dictator and the conspirators of 20 July 1944.

Two chapters in the last section of the book reveal the fundamental change in Germany's position in world politics after the caesura of 1945. Specifically, these deal with the relationship of the Federal Republic of Germany with the powers on the flanks of the continent, the French great power and the Soviet world power. They also reflect the persistent fear of the aged Konrad Adenauer about a renewed co-operation between the victors of the war, to the detriment of the young and insecure Bonn republic.

The book concludes with a comparative study of Germany history in its European context during the nineteenth and twentieth centuries, though reference is also made to earlier epochs. The specific historical facts of German development over long periods are presented as a German *Eigenweg*, Germany's 'own path' through the history of Europe, which led – by no means inevitably, but under certain conditions which can be recognized with hindsight – to the Nazi dictatorship of 1933–45. It is the hope of the author that this chapter, alongside the other studies in the book, will help to increase the understanding of the reader in two respects. First, the studies demonstrate the many historical forms which can be taken by the history of world politics between the twin poles of *Staatskunst und Systemzwang* (statesmanship and the constraints of the system); and secondly, they reveal that a historiography which begins with the problems of the world of states may also open the route to other spheres of historical experience and inquiry, to the history of society and the economy, of culture, of ideologies and of mentalities.

*The European Order
between German Unification
and the
First World War*

1

Great Britain and the foundation of the German Reich

I

In the history of the twentieth century, Anglo-German antagonism[1] has been a factor of crucial significance. Historians have consequently devoted a great deal of attention to the relationship between Great Britain and Prussia-Germany, and particularly to its origins and development in the course of the last century. During the Second World War, when he was editing a selection of the correspondence between the British ambassadors in Berlin and Foreign Secretary Granville during the years 1871–4 and 1880–5, Paul Knaplund commented:[2] 'How these great nations became rivals and finally enemies has challenged and will perhaps for all time challenge the curiosity of students of history.' In analysing the relationship, historians are confronted by a fundamental problem: how far, if at all, was the *kleindeutsch* (Little German) national state ever compatible with the interests of its European neighbours and of Great Britain, then at the height of its power? A few years ago, in his survey of the short history of the German Reich which had to all intents and purposes been destroyed in 1945, the English historian James Joll gave the following answer:[3]

> The present European community would, I believe, be impossible to maintain in its present form if Germany were ever to be reunited, since in that case we would be presented with a recurrence of the historical situation which we have already experienced before 1914 and between the wars, in which the natural economic, demographic and geographical strength of Germany would be such as to threaten the European balance, and thus make the only form in which Europe might possibly unite that of a Europe under German hegemony. On the other hand, we can also speculate whether the reunification is as inevitable on historical and political grounds as most Germans have to maintain that it is. After all, the Germany the reunification of which is demanded only existed as a unified state for 75 years. Must we necessarily accept this as a fixed historical pattern to which we are bound to return?

These comments oppose any reunification of the *kleindeutsch* national state which had been created on 18 January 1871, destroyed in the Second

3

World War and subsequently divided. The argument was linked to a conviction that a divided Germany would probably contribute more to the maintenance of peace – 'peace in pieces'[4] – than a united German national state. This latter belief is very widely held and has proved extremely difficult to repudiate. At the root of these assessments of the 'German Question' lie real doubts about the feasibility of, and justification for, the Bismarck state. They were stimulated by ideas of the kind put forward by the German historian Siegfried A. Kaehler under the direct impact of the 'German catastrophe' of 1945.[5] Kaehler wondered then whether Germany's responsibility for the loss of European power[6] – and thus for the fate of the world – was in fact due primarily to the policies pursued by the German Reich; might it not ultimately have been Germany's very geographical, demographic and economic existence which constituted its 'guilt'?[7] Kaehler himself raised this question with the very greatest caution and hedged it round with a whole series of qualifications. Nevertheless, it provoked a strong response from the English historian Geoffrey Barraclough.[8] At the same time, Barraclough provided a clear – though controversial – answer to the various options on the 'German Question' which had been considered during the nineteenth century and have become a live issue again during the postwar period. Barraclough remained unconvinced by the alternatives to the *kleindeutsch* solution achieved by Bismarck – namely, the possibility of German unity or unification in the form of *Grossdeutschland* (Germany and Austria), in *kleindeutsch* liberal form, or in central European federal form. He did not believe that any of these solutions would have been more tolerable for Europe. In Barraclough's judgement all of these possibilities, whether tending towards conservatism or liberalism, to a unitary or more federal state, would still have led to a concentration of power in central Europe which was bound to endanger peace. Accordingly, he expressed some astonishment that the Reich created in 1871, which he regarded as out of harmony with the 'spiritual map of Europe',[9] had not been dismembered after the First World War ended. The logic of his theories demanded that the victorious powers should have eliminated the alleged destroyer of European peace without hesitation. With hindsight, it does seem surprising that contemporaries were so ready to accept the continued existence of the Reich after the end of the First World War. Why did the victors of 1918 allow the *kleindeutsch* national state to survive? Was its survival not comparable to the unexpected 'miracle of the House of Brandenburg'[10] which had saved the Prussia of Frederick the Great in the eighteenth century? In truth, the threat of '*déstruction totale*' had always hovered over the Prussian-German state; in 1918 it was averted by the cataclysm of the October Revolution in Russia and the massive uncertainties that provoked. Barraclough's belief that the Reich was fundamentally incompatible with peace in Europe became common currency after the experiences of 1933–45, with the division of Germany as the consequence. After the First World War, however, the Anglo-Saxon powers in particular did not believe that the very existence of Germany had been responsible for the disastrous course of events in Europe. They held that its constitution and culture had also played a prominent role and that these might now be altered with favourable consequences for the future.[11] Naturally, the allies were also influenced by other important international and social motives (the factor of Soviet Russia and the perceived communist threat). Nevertheless, the course of events indicates that British statesmen at least, in the years 1918–20, thought that the German Reich was well worth preserving. During and after the Second World War, in contrast, they had come to believe that the continued existence of a unified German Reich was highly dangerous to peace and security. Nevertheless, these developments are an indication that the *kleindeutsch* national state had once been acceptable to and compatible with Europe, at least temporarily. It is against this background that the years when the German Reich was founded must be investigated. Did British statesmen *at that time*, in the 1860s and 1870s, regard Bismarck's Reich as compatible with their own requirements and with the existing international order in Europe? What significance did they attribute to Prussia, and then to Prussia-Germany, during the years 1860–80 – that is, *before* Great Britain came to regard Bismarck's colonizing activities in Africa during the 1880s as a threat to its world and its imperial interests, *before* Bismarck's successors in Wilhelmine Germany made a direct challenge to Great Britain by expanding the German navy, and *before* the two world wars did so much to convince Britain that the existence of the German nation-state was incompatible with European peace?

Historians have been too ready to allow their assessment of the British-Prussian and British-German relationship during the 1860s and 1870s to be distorted by their awareness of the disastrous course of Anglo-German relations in the following decades. As a result, they have tended to stress the special – and hostile – nature of Great Britain's attitude to Bismarck's Prussia and the young German national state.[12] In truth, at first sight the events of the 1860s appear to support such a judgement. In those years, Bismarck's Prussia was engaged in altering the map of central Europe by force and using war to revise the status quo in continental Europe. By contrast, Britain's main interest in foreign policy lay in maintaining the status quo so that the country could concentrate on domestic affairs relatively undisturbed and attend to the urgent need for reform. Thus, Great Britain favoured stability in foreign affairs so that it could safely give priority to internal change and reform; on the other hand, Bismarck was striving for revision in foreign affairs, at the same time managing to avoid the fulfilment of liberal demands for reform at home. Since the domestic and foreign policy interests of the two states diverged so widely, was future conflict between them not inevitable in Europe? Was the danger of conflict not bound to increase during the 1870s as Germany replaced France as a potential hegemonic power on the continent and began to confront Great Britain? There were also significant differences in the internal structure of the two states, between the liberal and parliamentary system of Britain and the conservative, monarchical government in Prussia. Were relations between the two not bound to be damaged by British suspicion and disapproval of the Prussian constitution? In this way, it can be argued that the outlines of future conflict were apparent even as the Reich was being established, long before Bismarck's shift towards conservatism at the end of the 1870s and long before the Reich took its momentous decisions on colonial and naval policy. According to these arguments, the hostility between the two states was rooted in internal political and ideological differences, which ultimately forced them into opposition in foreign affairs. Thus, for example, Raymond Sontag commented in his major study *Germany and England. Background of Conflict 1848–1894*:[13] 'Friendship was impossible between liberal England and Bismarckian Germany. To Gladstone, the Germans were foes of freedom; to Bismarck, Gladstone was a hypocritical demagogue.' If these arguments hold water, then British non-intervention policy in the 1860s and early 1870s was weak and inadequate in permitting the German Reich to be founded at all. Surely Britain should have intervened resolutely to prevent the creation of the new German national state in central Europe?[14] After the experiences of two world wars, and of the Anglo-German conflicts which had contributed to their outbreak, it is easy to believe that the creation of the German national state had always been incompatible with British interests for economic, demographic, geographical, political and ideological reasons. But was that how the situation appeared to British statesmen at the time the Reich was founded, in the 1860s and 1870s?

There is no room in this chapter for a full analysis of the history of British-German relations during these years. Instead, some of the fundamental features and problems of British world politics will be examined from a domestic and foreign policy perspective; Great Britain's attitude towards Prussia, and later to the German Reich, will be investigated against this background.

II

There is an obvious need for revision of the view of earlier German historians, who believed that Great Britain had consistently opposed the creation of a German national state ever since the unification attempts of 1848–50.[15] Even in 1876, Heinrich von Treitschke had written in the *Preussische Jahrbücher* condemning 'the deplorable, hypocritical policy of England'; in his view, it had 'always been hostile to the gathering strength of the German North during the last two generations'.[16] Erich Marcks made similar remarks in a lecture given in London in 1900:[17] 'Directly or indirectly, wholly or in part, it [England] has always been among the opponents, never among the friends of our unification.' This view continued to be widely held for many years, until after the Second World War in fact. Yet despite the force of prevailing opinion, there had been some comparatively early attempts to correct the balance. For example, Wolfgang Michael, an expert in British history and professor at the University of Freiburg, responded to the Morocco Crisis of summer 1911 (Agadir) by writing an article on the subject which he hoped would open up the possibilities for future co-operation between the two countries. In the article, which appeared in the December edition of *Contemporary Review* and was reprinted in *Deutsche Rundschau* the following year, Michael offered this opinion:[18]

> How did England behave towards the growing unity of Germany? That it energetically encouraged it, one could not say, but nor did it obstruct it. It was understood that a strong Germany would pose few dangers for the continent, that it could therefore be more easily tolerated by England than an over-mighty France. Castlereagh thought so, as did Palmerston. Thus Bismarck was able to complete his great work, unhindered by England and dealing with the continental powers by means of his wars and his masterly diplomacy: the new German Reich entered the circle of European great powers. After the foundation of the Reich there could be no question of a deeper conflict of interest between the new nation of Germany and the British Empire.

And even during the Second World War, in a book on 'Bismarck and England' which went through several editions, the journalist Maximilian von Hagen argued:[19] 'Hence in the main question of German history at that time, the German Question, the England of Palmerston and Russell did not unconditionally oppose Bismarck's foreign policy despite their great mistrust of his political methods ... On the contrary, even later than that, under the Russell-Clarendon régime, it favoured the unification of north Germany at least under the leadership of Prussia.' Opinions such as these remained very much in the minority, however. The mainstream of German historical writing and journalism continued to emphasize British hostility towards the foundation of the Reich.

Today, particularly since the work of Veit Valentin and the studies of Werner Mosse and Richard Millman,[20] views have changed. We know that Great Britain was not so hostile to the principle of German unification from the days of Palmerston to the time of Lord Clarendon, that is from the middle of the century until the Franco-Prussian War. Naturally there were differing views about the form it should take, but the process of unification was actually welcomed for a time by the British government and both political parties. Their view was strongly influenced by the prospects for a self-contained economic zone in central Europe; freed from onerous customs barriers, this might become an attractive trading partner for Great Britain. In addition, British statesmen hoped that a strong power was emerging in the centre of Europe as a counterweight to France, Britain's traditional rival on the continent. Both these ideas appeared frequently in the thinking of the country's statesmen and diplomats and persuaded them not to place fundamental difficulties in the way of unification attempts.[21] Britain's attitude towards German efforts at unification was sometimes benevolent and sometimes indifferent, but there was a general willingness to let events take their course. It is unlikely that this approach concealed a more hostile special relationship, as representatives of the older German historiography tended to assume.

In fact, especially after the end of the 'Age of Palmerston' in 1865, much of British energy and attention was directed towards domestic political problems. The country had witnessed scenes of tumult not far removed from civil war. In the eyes of many British statesmen, the great electoral reform of 1867 had provided only a first, temporary solution to these difficulties.[22] Even the Reform Act was only the prelude to the reforming policies of Gladstone's 'Great Ministry' in the years between 1868 and 1874. The 1850s and early 1860s had seen a period of domestic immobility, when the disparity between economic and social development on one hand and political representation on the other had grown increasingly apparent. Disquiet at the course of events, and particularly the state of the franchise, was widespread. Political energies were therefore devoted largely to domestic affairs, a situation which encouraged the adoption of a policy of restraint in the field of foreign policy. This sentiment was widespread in the country and was expressed by Lord Stanley, Conservative Foreign Secretary in 1867 – for Britain the year of the Reform Bill, for Europe the year of the Luxemburg crisis:[23] 'We are unusually free from diplomatic trouble: which is fortunate, as there will be plenty of parliamentary work on hand.' British statesmen in the second half of the 1860s and at the beginning of the 1870s were already tending to follow the principles which characterized Lord Salisbury's policy of 'splendid isolation' in later years:[24] 'However strong you may be, whether you are a man or a country, there is a point beyond which your strength will not go. It is courage and wisdom to exert that strength up to the limit to which you may attain; it is madness and ruin if you allow yourself to pass it.' (At this stage, however, Salisbury himself was highly critical of the foreign policy pursued by British governments, which he considered excessively passive.[25])

In so far as foreign issues occupied British politicians, the affairs of continental Europe did not even rate very highly. Thus on 29 April 1866, when the Austro-Prussian conflict was causing deep concern in the cabinets of Europe, the English Prime Minister Earl Russell informed his Foreign Secretary that he thought Great Britain's relations with the United States of America were 'more important than those with Europe'.[26] Central Europe was not a major area of interest for British foreign policy. Besides, relations with Prussia in the 1860s were never remotely as important to Britain as those with a number of other nations. Britain was much more concerned about the strongest power on the continent, France (the problem of hegemony; Belgium; the naval issue; south-east Europe; the Near East); about its global rival, Russia (the North-West Frontier of India; route to the subcontinent; the straits; the expansion of the tsarist empire in central Asia); about the United States (Canada; the Fenian problem; the Alabama Question; trade in Central and South America; naval rivalry); and also about issues affecting British interests in Asia (China trade). Britain's obligations throughout the world, and the need for internal reform, encouraged its politicians to avoid taking on too many extra burdens and ties in foreign affairs – a tendency strongly reinforced by the lasting effects of Britain's negative experiences in the Crimean War. The role of world's policeman, which Palmerston had attempted to adopt for a time, was abandoned. It was hoped that the country could avoid becoming involved in worldwide conflicts through a policy of 'meddle and muddle'. Such a policy could lead only too easily to an over-commitment in foreign affairs, thus endangering the existence of Britain's overseas possessions – especially India – and reducing its influence in Europe. Over-commitment in foreign affairs might also have blocked those domestic reforms which were widely regarded as necessary, with disastrous consequences for the British parliamentary system.

Awareness of the interrelation between domestic and foreign policy increased the inclination of the British ruling class and public opinion towards non-interventionism. However, it was the independent development of international affairs in Europe which made the temporary restraint in British foreign policy possible. Bismarck's conduct in foreign affairs in central Europe between 1866 and 1870 diverted the attention of France and, to a certain extent, Russia – although the latter was also preoccupied with its own domestic problems. In consequence, Britain could afford to maintain its neutrality in foreign policy and keep its distance from events in Europe without in any way damaging its vital interests. British non-intervention policy thus became one of the important preconditions for the foundation of the German Reich, just as Bismarck's policy of revision and unification contributed to a situation which permitted the British to follow the course they had chosen.

In view of these facts, it is not tenable to claim that British interests in Europe were endangered by the belligerent conduct of Prussia. Britain certainly did not feel impelled to depart from its policy of 'dignified intelligent non-intervention'.[27] The behaviour of Prussia, in its exclusively continental dimension, did not damage any vital British interest – not its hegemony, nor its colonies, nor its naval position. The policy of non-intervention, conceived as restraint, also created a foundation for internal political reform, which preserved for the country its parliamentary character and secured it from the dangers of revolutionary upheavals and Caesarist solutions[28] alike. Domestic considerations were at least as important as foreign ones in promoting the adoption of the policy. Yet non-intervention was never a dogma of the kind found in the ideas of Richard Cobden; it always remained a function of the country's national interest. This meant that Britain remained ready, even during this period, to undertake political and military intervention should it prove necessary. The Abyssinian expedition of 1868 proves that this was certainly the case outside Europe. But the possibility of intervention on the continent also remained a possibility, to safeguard the 'essentials' of Britain's world power – for example, the neutrality of Belgium or the position of Constantinople. Non-intervention policy was never an expression of weakness or decadence. Nor was it a sign that Britain had abdicated from its role as a great power, as Bismarck himself had once assumed when he misjudged the effects of the Reform Act of 1832. In his view, Great Britain since then had become a country where government by statesmen and diplomats had been overthrown in favour of rule by the 'rascals of the press'.[29] Such criticism, echoed in Britain itself by admirers of Bismarck such as Lord Napier and Lord Lytton, gradually made its mark on academic literature and thus influenced historical assessments of the period.[30]

Similar sentiments were expressed by Odo Russell, one of the most capable of the younger British diplomats. Russell had been special ambassador of the British government negotiating with Bismarck at Versailles since the reopening of the Pontus Question and was to be British ambassador in Berlin from 1871. He had been profoundly affected by the personality of the Prussian statesman.[31] Under the impact of the Prussian-German defeat of France, he commented in a letter to his brother Arthur, Liberal Member of Parliament and adherent of the 'Old Whig' wing of the party, on 11 February 1871:[32] 'My impression is that we have too readily accepted the position of a second class power Bismarck has assigned to us. We have scarcely had the courage of our opinion and have looked on too patiently from our "Happy England" als unten tief in die Türkei die Völker aufeinander schlugen. Gladstone's foreign policy is "la politique de la décadence"'. Lord Lytton, then still at the embassy in Vienna, but from 1876 viceroy in India, shared this view. On 22 January 1872 he wrote to Sir Robert Morier, one of the Foreign Office's leading experts on Germany, criticizing the foreign policy of his country in general terms:[33]

To tell you the truth, I have absolutely no belief in the possibility now, or at any future time, of an energetic foreign policy on our part, – even on behalf of peace . . . I don't think our international nihilism can fairly be laid at the door of any particular cabinet. It is the result of social and political conditions which will not be changed by any change of ministry. We are no longer a homogeneous nation. There is no one class of English society which is in a position to speak or act, towards foreign nations on behalf of all others. And there is not a single foreign question on which even the individual members of the same class are unanimous.

Lord Lytton's criticism of British foreign policy and its domestic foundations was influenced by doubts about the compatibility of democratic tendencies with the country's imperial obligations. These had already been outlined in 1859 by Lord Malmesbury, Tory Foreign Secretary until the change of government in June of that year. Referring to the current debate about reform of the parliamentary system and the extension of the franchise, he argued 'that in a country ruled by the £10 householders *la grande politique* was impossible'.[34] The British parliamentary system had previously been wholly compatible with the global tasks of the 'Pax Britannica', each nurturing and promoting the other; from now on, however, the relationship between democracy and empire became the cardinal problem of British politics.

Critics of British foreign policy and the parliamentary system found them wanting in comparison with the powerful, warlike and victorious conduct of Bismarck and Prussia. Moreover many Conservatives, and some 'Liberal Imperialists' like Morier and Seeley, feared that Britain's moral, military, political and economic superiority over other states was in jeopardy in the 1860s and 1870s. But these critics did not represent the majority sentiment of the British ruling class and its political representatives. Non-intervention was a popular policy throughout the country, for domestic as well as foreign policy reasons. It seemed both beneficial and reasonable to protect Britain and the empire, internal constitution and overseas possessions, while the country was adopting a productive policy of domestic and external change.[35] In a conversation of 1 April 1866 with the queen, who was always more committed to the continent and more inclined to intervention, Earl Russell outlined the limits of British power and possibilities. Taking into account the need for domestic reform and the fulfilment of worldwide obligations in foreign policy, he argued:[36] 'The military and pecuniary resources of England must be husbanded with the utmost care.' He was not alone in his opinion. On 23 April 1866, Lord Stanley recorded a conversation he had held with the Earl of Caernarvon, Colonial Secretary in the Earl of Derby's Conservative Cabinet. Caernarvon clearly understood the mutual dependence of domestic and external developments; referring to an England 'in a state of transition', he wondered how capable of resistance the country would prove to be in the event of a major internal or external crisis:[37] 'all is well while we are quiet, but in the event of a foreign war or domestic agitation what would be the resisting power of our institutions?'

British statesmen believed that unfavourable external developments could set off a chain reaction which, once it had begun, could be controlled only with the greatest difficulty. The threat to the status quo of Great Britain, in both foreign and domestic matters, might then become immense. Consequently, they paid careful attention to events abroad and adjusted their objectives and political conduct accordingly. In particular, British statesmen tried to avoid becoming embroiled in international problems which affected Britain – in contrast to the continental states – only indirectly, and to which a cautious approach seemed sensible. A policy of maintaining the peace offered many advantages for Great Britain, while a military conflagration could easily increase the dangers the country faced. Lord Stanley's view, noted in his diary on New Year's Day 1867, reflected this assessment:[38] 'Nothing except a war can check our prosperity.' In other words: war would indeed become a crime once it ceased to be a necessity.[39] Nevertheless, it would be quite incorrect to regard this policy as being identical with a pacifist or ideological rejection of any and all wars. Within the sphere of the Pax Britannica, a readiness to wage war remained a constant element in the political calculations of British governments. A policy of peace at any price was never adopted. Britain's global blueprint for order included the possibility of a *casus belli* as well as the principle of the European balance of power. British policy therefore consistently aimed to avoid war, whilst accepting that it remained a possibility.[40]

Apart from the priority of domestic reform, prompting it to withdraw temporarily from events on the continent, Great Britain had already ceased to regard itself primarily as a European power when the Reich was founded. Disraeli emphasized precisely this fact in a speech on the occasion of the take-over of government by Lord Derby's Cabinet in June 1866, in which he gave a concise description of the policy of non-interventionism:[41]

> The abstention of England from any unnecessary interference in the affairs of Europe is the consequence, not of her decline of power, but of her increased strength. England is no longer a mere European Power; she is the metropolis of a great maritime empire, extending to the boundaries of the farthest ocean. It is not that England has taken refuge in a state of apathy, that she now almost systematically declines to interfere in the affairs of the Continent of Europe. England is as ready and as willing to interfere as in old days, when the necessity

of her position requires it. There is no power, indeed, that interferes more than England. She interferes in Asia, because she is really more an Asiatic Power than a European. She interferes in Australia, in Africa, and New Zealand, where she carries on war often on a great scale. Therefore, it is not because England does not recognise her duty to interfere in the affairs of the Continent of Europe that persons are justified in declaring that she has relinquished her imperial position, and has taken refuge in the *otium cum dignitate* which agrees with the decline of life, of power, and of prosperity. On the contrary, she has a greater sphere of action than any European Power, and she has duties devolving on her on a much larger scale. Not that we can ever look with indifference upon what takes place on the Continent. We are interested in the peace and prosperity of Europe, and I do not say that there may not be occasions on which it may be the duty of England to interfere in European Wars.

The restrained and detached interest of British statesmen and politicians in Bismarck's foreign policy can be understood only in the context of the country's non-intervention policy in the 1860s and 1870s, and of the domestic and imperial concerns which caused it to be adopted. Ultimately, Bismarck's revisionism scarcely affected or damaged British interests at all, and the results of Prussian belligerence were actually regarded as compatible with the requirements of British world policy. British statesmen were committed to this perspective. Lord Clarendon's comment on the eve of the Austro-Prussian War in 1866 should therefore come as no surprise:[42] 'However much this country may regret to see Germany prey to civil war, yet so long as the war is confined to Germany there is no British interest of sufficient magnitude to render imperative the tender of British good offices.' In other words, 'the victory or defeat of one or other party'[43] was scarcely critical to British interests. Whatever the result, Britain foresaw the prospect of a new balance of power, and thus the desired stability, in central Europe – all of which could only be to the advantage of political order in the world.

In all, Great Britain in the 1860s had many more pressing concerns, more important things to do than to meddle in central European affairs, particularly those which seemed more likely to strengthen than endanger the European balance of power. In continental Europe in general, and Prussia-Germany in particular, this fact was frequently not understood, although Bismarck himself had recognized it in 1862.[44] For example, on 25 June 1866, the *Saturday Review* commented that Britain had no interest in how the Austro-Prussian War might alter the situation in Europe, since Britain was 'no longer a European Power as in the days of Wellington', but an Asiatic and maritime power. Consequently, the paper argued, affairs in Burma, Afghanistan and Nepal were more important for Britain than those in Württemberg, Hanover and Hesse-Cassel.[45] Britain's attitude towards the foundation of the German Reich was therefore dominated by two factors: first, by a lack of interest in specific events in central Europe; secondly, by its interest in the establishment of a stable new order there in general.

In the course of the nineteenth century, a whole series of German diplomats and statesmen had complained about British indifference to German issues and problems. For example, the long-serving Prussian envoy to London, Baron Bunsen, and his colleague from Saxony, Graf Vitzthum von Eckstädt, were both eloquent on the subject.[46] And when Bismarck visited England in 1862 whilst Prussian envoy in Paris, he received a similar impression of the knowledge of even leading British politicians about German matters. He wrote to his wife that the ministers of the country knew less about Prussia than about Japan and Mongolia, and told the Prussian Minister of War, van Roon, that people in England were better informed about China and Peru than about Prussia.[47] This lack of interest in German affairs, so widespread in London, provided the background to Disraeli's assessment of Prussia in 1863. The future Tory leader was aware of the vulnerability, fragility and perilous position of the Prussian '*Rationalstaat*':[48] 'Prussia without nationality, the principal of the day, is clearly the subject for partition.' This burden, of being forced to cope with its central position as a 'great power without a *Staatsidee*',[49] was also to be faced by the 'incomplete'[50] German national state.

Despite this indifference towards German problems, British politicians had no objections in principle to the 'appearance of a new central European great power,[51] i.e. the emergence of a German national state which was beset with so many problems. Their willingness to let events take their course was influenced by the hope that the development might offer the basis for a new stability in central Europe. It had long been clear to the makers of British foreign policy that the German Confederation was no longer capable of maintaining peace and the balance of power in Europe. Instead, the rivalry between the two German great powers, Austria and Prussia, was leading to instability in central Europe and to war. From a British point of view, the duel between Austria and Prussia in the summer of 1866 therefore had some positive results. It settled the persistent conflict between the two leading German states, determined spheres of influence in central Europe, and might ultimately – in the form of a new co-operation between Vienna and Berlin – create a functioning balance in central Europe to offset the powers on the west and east of the continent. On these grounds, Foreign Secretary Lord Stanley did not insist that the agreements of 1815 should be adhered to, since they were so obviously in need of revision. At the end of the Austro-Prussian War, on 21 July 1866, he let it be understood that it would not be appropriate[52] 'to appeal to those Treaties as being still binding'. His comment shows that Britain was still keeping its distance from affairs on the continent, and also provides some evidence to support Disraeli's conviction that Great Britain was currently to be judged primarily as an Asiatic power.[53] Thus, Hermann Oncken concluded:[54] 'In the event of a conflict, in British world policy during the sixties the Asiatic and not the European motive would take precedence.' Yet to avoid such a conflict, the country must defend its European interests so as not to lose undue influence at the centre of world politics. In the final analysis, Lord Stanley remained committed to the traditional British policy of the balance of power. However, he did not pursue it in the way that British governments had done during the first half of the nineteenth century when England, the 'third German great power',[55] appeared much more willing to intervene in the affairs of central Europe. With the international situation very much changed from the circumstances which had prevailed during the preceding decades, non-interventionism now seemed much more likely to help create the desired balance in Europe.[56] If Britain had intervened by force and meddled in affairs on the continent, it could easily have become entangled and been forced to accept the consequences of its participation. Politicians in England saw neither the occasion nor the possibility for them to abandon the role of umpire for that of policeman. A balance beneficial to Britain appeared to have been re-established without any activity on its part, not least as a result of the victory and growing strength of Prussia. To British satisfaction, the continued existence of Austria was never in doubt. Moreover, Austria's own future development appeared much more promising after the changes of 1866–7. The hope of co-operation between the two German great powers seemed to have been thoroughly justified.

For the rest, the first priority of British governments was to ensure the security of the central pillars of the empire. This was particularly true after the Indian Mutiny of 1857; in its aftermath, elements of a 'new Imperialism'[57] began to emerge long before the 'Great Depression' which is often regarded as a turning-point.[58] As has been noted elsewhere,[59] British statesmen were anxious to ensure continued control of the route to India by countering the plans of Napoleon III to make the Mediterranean into a 'French' sea. They also paid the most careful attention to Russian expansion in central Asia. (In 1860, according to the Prussian envoy in St Petersburg, von Bismarck, this was only about eighty miles from the northern frontier of British India.[60]) However, they did not seriously consider the ideas of British military circles for a 'forward defence' on the North-West Frontier, in Afghanistan or in Persia. No one in the British Cabinet really believed that the tsar intended[61] to seize Britain's wealthiest and most important colony. On the contrary, British governments of the period were determined to settle problems arising from the global conflict of interests with Russia through co-operation and agreement rather than through confrontation. This attitude remained a constant feature of both British and Russian policy. It became apparent after the Heidelberg meeting between Clarendon and Gortchakov in the late summer of 1869, and was maintained despite setbacks on eastern issues. The commitment was adequately recognized by Prussian-German statesmen only after long delay, and probably too late.

Britain had other obligations as well: to sustain Canada against the United States of America and at the same time to retain the South American market for British trade. Since the 'Age of Palmerston', it had pursued both these objectives by means of a defensive policy – indeed, Kenneth Bourne has described Lord Aberdeen's policy towards America in the 1840s as one of 'appeasement'[62] – towards the United States, which for its own domestic reasons was judged to be predisposed towards spectacular acts of aggression against Canada. Great Britain therefore withdrew from Central America and carefully avoided armed action, all with the aim of maintaining its political position in Canada and its economic position in South America. London also had to ensure that the European continent remained in a state of balance, that the integrity of Belgium was not damaged and – at least at this stage – that the Ottoman Empire and Constantinople were maintained intact. In addition, Britain was attempting to control the activities of the Fenians in America and Europe, and to find a tolerable solution to the Irish disturbances. Last but by no means least, its politicians were committed to the introduction of the necessary domestic reforms; for example, in the franchise, in education, training and university life, in the army, in local government and in social affairs. Britain was therefore forced to avoid involvement in most of the affairs of Europe, including the foreign policy of Bismarck, in order to deal with its major priorities in domestic and foreign policy. These priorities were concentrated on the defence and strengthening of the empire and the adjustment and improvement of British political institutions to meet the demands of the modern world.

At this point it is useful to widen the theme and investigate British methods of dealing with political and economic crises during these years. An attempt can then be made to integrate this analysis into a discussion of the theory of social imperialism as an apparent response to the crisis of industrial capitalist society.[63] Over a much longer period than covered here, the British ruling class developed a characteristic response to the problems caused by the growing chasm between economic and social changes on the one hand, and political representation on the other; the route adopted, and the solution chosen, was one of gradual reform in domestic affairs in order to restore political and social harmony. To this end, British statesmen continued to monitor the international situation with great care, whilst temporarily reducing the foreign policy activities of the country to the minimum level required to maintain the empire. Even in Gladstone's great Reform Cabinet, there was no serious prospect that the existence of the major pillars of the empire would be placed in jeopardy. It is true that, especially in the latter half of the nineteenth century, some political theorists and active politicians argued that a bold, imperialist foreign policy should be adopted to overcome domestic crises. Among these men were Joseph Chamberlain, Lord Rosebery and Cecil Rhodes. Some of them were clearly anti-parliamentarian in outlook, arguing that there was a fundamental incompatibility between parliamentarianism and imperialism, between democracy and empire; they regarded democratic tendencies as a threat to the continued existence of the British Empire. Criticism of this kind, favouring the use of social imperialist methods to overcome domestic crises, increased during the 'Age of Imperialism'. However, it was never the majority opinion of the British ruling class – a fact which was ultimately decisive for the subsequent course of British history. Instead, the policy of the country continued to be dominated by the tendency to settle domestic crises by means of political and social reforms. In this sense there was a natural limit to Britain's imperialist foreign policy, one which came into play whenever imperialism threatened to do real damage to the conditions and requirements of the traditional parliamentary system. These political facts of life ultimately had to be accepted by Joseph Chamberlain, by Lord Rosebery and by other powerful representatives of British imperialism.[64] It can be argued that the characteristic British method of dealing with crises provides evidence that industrial capitalist systems are not bound by historic necessity to adopt Caesarist forms of government, nor to resort to social imperialism, as a means of retaining power. During and after the period under investigation, Great Britain chose the opposite method; its statesmen dealt with the problems caused by industrialization within the framework of the existing political system, by adapting the institutions of the country to meet the challenge of the modern world. Internal difficulties, as a rule, were not deliberately diverted to the outside. In fact, rather the opposite was the case: foreign policy activity was reduced to allow the introduction of controlled reform through parliament, with the aim of achieving the desired social and political integration. It therefore appears that it is not industrial capitalism in itself, nor its nature at a some specific, ill-defined stage of development, which decisively affects the shape and definition of any policy. The decisive factor is the traditional political system of the country concerned, in which certain values, well-tried methods and the 'unspoken assumptions' of a ruling class play a vital role. In Britain, past experience and the conditions of the country's political culture played their part in influencing the decisions of the responsible politicians. They were persuaded that foreign policy should generally be conducted within the limits drawn for it by the parliamentary system; that parliamentary government should be regarded as the most suitable and efficient form of political constitution for Great Britain, in domestic and in foreign policy; and that the parliamentary system should not be damaged by the conduct of foreign affairs.

To return to our particular theme: between 1864 and 1871, Prussia's aggressive revisionism did not disturb any of the important interests of British world policy. However, one of the most experienced diplomats of the day, Lord Cowley, did define the acceptable limits of Prussian conduct when he wrote from his post as ambassador in Paris on 30 July 1866, on the eve of the Austro-Prussian War. Once these limits were overstepped, the likelihood of conflict with Great Britain would increase. Unlike the British Foreign Secretary, Lord Stanley, he regarded the increase in Prussian power with trepidation, and prophesied:[65] 'if ever she [Prussia] becomes a naval power she will give us trouble.' In the international arena, which was of primary interest in any British assessment of Prussia, Bismarck's revisionism and the British desire for peace were temporarily compatible. Most British statesmen distrusted the domestic politics of Bismarck's 'Junker Regiment'.[66] Indeed, they still hoped for a liberal development along British lines once the old king and that dreadful man of 'blood and iron' ('the real king of Prussia'[67]) were finally out of the way and the crown prince (whose intentions and abilities were overestimated) was in charge.[68]

Gradually, however, objections to the traditional hope for the liberalization of a united Germany began to be heard in Britain. The view was far from representative, and did not supplant the ideological distaste for Bismarck's policies. Nevertheless, it appears that Queen Victoria's warnings about the potential dangers of a united Germany were not directed solely against Bismarck, though she remained deeply suspicious of him. On 24 April 1867, when she committed her fears to paper, her comment was much more general than that:[69] 'I am afraid the time may come when Europe will wish France to be strong to keep the ambition of Germany in check.'

On 20 April 1867 the crown princess of Prussia had written a letter to her mother[70] which revealed that it was not only Bismarck – and perhaps not even mainly him – who would pose problems for the future development of Europe. Despite his lack of scruple, Bismarck had actually continued to show evidence of moderation in his foreign policy. This moderation was not shared by the liberals. The crown princess held views on the German Question, and on the relationship between France and Prussia, which were substantially those of the liberal opposition at court and throughout Germany. These views would become highly influential if a future German state ever adopted Great Britain as its constitutional model, and quite clearly contained elements threatening to Britain. The crown princess wrote: 'For my part, if the peace cannot be maintained I think it better the war should be now than later – horrible as it is. A war with France will be a very different thing than a war with Austria but if our honour is at stake – for the sake of Germany we must not hang back. That is my feeling and Fritz's and most people's here.' Up to this point in the letter, Victoria may have been surprised and concerned by the frequent revelations of her daughter's willingness to wage war. In general, though, the arguments may have appeared understandable. However, the crown princess then put forward with astonishing resolution her conditions for the solution of the German Question. Beyond doubt, these suggested a dismal outlook for the future of Europe: 'I think the great united empire of Germany will never consolidate itself in peace – before France is reduced to a second power on the Continent. I consider that as desirable for England as it is for us Germans.' She was certainly aware of the significance of her remarks, which Bismarck did not approve and would have condemned, and therefore declared them to be strictly her private opinion.

What future prospects did this document hold out to Queen Victoria? It appeared to give an insight into the political convictions of a section of the liberal opposition to Bismarck's 'Regiment', the very people regarded as the 'better' Germany by prevailing sentiment in Britain. But the liberals seemed certain that German unification would be achieved only by war, that the position of France would have to be degraded and that the 'great united empire of Germany' could then become the first power on the continent. Could such a prospect really be beneficial to Great Britain, as the crown princess argued? Was she not actually demanding hegemony for Germany in Europe, for which Bismarck himself had made no claim? Once this united Germany had become the major power on the continent, where would its expansion end? The letter from the crown princess raised a whole series of unpleasant questions, all of which cast a shadow over the (admittedly distant) future. It seemed that the ideas of the liberal opposition, the possible future rulers of Prussia and Germany, were not compatible with the interests of the British world power.

For the time being, however, such arguments were expressed only in private. They were not sufficient to persuade British statesmen to change the course of their policy towards Germany, and did not give them cause to take up the fight against German unification. Indeed, many of them continued to have faith in the blessings of a liberal reform of Germany. Within the Foreign Office, however, despite continued distrust of Bismarck's regime, officials became more accustomed to his policies and more prepared to accept them. Some British observers were beginning to understand the dangers to Britain and Europe posed by the dynamism of the liberal forces in Germany. In domestic politics, Bismarck was increasingly forced to work with the national liberals, and to attempt to restrain their foreign policy demands. The course of Prussian and German history was soon to show that national liberal objectives were a much greater threat to British interests than the policy of the 'wicked man'[71] who had created the *kleindeutsch* national state.

III

It is often assumed that Great Britain adopted a fixed (and hostile) attitude to the newly founded German Reich after 1871.[72] In assessing whether this is true, due heed must be paid to the opinions expressed by many British politicians and diplomats after the Prussian-German victory over France and the annexation of Alsace-Lorraine,[73] though it is vital to weigh their comments appropriately. With hindsight, many contemporaries might have asked the question posed later by the American historian Raymond J. Sontag:[74] 'Would Germany, intoxicated by success, develop napoleonic ambitions?'

Positive assessments of the new Reich were certainly in the minority on the British side, and very few shared Thomas Carlyle's view of the Prussian victory over France as 'the hopefullest fact that has occurred in my time'.[75] The French defeat and the German triumph were generally greeted with a certain trepidation. Thus, the English diplomat Henry Bulwer prophesied that instead of a 'mistress', Europe had gained a 'master'.[76] And the opposition leader, Disraeli, described the consequences of the 'German Revolution' in sombre terms in an effort to jolt the country out of its 'Gladstonianism' and its preoccupation with internal reform and to remind it of its tasks in foreign affairs.[77] Rumours of a German landing on the coast at Dover were rife in the form of 'battle of Dorking fever',[78] in much the same way that rumours of invasion by other continental powers had spread in earlier years. However, these rumours were immediately consigned by the government to the realm of political fiction.[79] With surprising speed, the Cabinet and Foreign Office reached a common, sober assessment of the British attitude towards Bismarck's Germany.

The power of the new national state was unmistakable. Odo Russell was describing a widespread feeling when he wrote:[80] 'The importance of Berlin will be great a few years hence when the power of Germany is felt by all Europe.' However, it would not be accurate to say that the German Reich had immediately assumed an extraordinary or special significance in British world politics. Such a change in the bilateral relations of the two states began only slowly and cautiously at the beginning of the 1880s, as 'the opening of the Egyptian Question and the development of Bismarck's colonial policy brought Britain into new relations with Germany'.[81] This tendency was accelerated after Bismarck's departure, when it finally achieved its full negative development. During the period dealt with here, however, the attitude of the British world power to the German Reich can still be described as normal.

Admittedly, it is clear that the interest and the sympathy of British public opinion during the 1870s were turning increasingly towards France.[82] French culture and the French way of life were prized whereas Germany – once admired – was believed to have sacrificed the spirit of philosophy and intellectual inquiry to the power of the military and the economy. On 3 February 1871, after the battle of Sedan and once Prussian plans to annex Alsace and Lorraine became known, Lord Arthur Russell gave expression to this widespread sentiment in a letter to Sir Robert Morier:[83] 'Many friends of the Germans have been disappointed because they had always believed that all Germans were philosophers. In the same way all those who thought that wars were impossible, have been painfully surprised – these cases are not mine.'

There was no prospect that the neutrality towards continental affairs which had proved beneficial for England would be abandoned, nor that a firm political and military view of the new Reich as the 'enemy' would henceforth be adopted. However, shortly afterwards – on 16 February 1872 – Lord Arthur Russell made an assessment of Prussia and Germany which almost certainly reflected opinion in Britain with some accuracy. Its ideological aspect was striking and, regarding the future of Anglo-German relations at times of potential international conflicts, revealing:[84]

> Prussia now represents all that is most antagonistic to the liberal and democratic ideas of the age; military despotism, the rule of the sword, contempt for sentimental talk, indifference to human suffering, imprisonment of independent opinion, transfer by force of unwilling populations to a hateful yoke, disregard of European opinion, total want of greatness or generosity etc. etc.

Though the accusation was somewhat exaggerated, the sentiments were widely shared in Britain. Odo Russell was in general agreement with it:[85] 'The change that has come over the Germans is very "unerquicklich". They are going for luxury and financing and no longer read their poets.' Internal conditions in the new *Kaiserreich* provided much cause for criticism, particularly when its measures were compared with an ideal image of that 'spiritual' Germany which had never actually existed. Ambassador Russell expressed real anxiety about the future political course Germany was likely to adopt in foreign affairs. Nevertheless, he remained largely calm about existing relations between Britain and Germany – officially, semi-officially and privately. Admittedly, on 1 February 1873 he told Hammond, permanent under secretary of state in the Foreign Office, of his fear[86] that the Germans might soon become the 'Bullies of Europe' and 'give advice where it is not wished for'. Yet he went on: 'All things being quiet and satisfactory for the present thank God ...'

In the atmosphere of the bilateral relations of Britain and Germany, at least, an unmistakable deterioration had set in. Traces of it are evident wherever one investigates British opinion of the German Reich in this period: 'Englishmen don't like Germany', reported Lord Arthur Russell to his brother Odo, ambassador in Berlin, on 10 December 1872,[87] 'they like Paris and have friends there.' He went on: 'Gladstone doesn't like Germans – Salisbury hates them. Derby doesn't care for them.' Though attitudes such as this had important implications for the future, in the 1870s such phobias must be seen in the context of the British tendency to adopt a cautious, critical and even hostile attitude towards any potential hegemonic power on the continent. Consequently, the new Reich was accused of every negative attribute, of being power-crazed, of immorality, of avarice, of loose living – all the accusations which Victorian England had made against the France of Napoleon III during the 1850s and 1860s.

Thus, after a conversation with a Dutch diplomat in London, Lord Arthur Russell wrote to his brother in Germany on 13 September 1871, complaining about the apparent decline in morals in the new German Reich:[88] 'He says, luxury, ostentation, extravagant imitation of Paris are now raging in Berlin & will lead to the decay of that hardy and self controlled race of Brandenburgians.' And six months later he summarized his disappointment over the ostensible abdication of the spirit in the face of newly acquired power – a theme which occupied contemporaries in Britain and abroad when they reflected on the state founded by Bismarck:[89] 'The liberal party in England has been grievously disappointed by the absence of all selfcontrol and moderation with which philosophical Germany gratified the passion of vindictiveness upon the French – and the blindness with which she introduces the evils & luxuries of Caesarism which have been the curse of France.'

As we have already seen, many of these criticisms of the German Reich are to be understood as British propaganda against a potential new hegemonic power. They can therefore be compared with earlier British attacks on France and, before that, against Spain in the form of the *'leyenda negra'*.[90] Yet their reflection of the beginnings of a real change of attitude gives them historical significance. The persistent negative judgements of Bismarck, Prussia and Germany must therefore be weighed appropriately. Historians have tended, when analysing the causes of Anglo-German antagonism in the Age of Imperialism, to attach too much importance to them, at least in the years when the Reich was founded. For at first the foreign policy attitude of Great Britain towards Prussia, and then Germany, did not change. Anti-German sentiments became significant only in the following decades, as colonial, naval and international tensions placed a critical strain on Anglo-German relations.

During the period in question, these developments lay in the future. Despite British anger during the war of 1870–1 at the German siege of Paris, despite disapproval of the annexation plans for Alsace-Lorraine, Great Britain was never even tempted to intervene. Lord Arthur Russell noted this fact on 12 January 1871 in a letter to Sir Robert Morier which calmly considered British interests:[91] 'I do not believe the transfer of so small a province in central Europe to be a sufficient English interest to plunge this country into a war with Germany.' And in the summer of 1875 Lady Derby wrote to Sir Robert Morier on the issue; her letter summarized the maxims of British foreign policy during this period with a lack of sophistication which does not disguise the fundamental accuracy of her remarks:[92] 'Let the foreigners fight it out – they won't hurt us.' Realistically, what if anything had happened to change the British approach following the foundation of the Reich?

Instead of the France of Napoleon III, Great Britain now had to deal with the potential domination of the European continent by the German Reich. Thus far, it was obviously necessary to pay much greater attention to the *Kaiserreich* than had been given to Prussia during the 1860s. At that time, Bismarck had been engaged in altering the status quo in central Europe and pursuing an aggressive foreign policy. But his conduct had not ultimately been a threat to Britain; indeed, it had even offered distinct advantages as far as the balance of power was concerned. After 1871, Germany had become a new 'half-hegemonic' power on the continent. British statesmen therefore had to ensure that British interests were protected, within the framework of normal relations between the two countries. Accordingly, British hopes for bilateral relations ranged from a relationship of 'cordiality' to one of loose *entente*. In any case, British statesmen would attempt to resolve conflicts by means of agreement rather than through confrontation.

The British attitude was decisively influenced by Bismarck's affirmation that the German Reich was a 'satiated state'. The Reich Chancellor renounced naval power, did not adopt a policy of colonial acquisition and ignored the invasion scares which erupted in the English press. Though even a sensible observer of the German scene such as the ambassador Odo Russell felt that the German military might have aggressive designs on British wealth, he retained his optimistic faith in the power of diplomacy:[93] 'Happily, however, for the peace of the world, armies are instruments in the hands of diplomacy and the statesmen of Germany earnestly desire friendship with England rather than war.'

Odo Russell expressed equal confidence in a long letter to his uncle, the former Prime Minister Earl Russell. His excessively friendly comments about Germany may well have been influenced by his awareness of the current pro-Protestant and pro-Bismarckian sentiments of the old statesman, as revealed in his open support of Bismarck in the *Kulturkampf* with the Catholic Church. With reference to Franco-German relations, which were observed with keen interest in Britain, the ambassador emphasized the defensive approach adopted by the Reich towards French révanchism:[94]

> you ask me what the opinion in Berlin is with regard to the future of France? The universal opinion seems to be that whatever gov[t] follows that of Mr. Thiers and nobody pretends to guess what that will be the French nation will for the next few years be intent on preparing a war of revenge and that the rulers of France, whoever they are, will seek popularity in promoting the national wish – . For that reason the Germans think it their duty to increase and improve their military defences so as to be prepared for a second attack if it sh[d] come, and not be unprepared as they were from neglect after the military glories of Frederic the Great in 1806 ... There is no wish in Germany to interfere with the internal affairs of France, – but a second war would inevitably lead to the policy recommended by General Blücher of materially weakening France so as to ensure the future peace of Europe.

The ambassador then surveyed the situation on the European continent in general. Since it was recognized in Britain how dangerous the combined might of Russia, France and Austria could be to the new Reich in central Europe,[95] Russell was undoubtedly exaggerating German power when he declared: 'In fact the so-called balance of power in Europe is over, for Germany has become invincible and can turn out an army of one million men in ten days.' He then described the power of attraction which the German Reich exercised over the German-speaking parts of the population of Austria-Hungary, whilst the Slavs of the Dual Monarchy were being drawn towards Russia. Nevertheless, Russell did not argue that the German *Kaiserreich* posed any acute danger to Europe, and he seemed sanguine about the prospects for his own country and for British-Prussian relations: 'The wish for peace is deep and sincere in Germany and their military preparations are merely the result of prudence and forethought, the wisdom of nations. Thanks to Lord Granville's able and skilful policy our relations with Germany are very good and the new German ambassador Count Münster will contribute to keep them so.'

In this letter, Russell's assessment of German policy was extremely positive. However, on other occasions during the years 1871–5 and certainly until the 'War in Sight' crisis of 1875, the ambassador continued to express deep mistrust about the political intentions of Bismarck and the course being followed by the German Reich. His fears were summarized in a speculation about the foreign policy objectives of the

German Chancellor, sent in a 'semi-official' letter dated 14 March 1873 to the British ambassador in Paris, Lord Lyons (this document has probably been relied on too heavily by historians of the period). Russell wrote:[96] 'The two great objects of Bismarck's policy are: 1. The supremacy of Germany in Europe and of the German race in the world...' He continued to distort Bismarck's policy until 1875 at least, as his uncertain assessment of the German Chancellor slowly took shape. Even in Versailles in 1871, he had been fascinated by the inscrutable Prussian statesman:[97] '"Das Dämonische"' is stronger in him than in any man I know'. Such judgements contributed to the general mistrust of Bismarck in the British political ruling classes and in public opinion, although in 1881 the British diplomat was to complain that he had spent ten years in an unsuccessful attempt to win trust for the German Chancellor in England.[98] Despite the long-term implications of such assessments, the fact remains that relations between Germany and Great Britain were fundamentally untroubled throughout the 1870s. Though crises did arise from time to time, either Anglo-German relations continued undisturbed or normality was quickly restored.

Great Britain was well accustomed to using diplomatic, political and military means to deal with the hegemonic ambitions and efforts of continental states. British statesmen thus handled the 'War in Sight' crisis of 1875 with resolution and in 'concerted movement' with the other states of Europe.[99] Though this drama dominated the weeks of spring 1875, once it was over it could even be regarded as of benefit to Britain because it had demonstrated to the new Reich the limits of its power. From then on, Bismarck's policy of maintaining peace and the status quo won increasing trust. Arthur Russell's confident comment, influenced by an awareness of Britain's history and its current position, thereafter reflected the British attitude towards foreign policy in general and the German Reich in particular:[100] 'We have had *our full share* of military and naval glory and now England has other interests to attend to, other duties: Australia, India, trade, pauper populations etc. etc. etc.' Moreover, even the 'half-hegemonic' land power of Prussia-Germany ranked below the domestic political and social questions to which Britain was now devoting its attention from the security of its splendid isolation. British governments in general were not prepared to allow their politics to be too much dictated by foreign policy issues, and particularly not by continental ones. Hence Arthur Russell's comment:[101] 'We must in all we do, never care *in the least* about continental or American opinion.' Such a maxim truly expressed a widespread confidence in the superiority of British civilization. Russell himself was able to comment on this sentiment with a certain ironic criticism, but his remarks actually expressed the prevailing mood of a considerable section of public opinion in the country:[102] 'these Germans must not forget that Lancashire is the centre of the world.' British foreign policy was made in an atmosphere of strong national identity and proud self-confidence. It is therefore understandable that scarcely any of the country's leading statesmen and diplomats were inclined to overrate Germany, temporarily 'satiated' and adopting a policy of peace under Bismarck, in either a negative or a positive sense. The Conservative leader of the opposition, Disraeli, certainly complained on a number of occasions before 1874 that the country was devoting too much of its energies to 'domestic legislation' and taking too little interest in external affairs. Yet he too remained proud and confident, despite all the changes in continental affairs:[103] 'there never was a moment in our history when the power of England was so great and her resources so vast and inexhaustible.' In the sphere of international politics, German's 'dazzling pre-eminence in Europe'[104] scarcely posed any real threat. British governments had become well accustomed to dealing with nations in continental Europe which were suspected of harbouring hopes of hegemony, and Anglo-German relations appeared to fit comfortably within this framework. At this stage, the relationship was normal and even friendly.

Gradually, the domestic politics of 'Bismarckism'[105] were also being reassessed in Britain, and the leadership of the Reich Chancellor was seen in a more favourable light. As time passed it became increasingly clear that the political alternatives to Bismarck's policies in Germany were far from attractive for Great Britain. First, Bismarck now seemed to be a reliable bulwark against 'red anarchy', which the English political elite had feared and abominated since the Paris Commune.[106] Events in Paris between February and May 1871 wrought a change in British opinion towards France and Germany. Pro-French sentiment, which had prevailed since September 1870, was replaced by a return of sympathy for the Germans of the kind they had enjoyed before Sedan. Such feeling helped 'to ease the entry of the new great power into the European community of states'.[107]

Secondly, politicians in London grew more aware that it was *Zornebock* – as Sir Robert Morier privately described Bismarck[108] – who was the author and embodiment of the welcome policy of external 'satiation'. Though the national liberals were demanding the introduction of the parliamentary system Britain would have welcomed, they were also eager to overcome the 'incompleteness' of the new national state by other, much less desirable means. The national liberal demand for territorial adjustments in central Europe was regarded with disapproval in Britain, their desire for a naval, colonial and world policy as unacceptable. Ambassador Odo Russell was particularly concerned, as he revealed in his report for the Foreign Office on 7 February 1874; the question was whether Bismarck could deal with liberal demands, in view of the chorus of complaint about the 'incompleteness' of the young Reich, without running the risk of a new war:[109] 'I must again repeat that Prince Bismarck may find it impossible in the future to complete the unity of Germany as understood by the National Party, that is mediatation of the smaller courts and the annexation of the German speaking portions of Europe – without another appeal to arms.' And some months later he wondered whether Bismarck might even be forced into another war – this time against the Habsburg monarchy rather than France – 'for the consolidation and completion of German unity' as a result of national liberal demands for the incorporation of German Austria into the Reich.[110]

Anxiety in Great Britain was now being caused not only – and not even primarily – by Bismarck's own foreign policy. British statesmen and diplomats now regarded the co-operation of the Chancellor with the liberals, his increasing dependence on them, and their demands for expansion, as a real and serious danger: 'The aspirations of the great national party in Germany should... be taken into account', commented another report to the London Foreign Office from the Berlin embassy.[111] The programme of the national liberals was now 'the completion of German unity before everything else'. Peering uncertainly into the future, the report continued: 'Will they be satisfied with anything less than the annexation of all the territory inhabited by German-speaking people?' Politicians in Britain were having to face the fact that the growing threat to British interests in continental, naval and colonial affairs was not emanating from Bismarck at all. His policy of 'satiation' was beyond question in all issues outside the European continent. After his appearance at the Congress of Berlin in 1878 in particular, the Chancellor won high approval in Britain as the guarantor of peace and the existing European order, which was increasingly identified with the 'Bismarck System'. In contrast, the national liberals in Germany were making vigorous demands for an end to the 'incompleteness' of the new national state, and not mainly by the introduction of a parliamentary system of government. They were directing much of their attention towards changes in foreign policy which would offset those aspects of the foundation of the Reich which they found unsatisfactory. Any fulfilment of their unreasonable demands would inevitably damage Britain's global and European interests and compel it to act. Britain had observed with some approval the creation of a flexible centre in Europe,[112] resting on co-operation between Germany and Austria-Hungary and forming the balance to the powers on the periphery; it would have been most unwilling to see this jeopardized by a new division of the Habsburg monarchy into its German and Slav territories. Changes such as this would come close to a revolution in the European order, leading to a growth of international anarchy with all its potential domestic dangers. British statesmen had to ask themselves whether a liberalization of Germany could actually be regarded as beneficial to British foreign policy. Instead, perhaps it would be wise to accept 'Bismarckism' despite its undoubted imperfections in domestic politics, since in international terms it acted as a guarantor of European stability. 'Bismarckism' was the embodiment of the concept of national satiation which was so useful to Britain and which made such a positive contrast to the foreign policy demands of liberal and democratic groups in Germany.

At this stage, certain parallels between British attitudes towards the foundation of the Reich during the 1860s and 1870s, and British policies towards the German Question in the period 1848–50, are clearly apparent. In 1848–50, the British reaction to German struggles for unification was not initially negative. On the contrary, it began in a comparatively positive manner, continued with caution and grew hostile only when the Schleswig-Holstein question became acute and the naval building plans of the Paulskirche gave an alarming insight into the foreign policy ambitions of the parliamentarians assembled at Frankfurt. Just as the change in British policy towards the German Reich at the turn of the century was influenced by the naval and international ambitions of certain 'bourgeois' groups, so there were comparable demands from the liberals in 1848–50 which eventually provoked a hostile response from Great Britain. There was thus a paradox in Anglo-German relations in the nineteenth century, centred on the different domestic and foreign policy perspectives of the two states. Bismarck's domestic policies were rejected by a majority of the British ruling class. In foreign affairs, however, the situation was very different; in fact, only Bismarck's solution to the German national problem – that of imposing the German Reich from above and restricting it to Little Germany – was compatible with British interests in European and world politics. Thus, the introduction of a parliamentary constitution in the new national state would certainly have been welcome to Great Britain from a domestic political perspective. In foreign affairs, by contrast, it would have meant the triumph of (national) liberal and democratic demands which had been apparent since 1848–50 and were scarcely compatible with British interests. Ironically, only the monarchical-constitutional solution imposed by Bismarck guaranteed – at least for a time – that restraint in foreign policy which made the new German national state tolerable to Great Britain and Europe. Whatever its domestic policies, the 'Bismarck System' ensured that the new German Reich was founded, and conducted itself, with moderation. Consequently, British statesmen came to regard it as a factor promoting peace and order in the international system under the rule of its chancellor. A comparison with 1848–50 is instructive; then, 'the ambition of Prussia ... [was] feared much less ... in London than the patriotic desires and fantasies about the future of the democratic liberal people's movement'.[113] Similarly, in the years between 1860 and

1880 it is arguable that the *kleindeutsch* national state could have been created and sustained only by the pursuit of policies which were widely regarded as being against the spirit of the age. After Bismarck's departure, the German Reich took the line demanded by much of its political, social, economic and academic elite, at least in foreign affairs; in tune with the prevailing ideas of the epoch, it strove to emulate other states by conducting an imperialist foreign policy. With hindsight, the decision was a fateful one. Would the development of a parliamentary system at this stage have arrested this fatal development, or merely accelerated it? The question remains hypothetical. However, in view of the popular demand for hegemony and a significant role in world politics for Germany – both of which would have endangered the European balance of power – it is certainly not safe to assume that a genuine parliamentary system would automatically have saved the Reich from its disastrous course.[114] Indeed, there are at least as many arguments to support the opposite point of view. Since their view of what was desirable in German foreign policy was so different from what they would have liked to see in internal affairs, British statesmen decided to accept the domestic political status quo in the Reich and to enjoy the stability in foreign affairs which resulted from it. Indeed, they adopted a more cautious approach towards the German liberal party as a result of its demands in the sphere of foreign policy. As long as Bismarck headed the government, so it seemed to Lord Odo Russell, there would be a 'frank and cordial understanding' between the two states.[115] Despite this assessment, the British ambassador never overlooked the potential negative consequences of the 'military spirit'[116] which was becoming dominant in Germany. Developments such as this, linked with the undeniable though latent hegemonic ambitions of the Reich, might some day come out into the open as a result of the unresolved tensions caused by the disparity between social and economic developments and the constitutional structure of the Reich.[117]

However, the most important long-term threat to Great Britain, and the revolutionary implications of the foundation of the Reich,[118] lay in the fact that Bismarck had achieved unification through war, in three greatly admired military campaigns. In accepting the new national state, Britain had followed a constructive policy[119] of the kind applied elsewhere, with the exception of the nationality issue in the Ottoman Empire. Its statesmen had accommodated the timely German demand for unification with general goodwill, though without excessive interest. Their conduct had revealed no significant sign of a conservative 'fear of catastrophe'[120] resulting from political change, which could frequently be detected on the continent. British policy in general, despite differences of detail in Europe and overseas, aimed to avoid revolutionary change and worldwide disorder in the international order; at the same time, there should be adjustment to unavoidable necessities in world politics by means of a policy of peaceful change in accordance with the country's own domestic political principles. Consequently, British policy did not simply call for a reactionary suppression of all demands for change. The attempt was made to work together with the developing powers of the era rather than in opposition to them, and to accommodate efforts to achieve freedom within the empire and the international order alike. As Henry Kissinger once noted critically,[121] British policy was not directed towards a bold historical vision. Instead, it was based on faith in the superiority of the country's political culture and the attraction of its maxims of progress and 'improvement'. Even more important, it was rooted in British history and experience during the course of the century, which showed the nation the way to avoid mistakes through careful willingness to compromise and make necessary changes. The catastrophe of the American War of Independence, in particular, was believed to provide support for such a policy.

This British attitude, this willingness to adjust to the national strivings of other peoples, may be regarded as an important precondition for the foundation of the German Reich. The fact that unification was achieved by means of war, however, was to pose a grave challenge to Great Britain which became more apparent with the passage of time. The brilliant military successes of Prussia undeniably influenced the international atmosphere and the thinking and conduct of other European states. The use of force to resolve political disputes became an increasingly attractive proposition, in Prussia as elsewhere. The ideal of 'blood and iron' based on military strength thus came to the fore, against Bismarck's own convictions and intentions. In so doing, it offered an alternative model course of development to that provided by Britain with its 'way of life' and political constitution. At this early stage, the potential attraction of the Prussian model was not yet clear, and was in any case difficult for British politicians and public opinion to understand. Nevertheless, to this extent there was a misjudgement in British foreign policy which had far-reaching consequences. Though this wrong assessment was made when the Reich was being established, its consequences did not become acute until much later, as a result of fateful political decisions by the German side.

Contemporary British policy was not yet affected by these factors. Until the beginning of the 1880s, Bismarck continued to be seen as the guarantor of the naval and colonial restraint of the German Reich. It was significant that, on the whole, the German Chancellor regarded the European order as legitimate. Moreover, British interests were well served by the balancing power of France and Russia, which prevented the possible development of hegemonic ambitions by the Reich.[122]

It is vital to remember that British assessments of the German Reich and the European continent were, in the 1860s and 1870s, made at a time when British power was unbroken and British confidence at its height: 'England alone remains unconquered and unconquerable with her neutrality, her fleet and her freedom', claimed Ambassador Odo Russell in his report to the Foreign Office of 30 October 1872 regarding the British attitude towards Bismarck's Germany. He continued proudly:[123] 'Three black spots on his [Bismarck's] horizon. Her neutrality, because it might again prove benevolent to France, – her fleet, because Germany has none to rival it, – her freedom, because the example of freedom so near Germany is fatal to the rule of blood and iron.'

IV

British observers such as Lord Odo Russell and Sir Robert Morier, both leading experts on Germany in the Foreign Office, recognized the pressures on the new, exclusively European great power. In their view, Germany would be forced to adopt a world policy in future in order to hold its ground and compete against the other powers after its belated unification. However, a policy of expansion would most probably bring about international conflicts which might alienate Great Britain and Germany from each other. Consequently, even in the first years after the creation of the Reich there was some anxiety in Britain about the future course of relations between the two countries. In particular, British statesmen wondered how long Bismarck could succeed in guaranteeing the 'satiation' of the young national state, encumbered as it was with the 'burden of immobility'.

To British statesmen and diplomats, Bismarck appeared more and more as the domestic guarantor in Germany of the interests of British world policy. At the same time, they grew to realize that of all the options for the solution of the German Question, only the monarchical-constitutional German Reich created by Bismarck was tolerable to the great powers of Britain and Russia, and actually beneficial to Great Britain for pragmatic and even ideological reasons.

At this point it is useful to widen our narrow investigation of Anglo-Prussian and Anglo-German relations and examine the broader European context. Liberal attempts to unite Germany failed because their territorial claims were too extensive and their ideological orientation aroused suspicion in St Petersburg.[124] Furthermore, liberal demands were even more threatening to the existence of the Habsburg monarchy than the *kleindeutsch* state created by Bismarck. For the time being, Bismarckism at least served to restrain the demands of the national movement in Germany on the German-speaking regions of Austria-Hungary.[125]

The plans of Schwarzenberg and Bruck for the creation of an empire of 70 million people in Europe were scarcely compatible with the interests of the other powers. It is in fact doubtful whether Schwarzenberg's bold ideas, so much 'against the spirit of the age',[126] could ever have succeeded in substituting Greater Austrian politics for national politics. Similarly, the ideas of Constantin Frantz for a Greater German universalist Reich, organized on a federal basis, would not have been welcomed by the European powers because of the territorial extent and associated economic and political potential of such a state.[127] It seems unlikely that a federal structure in central Europe would have succeeded in removing fears about the sheer aggregation of power involved.[128] If a loose federal state had been adopted it would have proved incapable of concerted action in foreign policy. A state which was immobile and weak, resembling the old German Confederation, would not have provided the stable but flexible centre required by Britain. On the other hand, an effective and tightly organized structure would have become a problem for Europe simply because of its size and power in international affairs.

The national and international situation, the conditions and demands of the period, meant that only the Bismarckian solution to the national problem of the Germans offered any real prospect of success and permanence. Constitutionally, a 'liberal' Reich would have been more welcome to many Germans as well as to Britain (and to France, though not to Russia). The foreign policy of the liberals, however, was unacceptable to them. Even in 1848–50 it had been the representatives of German liberalism who had blocked the creation of German unity by the extreme nature of their foreign policy demands. In contrast, before 1870 Bismarck revealed a certain moderation in foreign affairs; once the Reich was founded, moreover, his policy of 'satiation' led him to be accepted and eventually even admired in Britain. After his clever conciliation during the 'War in Sight' crisis of 1875 and his role as 'honest broker' at the Congress of Berlin in 1878, his stock was high. To the advantage of European peace and the Pax Britannica alike, the German Chancellor worked with Austria-Hungary to provide a stable and flexible centre in Europe, a continuation by other means of the 'Metternich System' of the first half of the eighteenth century.

In order to fulfil this international function – which secured and even legitimized its national existence – the German Reich had as much as possible to keep a 'free hand'. In particular, it must remain neutral to the extent that none of the great powers felt impelled to take the step of military intervention against Germany. Even a conflict of interest between Britain and Russia – in the event that German policy was at all capable of pursuing an independent line – must not lead to a *casus belli* between the two powers, as this could all too easily endanger the international order in Europe which was so important in sustaining the existence of Germany.

As Prussia had been to a lesser degree in the 1860s, the German Reich was clearly less able than the other great powers to display its strength and exercise it with relative freedom. Germany was forced to respect the limits imposed upon it by Britain and Russia in particular; otherwise, it faced the possibility of an intervention which would threaten its very existence, as the events of spring 1875 revealed. The conditions of the 'Crimean War Situation',[129] the temporary alienation between the two world powers, had created a 'wave trough' (L. Dehio) of history which assisted the creation of the *kleindeutsch* state in central Europe. Yet although these external conditions helped to guarantee the continued existence of the German national state in the sense of maintaining the national status quo, they also restricted its development by depriving it of the ability to compete on equal terms with the other states of Europe.

The German Reich was constantly being reminded that it owed its creation and continued existence to a specific international situation and that it was dependent on Britain and Russia. Its existence could therefore be traced more to its compatibility with the interests of the world powers than to its own character and power. The European dimension of the system developed by Bismarck during and after the foundation of the Reich, the 'Bismarck System', was beneficial to the other powers in so far as it helped to prevent revolutionary upheaval and destruction of the status quo in Europe; above all, from the British viewpoint, it satisfied the requirement for stability and order within the framework of Britain's global policy of 'peaceful change'.

The sole chance for a solution of the problem of German nationhood lay in a linkage of the German Question with the requirements of international politics. *Rebus sic stantibus*, it could only be made reality in the Bismarckian sense during the 1860s. If a united Germany was to take its place within the global Pax Britannica at all, it would have to be in a territorially limited form and with a monarchical constitutional framework. Only in this form did it correspond with the requirements of British *raison d'état*, with those 'British interests'[130] which were so important to its creation and continued existence.

It is therefore not accurate to claim that, during the 1860s and 1870s, the foundation of the German national state was *a priori* incompatible with British interests – on economic, demographic, or political grounds, or because its domestic arrangements were in such contrast to the parliamentary system of Great Britain. On the contrary: it is clear that British relations with Prussia, and then with the German Reich, could be described as normal in these years. In principle and in practice, relations between them were far from impossible.

Such facts throw fresh light on the accusation which is sometimes made against British non-intervention policy, to the effect that it was weak and had missed the opportunity to prevent the foundation of the German Reich by a timely intervention.[131] The accusation is clearly inappropriate. First, non-interventionism was a comprehensive response to the domestic, party and foreign policy interests of the country. And secondly, the threat which Germany was later to pose to Britain, to the European balance of power and to the British Empire had not yet developed and was not clearly recognizable. Of course, there were tendencies and trends within Germany which posed a latent danger to Bismarck's peace policies. These could not be concealed from British politicians and might ultimately have serious implications for both countries. Yet in the last analysis it was political decisions, not the irresistible power of social or international forces, which first seriously damaged Anglo-German relations in the 1880s and caused them to deteriorate still further during the Wilhelmine era. Evidence that the British attitude towards the German national state remained comparatively open-minded was provided in *The Times* on 7 September 1876:[132] 'We have no jealousy of the new Empire. Within its own bounds we wish it every success. But we feel that an enormous power for good or evil has risen up somewhat suddenly in the midst of us, and we watch with interested attention for signs of its character and intentions.'

NOTES

1 Dehio, L., *Gleichgewicht oder Hegemonie. Betrachtungen über ein Grundproblem der neueren Staatengeschichte* (Krefeld: 1948), esp. p. 201.

2 Knaplund, P. (ed.), *Letters from the Berlin Embassy. Selections from the Private Correspondence of British Representatives at Berlin and Foreign Secretary Lord Granville 1871–1874, 1880–1885*, Annual Report of the American Historical Association for the Year 1942 (Washington, DC: 1944), p. 5.

3 Joll, J., *A Historian's View. The Twenty-Seventh Montague Burton Lecture on International Relations* (Leeds: Leeds University Press, 1969), p. 20.

4 Katzenstein, P. J., *Disjointed Partners. Austria and Germany Since 1815* (Berkeley, Calif: 1976), p. 4.

5 Kaehler, S. A., 'Neuere Geschichtslegenden und ihre Widerlegung (1948)', in S. Kaehler, *Studien zur Deutschen Geschichte des 19. und 20. Jahrhunderts. Aufsätze und Vorträge. Herausgegeben und mit einem Nachwort versehen von W. Bussmann* (Göttingen: 1961), esp. p. 311–12.

6 Hötzle, E., *Die Selbstentmachtung Europas. Das Experiment des Friedens vor und im Ersten Weltkrieg* (Göttingen: 1975).

7 Kaehler, 'Neuere Geschichtslegenden', pp. 311–12.

8 Barraclough, G., 'German reunification. An essay in revision', *Historical Studies IV*; papers read before the Fifth Irish Conference of Historians (London: 1963), p. 62 ff. On Barraclough's position see also Becker, J., 'Die Deutsche Frage in der internationalen Politik 1941–1949. Grundzüge und Hauptprobleme ihrer Entwicklung', in J. Becker, T. Stammen and P. Waldmann (eds), *Vorgeschichte der Bundesrepublik Deutschland. Zwischen Kapitulation und Grundgesetz* (Munich: 1979), p. 48.

9   On the use of this term by Kaehler see W. Bussmann, 'Europa und das Bismarckreich', in C. Hinrichs and W. Berges (eds), *Die deutsche Einheit als Problem der europäischen Geschichte* (Stuttgart: 1960), p. 156.

10 See a recent work by Kunich, J., *Das Mirakel des Hauses Brandenburg. Studien zum Verhältnis von Kabinettspolitik und Kriegführung im Zeitalter des Siebenjährigen Krieges* (Munich/Vienna: 1978).

11 British politicians and diplomats were certainly influenced by such beliefs, alongside other motives. See Headlam-Morley, Sir James, *A Memoir of the Paris Peace Conference 1919*, ed. A. Headlam–Morley, R. Bryant, A. Cienciala (London: 1972), p. XXVII (introduction by Agnes Headlam-Morley).

12 On this problem see also the article by L. Gall, 'Bismarck und England', in P. Kluke and P. Alter (eds), *Aspekte der deutsch-britischen Beziehungen im Laufe der Jahrhunderte. Ansprachen und Vorträge zur Eröffnung des Deutschen Historischen Instituts London* (Stuttgart: 1978), p. 48 ff. Examining Anglo-German relations from Bismarck's standpoint, this refuted the idea of a 'special relationship' between the German Reich and Great Britain.

13 Sontag, R. J., *Germany and England. Background of Conflict 1848–1894* (New York: 1964; first edn, 1938), p. 94.

14 The author is preparing a monograph, based on extensive archive research in England, on 'Great Britain and the foundation of the Reich. The 'German Question' in English non-intervention policy (1865–1875)'. It will deal with this issue in particular. See also K. Hildebrand, 'Die deutsche Reichsgründung im Urteil der britischen Politik', in *Francia. Forschungen zur westeuropäischen Geschichte* 5 (1977) (Munich: 1978), p. 399 ff. The observations below are based in part upon this article.

15 See more details in Hildebrand, K., 'Von der Reichseinigung zur "Krieg–in-Sicht" Krise. Preussen-Deutschland als Faktor der britischen Aussenpolitik 1865–1875', in M. Stürmer (ed.), *Das kaiserliche Deutschland. Politik und Gesellschaft 1870–1918* (Düsseldorf: 1970), p. 215, esp. n. 78.

16 Treitschke, H. von, 'Preussen auf dem Wiener Kongress III (1876)', *Preussische Jahrbücher*, vol. 37, p. 285, quoted by E. Leipprand, 'Treitschke's Stellung zu England' (dissertation, Tübingen: 1928), pp. 57–8.

17 Marcks, E., *Englands Machtpolitik. Vorträge und Studien. Neu herausgegeben und eingeleitet von W.Andreas* (Stuttgart/Berlin: 1940), p. 52.

18 Michael, W., 'Deutschland und England', *Deutsche Rundschau* CL (1912), pp. 221–2.

19 Hagen, M. von, *Bismarck und England* (Stuttgart/Berlin: 3rd edn, 1943), pp. 44–5.

20 Valentin, V., *Bismarcks Reichsgründung im Urteil englischer Diplomaten* (Amsterdam: 1937); Mosse, W. E., *The European Powers and the German Question 1848–1871. With Special Reference to England and Russia* (Cambridge: 1958); Millman, R., *British Foreign Policy and the Coming of the Franco-Prussian War* (Oxford: 1965).

21 See, for example, Palmerston's observations in his 'Memorandum on relations with Germany' of 16 September 1847. This did not oppose German unification on principle, but warned emphatically of the incalculable dangers for Britain of a protectionist policy by the *Zollverein*. Extracts reprinted in Bourne, K., *The Foreign Policy of Victorian England 1830–1902* (Oxford: 1970), p. 277 ff.

22 On this issue in general see Smith, F. B., *The Making of the Second Reform Bill* (Cambridge: 1966); Cowling, M., *Disraeli, Gladstone and Revolution. The Passing of the Second Reform Bill* (Cambridge: 1967).

23 Public Record Office (cited as PRO), Foreign Office (cited as FO) 256/33, Stanley to Bloomfield, 12 March 1867. There has been some modernization of spellings and correction of obvious mistakes in the archive sources.

24 On this subject see Cecil, G., *Life of Robert, Marquis of Salisbury*, Vol. I: *1830–1868* (London: 1921), p. 301 ff; Thiersch, R., 'Bismarck im Urteil englischer Politiker und Diplomaten seiner Zeit 1862–1890 (dissertation, Munich: 1939); Frauendienst, W., 'England und die Bismarcksche Politik', *Probleme britischer Reichs–und Aussenpolitik, herausgegeben von der Hochschule für Politik, Forschungsabteilung* (Berlin: 1939), p. 14.

25 Quoted in Taylor, R., *Lord Salisbury* (London: 1975), p. 133.

26 Bodleian Library, Oxford (cited as BLO), Clarendon Papers dep. c.93, Russell to Clarendon, 29 April 1866.

27 Wemyss, R. (ed.), *Memoirs and Letters of the Rt. Hon. Sir Robert Morier, G.C.B., from 1826 to 1876* (London: 1911), Vol. 1, p. 408.

28 On the use of theories and terminology of Bonapartism and Caesarism see Gall, L., 'Bismarck und der Bonapartismus', *Historische Zeitschrift* 223 (1976), p. 618 ff.

29 Quoted in Eyck, E., *Bismarck* (Erlenbach-Zurich: 1941), Vol. I, p. 276. This mistaken assessment of Great Britain, its political culture and its foreign policy by (Prussian) German historians, lasted for many years as the 'continuity of error' in the German history of the Bismarck era. In this connection see, for example, Kurt Rheindorf's assessment of a 'degenerate' England in this period, in Rheindorf, K., *Die Scwarze-Meer-(Pontus) Frage vom Pariser Frieden von 1871. Ein Beitrag zu den orientalischen Fragen und zur Politik der Grossmächte im Zeitalter Bismarcks* (Berlin: 1925), pp. 62–3. See also the study by Brüns, G., *England und der deutsche Krieg 1866* (Berlin: 1933), p. 211, which relies on the comments of Heinrich von Treitschke. See esp. p. 213.

30 See Bourne, *Foreign Policy*, p. 116; also Burckhardt, H., *DDeutschland, England, Frankreich. Die politischen Beziehungen Deutschlands zu den beiden westeuropäischen Grossmächten 1864–1866* (Munich: 1970), esp. p. 267.

31 PRO FO 918/85, Odo Russell to his mother, Lady William Russell, typewritten copy, 23 November 1870: 'a man of genius'. Odo Russell's estate was made available to researchers only in the later 1960s and the Ampthill Papers have yet to be evaluated systematically.

32 PRO FO 918/84, Odo Russell to Arthur Russell, typewritten copy, 11 February 1871.

33 Balliol College Library, Oxford (cited as BCLO), Morier Archive, Lytton to Morier typewritten copy, 22 January 1872.

34 Quoted in Beales, D., *England and Italy 1859–1860* (London: 1961), p. 172.
26 35 In contrast, see Craig, G. A., 'Britain and Europe (1866–1869). A study in the application of non intervention' (PhD thesis, Princeton, NJ: 1941). Craig produced a powerful and scholarly criticism of non-intervention policy as a policy of weakness with far–reaching consequences for Britain and the international system.

36 Royal Archives Windsor (cited as RA), I 43/161, Russell to Queen Victoria, 1 April 1866. The document is mentioned, but without the above quotation, in Mosse, *The European Powers*, p. 230, n. 6.

37 Vincent, J. R.(ed.), *Disraeli, Derby and the Conservative Party. Journals and Memoirs of Edward Henry, Lord Stanley 1849–1869* (Hassocks: 1978), p. 249.

38 Vincent, *Disraeli, Derby*, p. 283.

39 Thus the English diplomat Lord Augustus Loftus once paraphrased the issue; see Valentin, *Bismarcks Reichsgründung*, p. 150.

40 On this realistic assessment of power politics and warfare see the reflections of Aron, R., *Frieden und Krieg. Eine Theorie der Staatenwelt* (Frankfurt-am-Main: 1963), p. 162.

41 Monypenny, W. F. and G. E.Buckle, *The Life of Benjamin Disraeli, Earl of Beaconsfield*, new and revised edn, 2 vols. (London: 1929), Vol. 2, p. 201.

42 RA I/44 2. Copy. Extract. Circular Dispatch to Minor German States. Relations between Austria and Prussia. This quotation, cited as PRO FO 181/422, also appears (as a copy appended to a letter from Clarendon to Buchanan of 18 April 1866) in Mosse, *The European Powers*, p. 236, n. 7.

43 Morier to Lady Salisbury, 15 March 1866 (with reference to the German-Danish War). Quotedd in Mossse, *The European Powrs*, p. 214.

44 See Gall, 'Bismarck und England', p. 49.

45 Quoted by Brüns, *England und der deutsche Krieg*, p. 103.

46 See a summary in Dawson, W. H., *The German Empire 1867–1914 and the Unity Movement* (London: 1966; first edn, 1919), Vol. 1, pp. 281–2.

47 See Gall, 'Bismarck und England', p. 49.

48 Quoted in Dawson, *The German Empire*, p. 282.

49 Plessner, H., *Die verspätete Nation. über die politische Verführbarkeit bürgerlichen Geistes* (Stuttgart: 5th edn, 1969), p. 39.

50 Illuminating on the 'category of the incomplete' is Scheider, T., 'Grundfragen der neueren deutschen Geschichte. Zum Problem der historischen Urteilsbildung', in H. Böhme (ed.), *Probleme der Reichsgründungszeit 1848–1879* (Cologne/Berlin: 1968), esp. p. 27 ff.

51 Rothfels, H., *Bismarcks englische Bündnispolitik* (Stuttgart: 1924), p. 9.

52 Stanley to Bloomfield, 21 July 1866, published in Temperley, H. and L. M. Penson (eds), *Foundations of British Foreign Policy from Pitt (1792) to Salisbury (1902)* (Cambridge: 1966), p. 307, doc. 118 (a).

53 See above, p. [/].

54 Oncken, H., *Die Sicherheit Indiens. Ein Jahrhundert englischeer Weltpolitik* (Berlin: 1937), p. 27.

55 Gruner, W. D., 'Europäischer Friede als nationales Interesse. Die Rolle des Deuschen Bundes in der britischen Politik 1814–1832', *Bohemia. Jahrbuch des Collegium Carolinum* 18 (1977), p. 101.

56 On the problem of 'balance of power' and 'non-intervention' see also Bourne, K., 'The Foreign Secretaryship of Lord Stanley, July 1866–December 1868' (PhD thesis, London University: 1955), p. 38. From a more fundamental persppective, see also Wight, M., 'The balance of power', in M. Wight and H. Butterfield (eds), *Diplomatic Investigations. Essays in the Theory of International Politics* (London: 1966), p. 159 ff.

57 On this subject see the interesting and thoughtful article by Rohe, K., 'Ursachen und Bedingungen des modernen britischen Imperialismus vor 1914', in W. J. Mommsen (ed.), *Der moderne Imperialismus* (Stuttgart: 1971), pp. 75–6.

58 See Wehler, H.-U., *Bismarck und der Imperialismus* (Cologne/ Berlin: 1969), p. 39 ff ('socio-economic period of crisis'), for England pp, 47–8. See also Saul, S. B., *The Myth of the Great Depression, 1873–1896* (London: 1969).

59 See above, p. [/].

60 Zechlin, E., *Die Reichsgründung* (Frankfurt-am-Main/Berlin: 1967), p. 29.

61 See the judgement of Arthur Russell, very typical of the assessment of British policy towards tsarist Russia, in a letter to his brother Odo, British ambassador in Berlin, dated 4 February 1873. He described the Russian danger to India: 'The annexation of India is a favourite plan of the Muscovite press, though perhaps not of Russian statesmen.' Blakiston Private Collection, London, Arthur Russell to Odo Russell (1871–1883), 4 vols (copies) (cited as Arthur Russell to Odo Russell). Through the friendly mediation of archivist Dr Wilhelm Lenz (now of the Bundesarchiv Koblenz), in 1970–1, I was given access to the typewritten copies of the letters from Arthur Russell to his brother which are in the private possession of the Blakiston family. The letters had not previously been available to researchers. On Lord Arthur Russell see A. Ramm, *Sir Robert Morier. Envoy and Ambassador in the Age of Imperialism 1876–1893* (Oxford: 1973), pp. 4–5.

62 Bourne, *The Foreign Policy*, p. 50 ff. On the origins of the term 'appeasement' in the period under discussion see also Kennedy, P., 'The tradition of appeasement in British foreign policy 1865–1939', *British Journal of International Studies* 2 (1976), p. 195 ff, esp. pp. 199–200. It can be useful to understand 'appeasement' as a feature of British foreign policy which spanned long periods in the nineteenth and twentieth centuries; thus it could be observed before Great Britain had to deal with the 'revisionist' states of the interwar years in the twentieth century, and perhaps characterized British policy towards the United States of America and the Soviet Union in the 1940s and 1950s. Nevertheless, the term should not be used indiscriminately. After all, as Gustav Schmidt has rightly pointed out, Britain had to deal with Hitler only once. On this subject see Gruner, W. D., '"British Interest" in der Zwischenkriegszeit. Aspekte britischer Europapolitik 1918–1938', in K. Bosl (ed.), *Gleichgewicht-Revision-Restauration. Die Aussenpolitik der Ersten Tschechoslowakischen Republik im Europasystem der Pariser Vorortverträge* (Munich/Vienna: 1976), p. 89, n. 13. In future, it will be the task of research to make individual investigations of the permanent and temporary features of British appeasement policy, to indicate which were a response to specific events and to make the distinctions clear. In this connection see the major work by Gustav Schmidt on British appeasement in the 1930s.

63 Wehler, *Bismarck und der Imperialismus*, has claimed that the theory of 'social imperialism' is applicable to the course of British history after the so-called economic 'disturbances of growth' from 1873. In my opinion, the theory is not satisfactory.

64 For Joseph Chamberlain see Kubicek, R. J., *The Administration of Imperialism. Joseph Chamberlain at the Colonial Office* (Durham, NC: 1969), esp. pp. 175–6; for Rosebery see Hamer, D. A., *Liberal Politics in the Age of Gladstone and Rosebery. A Study in Leadership and Policy* (Oxford: 1972), p. 248 ff. It is also true of 'Alfred Milner's criticism of the political system of England', the effectiveness of which ultimately condemned him to 'failure'. On this subject see also the interesting, if problematic, contribution of Schröder, H.-C., *Imperialismus und antidemokratisches Denken. Alfred Milners Kritik am politischen System Englands* (Wiesbaden: 1978), p. 81.

65 PRO FO 519/233, Cowley to Bloomfield, 30 July 1866; also quoted in Millman, *British Foreign Policy*, p. 36, n. 3.

66 See the almost completely negative assessments of Bismarck in this respect by the British royal family, the Prime Minister, the Secretaries of State for Foreign Affairs, the ambassadors in Berlin and other prominent individuals in Britain, in Thiersch, R., *Bismarck im Urteil englischer Politiker und Diplomaten seiner Zeit 1862–1890* (Kulmbach: 1941), *passim*, esp. pp. 19, 36–7, 60, 72, 93. In view of such assessments of Bismarck and Prussia by representatives of the British ruling class, the Prince Consort's comment via the Prince of Wales to the Prussian King Wilhelm on 9 September 1861 begins to grow in significance: 'It is not a Cavour that Germany needs but a Stein.' Quoted in Valentin, *Bismarcks Reichsgründung*, p. 161, n. 1. Later Queen Victoria, in a letter to Augusta, took up a remark of her dead husband's that it would be better if 'Prussia was incorporated in Germany, not Germany in Prussia'. Concerned, the queen went on: 'Will people understand that with you?' RA I 46/157 Victoria to Augusta, copy, 8 August 1866. Of course, the weight of such opinion must not be underestimated. But without presenting Great Britain's relationship with Prussia and Prussia-Germany in too harmonious a light, it must be remembered that Prussia – and *mutatis mutandis*, the infant German Reich – possessed no first-ranking interest for British politicians. In addition, moral and ideological reservations about a foreign policy partner appeared decisive for Britain only if there were other important conflicts of interest in the field of bilateral relations or international politics.

67 PRO FO 356/33, Clarendon to Bloomfield (private), 28 March 1866; also cited by Millman, *British Foreign Policy*, p. 14.

68 On this British attitude in general see Sontag, *Germany and England*, p. 82, and Hollenberg, G., *Englisches Interesse am Kaiserreich. Die Attraktivität Preussen-Deutschlands für konservative und liberale Kreise in Grossbritannien 1860–1914* (Wiesbaden: 1974), p. 18. Hopes for a liberalization of Prussia were a consistent theme of the letters between Queen Victoria and her daughter, wife of the Prussian crown prince. However, such hopes were not restricted to court circles. Perhaps less well known, but certainly more relevant politically, they also appear as policy perspectives in the ideas of Foreign Secretary Clarendon. It seems to have been these which persuaded the liberal Lord Clarendon that Britain – not fundamentally threatened – should adopt a cautious approach until Bismarck's minister-presidency was over and Prussia had adopted parliamentary institutions. See also Thiersch, *Bismarck im Urteil englischer Politiker*, p. 93. Clarendon believed that civilized humanity was moving towards what was reasonable and liberal – in short, towards British conditions. His attitude appears very clearly in the disarmament initiative of the winter of 1869–70, which Bismarck rejected for understandable reasons. Whatever the nationalist desires of broad circles of the Prussian and German middle classes, and the actual constitutional position in Prussia, Clarendon felt that the taxpaying bourgeoisie would one day refuse to make more money available for unproductive armies and would leave the governments no alternative but to disarm. Thus a letter from Lord Clarendon to Lord Augustus Loftus of 20 October 1869 contained the comment: 'I quite agree with you that the king [Wilhelm I] is *inabordable* about military reductions but I hope that the taxpayers bring him to understand their difficulties.' BLO, Clarendon Papers dep. c.474, Clarendon to Loftus, 20 October

1869; also quoted in Millman, *British Foreign Policy*, p. 155. Interestingly, he thought that the crown prince shared his opinion in the matter. BLO, Clarendon Papers dep. c.148, Clarendon to Lyons, 18 December 1868. See also Sontag, *Germany and England*, p. 83, and my chapter in this book, 'Lord Clarendon, Bismarck and the problem of European disarmament, 1870. Possibilities and limitations in British-Prussian relations on the eve of the Franco-Prussian War', p. [/].

69 Fulford, R., *Your Dear Letter. Private Correspondence of Queen Victoria and the Crown Princess of Prussia 1865–1871* (London: 1971), p. 130.
70 Fulford, *Your Dear Letter*, p. 129.
71 Quoted by Hollenberg, *Englisches Interesse*, p. 19.
72 See above p. [/]. Critical of this view is Hollenberg, *Englisches Interesse*, p. 4.
73 There is a short summary in Hollenberg, *Englisches Interesse*, p. 20 ff.
74 Sontag, R. J., *European Diplomatic History 1871–1932* (New York: 1961; first edn, 1933), p. 3.
75 Cited by Eyck, E., 'Bismarck', in W. N. Medlicott (ed.), *From Metternich to Hitler. Aspects of British and Foreign History 1814–1939* (London: 1969; first edn, 1963), p. 168.
76 Morley, J., *The Life of William Ewart Gladstone* (London: 1903), Vol. 2, p. 357.
77 Monypenny and Buckle, *The Life of Benjamin Disraeli*, Vol. 2, pp. 473–4.
78 See the study by Clarke, I. F., *Voices Prophesying War 1763–1884* (London: 1966), p. 30 ff, on the article by the well-known military author G. T. Chesney, 'The battle of Dorking. Reminiscences of a volunteer', which appeared anonymously in *Blackwood's Magazine* in May 1871; by December of that year 200,000 copies had been circulated .
79 On the reaction of *The Times* against the alarmists see Meine, K., *England und Deutschland in der Zeit des übergangs vom Manchestertum zum Imperialismus 1871 bis 1876* (Vaduz: 1965; first edn, Berlin, 1937), p. 56; on the rejection by Prime Minister Gladstone in his speech in Whitby on 2 September 1871 see Clarke, *Voices*, pp. 28–9.
80 PRO FO 391/22, Odo Russell to Hammond (private), 21 September 1872.
81 Taffs, W., *Ambassador to Bismarck. Lord Odo Russell, First Baron Ampthill* (London: 1938), p. 383.
82 On this subject see also Schramm, P. E., 'Englands Verhältnis zur deutschen Kultur zwischen der Reichsgründung und der Jahrhundertwende', in W. Conze (ed.), *Deutschland und Europa. Historische Studien zur Völker–und Staatenordnung des Abendlandes. Festschrift für Hans Rothfels* (Düsseldorf: 1951), p. 138.
83 BCLO, Morier Papers, Arthur Russell to Morier, typewritten copy, 3 February 1871.
84 BCLO, Morier Papers, Arthur Russell to Morier, typewritten copy, 16 February 1871.
85 PRO FO 918/84, Odo Russell to Arthur Russell, typewritten copy, 9 December 1872.
86 PRO FO 391/22, Odo Russell to Hammond (private), 1 February 1873.
87 Arthur Russell to Odo Russell, typewritten copy, 10 December 1872.
88 Arthur Russell to Odo Russell, typewritten copy, 13 September 1871.
89 Arthur Russell to Odo Russell, typewritten copy, 29 February 1872.
90 On this subject see the study by Powell, P. W., *Tree of Hate. Propaganda and Prejudices Attacking United States Relations with the Hispanic World* (New York/London: 1971).
91 Arthur Russell to Odo Russell, typewritten copy, 12 January 1871.
92 BCLO, Clarendon Papers, Lady Derby to Morier, typewritten copy, 13 June 1875.
93 PRO FO 64/748, no. 360, Odo Russell to Granville (secret), 24 December 1872.
94 PRO FO 918/10, Odo Russell to Earl Russell (private), 5 May 1873.
95 See below, n. 122.
96 Newton, Lord *Lord Lyons. A Record of British Diplomacy* (London: 1913), Vol. 2, pp. 41–2, published more recently in Röhl, J. C. G., *From Bismarck to Hitler. The Problem of Continuity in German History* (London: 1970), p. 25.
97 PRO FO 918/85, Odo Russell to his mother, Lady William Russell, 10 February 1871.
98 Taffs, *Ambassador to Bismarck*, p. 297.
99 On the motives and objectives of British foreign policy, see the work of Taffs, *Ambassador to Bismarck*, p. 74 ff. See also the report on the 'War Scare' by Arthur Russell, written in June 1887 on the occasion of renewed discussion of the 'War in Sight' crisis. This was based on the author's memories of discussions with his brother

during their visit to Potsdam in 1876. PRO FO 918/80, document of 13 June 1887, pp. 151–71. For an assessment of the European dimension of the 'War in Sight' crisis see Hillgruber, A., 'Die "Krieg-in-Sicht" Krise, 1975. Wegscheide der Politik der europäischen Grossmächte in der späten Bismarck-Zeit', in E. Schulin (ed.), *Gedenkschrift Martin Göhring. Studien zur europäischen Geschichte* (Wiesbaden: 1968), p. 239 ff.

100 Arthur Russell to Odo Russell, typewritten copy, 11 January 1871.

101 Arthur Russell to Odo Russell, typewritten copy, 8 June 1884.

102 Arthur Russell to Odo Russell, typewritten copy, 20 December 1872.
This report is in many ways so typical of the British relationship to the German 'upstart' that it is repeated here: 'This afternoon I attended a meeting of our Freetrade Conference Committee. A letter from our envoy Cartwright was read reporting that all the German liberals highly approved of the plan of holding a Freetrade Conference, but that each of them declared that he w^d not be able to attnd in London, because of the Vienna exhib[ition], next year, and C. said that the German Freetraders suggested that instead of *their* coming to London *we* might come to *Vienna*!! The amusement which this impertinent proposal afforded to our Manchester liberals, was great. The disciples of Cobden are ready to admit that all men are equal, but in return these Germans must not forget that Lancashire is the centre of the world.'

103 Quoted by Meine, *England und Deutschland*, pp. 98–9.

104 Taffs, *Ambassador to Bismarck*, p. 75.

105 On the use of the term 'Bismarckism' at the time see Meine, *England und Deutschland*, p. 71 ff.

106 This point of view is emphasized by Millman, *British Foreign Policy*, p. 222: 'An unprincipled Bismarck was better than a democratic Lassalle.'

107 Kolb, E., 'Der Pariser Commune-Aufstand und die Beendigung des deutsch-französischen Krieges', *Historische Zeitschrift* 215, (1972), pp. 293–4.

108 Perhaps understandably, the British ambassador Lord Ampthill [Lord Odo Russell] may have been estimating Bismarck's powers too highly when he wrote to Sir Robert Morier on 20 March 1881: 'Zornebock is in great force and completely dominates the situation having inspired all classes from the *very highest* to the lowest with the "sogenannte Scheissangst der Deutschen". – He is in excellent health, "eats for four" "and drinks like a hole" and gloats over the absolute power he has given himself. Hab meine Freude dran!!! All the great powers bow before him and come and ask his leave before they venture to do anything. Voilà!!' BCLO, Morier Papers, Odo Russell to Morier, 20 March 1881. On the nicknames 'Zornebock' and 'Z' which Morier called Bismarck, see Ramm, *Sir Robert Morier*, p. 7.

109 PRO FO 64/802, no. 67, Odo Russell to Granville (secret), 7 February 1874, also mentioned by Taffs, *Ambassador to Bismarck*, pp. 68–9.

110 PRO FO 64/807, no. 313, Odo Russell to Derby (confidential), 30 November 1874.

111 PRO FO 918/13, 'The ideas of a German "old liberal"', 1874 (?).

112 On this subject see also Muralt, L. von, 'Deutschland und das europäische Gleichgewicht', in W. Hofer (ed.), *Europa und die Einheit Deuschlands. Eine Bilanz nach 100 Jahren* (Cologne: 1970), pp. 20, 28.

113 Ritter, G., *Europa und die deutsche Frage. Betrachtungen über die geschichtlichen Eigenart des deutschen Staatsdenkens* (Munich: 1948), p. 76.

114 See also Hildebrand, K., 'Staatskunst oder Systemzwang? Die deutsche Frage als Problem der Weltpolitik', *Historische Zeitschrift* 228 (1979), p. 642.

115 Odo Russell to Lord Derby, 3 January 1876, quoted by Taffs, *Ambassador to Bismarck*, p. 122.

116 Arthur Russell to Odo Russell, typewritten copy, 3 March 1871: 'The military spirit has become *too strong* among them.'

117 One of Odo Russell's predecessors as ambassador to Berlin, Sir Andrew Buchanan, had already reported in summer 1864 on the relationship between internal and external policy in Prussia, attributing the following comment to Bismarck on the subject of the relationship between internal revolution and external war: 'He [Bismarck] said he was not afraid of these eventualities [war with Europe and Great Britain], that it was better for Prussia to incur any risks from a foreign enemy than from

revolutionary movements in Germany, and that while France remained neutral, which he felt assured she would do, it would be wiser to accept foreign than domestic war.' Buchanan to Foreign Secretary Lord John Russell, 18 June 1864, published in Valentin, *Bismarcks Reichsgründung*, appendix doc. no. XXIII, p. 521. Though Odo Russell continued to regard the issue of 'incompleteness' as crucial in determining the predisposition to war of the new Reich, he also provided a useful insight into the possible domestic, social and economic factors at work, in a report of 9 January 1874: 'I quite agree with General Walker [Major General Walker, British military attaché in Berlin] in thinking that there is no intention of going to war at present however angry the tone assumed towards France by ministers and military men, or by the official press may be:– Say what they will, there is no necessity for a war of defence, and no excuse for a war of aggression . . . But while I share General Walker's confidence in the present maintenance of peace, I do not feel sure of the future. To my mind, the danger will grow out of the national temptation to complete with so invincible an army the unification of the German speaking population of Europe under one hand:–and besides the patriotic aspirations of the people to realise their national ideal of unity it should not be forgotten that unfortunately for other nations, war has proved to be a profitable business to those who carry it on with a military system like that of Prussia. The Prussians have not only tasted glory, they have also tasted money:– Their glory has been crowned with wealth: From a poor kingdom Prussia has become a rich empire. From needy younger sons, their generals have become wealthy landowners having invested their war donations in landed estates with titles of nobility . . . Such, and many other examples fire the ambition of the rising generation of officers, – whilst the financial world, – so powerful in modern Germany, – would not object to another war indemnity, of five milliards to revel once more in the delights of sensational speculation. Military glory and sudden wealth have not, I fear, improved the character, or satisfied the ambition of the Prussians.' PRO FO 64/801, Odo Russell to Granville (secret), 9 January 1874; the document is also mentioned by Taffs, *Ambassador to Bismarck*, p. 67.

118 On this subject see also Howard, M., *The Franco-Prussian War. The German Invasion of France 1870–1871* (London: 1962), pp. 455–6.
119 Freyer, H., *Weltgeschichte Europas. Zweiter Band* (Wiesbaden: 1948), p. 915.
120 Boldt, H., 'Deutscher Konstitutionalismus und Bismarckreich', in Stürmer, *Das kaiserliche Deutschland*, p. 128.
121 Brandon, H., 'The cool sound of international accord', in The Sunday Times, 5 November 1972, p. 33.
122 See Arthur Russell's assessment of the international situation in February 1871: 'W. C. [William Cornwallis Cartwright, Liberal MP 1868–85, wealthy landowner, member of the Carlton Club; see Ramm, *Sir Robert Morier*, pp. 4–5 who comes straight from Berlin tells us that all political men expect a war with Russia in a few years. Great military states fight their neighbours now and then, by a law of their existence, France of course, will work day & night for an intimate alliance with Russia henceforth – All Russian society is French – the Czar alone is Prussian.' Arthur Russell to Odo Russell, typewritten copy, 11 February 1871.
123 PRO FO 64/747, no.285, Odo Russell to Granville (secret and confidential), 30 December 1872. See also the assessment of the *Saturday Review* of 29 July 1876, which clearly reveals the prevailing British view of the different degrees of civilization in the two countries: 'The Germans have got in them the stuff out of which civilized nations are formed; but at present they are not forward enough to rival nations which, like England and France and Italy, have an old civilization.' Quoted by Meine, *England und Deutschland*, p. 205.
124 Jelavich, B., 'Russland und die Einigung Deutschlands unter preussischer Führung', *Geschichte in Wissenschaft und Unterricht* 19 (1968), p. 529.
125 Diószegi, I., *Österreich-Ungarn und der französisch-preussische Krieg 1870 bis 1871* (Budapest: 1965), p. 9 ff.
126 Schieder, T., *Staatensystem als Vormacht der Welt 1848–1918* (Berlin: 1977), p. 84.
127 Of fundamental importance here is Ritter, G., 'Grossdeutsch und kleindeutsch im 19. Jahrhundert', in W. Hubatsch (ed.), *Schicksalswege deutscher Vergangenheit. Beiträge*

zur geschichtlichen Deutung der letzten hundertfünfzig Jahre. Festschrift für S. A. Kaehler (Düsseldorf: 1950), pp. 77–8.

128   On this subject see also Rumpler, H., 'Föderalismus als Problem der deutschen Verfassungsgeschichte des 19. Jahrhunderts (1815–1871)', *Der Staat* 2 (1977), p. 125 ff.

129   On the paradigmatic significance of this term see Hillgruber, A., *Otto von Bismarck. Gründer der europäischen Grossmacht Deutsches Reich* (Göttingen: 1978), p. 107.

130   On this subject see Hildebrand, K., ' "British Interests" als Staatsräson. Grundglagen britischer Aussenpolitik im 19. Jahrhundert, untersucht am Beispiel der Beziehungen zwischen Grossbritannien und Preussen in den Jahren 1866–1870', *Mitteilungen der Gesellschaft der Freunde der Universität Mannheim eV* 22 (1973), p. 2 ff; and Hildebrand, K., '"British Interests" und "Pax Britannica". Grundfragen englischer Aussenpolitik im 19. und 20. Jahrhundert', *Historische Zeitschrift* 221 (1975), p. 623 ff. Klaus Wormer has investigated the concept of "British interests" as part of a description of British foreign policy in the years preceding the First World War: Wormer, K., 'Russland, Deutschland und das Empire. Studien zur englischen Aussenpolitik vor dem Ersten Weltkrieg, (dissertation, Mannheim: 1975), p. 22 ff. Wolf D. Gruner has continued these reflections with reference to the interwar years of the twentieth century: Gruner, '"British Interest"', p. 85 ff.

131   For example, see a summary of relevant opinions in Picot, M.-L., 'England und Preussens deutsche Politik 1856–1866' (dissertation, Munich: 1934), p. 60; also Lord Strang, *Britain in World Affairs. A Survey of the Fluctuations in British Power and Influence. Henry VIII to Elizabeth II* (London: 1961), esp. p. 197.

132   Quoted in Meine, *England und Deutschland*, p. 205.

2

Lord Clarendon, Bismarck and the problem of European disarmament, 1870.

Possibilities and limitations in British-Prussian relations on the eve of the Franco-Prussian War

I

The role of the British Foreign Secretary Lord Clarendon during the disarmament episode of winter 1869–70 remains a controversial one. Why did he act as a comparatively committed spokesman of French disarmament proposals, though remaining sceptical about the prospects for the success of his initiative?

Representatives of the older school of German history often assumed[1] that the English diplomat had simply acted as the henchman of French policy. His personal goodwill, his pursuit of high humanitarian objectives, were not doubted. However, it was argued that he was too naive, allowing himself to fall into the trap set by cunning French statesmen. In contrast, more recent works such as those of R. Millman and E. Kolb[2] have claimed that Lord Clarendon had much more practical objectives. According to this analysis, he hoped that a partial disarmament of the two continental powers, France and Prussia, would bring about a relative improvement in the weak military position of his own country, thus relieving Britain of the need to rearm. Then, in 1972, J. L. Herkless[3] drew more attention to the international background to the British disarmament initiative, and particularly to the connection between the British proposal and the progress of German unification. In his view, Lord Clarendon was strongly motivated by the desire to maintain and extend the *entente* with France. He was therefore willing to accede to French requests and support the disarmament initiative which accorded so closely with the domestic and external requirements of France. At the same time, also in accordance with French wishes, he adopted a very distant attitude towards Prussian and German demands for national unity.

43

It remains to be seen whether any of these interpretations are sufficient to explain Lord Clarendon's conduct, either solely or in combination, or whether he had some other motives and objectives. In any case, the affair can throw light on the political concepts of the British Foreign Secretary and on an outlook which was concerned with much more than a pragmatic handling of the everyday business of politics.

First of all, some assessment of the earlier arguments of historical research is necessary.

(1) Accusations of unworldliness and naiveté against Lord Clarendon, which must be examined closely, relate to the liberal principles that underpinned his political convictions. Yet both the British political parties were aware of his long diplomatic experience and regarded him as the country's most experienced exponent of foreign affairs, an assessment shared by the representatives of the foreign powers. In such circumstances, the theory that Lord Clarendon allowed his humanitarian instincts to blind him to the cunning of French diplomacy really does not hold water. There was undeniably a strong theoretical dimension to his thinking which went beyond a concern with day-to-day political tasks; however, this element served to complement a realistic judgement of politics and was so carefully applied that it remained compatible with the requirements of British foreign policy.

(2) Millman and Kolb argued that, in the first instance, Lord Clarendon advocated disarmament in pursuit of British interests. It is probable that this was indeed one of the Foreign Secretary's motives. A process of disarmament had already begun in the British navy and army, and remained extremely controversial in leading political circles in the country. It is obvious that a partial disarmament of the great continental powers, France and Prussia, would therefore have been greeted with satisfaction in Great Britain and automatically served to reduce the relative weakness of the country in military affairs.

Nevertheless, one is bound to ask whether Lord Clarendon's exceptionally discreet handling of the disarmament affair can be fully explained by any of these arguments. If he was motivated either by personal idealism or by the limited desire to improve the disadvantageous position of his own country by encouraging the disarmament of other states, why did he not advocate a European disarmament as early as 1868? At that stage, by contrast, he had argued forcefully against a similar Austrian initiative. It seems certain that there were other motives behind Lord Clarendon's conduct, closely connected with his own political beliefs.

(3) Even the interpretation of Herkless, that Lord Clarendon's disarmament policy should be understood as part of his attempts to nurture

the *entente* between Great Britain and France, does not fully explain his actions. His major objectives in the disarmament issue ultimately went beyond the scope of normal diplomatic manoeuvring and power politics. Nor did they involve the kind of crisis management which Lord Clarendon had practised so successfully in the Franco-Belgian railway conflict of 1869.

His involvement in this dispute had shown the Foreign Secretary just how fragile the European peace was, and just how warlike the atmosphere on the continent was becoming. In such conditions, it seemed that revolutionary movements could gain ground only too easily both at home and abroad. A fundamental therapy seemed to be necessary in order to liberate Europe from at least some of the burdens which threatened to ruin the trade and commerce of its member states. In contrast to the (retrospective) judgement of Friedrich Thimme,[4] the Foreign Secretary did not believe that the situation had deteriorated too far for the attempt to be possible, although he approached the entire undertaking in a mood of sceptical realism. In some ways, conditions at the beginning of 1870 even appeared relatively favourable, particularly as the European conflict over Belgium had just been successfully solved and there was something of a 'pause for breath'[5] in international politics. Admittedly, Britain itself faced a number of difficulties, large and small, with Russia and the United States of America; however, these had been a routine feature of British foreign policy for a number of years and played no part in the pending disarmament affair.

Great Britain was enjoying good relations with both France and Prussia – in itself a favourable precondition for the initiative of the British Foreign Secretary. Moreover, since the visit of the Prussian crown prince to London in 1868, Lord Clarendon supposed – not entirely accurately – that the taxpaying bourgeoisie in Prussia as elsewhere was in revolt against the 'monster armies' which were so damaging to civilized progress. He was aware that the Prussian king was not remotely interested in disarmament. However, he hoped that the monarch would eventually be forced to revise his position as a result of domestic and external pressure. Lord Clarendon apparently overlooked certain facts of political life in Prussia and Germany. Despite a liking for the idea of cost-saving disarmament, the liberals there were more vehement in their demands for the unification of the fatherland than Bismarck himself, who remained comparatively moderate. At this stage, all the other demands of liberal philosophy were being subordinated to the longing for a German national state. The delegate Lasker was expressing widely held sentiments when, during a debate in the North German Reichstag on 5 November 1869, he emphasized the primacy of national unity ahead of the objective of European disarmament:[6] 'I do not entertain hopes for a systematic disarmament until the time when Germany has won its proper impressive position, [so] that all the surrounding powers know: there is no further subject for war here.' It would consequently be difficult to play off Prussia and Germany against each other on the issue of disarmament as Lord Clarendon was proposing. In fact, the British ambassador in Berlin, Lord Augustus Loftus, specifically warned him that the national liberals would always rate disarmament below the great objective of unity. Despite this, the Foreign Secretary saw other positive signs on the European scene, which persuaded him to persevere with his disarmament initiative.

In particular, Lord Clarendon was greatly encouraged by the development of France, some weeks before, into an *'Empire libéral'*. He assumed that its existence would effect a quite fundamental change in the political culture and mentality of the French. Moreover, he introduced his attempt with such discretion that there were hardly likely to be problems of prestige for the participating powers which would increase the risk of war. The Foreign Secretary was determined that a rejection of his proposal by Prussia, which he always regarded as possible and even probable, should under no circumstances lead to a French reaction of the kind described by Émile Ollivier with the threatening phrase:[7] 'Un échec c'est la guerre.'

Conditions for the initiative thus appeared moderately favourable and the risks at least calculable. Lord Clarendon's proposal for a partial disarmament was motivated to a considerable degree by a personal philosophy which appeared in his arguments on many occasions:[8] 'The maintenance of peace should be the paramount purpose of every European Gov*., notwithstanding their monster armaments that are a disgrace to our age and civilisation, and none should be ashamed of avowing that purpose and adapting its policy to the end in view.' His convictions were characteristic of the political thinking of his country at that stage of its development. This held that the modern era was simply incompatible with high levels of armaments, which threatened to stifle normal civilian life and encouraged war and revolution. A partial disarmament, in contrast, would put the rivalry between the peoples back on a more peaceful and reasonable footing. At the same time, Lord Clarendon believed that Britain's superiority in the field of economic and political competition between states would be accentuated almost automatically, since he and others regarded its 'way of life' as unquestionably superior. Success in the disarmament issue would bring a new morality into international relations and an even stronger orientation towards Great Britain as a model of liberal civilization, thus underlining its own 'natural' claim to pre-eminence in this sphere. The Foreign Secretary's disarmament initiative can therefore also be seen as an attempt to make the policy of 'peaceful change', followed by Britain in both domestic and foreign policy, more widely accepted in Europe than it had previously been. In other words, he hoped that reliance on military armament and recourse to war could be replaced by the British ideas of economic competition and social progress, of freedom and the parliamentary system. Lord Clarendon felt that the disarmament initiative of winter 1869–70 would improve the prospects for peace in Europe. But he never became so immersed in the ideological element of his concept that he could not at any time return to its other pole, to pragmatic diplomatic crisis management *ad hoc* in order to save the peace.

What effects did Lord Clarendon's disarmament proposal have on the relationship between Britain and Prussia? Would disagreement on this fundamental issue damage the existing compatibility between British world policy and Prussian revisionism, which was politically moderate although it was being achieved by war? There remained many possibilities for British-Prussian co-operation within the international system; however, the disarmament episode of 1870 revealed the fundamental limitations of the relationship more clearly than before.

II

In a letter of 2 February 1870[9] to the British ambassador in Berlin, Lord Augustus Loftus, the Foreign Secretary took the first important step to explore the prospects for disarmament. He emphasized the private character of his inquiry, but did not indicate that he was acting in agreement with the French government. Lord Clarendon stressed that he had no desire to interfere in the internal affairs of Prussia, but brought Bismarck's attention to a problem which had long preoccupied him and which he was now addressing in the interests of Europe, of peace and of 'humanity'.[10] This concerned the reduction of the enormous standing armies. In Clarendon's view their existence placed Europe in a position which was neither war nor peace, 'but which is so destructive of confidence that men almost desire war with all its horrors in order to arrive at some certainty of peace'.[11] The situation prevented 'millions of hands'[12] from doing productive work, it burdened the population with massive taxes and made them dissatisfied with their rulers. It appeared to Lord Clarendon that no reasonable person could regard this state of affairs without anxiety and even alarm. With his attitude shaped by British developments, he assumed – not always correctly – that the methods which had proved successful for his own country would be accepted as equally valid by other states. Thus he continued:[13] 'This system is cruel, it is out of harmony with the civilization of our age and it is pregnant with danger.'

Even at this point one is inclined to ask how the British Foreign Secretary could assume that his assessment of the problems would be shared by Prussia. In any case, he suggested that Berlin should take the lead in changing the miserable situation of Europe by showing its willingness to disarm. Such a move would provide irrefutable proof of Prussia's 'morality and power'.[14] Although he did not underestimate the difficulties of adopting such a policy, particularly given the attitude of King Wilhelm, he nevertheless claimed that a partial disarmament was possible because 'the moment is a singularly propitious one for the purpose'.[15] Specifically, Clarendon argued that the massive French standing army had become less threatening since the political changes in the government in Paris; the new 'responsible Government'[16] there would ensure that France was more ready for peace than at almost any time in its history. Here Lord Clarendon was expressing his own conviction that parliamentary governments tended in principle to be peaceful ones, a point of view which is historically contestable and could indeed by refuted by an examination of British history itself. He was certainly aware of the quite different symptoms in France. Nevertheless, Lord Clarendon boldly claimed that once France was set fully on the British path of development, determined to achieve national glory through trade and business rather than by the sword, then the government in Paris would seek popularity and strength in a policy of peace 'and in economy',[17] particularly given the wealth of the country and the notorious indifference of the French towards their tax obligations. Consequently, France would certainly consent to the proposal for an proportionate disarmament with Prussia. He, the British Foreign Secretary, declared himself ready to make soundings in Paris if Prussia would agree to it. Bismarck was thus not told that France had stimulated Lord Clarendon's initiative in the first place. Although the Prussian Minister-President and Chancellor of the North German Confederation had been expecting the French to make some move of this kind, he was unaware of the close links between Lord Clarendon and the French Foreign Minister.

On 5 February 1870, Lord Augustus Loftus brought Clarendon's letter to the attention of Count Bismarck.[18] The latter did not reject the British proposal point-blank, but immediately listed a whole series of factors which would make European disarmament difficult to achieve. He declared that it was quite impossible for him to inform King Wilhelm of the British proposal, as the monarch might easily respond by adopting an anti-British policy. In fact, Bismarck did inform Wilhelm I of the initiative, but was hoping that his statement to the British ambassador would prevent it from becoming an official matter. For the rest, he promised to answer Lord Clarendon's letter in a private communication to the Prussian ambassador in London, Count Bernstorff. In this way, he was adhering to the form of unofficial diplomatic exchange chosen by Lord Clarendon.

Bismarck's conversation with the British ambassador on 5 February contained all the arguments which he was to use throughout the disarmament initiative. In particular – and without receiving an answer – he asked what guarantees Great Britain could give Prussia in the event that it was prepared to disarm. In this connection, he pointed out to Lord Augustus Loftus that the natural circumstances of British and Prussian (or German) foreign policy were entirely different. Thus, he contrasted the island position of Great Britain with the central location occupied by Prussia and Germany in Europe, which made them vulnerable to every political change and dangerously dependent on fluctuations in the international situation. These geographical facts, Bismarck argued, had been largely responsible for the fact that his country had constantly been in fear for its existence since the eighteenth century. 'You', he said – according to Lord Augustus Loftus's report on his conversation with Bismarck[19] – 'live in a happy island and have not to fear an invasion.' On the other hand, Germany had been exposed to attacks by the French for 250 years and had suffered from it. Nobody could accuse the Germans of being aggressive. 'Germany, as now constituted, has all that she wants, and there is no object of conquest for her', so at any rate Lord Augustus Loftus reported Bismarck's comments to London.[20] Here, the Prussian statesman was speaking about and on behalf of Germany, not simply for Prussia or the North German Confederation. His remarks indicated – comfortingly for the British – that the north and south of Germany, meaning Little Germany without Austria, should be seen as satiated. But he was also assuming that this Germany was already to be regarded as a unity, at least to the point that it could no longer be an object for the ambition of external powers. Bismarck drew particular attention to the encircled central position of Germany, whose position within the international system was 'an exceptional one':[21] 'We are surrounded by three great Empires, with armies as large as our own, any two of whom might coalesce against us.'

Furthermore, Bismarck made it clear that he regarded the domestic situation of France, threatened by socialism, as extremely uncertain. He consequently thought it possible, he continued, that the French emperor would have to resort to the method the two men had discussed during a long conversation in 1867. If the route of granting 'more internal liberty'[22] no longer helped the emperor to secure and maintain his rule in the face of internal unrest and the threat of socialism, then only war was left as a method of overcoming internal difficulties. The danger of such a war had first become acute ten months previously in the shape of the Franco-Belgian railway conflict. And who, asked Bismarck, could be certain that the threat would not soon be repeated? He therefore regarded it as the best guarantee of peace if people in Europe were aware that Prussia was ready and able to defend itself at any time. He pointed to the fact that Austria-Hungary had recently changed its military organization so that 800,000 men now stood at its disposal. Furthermore, he spoke of the possibility of an alliance between France and Russia directed against Prussia, and he left no doubt that defence against such an attack would be possible only if the present military system, 'now in vigour for the last 50 years in Prussia',[23] was retained unchanged.

To make his arguments against disarmament still more convincing, Bismarck claimed that the 'Muscovite Party'[24] in Russia was extremely anti-German and that, in view of the notorious antipathy of the tsarevitch to Prussia, relations between Russia and Prussia were certain to deteriorate after the death of Tsar Alexander II. He then offered the comforting assurance that Prussia did not intend to incorporate the south of Germany into the north by force:[25] 'that, if the great majority of the population asked to enter the North German Confederation, no refusal could be given, but that no force would be employed'. All in all, Bismarck underlined the need to maintain the current military strength and military system of the country in order to safeguard its defensive capability.

Bismarck was unimpressed by the reproaches of Lord Augustus Loftus, who argued that the new government in France ought to be strengthened by means of an accommodation and that a step towards disarmament would be applauded particularly by the 'Liberal Party' in Germany.[26] In truth, both he and the Prussian king were determined not to alter the superior, proven military system of Prussia in any way, for reasons of foreign policy. If their attitude had been determined by domestic considerations, by the need to secure their rule at home, then smaller military forces, differently organized, would have sufficed.

At this stage, Lord Clarendon could hardly conceal his disappointment at French policy. It had become clear that Paris was eager to brand Prussia as the guilty party in the event of a rejection by Bismarck of the disarmament proposal. He gave a clear instruction to Lord Lyons, the British ambassador in Paris, for his discussions with Foreign Minister Daru:[27] 'it would be most imprudent on the part of the French Gov^t. to make any official proposal to Prussia this year for disarmament with the foreknowledge of what the answer will be.' For the rest, France had enough to do with its own affairs, and must not become involved outside its own borders. If the Paris government went rashly ahead with the disarmament issue, and if it should then be rejected, then the French army could not be restrained from military action. But war, Lord Clarendon argued presciently, 'would be just what the Revolutionists would most desire'.[28] The British Foreign Secretary had thus made a realistic assessment of the situation in France as well as the general position and had warned that war could accelerate the process of internal upheaval in that country. Indeed, he believed that the other states of Europe might also become involved if the twin perils of war and revolution spread from France to ravage Europe, as they had done after the great convulsion of the eighteenth century.

On 9 February 1870, Bismarck provided a detailed reply to Lord Clarendon's confidential letter, in the form of an ostensibly private letter to Count Bernstorff.[29] As a result of technical delays, this did not reach the British Foreign Secretary until 17 February. The letter contained much the same information that had already been sent to Lord Clarendon by Lord Augustus Loftus after his conversation with Bismarck on 5 February. In the letter, Bismarck argued that the Prussian military system was fundamentally more open than the methods of army recruitment and organization adopted by other states and therefore offered fewer possibilities for concealed rearmament. His claim was never contradicted during the disarmament soundings, since its accuracy was clearly apparent. In contrast, he questioned the British assessment of the geopolitical motives and military strength of the other powers.

Bismarck expressly warned the British that disarmament would endanger the position of Prussia in Europe. 'A weakening of the position of Prussia [however], a disturbance in the balance of power on the continent, can scarcely be in the interest of England.'[30] Once again he questioned the fundamental assumption of British policy, that a peaceful regime had been established in France. Bismarck was less than convinced by the proposition, mentioning a whole series of historical possibilities which can incite peoples and compel their rulers to make war against their will. A state such as Prussia, exposed and vulnerable on political and geographical grounds, could never afford to rely on unproven speculations of this kind. Nevertheless, Bismarck did not break off contact with London on the disarmament issue. His most urgent request was that confidentiality be maintained as Lord Clarendon had suggested.

In a document to Count Bernstorff the same day,[31] Bismarck explained his hostile attitude to the proposal in more detail. It was emphasized that his comments referred exclusively to the external and security questions raised in his combative letter, whilst domestic political problems of securing power were not mentioned once. Bismarck made a personal assessment of British conduct within the framework of the relations between Berlin and London and between Britain and France. He did not believe, he wrote,

> that Lord Clarendon had so consciously made himself into an instrument of the plans of Emperor Napoleon. Rather I consider the thinking of Lord Clarendon to be one of those Utopias such as occur to English statesmen, which always regards the conditions of the continent from a distorted angle and is often guided more than is reasonable by muddled humane ideas which are wont to prevail in public opinion.[32]

51

None of the governments involved could dare to entrust the security and independence of their country to the goodwill and sincerity of its neighbours. 'To put it mildly', so Bismarck assessed the British proposal,[33] 'in taking this step Lord Clarendon gives me the impression of a cool friend who feels no great scruples if he puts our neck at risk. France's disarmament proposals have no other meaning for us than a request from the wolves for the removal of the sheepdogs, a[nd] to see England as a willing party to such efforts is a saddening experience for me.'

Shortly after, on 11 February 1870, Ambassador Lord Lyons reported to Lord Clarendon[34] on the French response to Bismarck's first negative reaction. The Foreign Minister in Paris, Count Daru, had referred to the growth of Prussian power in the preceding years and attempted to refute Bismarck's claim that Prussia was not a 'conquering power'.[35] In addition, he offered the prospect that France might unilaterally disarm and call up only 90,000 men per annum instead of 100,000. French diplomacy, Daru noted, would thus be directed towards that party in Germany which was arguing against the burdens of military spending. Lord Lyons was convinced of the good sense of this proposal; in particular, it strengthened his own belief that the disarmament initiative could be successful only if public opinion in Germany could be persuaded to bring pressure to bear on the governments of Prussia and the other German states. As we have seen, it remains doubtful whether British statesmen and diplomats ever seriously considered what would be more important to the population in Germany in the event of conflict: national unity or military disarmament, security against a potentially belligerent France or the promotion of trade and commerce. After all, British politicians approached the problem as representatives of an 'old' national state and the most advanced civilization of the age; they came from a political culture which was very different to that of Prussia and Germany. Bismarck had given Lord Augustus Loftus an important insight into the Prussian response to the British disarmament proposal, which the British ambassador reported to London on 12 February:[36] 'Until the German Question is finally solved – (and we are a long way from that) – there is no chance of any reduction in the Military strength of the North German Confederation.'

By now, the French government was pressing with increasing urgency for the Prussian rejection of the disarmament proposal to be made public. Lord Clarendon reacted to these demands with some irritation and again urged the French government not to interfere in German affairs in any way. A French policy of restraint towards Germany would ultimately do more to force Prussia to disarm than any other measure. Lord Clarendon's response to the strained relations between France and Prussia (and Germany) is revealed in his recommendation that France should take a more detached approach to the German Question, and that Prussia-North Germany should not make any move to the south for the time being. The objective, as seen from Britain, was to maintain the status quo in central Europe for the foreseeable future; this would give Paris time to become accustomed to what London saw as the unavoidable and perhaps even natural unification of North and South Germany. However, if France was now seeking to use or misuse the disarmament contacts as a tool of its policy towards Germany, these would be doomed to failure from the outset. Lord Clarendon was in no way hostile in principle to the national union of Germany. Instead, he advocated a slackening of the pace towards it, in order to achieve his own primary goals of peace and disarmament. Perhaps his initiative for partial disarmament would have been more successful if he had tried more actively to persuade France to accept German unification beforehand. At this stage, however, it was impossible to introduce such thinking into the conversation even at a general level. Bismarck's own patience in considering British appeals for a reduction in the tempo of unification met with no reciprocal French generosity, no willingness to accept the foundation of a German national state. The British disarmament initiative did not fail simply because it was rejected by Prussia; even more important was the fact that whilst Britain saw the proposal as a progressive goal of foreign policy in itself, for its *entente* partner it was only a means to achieve an advantage in the field of power politics.

The disarmament proposal of the British Foreign Secretary had failed. Nevertheless, on 9 March he began a second attempt.[37] 'I have fired another shot at Bismarck about disarmament', he commented three days later,[38] though once again he had no great hopes for the success of his undertaking. First of all, he repeated the previous arguments made by the British side. However, he then put forward a new idea which must be examined more closely. The extent of his willingness to dispel Bismarck's fears for Prussia's security in Europe is of particular importance here.

Lord Clarendon firmly denied that he had any desire to damage the independence and power of Prussia in any way. To this end, he protested, he would not suggest the disarming of a single regiment. In fact, Prussia's strength appeared to him to be 'essentially beneficial' to Europe. Did not this comment itself perhaps contain an indirect, but none the less important, commitment to the continued existence of Prussia, which Bismarck simply underestimated? At the beginning of the 1860s, Disraeli had vividly described the fear of '*déstruction totale*' with regard to Prussia.[39] But might it not be the case that this fear now lived only in the fantasies of Prussian politicians and diplomats? Did it have any basis in reality any longer?

Perhaps Lord Clarendon's comment did have some positive significance for the future of Prussia and Germany; it may have been an indication that the existence of Prussia was now generally accepted and that the state had some room for manoeuvre in Europe. At the time, however, there were no reliable signs of safety and security for the artificial '*Rationalstaat*' in the centre of Europe. Moreover, since 1866–7 Prussia had clearly been engaged in the creation of the German national state. These policies reduced the chances for disarmament from a quite specific national perspective and should therefore be regarded as just as important in Bismarck's rejection of the British proposal as the traditional Prussian 'security dilemma'.

Prussia was and remained the parvenu of Europe. In the preceding years its rise had been so dramatic that its leading statesman thought it even more in danger than before. Over the longer term, Lord Clarendon's remarks may have intimated a change in the European assessment of Prussia; perhaps the state which had lived with the threat of destruction since the eighteenth century was coming to be regarded as natural and even indispensable by the other European states. But Prussia could not possibly take a decision to disarm simply on the grounds of such generalized and vague hopes as these, particularly as Lord Clarendon always refused to talk about concrete guarantees in the event of disarmament on the grounds that the procedure was too protracted. Not unnaturally, Bismarck could not rely on references made *en passant* to the fact that Prussia's position in the circle of European nations was apparently no longer in question.

Lord Clarendon's opinion that Prussia was not in real danger from any direction was offered from the safety of Great Britain, then at its height as a world power and adopting a position of neutrality in Europe. Not surprisingly, the situation looked very different from Prussia, surrounded in central Europe, regarded with distrust by its neighbours, and with a population making a demand for unity that was echoed in the other German territories. Though British statesmen were aware of the anti-German attitudes of significant circles in Russia, Lord Clarendon attempted to play them down. He argued, for example, that the Russians had for some time been devoting all their energies towards the east. The Foreign Secretary omitted to add that however extensive these Asiatic ventures might be, they could never completely replace Russian ambitions in Europe. Lord Clarendon would not accept that the military strength of Austria was a serious danger to Germany, though he conceded that 250,000 men stood ready for action at any time there. As far as France was concerned, he pointed out that it had to maintain troops in the colonies and that, for the rest, its regiments were needed to ensure 'the maintenance of order'[40] in larger cities such as Lyons. His conviction that France posed no major threat to Prussia was less than convincing. With hindsight, he was overestimating the desire for peace in France, which he characteristically linked to the political changes in the French government. In so doing, he failed to take into account that parliamentary and democratic governments, under pressure from the masses, can sometimes behave in a more chauvinistic manner than authoritarian political systems.

Liberal conviction also underpinned Lord Clarendon's persistent argument that the best guarantee for disarmament, security and peace would be gained by 'anglicizing' constitutions:[41]

> Count Bismarck will admit, and I am sure that a statesman so liberal and far-sighted will admit without regret, that the people everywhere are claiming and must obtain a larger share in the administration of their own affairs, and that, in proportion as they do so, the chances of causeless wars will diminish. The people well understand the horrors of war, and that they, and not their rulers, are the real sufferers: they equally understand and will daily become more impatient of the taxation for these costly preparations for war which in themselves endanger peace, and I believe that there is at this moment no surer road to solid popularity for Government than attending to the wants and wishes of the people on the subject of armaments.

Lord Clarendon's liberal credo was one of the foundations of his political conduct, existing alongside his routine business of political crisis management. As far as power politics and the balance of power were concerned, there was no cause for friction between Britain and Prussia at this time. However, clear differences opened up between the two states when the other, more theoretical dimension of Lord Clarendon's policy was applied, postulating the preconditions of the British parliamentary system as a universal model and suggesting its extension to Prussia. These differences were the result of the entirely dissimilar political and, especially, geopolitical circumstances of Great Britain and Prussia. It was an axiom of Lord Clarendon's liberal outlook that a government controlled by the people would automatically pursue a peaceful policy and that appropriate political changes were necessary everywhere. Yet in these years, in conditions other than those prevailing in Britain, precisely the opposite could be the case.

If Bismarck had given in to popular foreign policy demands in his country on the eve of the Franco-Prussian War, these would have been unlikely to lead to disarmament. Certainly, there were many complaints in Prussia about the burden of taxation. Nevertheless, many German liberals supported the achieving of German unification by means of a fervent national war against France. Evidence of the proverbial *furor teutonicus* had been provided as far back as 1848–50 when the broad liberal group in the Paulskirche made extensive territorial demands in Europe; these sentiments, which had since been kept in check by Bismarck, might then have been unleashed on the continent in full force.

Bismarck's style of government, much disliked in Great Britain, was to rule together with the parliament and the king, to balance the domestic political weight of each against the other, and thus to win a high degree of authority for himself. He refused, on grounds of ideological and political principle, to allow the people to participate at all in decisions on foreign policy. However, there were also significant practical reasons for his conduct. By retaining control of foreign policy, he could ignore demands within Germany for impetuous moves to achieve unification by force against the rest of Europe. Instead, Bismarck continued to seek unification with more circumspection, in concert with Europe where this remained possible. To this extent, the foreign policy and international circumstances of Prussia, and later of Prussia-Germany, almost demanded a monarchical-constitutional form of government of the kind practised by Bismarck. His domestic policies made him the object of considerable mistrust in Britain. Nevertheless, Bismarck's moderation in foreign affairs was convincingly demonstrated to Britain in the peace treaties of Nikolsburg and Prague in 1866. From an international perspective, this policy of moderation was generally beneficial to both Britain and Europe.

Once again, Bismarck had opposed disarmament. Yet he was certainly not endangering peace more than would have been the case if he had allied himself with the demands of the liberals. In Prussia, the national liberals continued to advocate disarmament, but also to exploit nationalist sentiment, calling for the unification of Germany by force in a war against France. Lord Clarendon's disarmament diplomacy took insufficient account of the compatibility between the political objectives of Britain and Prussia, despite the obvious geopolitical, historical and ideological differences between them. This compatibility was accentuated by Bismarck's desire to move towards German unification in harmony with Great Britain and Europe. In the longer term, potential dangers began to emerge during the disarmament debate, arising from the ideological and political contrast between the two states. There was a possibility that Prussia-Germany would one day come to be regarded as the power in Europe which clung to unproductive armaments and thus forced other states to bear useless costs. However, diplomatic discretion was still preventing such reactions, though at the conclusion of his letter Lord Clarendon indicated the possibility as a danger for Prussia. For the time being, the British statesman exercised his skill and intelligence to avoid publicity and prevent the danger becoming acute; he was honestly concerned with disarmament itself, not the propaganda effect which could lead all too easily to a general European conflagration.

On 11 March Lord Augustus Loftus brought Bismarck the new letter from Lord Clarendon,[42] containing the second 'shot' he had 'fired at Bismarck' over disarmament. In reply, the Prussian statesman largely repeated the arguments he had already put forward during the dialogue. Lord Clarendon expressed some surprise at the way Bismarck had been able to maintain such a steadfast opposition to the disarmament proposals, such a refusal to be swayed by argument. He was having to accustom himself to the idea that the Prussian Minister President was not under such strong pressure to disarm from public opinion in Germany as the British had supposed. In any case, Lord Clarendon now asked the British ambassador in Berlin:[43] 'Can you tell me how military reduction would be viewed by the liberal party in Germany? Do they sympathize with the popular impatience of taxation or do they like the notion of Germany overawing Europe?'

Lord Augustus Loftus responded two days later, on 18 March 1870,[44] in a long and informative letter to his Foreign Secretary. He described the basic assumptions of the Prussian and German liberals, so different to those of their counterparts in British liberalism: 'As regards the feelings of the National Liberal Party on this subject, they are decidedly on principle in favour of a reduction, but they will support the existing establishment if they could be assured of the firm intention of Count Bismarck to carry out at no distant date the completion of German Unity.' Loftus was accurately conveying the prevailing sentiments and opinion of wide circles of the population, not merely the adherents of the liberal party. The national liberals might indeed encourage disarmament on principle, and demand reductions in the burden of taxation. But when the chips were down and they had to choose between national unity and European disarmament, or if they believed that unification could be achieved as long as demands for disarmament took second place for a time, then it was certain that the majority of Germans would decide against disarmament. Lord Augustus Loftus gave a vivid description of the attitude of the national liberals on this issue:[45] 'There are no sacrifices this party will not incur to satisfy their national aspirations. And they would tomorrow cross the Maine and admit the Grand Duchy of Baden into the North German Confederation, at the risk even of a War with France.'

British statesmen and diplomats began to realize that the direct danger of war and the most vehement demands for unification were coming much more from the progressive, liberal and pro-parliamentary forces in Germany; in contrast, Bismarck was actually a moderating influence in foreign affairs. Should his domestic critics ever achieve control of the government and replace the existing monarchical-constitutional system of Prussia with a parliamentary system similar to that of Britain, then Great Britain – however hostile to Bismarck's domestic policies – would have to adjust to a completely new and probably highly dangerous development in the international field. For it was the existing political system in Prussia, with Bismarck at its head, which embodied that restraint in foreign affairs which was of benefit to both Britain and Europe. Thus Lord Augustus Loftus emphasized:[46] 'The danger is that Count Bismarck may find himself overpowered by pressure from this Party, and may be forced into a Policy of action, which he has hitherto successfully resisted.'

Persistence in the disarmament issue, warned the British ambassador in Prussia, might even do more to provoke war than to secure peace.

This was not a completely idle speculation. In a conversation between Bismarck and Lord Augustus Loftus that same day,[47] there was again no progress on the disarmament issue. Bismarck merely stated his own views more clearly than before. During the conversation, the Prussian Minister–President referred to his domestic difficulties in maintaining his authority and the resulting limits on his freedom of action. (Of course, he may also have been exaggerating these in order to justify his conduct.) His difficulties, he argued, included his relations with the king as well as the liberals with their demands for national unity. Wilhelm I, claimed Bismarck, had steadfastly refused to change the Prussian military system since 1862. There were only two ways to reduce the 'North German army':[48] first, to change the appropriate laws and thus the entire organization, and, second, to reduce the period of service to two and a half years. There no point in talking about the first option, as it was simply impossible. Such a step would damage Prussia's security. The king had already opposed the alternative option for a number of years and had repeatedly said that he would rather risk his throne than give way in military affairs. So there was no chance of implementing that option either.

For the rest, the monarch already regarded the British disarmament proposal as an undertaking which promoted the policy of France and correspondingly damaged the position of Prussia. Bismarck continued with another reference to the very different situations facing Britain and Prussia:[49] 'It is all very well for you . . . living in an island where nobody can attack you to preach disarmament.' Seizing the initiative in the negotiations, he asked the British ambassador what people in Britain would say if somebody told them[50] 'that your navy was too large?' What would be the reaction on the other side of the Channel if Britain was accused of devoting considerable tax revenues to ships which, considering the balance of power in Europe and its requirements, were simply not necessary? The ambassador's pertinent reply, that Britain was actually in the process of disarming, was ignored. Bismarck summarized his position by saying that partial disarmament of the type suggested would damage Prussian interests in a fundamental way. Lord Augustus Loftus again stressed that his government was dealing with this issue in the hope of promoting the welfare of Europe. Above all, however, he was anxious to remove the suspicion that Britain's objective was the same as that of France, to prevent German unification. On the authority of Lord Clarendon, the ambassador described the British attitude to the German Question and outlined British wishes for a future German national state in Europe. For Great Britain, this historical event was not closely connected with the desire for partial disarmament. In contrast,

French policy had endeavoured to use the disarmament issue in order to prevent the unification of Germany. The British government had no desire to be identified with such a policy. 'Your Lordship was desirous', so the British ambassador in Berlin outlined the position of Clarendon towards the problem of a future German national state,[51] 'of seeing Germany strong, united and prosperous; strong, because her geographical position would enable her to maintain the Peace of Europe, united, because 'L'union fait la force', and prosperous, because in her prosperity we should find our own.'

Once again Lord Augustus Loftus concluded by emphasizing the private character of the disarmament soundings, which had been made in an effort to reduce general tension. However, he adopted a resigned tone when reporting to the Foreign Secretary, claiming that he saw 'no chance'[52] for disarmament. He urgently advised Lord Clarendon not to take any further steps as these would only increase the danger of war and, from a political point of view, would persuade King Wilhelm to turn away from England and move even closer to Russia. This process would be most unwelcome, particularly since relations between Britain and Prussia had been good; indeed, in the course of 1869 Berlin had ceased to adopt as a matter of course the Russian view in the eastern question.

After receiving this news from Berlin, Lord Clarendon realized that further pursuit of the disarmament proposal would do 'more harm than good'.[53] On 7 April 1870, the British Foreign Secretary finally stated:[54] *'cadit quaestio'*.

Prime Minister Gladstone's indignation at the Prussian rejection did not alter the decision. Lord Clarendon was encouraged[55] to point out – with reference to Bismarck's allusion to naval disarmament – that this was already being put into practice and that Britain was not merely recommending armaments reductions to others. Independently of this, Lord Clarendon made another reference to Bismarck's reproaches in a letter to Lord Augustus Loftus,[56] in which he pointed out that European armies could not be compared with the British navy. British naval supremacy posed no threat to the peace of Europe, but served to defend the motherland and to protect the colonies and trade. Despite these global tasks, Britain had been making considerable economies in the sphere of naval armaments and intended to continue this course in future. He stressed yet again that it had been neither Britain's intention nor was it in British interests[57] 'to diminish the power and prestige of Prussia in Europe'. In this way, Lord Clarendon was seeking to regain the political and diplomatic status quo ante between the two states. Though the disarmament proposal had failed because of the very different attitudes of Great Britain and the continental powers, and the hostility between Prussia and France, he hoped that co-operation with Prussia on day-to-day affairs could now be resumed.

In contrast to previous years, British activity in foreign policy was increasing. However, Britain's commitment never went beyond the point at which the country's interests might be damaged. This was as much the case in the disarmament issue as it was in the equally contentious Greek Question:[58] 'We must be cautious not to involve ourselves in European difficulties.' As often before in the 1860s, British willingness to intervene, within the framework of a general non-intervention policy, had reached the natural limits defined by British interests. Great Britain was concerned to avoid war, and indeed to reach satisfactory solutions to international issues where possible, as it had hoped to do in the disarmament affair. But these efforts were under no circumstances to be made at the price of forcing Britain to give up the course of neutrality which accorded so closely with 'British interests'.[59]

III

The disarmament episode of 1870 revealed a fundamental incompatibility in the standpoints of Great Britain and Prussia. Yet an equal incompatibility between Britain and France had also become apparent. The politicians in Paris had intended to use disarmament as an instrument of power politics for their own advantage; Great Britain, on the other hand, regarded it as a genuine objective of foreign policy, aimed at replacing military armament with competition between economies and civilizations, in order to promote both the welfare of Europe and the needs of Britain.

In view of its vital security requirements and the German demands for unification, Prussia was compelled to oppose disarmament. Domestic motives, the need to protect the existing system of government, played no part in its decision. The affair had manifested an important dimension of British foreign policy, over and above the customary crisis management of the Foreign Office. It took the shape of an attempt to put new life into the peaceful competition between peoples by reducing their armaments, thus inaugurating a policy of 'peaceful change'. The policy was rooted in historical, economic, ideological and political conditions different from those which had created the foreign policy of Prussia. Moreover, it failed to recognize that the values of the British 'way of life', closely linked with its parliamentary system of government, were by no means accepted as generally valid by the continental great powers of Europe. Indeed, Lord Clarendon could scarcely foresee that the industrial, technical and material achievements of Britain could one day be exploited by a political culture very different from his own and for very different political objectives.

The failure of the disarmament dialogue did not disturb the relationship between Great Britain and Prussia. The different historical, political and – especially – geographical conditions of the two states had caused them to disagree in the disarmament issue; however, these same factors actually encouraged their relations in the field of power politics, since their different spheres of interest guaranteed that there was no rivalry between Great Britain and Prussia in the period under investigation. Moreover, Bismarck was careful to ensure that his foreign policy, although revisionist in nature and achieved through war, remained acceptable and even beneficial to Britain.

It remained true that the failure of the disarmament discussions had made the powers more closely aware of the possibilities and limitations of co-operation between Britain and Prussia-Germany. Within the Foreign Office, there was a sober recognition of the fact that these limitations were not only a question of conspicuous contrasts[60] whereby Gladstone appeared as the genius of the peoples, of free government and the law of nations and Bismarck was regarded as the embodiment of force, *raison d'état* and the policy of 'blood and iron'.

However, at this stage it was Franco-Prussian and then Franco-German relations – connected with French claims to intervene in South Germany and the German demands for unification – which had been damaged by Lord Clarendon's disarmament efforts. Despite the information reaching him from Lord Augustus Loftus, it seems unlikely that the British Foreign Secretary ever fully understood that the national question was more important to the Germans than the British goals of disarmament and parliamentary reform.

Lord Clarendon's disarmament attempt was an episode which did little lasting damage to relations between London and Berlin. As far as Bismarck was concerned, the decisive factor was Britain's continued acceptance of Prussia's German policy and the fact that her statesmen saw a united Germany as a flexible centre in Europe which could act as as a counterbalance to the other powers in Europe and therefore help to keep the peace. British statesmen were quite prepared to permit this development to occur, indeed even to provide cautious encouragement. However, it was important to them that it should if possible be carried through without war. When war actually broke out so soon, in summer 1870, it naturally influenced the relations of Great Britain with Prussia-Germany. Finally, the disarmament proposal of early 1870 was part of a concern with the problem of international disarmament (and of an international system of arbitration) which had emerged in Europe, since the end of the Crimean War in particular. In the remainder of the nineteenth century, and throughout the twentieth, it was to become an increasingly important factor in the domestic and external affairs of the nations.[61] A convincing solution to the problem, however, has yet to be found.

NOTES

1 See especially Rheindorf, K., 'Die englisch-preussischen Verhandlungen über eine Abrüstung im Frühjahr 1870. Unter Benutzung unveröffentlichten Materials', *Archiv für Politik ung Geschichte* 4 (1925), p. 442 ff; Nolte, K., 'Die Abrüstungsideen von 1867–1870 und die europäische Politik' (dissertation, Munich: 1925), esp. p. 105 ff; and Roloff, G., 'Abrüstung und Kaiserplan von 1870', *Preussische Jahrbücher* (1928), p. 183 ff. In this chapter, the footnotes are kept to a minimum and are generally used to show the source of the quotations. On the general background, see also my essay on Great Britain and the foundation of the German Reich, the first chapter in this book.

2 Millman, R., *British Foreign Policy and the Coming of the Franco-Prussian War* (Oxford, 1965), p. 153; and E. Kolb, *Der Kriegsausbruch 1870. Politische Entscheidungsprozesse und Verantwortlichkeiten in der Julikrise 1870* (Göttingen: 1970), p. 40, n. 47.

3 Herkless, J. L., 'Lord Clarendon's attempt at Franco-Prussian disarmament, January to March 1870', *The Historical Journal* XV (1972), esp. p. 468.

4 *Bismarck. Die gesammelte Werke. Politische Schriften*, ed. F. Thimme, Vol. 6b: *1869 to 1871* (Berlin: 2nd edn, 1931), p. 231.

5 Bodleian Library, Oxford (cited as BLO), Clarendon Papers dep. c. 478.

6 Quoted in Nolte, 'Abrüstungsideen', p. 92.

7 Lyons to Clarendon, 30 January 1870, in Newton, Lord, *Lord Lyons. A Record of British Diplomacy*, Vol. 1 (London: 1913), p. 249.

8 BLO, Clarendon Papers, dep. c. 474, Clarendon to Bloomfield (private), copy, 16 February 1870. From the Bloomfield Archive (PRO FO 356/33); also quoted in Millman, *British Foreign Policy*, pp. 154–5.

9 Clarendon to Loftus, 2 February 1870, in Newton, *Lyons*, p. 251 ff.

10 Clarendon to Loftus, 2 February 1870, in Newton, *Lyons*, p. 251.

11 Clarendon to Loftus, 2 February 1870, in Newton, *Lyons*, p. 251.

12 Clarendon to Loftus, 2 February 1870, in Newton, *Lyons*, p. 251.

13 Clarendon to Loftus, 2 February 1870, in Newton, *Lyons*, p. 251.

14 Clarendon to Loftus, 2 February 1870, in Newton, *Lyons*, p. 252.

15 Clarendon to Loftus, 2 February 1870, in Newton, *Lyons*, p. 252.

16 Clarendon to Loftus, 2 February 1870, in Newton, *Lyons*, p. 252.

17 Clarendon to Loftus, 2 February 1870, in Newton, *Lyons*, p. 252.

18 Loftus to Clarendon, 5 February 1870, in Newton, *Lyons*, p. 254 ff; Bismarck to Bernstorff, 9 February 1870, in *Gesammelte Werke*, Vol. 6b, p. 232 ff.

19 Newton, *Lyons*, p. 254.

20 Newton, *Lyons*, p. 254.

21 Newton, *Lyons*, p. 254.

22 Newton, *Lyons*, p. 255.

23 Quoted from the original of the letter from Loftus to Clarendon of 5 February 1870, which was published in abbreviated form in Newton, *Lyons*, p. 254 ff, in BLO, Clarendon Papers dep. c.478, Loftus to Clarendon (private and confidential), 5 February 1870.

24 Lyons, *Newton*, p. 255.

25 BLO, Clarendon Papers dep. c.474, Loftus to Clarendon (private and confidential), 5 February 1870.

26 BLO, Clarendon papers dep. c.474, Loftus to Clarendon (private and confidential), 5 February 1870.

27 BLO, Clarendon Papers dep. c.474, Clarendon to Lyons (private), copy, 9 February 1870.

28 BLO, Clarendon Papers dep. c.474, Clarendon to Lyons (private), copy, 9 February 1870.
29 Bismarck to Bernstorff, 9 February 1870, *Gesammelte Werke*, Vol. 6b, p. 232 ff.
30 *Gesammelte Werke*, Vol. 6b, p. 233.
31 *Gesammelte Werke*, Vol. 6b, p. 234 ff.
32 *Gesammelte Werke*, Vol. 6b, p. 237.
33 *Gesammelte Werke*, Vol. 6b, p. 237.
34 Lyons to Clarendon, 11 February 1870, in Newton, *Lyons*, p. 256 ff.
35 Lyons to Clarendon, 11 February 1870, in Newton, *Lyons*, p. 257.
36 BLO, Clarendon Papers dep. c.478, Loftus to Clarendon (private), 12 February 1870.
37 Clarendon to Loftus, 9 March 1870, in Newton, *Lyons*, p. 267 ff.
38 Clarendon to Lyons, 12 March 1870, in Newton, *Lyons*, p. 266.
39 On this subject see Dawson, W. H., *The German Empire and the Unity Movement* (London: 1966, first edn, 1919), Vol. 1, p. 282.
40 Clarendon to Loftus, 9 March 1870, in Newton, *Lyons*, p. 268.
41 Clarendon to Loftus, 9 March 1870, in Newton, *Lyons*, p. 268.
42 Loftus to Clarendon, 12 March 1870, in Newton, *Lyons*, p. 270 ff; Bismarck to Bernstorff, 25 March 1870, in *Gesammelte Werke*, Vol. 6b, p. 304 ff.
43 Public Record Office (cited as PRO), Foreign Office (cited as FO) 361/1, Clarendon Papers, Clarendon to Loftus (private), copy, 16 March 1870.
44 PRO FO 361/1, Loftus to Clarendon (private and confidential), 18 March 1870.
45 PRO FO 361/1, Loftus to Clarendon (private and confidential), 18 March 1870.
46 PRO FO 361/1, Loftus to Clarendon (private and confidential), 18 March 1870.
47 PRO FO 361/1, Loftus to Clarendon (private and confidential), 18 March 1870.
48 PRO FO 361/1, Loftus to Clarendon (private and confidential), 18 March 1870.
49 PRO FO 361/1, Loftus to Clarendon (private and confidential), 18 March 1870.
50 PRO FO 361/1, Loftus to Clarendon (private and confidential), 18 March 1870.
51 PRO FO 361/1, Loftus to Clarendon (private and confidential), 18 March 1870.
52 PRO FO 361/1, Loftus to Clarendon (private and confidential), 18 March 1870.
53 Clarendon to Lyons, 23 March 1870, in Newton, *Lyons*, p. 276.
54 PRO FO 361/1, Clarendon Papers, Clarendon to Bernstorff, 7 April 1870 (particulière), copy; see also Rheindorf, 'Die englisch–preussischen Verhandlungen', p. 475.
55 Gladstone to Clarendon, 9 April 1870, in J. Morley, *The Life of William Ewart Gladstone* (London: 1903), Vol. 2, p. 322.
56 BLO, Clarendon Papers dep. c.474, Clarendon to Loftus (private), copy, 13 March 1870.
57 BLO, Clarendon Papers dep. c.474, Clarendon to Loftus (private), copy, 13 March 1870.
58 PRO 30/22/16F, Russell Archive, Clarendon to Russell, 12 May 1870.
59 See the first chapter of this book, on Great Britain and foundation of the German Reich, p. [/], n. 130.
60 Sontag, R. J., *Germany and England. Background of Conflict 1848–1894* (New York: 1964; first edn, 1938), p. 80.
61 On this subject see Düffler, J., 'Die Haager Konferenzen von 1899 und 1907 in der internationalen Politik. Altes Grossmachtsystem oder neue Friedensordnung?' (thesis, Cologne: 1979).

3

Between alliance and antagonism.
The problem of bilateral normality in British-German relations in the nineteenth century (1870–1914)

I

The year 1873 saw the publication of the 'enlarged and revised German edition' of James Bryce's history of *The Holy Roman Empire*, the first English edition of which had appeared in 1864. Bryce made the following comment in the foreword:

> despite all the hasty and gullible comments of a certain sector of the English press, the successes which Germany has recently enjoyed in gaining its national unity, winning back provinces which had been lost long before, chastising a nation and a ruling dynasty which had been the eternal destroyers of peace in Europe, were observed by the majority of Englishmen, whose knowledge of continental history in the last four hundred years gives their assessment special value, with sincere sympathy and pleasure.[1]

Only a generation later, this positive British assessment had been overtaken by the course of events. Public sentiment was by then dominated by harsher and shriller voices, in the political exchanges between London and Berlin, in the educated circles to which Bryce was referring and more broadly in public opinion in Britain and Germany. In both countries, Machiavelli's instructions for political conduct in book II of the *Discourses* seemed to have been forgotten:[2] 'I hold it to be a proof of great prudence for men to abstain from threats and insulting words towards any one, for neither the one nor the other in any way diminishes the strength of the enemy; but threats make him more cautious, and insults increase his hatred of you, and make him more persevering in his efforts to injure you.' By contrast, both nations seemed more and more determined to prove the truth of the remark which had introduced Machiavelli's thoughts: 'Contempt and insults engender hatred against those who indulge in them, without being of any advantage to them.'

How did this development occur? What happened to change the climate? Why did hostility between Britain and Germany increase? These questions have been a constant source of interest for international historians in the twentieth century, and continue to be so. Much attention has been devoted to the actual or supposed turning-points in the Anglo-German relationship, and particularly to the unsuccessful alliance negotiations and soundings between the powers in 1879, 1889 and 1898–1901. The failure to achieve agreement on those occasions often seems to have prepared the way for a disastrous development in Anglo-German relations, by preventing a closer connection or an alliance and leading to antagonism and even enmity between London and Berlin. British-German antagonism has been a crucial factor in the history of the nineteenth and twentieth centuries. In the attempt to provide a comprehensive explanation, the hostility has sometimes been reduced to an ideological incompatibility between two very different political cultures; in line with this theory, some historians have traced the origins of British-German antagonism back to the Bismarck era itself. Interpretations of this kind have been made, for example, by historians ranging from Raymond J. Sontag through Erich Eyck to Paul Kennedy.[3] However, these interpretations inevitably tend to overlook, or to diminish the significance of, one unmistakable fact: the antagonistic development between London and Berlin only really got under way at the turn of the century and was not irreversible even then. Even after 1900, Anglo-German hostility was not made inevitable by the simple fact that Germany was attempting to force its way into the ranks of imperialist states. Instead, as Ludwig Dehio has already emphasized,[4] it was the insistence of German imperialism on challenging Britain by its own front door and threatening its vital (Channel, North Sea and Atlantic) naval supremacy, which profoundly damaged Anglo-German relations. This naval threat distinguished the German Reich from other, equally imperialist expanding states like the United States of America and Japan and also from Britain's European rivals such as France and Russia. Wilhelmine Germany was set on a path which raised the old problem of hegemony once again, as part of the re-continentalization of international politics after the turn of the century. The dual German challenge on land and sea – a challenge always visible as a morphological model when the European states have moved between hegemony and the balance of power – ensured that Germany became by far the most dangerous rival of Britain. In comparison, the traditional rivalry of France and Russia appeared much less of a threat.

In this chapter, the basic possibilities for Anglo-German relations during the period 1870–1914 will be examined once again. Part of the study will necessarily involve the concepts of alliance and antagonism between the two states to which so much attention has been paid in the past. However, much more importance will be attached to a comprehensive evaluation of the category of bilateral normality as a model for the regulation of the relationship between London and Berlin – a concept which has been studied much less and is also possibly more difficult to recognize and define. To put the issue another way: how inevitable was the route from the non-establishment of a 'closer connection'[5] during the Bismarck era, via the interlude of the unsuccessful alliance negotiations at the turn of the century, to the antagonism of the prewar years and the outbreak of war in 1914? Was the apparent normality in mutual relations during the 1870s and 1880s[6] inevitably condemned to disappear because powerful domestic, social and ideological forces were already preventing an alliance and tending towards antagonism?

There are other issues at stake here, one of which is currently the subject of much historical interest and research. It deals with how far the phenomena of foreign and international politics should be regarded as the results of internal factors in the societies of the states concerned. So long as the relationship between 'power politics and form of government'[7] is not understood purely as the dependence of foreign policy on internal factors, as frequently occurs in modern historical writing, but also has due regard for the influence on a domestic political culture of its international surroundings,[8] then many features of policy in both Britain and Germany become more comprehensible. Elements of feverishness and haste, of strain and the overstretching of resources, often characterized the German attitude towards foreign policy; these were undoubtedly due in large measure to the traditional situation facing Prussia-Germany and to German doubts that the existence of the Reich was secure. In contrast, the British Foreign Secretary Lord Stanley had commented in 1868 that the Channel had long been Britain's best ally;[9] the security of its position allowed the maritime power to appear more generous and accommodating in its attitude than land powers were able to do, even the old continental nations whose existence was never in doubt. However, this maxim concerning the attitude of maritime and land powers requires qualification and clarification. In general, the maritime power proves more accommodating only until one of the land powers prepares to challenge it directly and to make it vulnerable by means of naval expansion which would involve it in 'latent war'.[10] In that case, the naval power reveals unsuspected depths of vulnerability and shows itself more restricted in its conduct than the land power, which is able to exploit the advantage of the inner line and, at least for a time, to cope with the problem of supplies. When faced with the threat of being cut off from its supplies, the naval power reacts in a highly resolute manner.

Can this recognition of the morphology of continental, British and international politics in recent times help to explain the development of the Anglo-German relationship in the nineteenth and twentieth centuries? Is it not more satisfying than the attempt to interpret relations between London and Berlin as the result of the different internal political and social circumstances of the two industrialized states? Can Anglo-German antagonism really be explained by reference to the different societies and industrial interests of the two countries? Indeed, how great actually were the differences between the two states, particularly in the period after the departure of Bismarck and Salisbury? Were the differences in social structure and political regime so overwhelming that they made a decisive contribution to the development of conflict? If the common ground between the two countries remained considerable, its existence must surely qualify any explanation for the growing hostility between Great Britain and the German Reich based on differences in the systems of the two; in that case, other factors must surely have played an important part in the course of Anglo-German developments. Moreover, in addition to the notorious weaknesses of Prussian-German constitutionalism, the historian must also investigate the mistakes made by British politicians of the period, which led them to adopt an agitated and inflexible policy after the turn of the century. It can even be argued that British statesmen continued to operate on these principles long after the Age of Imperialism and the First World War had ended.

Finally, the historian must address the vexed question of the compatibility of the Prussian-German national state with a Europe which obtained its specifically European character from the multiplicity of its nations, and within the framework of a Pax Britannica whose representatives regarded the maintenance of the European balance of power as an important element of the international and domestic *raison d'être* of Britain.[11] In these circumstances, we must face the argument that Disraeli was right when, in the House of Commons in April 1848, he argued that Britain must oppose the beginnings of German liberation policies – "'that dreamy and dangerous nonsense called German nationality" – in the interests of European peace'.[12]

II

The causes of the emergence and development of Anglo-German antagonism must be dealt with individually, beginning with the argument which locates the origins of ideological and political alienation between the two states in the Bismarck era. This view was recently expressed most cogently by Paul Kennedy:[13]

Nevertheless, Bismarck's overall impact upon the Anglo-German relationship can only be described in negative terms. What 'Bismarckism' had done was to make every British government from the 1860s to the 1880s, whether Liberal or Conservative, so disapproving of its domestic-political arrangements, that a firm, public and binding Anglo-German alliance was out of the question. Although many individual Britons (especially imperialists) came to admire Bismarck's achievements, the 'Official Mind' only really leant towards Germany in these years for negative reasons, that is, out of concern for the more immediate threats posed to the British Empire by France and Russia. A pro-German policy on the part of the British government in the age of Bismarck took place, in other words, *despite* the Chancellor rather than because of him: which is hardly a resounding accolade for someone who was widely regarded as the greatest statesman Germany had ever produced.

One is inclined to doubt the validity of this judgement, even if only because Queen Victoria, Lord Salisbury and members of his Cabinet, always mistrustful of the person of the Reich Chancellor and contemptuous of the regime of 'Bismarckism', nevertheless regarded his departure as 'an enormous calamity of which the effects will be felt in every part of Europe'.[14] They believed that the fall of Bismarck meant the loss of the critical element of predictability and stability in Germany, which had been of such great importance for Europe. He had come to be seen as the creator of the 'Bismarck System' in foreign policy, which had maintained the peace and the flexibility of the 'little' (continental) European balance of power to the advantage of the 'great' order of world politics[15] protected by Britain and serving the interests of that country. It can be argued that the fall of Bismarck was a blow to Great Britain, since the Chancellor had guaranteed the 'satiation' of the new Reich and had been highly sceptical of the idea of offensive or preventive war. Moreover, Bismarck had found a justification and a role for the Little German national state in a great power policy which, though it occasionally exploited the hostility of the world powers of Britain and Russia, also sought to balance them. Though he sometimes intensified Anglo-Russian hostility, Bismarck more often sought to reduce the tension in order to postpone the need for Germany to opt to become a junior partner of one or the other power in the *Staatensystem* (lit., 'states system'). In this sense Bismarck, like Clarendon, Granville, Derby and Salisbury on the British side, regarded the maintenance of peace as the most vital task. He saw it as the *raison d'état* of Prussia-Germany and was therefore in harmony with the 'British interests' of the period. The Chancellor's attempt to maintain the status quo was far removed from a policy of 'any kind of territorial conquest'[16] with its risks of war 'out of which very dangerous chicks might crawl'.[17] It contained some clear parallels with Salisbury's equally sober and sceptical attitudes and his desire to maintain the existing state of affairs through a policy of moderation. As mentioned in Chapter 1, Salisbury expressed his convictions at the end of his period in government, during a conversation about the problem of a forward defence on the North-West Frontier of India:[18] 'However strong you may be, whether you are a man or a country, there is a point beyond which your strength will not go. It is courage and wisdom to exert that strength up to the limit to which you may attain; it is madness and ruin if you allow yourself to pass it.'

It can be argued that neither Bismarck nor Salisbury really desired a 'closer connection' or even an alliance, since such a step would have considerably limited the freedom of manoeuvre available within the two linked systems of the continental European and the global order. The policy of 'splendid isolation' and that of the 'free hand' were regarded by both representatives as beneficial. Consequently, the Anglo-German alliance soundings at the end of the 1870s and 1880s were not exclusive and perhaps were not even directed towards a genuine objective; instead they served to make the other great powers aware of the alternatives open to Berlin and London, and thus helped to maintain the existing *Staatensystem* and protect their own possible courses of action. Both statesmen held fast to this course, despite its great domestic political dangers – Bismarck until 1890 and Salisbury until the turn of the century – with basic success despite obvious encroachments. However, the question of alliance or antagonism between London and Berlin came to the fore again, more intensely than before, when a new generation of politicians came to power in both countries. These men valued the benefits of foreign policy freedom of manoeuvre less highly, they were prepared to gamble with it and, ultimately, they felt compelled to abandon it. It is beyond dispute that tensions already existed in the era of Bismarck and Salisbury, with the dangers of loss of direction on one side and incorrect decisions on the other;[19] statesmen were already facing the difficult task of seeking and exploiting the 'lasting and intensive possibilities for decision . . . in the border area between necessity and chance'.[20] In all probability, statesmen can only discharge this task at all if they constantly bear in mind the temporary and incomplete nature of their actions. For their part, both Bismarck and Salisbury acted in the sober understanding that they were not creating anything definitive or eternal, but could only hope to delay or ward off the inevitable. In this respect they differed from Bülow and Tirpitz, from Joseph Chamberlain and Lord Fisher, who adopted other approaches to the challenges of the day as they perceived them and sought to change the international, political, military and diplomatic status quo. Against the background of rapid international change, new leading statesmen, politicians and diplomats came to the fore on both sides of the English Channel. The change had a decisive impact on the course of Anglo-German relations.

In Germany the significant change took place after the interregnum of the Caprivi government, under the chancellorship of Hohenlohe, when Bülow and Tirpitz gained important positions in the government in 1897 and began to determine the new course. In Britain, events developed more slowly. The Salisbury era was followed by a period of transition, in which Arthur Balfour sought to do justice to the demands of a new era as well as to the legacy of his uncle. He came under constant pressure from the new forces represented by Joseph Chamberlain and the Liberal Imperialists, who believed that the abandonment of the policy of isolation was inevitable and demanded that clear fronts be drawn for the battles of the future. This line of development was confirmed and strengthened when Grey became Foreign Secretary after the Liberal election victory in 1905 and 1906.

These changes in international politics were connected with the climate of the era itself, with the heightened delirium of imperialism and the pressures of modern mass society. All these issues have been extensively researched in recent years. However, work remains to be done to investigate the significance of other factors. How much were the new leaders influenced by the feeling that, after a long period of peace which had apparently outlived its vitality, they must be ready to meet new challenges more aggressively? How closely was fear of the abyss connected with the inclination to take decisive action? Did the fear of confrontation decline because people found it difficult to imagine either the extent or the consequences of the coming war, and did they therefore adopt a very different approach to that of Bismarck and Salisbury? Despite the growth of domestic and social pressures for the creation of clearly defined fronts in the last years of the Bismarck era and of demands for a choice between alliance and antagonism, both Bismarck and Salisbury sought to resist such 'necessities' and to maintain their freedom to manoeuvre in foreign affairs. In consequence, even the colonialist period of the German Reich at the beginning of the 1880s did little to poison the relations of the two states over 'grand policy'. It must be said, however, that British politicians did not forget the conduct of Germany, which was later to be one of the issues which damaged bilateral relations between Germany and Great Britain.

Social forces in both countries were not yet so powerful that they endangered the fundamental structure of the 'Bismarck System' or Salisbury's policy of 'splendid isolation'. Thus Bismarck and 'Bismarckism' in no way endangered that normality in the Anglo-German relationship which was beneficial to both partners and, on the German side, was linked to the existence of Prussian-German constitutionalism. The belief that a liberalization and parliamentarization of Prussia-Germany would have led to a different, more peaceful and more desirable course in German and European history was held even by contemporaries and is often repeated today[21]. However, its validity is disputable. On closer examination, the picture of 'good Germany' and 'bad Bismarck' is not entirely convincing. In that case, why did Lord Salisbury regret the dismissal of the old Chancellor? Why did the under secretary of state at the Foreign Office, Sanderson, make it clear that he valued the results though not the methods of Bismarckian policy? It was those domestic conditions which were so very alien to British tradition and practice which allowed the Reich Chancellor to create his own powerful position and, as recent research has revealed,[22] to make certain significant compromises with the forces of liberalism. Though Bismarck was always the 'Kurbrandenburg vassal' dependent on his royal master, he could not have followed him unconditionally, *'treu bis in die Vendée'*. To a certain extent it was actually the system of 'Bismarckism' embodied in Prussian-German constitutionalism, so different from the parliamentary government of Britain and regarded with such mistrust by the British, which provided the preconditions for the policy of 'satiation' of the Reich in Europe, for the discreet nature of its supremacy on the continent, for its restraint in naval affairs and its moderation in colonial affairs. It must always be borne in mind that the forces pressing for parliamentary government and democratization in Germany, particularly after 1848, were also pursuing extensive foreign policy objectives which could damage the interests of Britain. It must remain an open question whether the introduction of a genuine parliamentary system in Germany would have promoted a stronger sense of political responsibility in the supporters of national liberalism and, by encouraging the reaching of responsible and reasonable decisions through the parliamentary process, have restrained their ambitions in foreign policy. In their attitudes towards issues of peace and war, parliamentary states are multivalent; they cannot be regarded as a priori peaceable or warlike. The point is surely a necessary one to make, in view of the history of Europe and indeed of Britain itself. From the specific perspective of foreign policy, Prussian-German constitutionalism was thus not wholly against the spirit of the time and even helped to preserve the peace. This function of preserving the peace is clearly apparent in Bismarck's decision (unmistakable after 1875) to avoid foreign wars as the precondition for maintaining the existence of the Reich. It also becomes obvious on examination of the spirit and mechanics of his foreign policy system; its various alliances were generally intended to maintain the peace and not to prepare for war.[23]

The fact that German and British foreign policies lost their flexibility after the caesurae of the years 1890 and 1900–2 is probably connected as much with the conditions of the time as with the abilities of the statesmen. Until 1890 at least, 'normality' prevailed in relations between Great Britain and Germany and the relationship was equally distant from both fixed alliance and irreversible antagonism. However, the opposing poles of alliance and antagonism can sometimes lie close together, a fact which is revealed by Joseph Chamberlain's dramatic switch from being a firm advocate of co-operation with Germany to a bitter opponent of the Wilhelmine Reich. The domestic constitutional condition of the two states played a comparatively small role in preventing them from reaching a 'closer connection'. As a general rule (though one with exceptions) it has been the power of political affairs and interests, not ideological affinities or differences, which has led to rapprochements and alliances or to alienation and hostility between states. The principle remains valid from the alliance between Francis I of France with the Turks in 1536, which received its remarkable ideological justification in a letter from the 'all Christian king' to Pope Paul III,[24] to the conclusion of the convention between parliamentary Britain and autocratic Russia in 1907. *After* a decision has been taken for political and military reasons, then ideological factors can naturally confirm and strengthen it. Ideological differences were not causal factors in Anglo-German relations, as a glance at the different state structures and coalitions of the Bismarck era and the interwar years should be enough to reveal. In any case, before the caesura of 1890, decision-makers were still able to pursue a foreign policy which was motivated by the mutual urge to keep the peace despite the growing strength of opposing forces. In this sense, the policy of Salisbury and Bismarck ensured that relations between London and Berlin can still be described as 'normal' – as far removed from 'closer connection' and alliance as from antagonism and enmity. Moreover, normality in Anglo-German relations during these years meant that the two powers did not seek to decide between alliance and antagonism, but were able to use both elements as possibilities in diplomatic practice and political conduct. Above all, the concept of normality included the implicit understanding that both sides accepted the existing European and global order, that neither side disputed the right of existence of the other, and that the existence of the great powers was a precondition for maintaining a flexible *Staatensystem*. Neither side saw the existing order as so intolerable or in such need of revision that it was forced into conduct which was unacceptable to the other side.[25] Great Britain and Germany did not question each other's right to exist and both recognized that the existence of the other offered more advantages than disadvantages. In order to ensure that this situation continued, it was necessary to avoid paralysis in foreign affairs, to retain a certain freedom to make spontaneous decisions and not to succumb to mechanisms of alliance politics. Foreign policy can all too easily become the slave of bureaucratic and military necessities, in which case apparent security may prove dangerously close to the threat of anarchy. Normality in the bilateral relations of Great Britain and Germany did not preclude conflicts, but it limited their objectives, extent and methods. Above all it served to consolidate the existing relationship of states and to give a firmer base to the existing order; it did not seek to transform the relationship between the two countries into a completely new situation – for example, one of either alliance or antagonism – which might have changed the entire status quo of the international order. Bismarck and Salisbury, who had rather more freedom to take political decisions than their successors, united elements of the opposing concepts of alliance and antagonism and used them to create a normality in Anglo-German relations which served to retain their freedom of manoeuvre and to maintain the peace. It was not primarily the different social and political structures which prevented the liberal ideal of a closer connection between Germany and Britain and ultimately caused the two nations to become antagonists. Instead, relations between Berlin and London – especially after the 'War in Sight' crisis of 1875 – tended to be characterized by the effort to achieve bilateral co-operation which would avoid all extremes whether of a positive or negative nature. In this sense the relationship between the two countries was normal until 1890. It is therefore entirely inappropriate for later historians to hold Bismarck responsible for preventing the establishment of a closer connection or an alliance with Britain. The system of 'Bismarckism' cannot be blamed for this apparent failure, since its existence was a major precondition for the normality of Anglo-German relations which was of such benefit to Britain. However, a relationship of normality between states is more difficult to maintain than a relationship based on alliance or antagonism, as is revealed by the course of developments during the Wilhelmine-Edwardian period. In those years, at domestic political and international level alike, the statesmen lost their freedom to manoeuvre. The political balance of power was dangerously restricted, ultimately becoming little more than a military balance; and the circumspection of the few came increasingly under the influence of the passions of the many.

Even in this period, it would be a mistake to believe that foreign policy decisions were too dependent on domestic political events. Domestic and foreign policy certainly became increasingly interlocked and urgent, and each exerted on the other an effect that was either paralysing or dynamic. Yet, from the British point of view, it was not Germany which was the main opponent or even enemy in the early 1890s. Under Bismarck, the Reich had performed a number of worthwhile services for Great Britain in the international arena; Germany could still be regarded as useful, despite the fact that increasing numbers of Britons were beginning to regard it as a 'nuisance'.[26] Nevertheless, as before, it was Russia and France who were Britain's actual adversaries as a world power. In 1892 these two nations appeared to the British Foreign Office to be 'the two restless powers in Europe', whilst 'the Triple Alliance of Germany, Austria and Italy' was regarded as 'the stable, calm group'.[27] Moreover, it was the development of a Franco-Russian rapprochement during the period 1892–4 (though with some German involvement) that was destroying the 'Bismarck System'[28] and beginning to move Europe from a position of diplomatic flexibility into one of paralysis and dependence on military factors. On a number of occasions, becoming fewer as time passed, there were opportunities to reverse the course of developments which had begun.

The international situation had begun to deteriorate. It was vitally affected by the decision of the German Reich at the end of the 1890s – despite its apparently chaotic political 'structure' in domestic and foreign politics – to challenge Britain at sea. This decision has been described by Ludwig Dehio as the 'unique dynamic . . . of the "peaceful" policy'[29] of the Reich. Almost every state was now infected by an expansionist fever, but none threatened Britain so directly as Germany. Its challenge now seemed to endanger even the motherland itself; in contrast, whatever the nature of French and Russian threats to the approaches to India, their policies were restricted to the periphery. German statesmen of the post-Bismarck generation took this first step consciously and with autonomy, but thereafter they exerted less and less control over the consequences of their original decision. Britain took notice of the German challenge rather earlier than is sometimes recognized[30] and decided on a resolute military response, though British statesmen never regained their old mastery of the arms race and its paralysing international and social consequences. Nevertheless, the period of British weakness which was revealed in the Boer War had been largely overcome by 1905 and British naval superiority largely restored. At that time it might have been possible for British statesmen to consider the consequence of the disastrous arms race and to search for a set of political alternatives which would not have endangered the existence and safety of the nations. Even so, it should not be forgotten that, whatever the fluctuations in German foreign policy as the relationship with Britain changed from normality to short-term alliance negotiations and then to the 'dry war',[31] the German side adhered firmly to *one* fixed goal: naval expansion. In response, the new generation of British politicians no longer shared the political concepts of Salisbury or Sanderson, or even of Balfour and Lansdowne. Their foreign policy was increasingly concentrated on the alternatives of *entente* and antagonism, of allies and enemy powers. The policy of the men at the head of the two armed and opposing structures in Europe, the Triple Alliance and the Triple Entente, helped to ensure that the old multipolar and moderate *Staatensystem* fell prey to division and took on bipolar, revolutionary characteristics.[32] In fact Germany and Britain, the two nations at the head of their groups of friendly or allied states after 1907, pursued

> very diverse objectives with all . . . the means available: at first sight their freedom to manoeuvre therefore appears much greater than in

a balance of power system. However, in reality the area of freedom is much narrower, since each of the two rivals is almost bound to pursue a hostile policy against its rivals, whilst in a balance of power system the larger entities can decide between (temporary) enmity and friendship.[33]

Furthermore, Stanley Hoffmann has described another dangerous feature of bipolar systems:[34]

This complete rivalry leads to a competition for alliance partners which undermines the hierarchy by making each of the two powers largely dependent on the support (or at least neutrality) of third states. Whilst the smaller states are subject to a direct or indirect domination more than in a functioning balance of power system, the situation also offers them opportunities for blackmail which are not available in the balance of power system.

Evidence of the consequences of this tendency was provided by Sir Edward Grey's anxious determination not to offend France during British discussions with Germany in the years before 1914, and by the development of Bismarck's limited 'option'[35] for Austria-Hungary in 1879 into the absolute 'Nibelung loyalty' of Wilhelmine statesmen towards Germany's last ally among the great powers, which made rapprochement between Berlin and St Petersburg impossible. As we are now well aware,[36] the reorientation of the 'Official Mind' in London was linked with the jingoist sentiments of the British masses; it had developed from the general fear of any kind of international rivalry and was also also a response to intensified economic competition. Yet again, the historian is forced to consider the question of the compatibility of empire and democracy.[37] Parliamentary system and world power, internal freedom within a limited framework and external power at global level – for many years these developments had gone hand in hand and had been part of the British self-image during the nineteenth century. However, towards the end of the Victorian Age the compatibility of domestic and foreign policy had become less secure. For example, the country had been forced to deal with the challenge of Milnerism, which had some parallels with the thinking of Rosebery and Joseph Chamberlain. Milnerism and similar ideas demanded adjustments in the parliamentary structure to take account of the new requirements for defence of the empire, and even proposed extensive alterations in the British political system. Of course, it should never be forgotten that the existence of the British parliamentary system eventually triumphed over all the claims of the empire.

In this context, it is important to note the strength of belligerent and jingoistic sentiments in the democratic elements of both countries, and to observe the influence they exerted on the more hesitant representatives of their respective governments. There were clear parallels to Milnerism within the German Reich. For example, after 1890 there appears to have been an excessive freedom of action for the various personalities, parties and groups in the Reich, uncontrolled by the crown or the Reichstag, which gave Wilhelmine Germany much of its unique and dangerous dynamism. This tendency also existed in other nations, and indeed in Britain itself, though to a lesser degree. All these elements undoubtedly intensified the arms race, but they did not initiate it, since it was the result of comparatively autonomous political decisions. Nevertheless, social and political dynamism was so rampant that in Britain it could be restrained only with difficulty, and in Germany hardly at all. The effect was to intensify negative developments in bilateral relations between the two states.

The historian is consequently forced to confront another fundamental problem, which was mentioned at the beginning of this chapter and involves an analysis of the differences and similarities between Wilhelmine Germany and Edwardian Britain. Roughly speaking, one school of historians emphasizes the internal differences between the two states and regards the foreign policy strategies of the German Reich and Great Britain as being more or less directly dependent on their internal political structures. At its crudest level, the liberal and open British parliamentary system is thought to have encouraged a policy based on avoiding conflict and promoting peaceful change; in contrast, the authoritarian and closed Prussian-German constitutional structure is seen as containing within itself a propensity for military conflict.[38] In contrast, other historians emphasize the similarities between the two countries.[39] In their view, the emergence and development of Anglo-German antagonism must be explained by reference to factors and events outside the domestic political structures – in particular, the international constellation and specific decisions in foreign policy. There were indeed many similarities between the two nations in the modern industrial age, between two states in transition 'from the politics of the notables to the political mass market, from cabinet politics to imperialist world politics, from the parties as "communities of sentiment" to popular parties integrating social interests'.[40] Weaknesses of leadership and instability of power structures as the consequence of deep-seated social and international change were not unique to the Prussian-German Reich 'created from above', nor to the constitutional structure created by Bismarck. They also appeared in parliamentary Britain. The domestic problems and conflicts of the two countries were very similar, especially after the turn of the century, as were the reactions to them in the 'class struggle from above'. Yet despite the obvious similarities in the problems and symptoms of Britain and

Germany, the British ruling elite always operated within the developing parliamentary system and seems to have been more prepared to make social and political compromises than its counterpart in Germany. In the Reich, the attention of the historian is therefore directed once more towards the interlocking of domestic and international motives. The specific course of modern German history is not a result of the general development of western capitalism, nor is it predominantly the consequence of particular economic and social conditions in Prussia and Prussia-Germany.[41] Within the framework of an intellectual climate which had been profoundly influential in Germany since the Reformation,[42] the course of modern German history has been, to a high degree, the product of international politics and the changing organization of the *Staatensystem*. Attempts to anchor the foreign policy of the German Reich and Great Britain in their domestic political and social structures cannot adequately explain the path the two nations took to conflict. They can, however, help to illuminate the growing stubbornness and apparent irreversibility of the arms race between them, which escaped more and more from the control of its initiators and protagonists. The investigation of lost opportunities and unsuccessful attempts to restore flexibility to the polarized and paralysed *Staatensystem* reveals that there were serious and sometimes almost unavoidable failures on the British side as well as the German. At no time during these years did British statesmen ever manage to rid themselves of the fear that the country was under threat. The German naval challenge ensured the persistence of the British 'security dilemma',[43] and the ideological gap between the two regimes, which had not originally caused the existence of hostility, now served to intensify and encourage it. A study of international relations shows that alliance systems 'resting on an ideologized hostility between different systems'[44] are very difficult to eradicate, even though 'the hostility of social systems . . . as such does not itself build foreign policy constellations'.[45]

For both sides it became increasingly difficult to return to the lost normality of their bilateral relations during the 1870s and 1880s. There were several attempts to reduce the level of antagonism. After 1909, and with greater intensity between 1912 and 1914, the Germans and also the British tried to regain the lost flexibility of Grand Policy by making political agreements at the periphery and trying to extend these inwards to Europe itself.[46] All these efforts failed and are little more than aborted alternatives to history. Nevertheless, the attempts to reach *détente* – or even, using modern vocabulary, antagonistic co-operation[47] – between the two powers are worthy of study.

As the power struggle between Britain and Germany took on an ideological form, it came closer to a point of no return. Previous doctrinal nonsense about conflicts of nature between British 'shopkeepers' and German 'heroes' now acquired a disastrous dogmatic rigidity. At this level of assumptions, it is also necessary to assess a fundamental conviction – and perhaps a fundamental error – of British policy, the roots of which lie deep in the nineteenth century and continued to have an influence into the 1930s. The attitude of leading British figures in international politics was deeply affected by the belief that an industrial and technical development along British lines would gradually also impart the other values of British political and social culture to the states involved.[48] This hope, as the course of European history demonstrates only too clearly, was an illusion. Germany's decision to challenge Britain at sea provided early evidence that the skills and techniques associated with international 'progress' could be used to serve objectives quite unrelated to the 'anglicization' of the domestic and particularly the international life of peoples. After all, it was the military victories of Prussia which had led to the foundation of the Reich; the 'Moltke treatment' – as Richard Wagner once described the effect of this triumph on the spiritual and political life of Germany[49] – had created important doubts about the previously almost undisputed moral, ideological and political predominance of Britain. The militarization of European thinking as a result of Prussia's victorious wars of 1864, 1866 and 1870–1 was thus begun by Bismarck and in future could be controlled only with difficulty. Even a state like Austria-Hungary, whose very existence depended on balance and law, was affected by the dominance of military strategic thinking.[50] In 1871 Count Andrássy, its new Foreign Minister, made a purely superficial imitation of the 'Iron Chancellor' and postulated:[51] 'The consequence of the last war is "might before right" . . . and that foreign policy is correct that is also strategically correct.' Thinking of this kind undermined the universal nature of the British values of the time, damaged the model of the British 'way of life' and called into question the concept of a civilizing mission based on ideas of 'improvement', 'reform' and 'peace'. This deep shift in the value structure of states and their representatives was observed by British statesmen with great reluctance and extreme difficulty. Indeed, many appeared unwilling to pay adequate attention to the tendency at all, until well into the twentieth century. They regarded the alternative to the liberal British understanding of civilization and politics as revolutionary, warlike and unreasonable; in such a situation, British politicians could see little alternative but to adhere to their own position of moral superiority, to their traditional beliefs and to their 'ostensible mission'[52] in the hope that time would gradually show the virtue of acceptable, progressive and Anglo-Saxon solutions. Finally, then, it is necessary to study the issue of the compatibility of the *kleindeutsch* national state with the existence of Europe and of the British Empire.

A reasonable and serious historical judgement of this question is possible only if the facts of *kleindeutsch* and European historical development are kept entirely separate from the contemporary argument for and against German reunification. Academic facts cannot properly be used to recommend or justify political decisions in any unconditional and simplistic way. Thus, arguments made after two world wars about the nature of the German national state and its incompatibility with Europe have no necessary connection with *contemporary* sentiments and impressions in Great Britain at the time the Reich was founded. In fact, British judgements at the time provide more evidence of the acceptability and even the desirability of the Bismarck Reich in the European and international framework. For example, Bismarck's policies of the balance of power and peace were highly advantageous to British interests.[53] Only after the fall of the first Reich Chancellor did the countervailing tendencies which had been visible in his time make a breakthrough, and the understanding of the need for moderation and self-limitation was gradually lost. The universal contemporary desire for expansion was the prelude to disaster for the German Reich. In the first instance, therefore, it was not the notorious backwardness of Prussian-German constitutionalism which isolated the German national state and allowed it to be regarded as a destroyer of the peace and even as an alien body in Europe. Instead, the isolation of Germany was due to the passionate and hasty desire of Bismarck's successors to catch up with modern developments, to abandon the apparently outmoded policies of the former Chancellor, and to make the breakthrough into *Weltpolitik*. Yet could the Reich have continued to exist at all in its limited form, infected with the virus of imperialism but continuing to suppress the outbreak of the fever in the Bismarckian manner? Fascinating though the question is, there can be no definitive answer to it. However, the possibility of prolonging the status quo of a Reich which voluntarily remained within its borders clearly decreased as time passed. And though it may be asked whether a more generous British attitude in the international arena might have softened the foreign policy demands of the young Reich, this possibility no longer existed once the German naval challenge had begun to threaten the existence of Great Britain. One cannot beat a potential partner about the head and still expect his understanding and his help. Germany, therefore, was forbidden to be like other states; the Reich could not be an imperialist power with similar attributes to those of Great Britain. Within the great framework of international politics, of course, there were alternatives to the Wilhelmine option of a total challenge to the existing *Staatensystem*. Ultimately, all of them amounted to the acceptance of the role of junior partner of one of the great world powers, Russia or England, in European and world affairs. The new generation in Wilhelmine Germany was no longer

79

willing to accept this restriction. In Bismarckian Germany this limited role had been made less burdensome by superior diplomacy, but had still been unavoidable for a state born out of the 'Crimean War situation'.[54] Wilhelmine statesmen were not content with a comparatively autonomous position of continental supremacy and sought to make Germany a world power, equal with and even overtaking Great Britain. They thus took the intellectual, political and military step which put the Reich on the road to defeat and even placed the existence of Germany, originally compatible with European and British requirements and fulfilling a useful function as far as British interests were concerned, in question.

The German challenge had inevitable consequences for British policy. Great Britain was more or less compelled to defend itself if it was not to capitulate without a struggle. However, the British response was restricted to increased military spending and the making of alliances, *ententes* and conventions. These very decisions imprisoned the nation in a box of iron necessities; even the liberal parliamentary system, with its inherent possibilities of renewal and regeneration, was unable or unwilling to liberate the country from its dilemma. Relatively independently of the structure of German constitutionalism and British parliamentarism, each of the two powers sought to impose its own concept of a world and European order on the other, in the name of the dubious concept of the world balance of power. In both countries, statesmen lost sight of the obligation of great powers to work together to construct and maintain order in the *Staatensystem*. After the departure of Bismarck and Salisbury, German and British statesmen irresponsibly neglected the universal desire for a minimum of order in the international system. This desire is so strong that it induces willingness to accept an order based on the measures and compromises of the great powers even when these are not always pleasant for third parties, rather than risk the collapse of any and all order.[55] In the years before the outbreak of the war, Great Britain and Germany failed in this task. However, the ability to order the world tends to be connected with possibilities for (domestic and international) peaceful change. Opportunities for such change depend greatly on the organization of the *Staatensystem* and the relations of the great powers within it. Excessively close ties or extreme antagonism between the leading states can obstruct both the development of a policy of 'peaceful change' and the establishment of a flexible order. For example, a powerful duumvirate of great powers may take on a hegemonic character, and is thus likely to be rejected by the other powers and overthrown. In contrast, intense hostility between two great powers can easily lead to catastrophe. For the great powers to fulfil their task of maintaining order, the relations between them must be based on the concept of normality; in turn, the maintenance of normality depends on the intensity with which the challenger opposes the power in possession.

'Challenge' and 'response' are part of the normality of relations between states. However, when the measure of what is reasonable and tolerable is lost, the challenger begins to strive for the entire legacy of the old power. In that case, the ability to compromise and reach satisfactory settlements automatically disappears, and politics degenerates into an arms race based on rigid alliance mechanisms. Nations and societies are sucked into this process and, preoccupied with the need to respond to actual or implied threats, are scarcely able to see the abyss of revolution and war ahead of them. Even with hindsight it becomes difficult to discover the opportunities for independent action in the 'inherent necessities' of domestic and international politics. Whatever the difficulties involved, the historian of the First World War must always confront this problem, since it is universal and is equally relevant to our own time.

The study of the emergence and development of Anglo-German antagonism in the nineteenth and twentieth centuries thus leads to conclusions which have a much wider applicability. The creation, maintenance and development of normal bilateral relations between states is one of the most difficult tasks of foreign and international politics, and one which is frequently not adequately recognized. 'Normal' relations must constantly be re-created as the international situation changes, since universal rules and precepts cannot be applied mechanically in every situation. However, an analysis of the period before 1914 can still help us to construct a model to guide the conduct of statesmen in domestic, foreign and international politics. Statesmen must never become mere accomplices of apparently overwhelming 'inherent necessities'. Instead, though aware that they are 'in part . . . prisoners of unavoidable circumstances', they should struggle 'to save an element of free choice from the pressure of circumstances'.[56] In the years before the outbreak of the First World War, the existence of rigid alliances and antagonisms as the model of international politics prevented statesmen from observing this requirement. In contrast, the existence of bilateral normality appears as the precondition, condition and consequence of reasonable conduct within the *Staatensystem*. Today, we are perhaps sceptical about the prospects for any normality in the bilateral relations of leading world powers. Has the emergence of totalitarian systems and their approach to foreign policy made the normality of inter-state relations into a phenomenon of history which belongs irrevocably to the past?

NOTES

1 Bryce, J., *Das heilige römische Reich* (Leipzig: 1873), p. VIII. For this reference I am grateful to the dissertation by Kleinknecht, T., 'Imperiale und internationale

Ordnung im historisch-politischen Denken von James Bryce (1838–1922). Eine wissenschaftgeschichtliche Untersuchung zum anglo-amerkianischen akademischen Liberalismus' (DPhil. thesis, Münster: 1980), written under the guidance of H. Gollwitzer; see in particular pp. 144 and 148.

2   Machiavelli, N., *Politische Betrachtungen über die alte und italienische Geschichte*, translated and introduced by F. von Oppeln-Bronikowski, 2nd edn ed. E. Paul (Cologne/Opladen: 1965), p. 21.

3   Sontag, R. J., *Germany and England. Background of Conflict 1848–1894* (New York: 1964; first edn, 1938), p. 94; Eyck, E., *Bismarck. Leben und Werk*, 3 vols (Erlenbach/Zürich: 1941–4), *passim*; Kennedy, P. M., *The Rise of the Anglo-German Antagonism 1964–1914* (London/Boston, Mass./Sydney: 1980), p. 82.

4   Dehio, L., 'Deutschland und die Epoche der Weltkriege', in L. Dehio, *Deutschland und die Weltpolitik im 20. Jahrhundert* (Munich, 1955), p. 15; Dehio, L., 'Gedanken über die deutsche Sendung 1900–1918', in Dehio, *Deutschland und die Weltpolitik*, p. 82.

5   Kennedy, *Antagonism*, p. 153.

6   On the German side, these facts are emphasized by Gall, L., 'Bismarck und England', in P. Kluke and P. Alter (eds), *Aspekte der deutsch-britischen Beziehungen im Laufe der Jahrhunderte. Ansprachen und Vorträge zur Eröffnung des Deutschen Historischen Instituts London* (Stuttgart: 1978), p. 46 ff; for the British side see Chapter 1 in this book, 'Great Britain and the foundation of the German Reich'.

7   Hintze, O., 'Machtpolitik und Regierungsverfassung', *Internationale Monatsschrift für Wissenschaft, Kunst und Technik* 7 (1913), col. 1067 ff (part I) and col. 1157 ff (part II). Reprinted in Hintze, O., *Staat und Verfassung. Gesammelte Abhandlungen zur allgemeinen Verfassungsgeschichte*, ed. G. Oestreich, with an introduction by F. Hartung, 3rd edn, revised and extended (Göttingen: 1970), p. 424 ff.

8   On this subject see Hildebrand, K., 'Staatskunst oder Systemzwang? Die deutsche Frage als Problem der Weltpolitik', *Historische Zeitschrift* 228 (1979), p. 624 ff, esp. p. 637 ff.

9   *The Times*, 14 November 1868, quoted by Craig, G. A., 'Britain and Europe (1866–1869). A study in the application of non-intervention' (PhD thesis, Princeton, NJ: 1941), p. 165.

10   On this argument by Widenmann see Dehio, 'Gedanken über die deutsche Sendung', p. 77.

11   See, for example, Paul Kennedy's lucid argument about the apparent incompatibility of the Little German national state with the shape of Europe in his book about the rise of Anglo-German antagonism: Kennedy, *Antagonism*, p. 204.

12   Faber, K.-G., *Deutsche Geschichte im 19. Jahrhundert. Restauration und Revolution. Von 1815 bis 1851* (Wiesbaden: 1979), p. 238.

13   Kennedy, *Antagonism*, p. 204.

14   Kennedy, *Antagonism*, p. 204.

15   On this subject see Muralt, L. von, 'Deutschland und das europäische Gleichgewicht', in W. Höfer (ed.), *Europa und die Einheit Deutschlands. Eine Bilanz nach 100 Jahren* (Cologne: 1970), p. 31.

16   On the interpretation of this passage from the Kissinger Diktat of 15 June 1877 see Gall, L., *Bismarck. Der weisse Revolutionär* (Frankfurt-am-Main/Berlin/Vienna: 1980), p. 517 ff.

17   Comment by Bismarck to the Free Conservative deputy Lucius a few days after the Kissinger Diktat, Gall, *Bismarck*, p. 519.

18   Taylor, R., *Lord Salisbury* (London: 1975), p. 133.

19   See also the well-reasoned arguments of Karl Rohe in his review of Paul Kennedy's book on the rise of Anglo-German antagonism,. The review appeared in the bulletin of the German Historical Institute in London. I would like to take this opportunity to thank Mr Rohe once again for allowing me to use his manuscript.

20   Kissinger, H. A., *Memoiren 1968–1973* (Munich: 1979), p. 64.

21   See, for example, Fehrenbach, E., 'Preussen-Deutschland als Faktor der französischen Aussenpolitik in der Reichsgründungszeit', in Kolb, *Europa und die Reichsgründung: Preussen-Deutschland in der Sicht der grossen europäischen Mächte 1860–1880*, Beiheft 6 der Historischen Zeitschrift (Munich: 1980) p. 137.

22   On this subject see especially Gall, *Bismarck, passim*, e.g. pp. 192, 333, 377, 379, 382, 394 ff, 466, 468, 492, 554, 575, 581, 587, 612, 716.

23   Hillgruber, A., *Bismarcks Aussenpolitik* (Freiburg i.B.: 1972), p. 159.

24 Alexandrowicz, C. H., *An Introduction to the History of the Law of Nations in the East Indies: Sixteenth, Seventeenth and Eighteenth Centuries* (Oxford: 1967), p. 236.

25 Kissinger, H. A., *Grossmachtliche Diplomatie. Von der Staatskunst Castlereagh und Metternichs* (Düsseldorf/Vienna: 1962), p. 7.

26 Kennedy, *Antagonism*, p. 182.

27 On Sir Edward Grey's retrospective assessment of the year 1892, made to the Committee of Imperial Defence in 1911 in the form of a memoir, see Petrie, Sir Charles, *Diplomatie und Macht. Eine Geschichte der internationalen Beziehungen 1717–1933* (Zürich/Freiburg i.B.: 1950), p. 282.

28 Kennan, G. F., *The Decline of Bismarck's European Order. Franco-Russian Relations 1875–1890* (Princeton, NJ: 1979).

29 Dehio, 'Gedanken über die deutsche Sendung', p. 77.

30 Kennedy, *Antagonism*, p. 247.

31 On the contemporary comment of Hans Delbrück see Dehio, 'Gedanken über die deutsche Sendung', p. 77.

32 Vital here is Hoffmann, S., *Gulliver's Troubles oder die Zukunft des internationalen Systems* (Bielefeld, 1970), p. 30 ff.

33 Hoffmann, *Gulliver's Troubles*, p. 31.

34 Hoffmann, *Gulliver's Troubles*, p. 31.

35 Hillgruber, *Bismarcks Aussenpolitik*, p. 156.

36 A recent survey is Kennedy, *Antagonism, passim*.

37 See in more detail in Hildebrand, K., '"British Interests" und "Pax Britannica". Grundfragen englischer Aussenpolitik im 19. und 20. Jahrhundert', *Historische Zeitschrift* 221 (1975), p. 623 ff.

38 See note 3.

39 Schmidt, G., 'Deutschland am Vorabend des Ersten Weltkrieges', in M. Stürmer (ed.), *Das kaiserliche Deutschland. Politik und Gesellschaft 1870–1918* (Düsseldorf: 1970), p. 197 ff; Schmidt, G., 'Innenpolitische Blockbildungen am Vorabend des Ersten Weltkrieges', in *Aus Politik und Zeitgeschichte. Beilage zur Wochenzeitung "Das Parlament"*, B20/70, 13 May 1972, p. 3 ff; Schmidt, G., 'Die Nationalliberalen – eine regierungsfähige Partei? Zur Problematik der inneren Reichsgründung 1870–1878', in G. A. Ritter (ed.), *Deutsche Parteien vor 1918* (Cologne: 1973), p. 208 ff; Schmidt, G., 'Politischer Liberalismus, "Landed Interests" und Organisierte Arbeiterschaft 1850–1880. Ein deutsch-englischer Vergleich', in H.-U.Wehler (ed.), *Sozialgeschichte heute. Festschrift für Hans Rosenberg zum 70.Geburtstag* (Göttingen: 1974), p. 26 ff; Schmidt, G., 'Parlamentarismus oder "Präventive Konterrevolution"? Die deutsche Innenpolitik im Spannungsfeld konservativer Sammlungsbewegungen und latenter Reformbestrebungen 1907–1914', in G.A.Ritter (ed.), *Gesellschaft, Parlament und Regierung. Zur Geschichte des Parlamentarismus in Deutschland* (Düsseldorf: 1974), p. 249 ff.

40 Schmidt, 'Parlamentarismus oder "Präventive Konterrevolution"', p. 250.

41 On this subject see Wehler, H-U., '"Deutscher Sonderweg" oder allgemeine Problem des westlichen Kapitalismus. Zur Kritik an einigen "Mythen deutscher Geschichtsschreibung"', *Merkur. Deutscher Zeitschrift für europäisches Denken* (1981), Heft 5, p. 478 ff.

42 Hennis, W., *Die deutsche Unruhe* (Hamburg: 1969), p. 128 ff.

43 Herz, J. H., 'Idealistischer Internationalismus und das Sicherheitsdilemma', in J. H. Herz, *Staatenwelt und Weltpolitik* (Hamburg: 1974), p. 39.

44 Löwenthal, R., 'Internationale Konstellation ind innerstaatlicher Systemwandel', *Historische Zeitschrift* 212 (1971), p. 57.

45 Löwenthal, 'Internationale Konstellation', p. 57.

46 See Schöllgen, G., 'Richard von Kühlmann und das deutsch-englische Verhältnis 1912–1914. Zur Bedeutung der Peripherie in der europäischen Vorkriegspolitik', *Historische Zeitschrift* 230 (1980), p. 294 ff, esp. pp. 306–7 and 332–3.

47 Link, W., *Der Ost-West-Konflikt. Die Organisation der internationalen Beziehungen im 20. Jahrhundert* (Stuttgart/Berlin/Cologne/Mainz: 1980), p. 86 and p. 216.

48 See in more detail in Chapter 2 of this book, 'Lord Clarendon, Bismarck and the problem of European disarmament 1870'.

49 Gregor-Dellin, M., *Richard Wagner. Sein Leben, Sein Werk, Sein Jahrhundert* (Munich/Zürich: 1980), p. 765.
50 Lutz, H., *Österreich-Ungarn und die Gründung des Deutschen Reiches. Europäische Entscheidungen 1867–1871* (Frankfurt-am-Main/Berlin/Vienna: 1979), p. 489.
51 Lutz, *Österreich-Ungarn*, pp. 488–9.
52 Dehio, 'Gedanken über die deutsche Sendung', p. 94.
53 Chapter 1 of this book, *passim*.
54 On this term, used paradoxically, see Hillgruber, A., *Otto von Bismarck. Gründer der europäischen Grossmacht Deutsches Reich* (Göttingen/Zürich/Frankfurt-am-Main: 1978), p. 100 ff, esp. pp. 107–8.
55 Bull, H., 'Von der Verantwortung der Weltmächte. Die Vereinigten Staaten, die Sowjetunion ind die Weltordnung', *Europa-Archiv* 18 (1980), p. 548.
56 Kissinger, *Memoiren*, p. 63.

4

The crisis of July 1914:

The European security dilemma. Observations on the outbreak of the First World War

I

More than seventy years have passed since the outbreak of the First World War. The events which led to it have been the subject of much research and many different interpretations in those years. At the time, the prevailing view among all the combattants was that they had been drawn into a defensive war and that the enemy had launched a war of aggression. Article 231 of the Versailles treaty, imposed by the victors, subsequently stated that the German Reich bore the sole guilt for the outbreak of war.[1] Almost unanimously, the Germans rejected the accusation as the 'war guilt lie', and during the interwar years German historians were understandably preoccupied with efforts to refute it. For a variety of motives, they received some assistance from foreign academics.[2] Now that the intense controversy of those years has abated, we can see that these arguments produced rich dividends in the literary, documentary and editorial fields, which are not always adequately heeded in contemporary discussions. Lloyd George's dictum that all the nations stumbled into the war[3] – coined partly to excuse his own policy before its outbreak – became widely accepted in the following years; one-sided accusations of guilt against one or another protagonist were replaced by a universal-historical view. There was a negative side to this development, since it ran the risk of creating the night in which all cats are grey. For example, sweeping and premature generalizations were made in which the 'old diplomacy' was accused of chief responsibility for the outbreak of war. The tendency gathered force in the years after the end of the First World War, reflecting the general enthusiasm for a democratization of foreign policy and the establishment of the League of Nations. In this atmosphere, the traditional forms of relations between states were demonized and condemned. However, there were also some positive results. It became possible to obtain an overall view of the *Staatensystem* and, in particular, to examine more closely the increasing, and ultimately overwhelming, influence of the system of alliances in the prewar period. In this way at least, researchers were offered an explanation of what had happened.

The subject requires the adoption of a differentiated approach by historians. An approach of this kind is often lacking in the various Marxist interpretations, which argue that capitalist imperialism was the decisive phenomenon, both internationally and domestically, in leading to the outbreak of war. To have tenable claims to academic validity, both the Marxist and universal-historical interpretations need to supply convincing reasons why the world war broke out in July/August 1914 and not earlier or later. The conduct of the responsible statesmen and diplomats must be examined closely. Where were the possibilities and limits of necessity and freedom, of diplomacy and the obligation to conform to the system,[4] of inevitability and recklessness, in their behaviour?

After the Second World War, attempts were made to utilize the results obtained in the interwar years after purging them of their national distortions. In the West, especially in view of the political consequences of the Second World War, a general approach was developed in which the responsibility for the outbreak of war in 1914 tended to be shared among all the nations involved in the July crisis, though to differing degrees. It was obvious that none of the five European great powers had been resolute enough in its desire for peace.[5] This interpretation of the July crisis of 1914 was dominant until 1961, when it was challenged by Fritz Fischer's book, *Griff nach der Weltmacht*[6] ('Germany's Aims in the First World War'). The debate which followed caused an uproar among the general public in West Germany,[7] but also enriched German history in the long term. In particular, it raised two specific issues: first, the old question of the sole guilt of Germany; and secondly, the question of the internal driving forces behind German foreign policy in the years before 1914, which many observers regarded as especially aggressive.

As far as the first question is concerned, it must be said that there was no sole guilt on the part of the German Reich. In some areas it did bear a very great responsibility, particularly over military mobilization as the July crisis reached a climax; in this specific case, German conduct was comparable to that of the Russian government. Nevertheless, the German offensive strategy was born out of a foreign policy defensiveness which no longer appeared reasonable.[8] It led the government in Berlin to encourage the pursuit of an aggressive foreign policy by Austria-Hungary, though Vienna had already responded firmly after the murder of the heir to the Austro-Hungarian throne. In many of its motives and aims, characterized equally by fear and arrogance,[9] German foreign policy seemed to bear many similarities to French, Russian and even British policy during these weeks.

The 'Fischer controversy' had a highly stimulating effect on research in many ways. However, universal-historical surveys of the outbreak of war are now a rarity in academic history,[10] though the issues they raise ought to be the subject of future research. For example, studies of the dependence of external policy on the internal conditions within a country gain real meaning only if they adopt a comparative perspective and seek to explain how far social dislocations and domestic political hopelessness determined the decisions of national foreign policy and the resolve to wage war. Comparative analysis might lead to the observation of similar phenomena in various societies: for example, it might be argued that the unwillingness of weakened aristocratic elites to give up their leading positions in the state[11] made them act in a way which ultimately provoked the outbreak of war. Such an analysis, even if limited chiefly to Russia, Austria-Hungary and Germany, would then approach such a degree of universality that it could not well serve as an explanation for the course of the July crisis.

As James Joll has recently argued,[12] the results of recent research have surely made necessary an examination of the events of summer 1914 from a supranational perspective. The effectiveness of the international system itself is an appropriate topic for inquiry. The need appears even greater as a consequence of the tendency of historians in the last twenty years, particularly in the Federal Republic of Germany, to investigate the internal political and economic preconditions of Bismarckian and Wilhelmine foreign policy. These historians frequently present the course of foreign policy and the decision to wage war as the consequence of domestic compulsions; moreover, they regard the failure to introduce a parliamentary system of government in the Reich as being responsible for its apparent choice of a '*Flucht nach vorn*', a flight from (intractable domestic problems into war).[13] However, as this explanatory model could also be applied to tsarist Russia and the Dual Monarchy it thereby loses much of its power to explain the specific conduct of Germany.

France and Great Britain had taken the parliamentary path, in Britain's case long and successfully. Yet even these nations were suffering from domestic political conflicts when war broke out. The internal position of Europe on the eve of the First World War has been accurately described by Donald Cameron Watt:[14] 'Most of the major powers in Europe stood on the edge of civil strife in the years before 1914. But not even Austria-Hungary, only Russia in fact had reached a state of disorder and division similar to that of affairs in Britain.' Notwithstanding the fact that 'each social order . . . has its own basic framework within which it solves the same or similar problems in its own distinct way',[15] and without wishing to insist too rigidly that the functional interrelationship between domestic crisis and foreign war, which is supposed to have obtained for the non-parliamentary powers Russia, Austria-Hungary and Germany, might have played its part in determining the affairs of the parliamentary powers Britain and France as well, this is a question which at least merits further investigation.[16] Quite possibly such an inquiry would produce results for British and French policy very similar to those well known to be true for Russian, Austro-Hungarian and German policy in these decades. In these latter countries there were military and political figures – and even some major economic figures – who concluded that the pressing problems of their respective countries could be solved only by war. In contrast, other leading figures were convinced to the contrary, believing that external war would certainly unleash internal revolution;[17] in the years before 1914, these men were at least as numerous and influential as their opponents.

This highly complex situation clearly requires further investigation and explanation. The events of summer 1914 must be placed in their historical perspective and examined against the background of the developments in the European system since the end of the Bismarck era. In this way, proper account can be taken of the structural and economic arguments which are used to support the theory of the 'primacy of domestic policy' during decisive events, but also of the conduct and failures of individual personalities. It can safely be assumed that the mechanisms of the international system, and the leading individuals on all sides who worked within them, played a vital role during the course of the July crisis.

In this analysis, it is not enough to examine the conduct of only one participant in international events, nor to concentrate solely on the internal crises which were apparent throughout Europe and which influenced the formation of national foreign policies to a greater or lesser extent. It is also necessary to investigate the details of historical development and the features of the international system which had an effect on the outbreak of war in 1914. First, how had the European system, and the thinking of European politicians and statesmen, changed since the end of the Age of Bismarck? Secondly, why did the July crisis in particular lead to war? Why had the first and second Morocco crises of 1905–6 and 1911, the annexation crisis in Bosnia-Herzegovina in 1908–9 and the Balkan and Adriatic crisis of 1912–13, not led to full-scale war? It can be argued that it was not the outbreak of war in 1914 which was surprising, but the fact that it had not happened earlier as the result of one of the crises which had shaken Europe during the preceding decade[18].

II

Though the system created by Bismarck was not ideal, it allowed its participants a considerable degree of flexibility and freedom of manoeuvre. Its order was based on the foundation without which peace is impossible, on the existence of a balance of power. The German Reich was certainly the strongest power on the continent. However, it was far from certain to remain so in the future, particularly since the two world powers on the periphery, Great Britain and Russia, were stronger than Germany in themselves, in co-operation with each other, or even in alliance with another great power.

The French tended to regard Bismarck's European order with some hostility, as '*la paix Allemande*'.[19] Yet the 'half-hegemony' of Germany did not mean that the Reich was actually hoping to achieve supremacy on the European continent in the manner of Napoleon I. Bismarck had made some cautious probes, without provoking conflict over the balance of power and hegemony, to discover what Europe might reasonably be expected to tolerate in this respect. It had been made clear to him – for example, in the 'War in Sight' crisis of 1875 and the central European plans launched against Austria-Hungary in the late 1870s – that any attempt to attain such an objective would threaten the very existence of the new Reich. Bismarck's system therefore permitted the German Reich neither more nor less than the preponderant position in the 'Concert of Europe',[20] but one which was limited in two important respects. The first restriction was a result of the fact that the German Reich had been founded 'in agreement with England'.[21] Britain's global interests after 1871 had been promoted by the unity of Germany; within Europe, moreover, the balance of power and peace established by Bismarck within the framework of the Pax Britannica had been to its advantage.[22] In addition, the predominant position of Germany was limited because Bismarck himself had imposed restrictions on its development. However, this self-imposed restraint was becoming increasingly difficult to justify and appeared to a growing number of his contemporaries in the new national state to be untenable in the future. The Chancellor's policy was based on an insight which many Germans found difficult to accept; it involved the understanding that the existence of the Reich could be guaranteed only if it acted as a junior partner of one of the two world powers, either the British or the Russians.[23]

One of the difficult tasks of foreign and international politics was to maintain this complex, comprehensive balance of power. It demanded an accurate assessment of power relationships which extended far beyond the purely military dimension. In addition it required 'absolute ruthlessness',[24] since statesmen must be prepared 'to sacrifice friendship, legality and every other consideration to the national interest'. The balance of power therefore presupposed 'an internal political structure' which permitted, and even encouraged, such conduct. For Germany, the state which for understandable reasons most made this strategy its own, it created the obligation to make neither lasting friends nor eternal enemies; the existence of either imposed too great a restriction on the freedom of manoeuvre necessary to maintain the balance of power.

The fact that the Bismarck system continued to function for two decades was partly due to the leading role played by its creator. In addition, the Reich Chancellor had capable partners within the Concert of Europe, who were able to make their own contribution to the balance of power. These partners included Salisbury and Giers – who was the equal of Bismarck 'intellectually and in the mastery of the issue and the methodology of the diplomacy of the period'.[25] At the beginning of the period, they also included Beust (though not Andrássy) and even Ferry. As a result, relations between states could be conducted in an atmosphere of normality which was equally far removed from the twin poles of alliance and antagonism. By and large, the nations accepted the European status quo.[26] Certain territorial alterations could be made within this framework and could even be achieved by war, as long as the objectives and methods involved had a constructive effect and actually sustained the existence of an order which remained fundamentally sacrosanct.

In every nation there were tendencies opposed to this model of international politics, which gained in influence as time passed. These included the '*Weltpolitiker*' and pan-Germans in the Reich; the protagonists of various imperialist policies, the adherents of imperial forward defence and later the military in Great Britain; the pan-Slavs in Russia; the révanchists in France; and the 'war party' at court in Vienna, even though Austria-Hungary was dependent on a climate of loyalty to treaties, liberality and conciliation.[27]

For all that, for two decades the moderation of the few prevailed over the fervour of the many, though sometimes only just. In this period, the 'political situation as a whole'[28] in Europe was generally balanced. Only Britain was permitted a certain degree of indirect supremacy in the global sphere. Even here, the 'Great Game' of British rivalry with Russia[29] was continued and the Pax Britannica was subjected to a powerful challenge in Asia. However, the British proved ready to accept these experiences and adjusted their policies accordingly. There were clear parallels here to the British reaction in the middle of the nineteenth century, when the belief that North America was unconquerable and that the British position in Canada, Central America and the Atlantic was relatively weak had resulted in a foreign policy of appeasement towards the United States.[30]

To obtain a genuine balance of forces, each of the five great powers had to strive to be one of the three partners who for a period – though not a long time – were superior to the other two to a relative but not an intolerable degree. The precondition for such a balance was that each great power must avoid fixed alliances which did not aim to keep the peace but were motivated by the prospect of victory in a coming war. Statesmen such as Salisbury, Giers and Bismarck were persuaded by historical insight and prophylactic pessimism that their best hope lay in creating continuity in their lifetime rather than in building for eternity. Nevertheless, there was no relapse into fatalism. They acted vigorously to prevent the spread of disorder and adopted policies necessary to maintain the balance of forces; that is, they concluded alliances in order to maintain peace, and not to prepare for war.

It was certainly not humanity or altruism which led them to behave in this way. Instead, caution and *Realpolitik* born of experience encouraged them to avoid war because it would bring chaos on both the international and domestic stages. They therefore strove to avoid the establishment of political relations on an ideological basis, since this might have the effect of solidifying temporary formations into permanent structures. Conduct of this kind was inimical to the necessary free play of forces in the balance; it would place excessive restrictions on the ability to change partners, the *'renversement des alliances'*, and would undermine the balanced order either directly and visibly or gradually and insidiously.

At the end of the 1880s and after the departure of Bismarck, developments of this kind first began to determine the course of European history. Until then, despite obvious contrary tendencies, statesmen had succeeded in maintaining the 'political situation as a whole' by means of shifts in the balance and the retention of flexibility and control. However, the international situation thereafter began to change, though not irreversibly. Nor were the likely consequences of the change recognizable. Previously, the international order had been stable because of its flexibility, but a new generation of statesmen and diplomats was emerging which was unable to recognize the threat to the international order. These men adopted the policies which seemed to them to promise the highest degree of security, but which in fact quickly created fundamental insecurity and proved very likely to lead to war. This European security dilemma[31] was the consequence of several factors: the creation of an antagonistic system of alliances which became immovable; an arms race which was fuelled by ideology; and above all, a catastrophic primacy of mobilization plans which were determined largely by purely military factors and became caught up in the fatal circle of 'power accumulation, power competition ... and use of force'.[32] The European statesmen who had conjured up this illusory security were unable to disentangle it or to divert it into constructive channels.

In line with the wishes of Bismarck though not those of Andrássy, the Dual Alliance of 1879 between the German Reich and the Habsburg monarchy was not concluded to prepare for a military conflict with Russia. Instead it was designed to achieve the result obtained in 1881, to provide a demonstration of political power which would draw tsarist Russia to the side of Berlin and Vienna and thus secure peace in Europe.

However, shortly afterwards politics in Russia and Germany came under the influence of men whose ideas and intentions differed fundamentally from those of Bismarck. The trend emerged clearly in 1888, when Russian actions began to undermine the reinsurance treaty agreed between the two countries the previous year. Giers, whose domestic political position was very different from that of the German Chancellor, no longer opposed the rapprochment with France,[33] though this had a permanently damaging effect on relations with the Reich well before Wilhelmine statesmen failed to renew the reinsurance treaty.

The Franco-Russian alliance began to develop strongly from this time and was given political and military form between 1891 and 1894. It also had a different quality from the agreements which had been made in the Age of Bismarck and made a significant contribution to the establishment of fixed alliance systems within Europe. The alliance was originally directed mainly against Britain, but later acquired an unmistakably anti-German character as the French began to revise their anti-British foreign policy after the Fashoda incident of 1898. This process culminated in the Entente Cordiale of 1904, an agreement which regulated the overseas interests of Britain and France but also had considerable significance within Europe itself. The Franco-Russian alliance paralleled the decision of Wilhelmine statesmen to depart from the course adopted by Bismarck and to regard Austria-Hungary as the indispensable partner and ally of the Reich. All the great powers sought increased security through close ties; though it was not obvious at the time, the process led to greater mutual dependence and thus brought with it a general insecurity, the opposite of what had been sought.

The militarization of politics had been encouraged involuntarily by Bismarck by the three victorious wars of 1864, 1866 and 1870–1. Thereafter, he was able to restrain this development only with great effort. Consequently, the tendency to regard 'any foreign policy' as 'correct, which is also strategically correct'[34] – described by Andrássy on 17 February 1872 – gradually gained the upper hand. The result was a profound change in the character and *telos* of the existing *Staatensystem*, though there were repeated attempts to reverse the trend taken in the years 1888–90 and 1891–4. It became more and more difficult for politicians to return to the classical and genuine balance of power. Their problems were increased after the turn of the century, when growing ideological hostility intensified the power political differences between the two great alliance blocs.

The alliances between the Dual Monarchy and the German Reich on one side, and between the French Republic and tsarist Russia on the other, took on an increasingly offensive shape. In part, this was the consequence of the growing belief of statesmen throughout Europe that the status of their own countries as great powers depended on loyalty to their respective partners. But it was also a response to the widespread 'cult of the offensive';[35] leading figures on all sides were influenced by a conviction that it was the task of diplomacy to prepare a position from which their country could achieve a strong attacking position as quickly as possible in the event of war.

For such a policy to be possible, it was vital that the allies of each country should be prepared to offer immediate and unqualified support in the event of conflict. In fact this support was to be more or less automatic, and was ultimately prepared by means of mobilization agreements. In the event of war in Europe, France therefore had to urge Russia to strike immediately against Germany, not to stand aside or concentrate solely on Austria-Hungary. For its part, if there was war in south-eastern Europe, Russia had to demand that France move directly into action against Germany. Germany, desperate to relieve its eastern flank, urged Austria-Hungary to be ready to march against Russia without delay. Finally, the Dual Monarchy needed Germany to move against Russia unconditionally, and not to concentrate solely on the war in western Europe. With hindsight, it is clear that politics and diplomacy were being placed at the service of military strategy, which was now almost entirely obsessed with the dogma of the offensive war. Politics and diplomacy therefore only increased the European security dilemma rather than alleviating it. This development, characteristic of the prewar period, was in fundamental contrast to the defensive, flexible *Staatensystem* of the 1870s and 1880s.

The development of ideology in power politics can be regarded as the great enemy of a multipolar balance of power. In this respect, the expansion of the German navy played the critical role in the splitting of Europe into antagonistic blocs, because it drew Britain directly into European quarrels. This process was not irreversible. For example, if the British had behaved with more generosity, especially after they had clearly assured their supremacy in this sector by 1911 at the latest, its effects might have been mitigated. Nevertheless, from the turn of the century German naval expansion was the uniquely problematic feature of the imperialist dynamic of the Wilhelmine Reich,[36] which otherwise was not greatly out of tune with the times.[37]. It was almost inevitable that a hegemonic and/or maritime challenge to Britain would be bitterly opposed and would bring Britain to the head of a powerful European coalition against the Reich. In earlier times, the Spaniards and the French had already suffered a similar fate; moreover, Frederick the Great had been able to count on English support during the Seven Years War only because he was not engaged in a struggle for hegemony and was not offering the kind of naval challenge which could have damaged relations between Britain and Prussia.

The British generally regarded German colonial demands and acquisitions as less of a danger. In fact, they even hoped that such a policy might supply a possible outlet for German expansionist drives which could not be satisfied by further territorial expansion in Europe. Only the expansion of the navy was aimed at the very heart of Britain, threatening to cut the motherland off from its empire and its trade links. The Reich was not fitting out a cruiser fleet, which could have served to assist the acquisition of colonies and to guard and maintain them. Bülow's policy of colonial restraint, which went hand in hand with the rapid extension of Tirpitz's battleship fleet, therefore had a much more explosive effect than Bethmann Hollweg's far greater ambitions in the colonial sphere; these actually promoted a relief of tension in the heart of Europe, *détente* with Britain and a measure of naval disarmament.

In contrast, the 'Tirpitz Plan'[38] challenged Great Britain directly in home waters and could cut its vital links to the empire and the world. The British, who were well aware of the extent of German naval construction in the years 1901–2,[39] came to believe that the young German Reich could offer a greater threat to India and the approaches to the subcontinent than their old global rival, Russia: 'This [i.e. the vulnerability of India] was Britain's basic international problem after 1885, and it remained so until the German naval threat took priority in the time of Grey.'[40]

Though Anglo-German naval rivalry was crucial, it was not the only factor which served to diminish British fear of the Russian danger. After the abandonment of 'splendid isolation' and the conclusion of the Anglo-Japanese alliance of 1902 and the *Entente Cordiale* of 1904, another element made a contribution to the Anglo-Russian rapprochement and the convention of 1907. This was the British fear of the historic invincibility and apparently growing power of the Russian empire. To both British and German statesmen and military leaders,[41] Russia seemed to be 'a formidable power [which] will become increasingly strong',[42] particularly after the tsarist empire had recovered from its defeat against Japan in 1905–6.

The British came to a very different conclusion from that reached by the Wilhelmine elite, which lacked the long British experience in relations between the great powers[43] and also faced a much more direct Russian danger[44] than the latent pressure on India feared by the British. Apparent Russian strength led British statesmen to conclude that they must reach a rapprochement with St Petersburg; 'British interests' required that an agreement be made with a rival who was too strong to be dominated. This tendency existed independently of and long before the Anglo-German naval rivalry in the 'dry war',[45] which masked and pushed into the background every other problem of British world politics. It became more clearly visible after 1895, when Salisbury organized the British retreat from Constantinople to the Nile Line,[46] which had become more important after the construction of the Suez Canal; it can also be recognized, in outline, in the dialogue between the world powers carried out by Gortchakov and Clarendon in Heidelberg during late summer 1869.[47] For deep-seated reasons which had now become pressing, Britain felt the need to seek the friendship of Russia in order to avoid its enmity. The British ambassador in St Petersburg, Buchanan, described this conviction of British foreign policy in exaggerated form: 'Russia is rapidly becoming so powerful that we must retain her friendship at almost any cost.'[48]

As has been noted elsewhere, the British had revealed themselves similarly ready to compromise and even to yield in their relationship with the Americans, who were regarded as both invulnerable and dangerous. Even at the beginning of the twentieth century, when it was becoming increasingly clear that the Pax Britannica would eventually be challenged more seriously by the Pax Americana than by the artificial Pax Germanica, the British decided to work against the weaker party and in co-operation with the stronger. 'In the eyes of the leading classes in London [American domination promised] to preserve something of the English hegemony'; on the other hand, 'German hegemony was perceived as alien, humiliating and unacceptable'.[49] It is not only the desire to retain power which drives nations into war.

After the turn of the century, the development of the German battle fleet meant that the position of Britain was more directly and acutely threatened by the Wilhelmine Reich than by its more powerful American and Russian rivals. By this stage Britain was already coming to an arrangement with the United States and Russia. The possibility that Great Britain would go to war against the USA because of quarrels in Canada or Central America had disappeared long ago; in addition, there was no current danger that Britain would become just a 'third-rate power'[50] after defeat at the hands of Russia and the loss of India. In both cases, the extent of the potential danger persuaded the British to adopt a conciliatory and prudent attitude. A generous reaction of this kind is peculiarly possible for a maritime power and is frequently characteristic of its foreign policy. However, in order for the island state to maintain this calm and composed approach, an invulnerable position is essential. If this is threatened, the maritime power generally reacts more sensitively than a continental power, which is more quickly prepared to come to terms and can also rely on the advantage of its inner line in the event of conflict. The sight of the German battle fleet sailing close to its harbours and coasts provoked an extremely nervous reaction in Great Britain, which displayed a strong sense of vulnerability and very little generosity. Its lack of composure in this instance was much more 'continental' than 'insular'. In short, the existence of the German 'risk fleet' led 'to a radical change in British strategic thinking'[51] and altered 'the whole basis of Anglo-German relations'.[52] To a certain extent, it is comparable with the British response to the challenge of Napoleon I, which encouraged the process whereby India came under direct British control almost as a preventive measure.[53]

The British Gulliver, tied down by its worldwide obligations, had less power at its disposal than before. Yet just as Wilhelmine statesmen had come almost to expect an 'English war of succession',[54] so their British counterparts began to make preparations for a seemingly inevitable 'battle of the titans' against the German upstart.[55] When there is no power political opposition to phobias of this kind, they are strengthened[56] and made very difficult to reverse. The British thus gradually lost the ability to maintain the necessary moderation in their response to the German challenge. Statesmen tended to lose sight of the great maxim that 'peace is the greatest of British interests'[57] in favour of preparation for a war which seemed increasingly unavoidable.

However understandable the response to the threat posed by the German navy may appear, not all the steps taken by the British can be justified as necessary or sensible. A brutal and threatening challenger can scarcely expect his rival to behave with restraint and moderation, and the response must clearly be resolute. Nevertheless, it can be argued that the response should not be so hard and uncompromising that the defender is himself injured; should there not be an attempt to find some way to accommodate the challenger, on grounds of self-interest? If the opportunity is missed, then it rapidly appears with hindsight to have been the point of no return. Great Britain had failed to react positively enough to the prospect of *détente*, which had been on offer since 1909 and was, at least in part, promoted by the personality and policies of Bethmann Hollweg. By 1911 such a reaction was at least theoretically possible because, despite the clamour of the 'diehards', supremacy in the naval sphere had been regained.

In the meantime the alliance between France and Russia, weakened in 1904–5, had recovered. After the humiliating outcome of the annexation crisis of 1908–9, the Russians rearmed with great vigour,[58] whilst France made no attempt to avoid the arms race with the Germans, and even deliberately sought it.[59] By this stage the British had lost far too much of their autonomy. The policy of 'splendid isolation' and the method of changing alliances according to opportunity had been abandoned; the plan for a comprehensive and flexible political balance had been sacrificed in favour of a knife-edged military balance based on the antagonism of two armed camps.

Once Salisbury's policy of independence was abandoned, the links with France and Russia developed into genuine alliances and took on an increasingly fixed and inescapable form. Ideological antagonisms intensified the development, as part of a distinct 'recontinentalization' of British and European politics after 1905. The world no longer served solely 'as the spoils of the Europeans'[60] and the imperialist spirit began to surge destructively back against Europe itself.[61] In both camps, and in all the great powers, there were a number of attempts to reverse the trend; for example, by the use of peripheral relief strategies[62] of the kind which had been adopted in the nineteenth century to divert European tensions to the outside world or to create new movement in an attempt to loosen the blocs and return to the old order. However, faced by a direct challenge at sea and by the threat of a continental hegemony of the German Reich, British statesmen believed that their freedom of action was limited. In their view, the present and future order depended on Britain making an alliance with France and Russia to bring the German 'enemy' to its knees – even at the cost of a war. At the beginning of 1907 there was a debate[63] between Thomas Sanderson, a foreign policy representative of the Salisbury era, and Eyre Crowe, a representative of the new anti-German course, which gained increasing influence after the reform of the Foreign Office in 1905–6. The debate was ultimately resolved in favour of Crowe, and Sanderson's advocacy of the old *Staatensystem* of Bismarck and Salisbury did not succeed in restoring its vitality. Crowe managed to see in German history nothing less than a 'direct and unmistakable hostility to England' and 'a disregard of the elementary rules of straightforward and honourable dealing'.[64] In the atmosphere of the time, his arguments found significant support; it seemed necessary to oppose the German danger with unconditional resolution, with the result that 'every German gain' appeared to be 'a British loss'.[65]

In contrast, Sanderson objected that 'the British Empire must appear in the light of some huge giant sprawling over the globe, with gouty fingers and toes stretching in every direction, which cannot be approached without eliciting a scream'.[66] Indeed, he regarded German conduct as understandable in some ways. Sanderson argued that Germany was a late-comer, 'impatient to realize various long-suppressed aspirations';[67] the Reich was therefore anxious to demand full recognition of its new position and was also haunted by the insecurity of its situation, marooned between 'two powerful, jealous and discontented neighbours'.[68] Whilst Crowe urged that the status quo should be defended without concessions or altered only for services in return, Sanderson recommended that a settlement be sought since 'a great and growing nation cannot be repressed'.[69]

The dilemma facing British statesmen was that they did not have even an approximate idea what the Germans really wanted. Was it a share of world power, its division, or the whole British inheritance? This uncertainty eventually strengthened their belief – fuelled by popular sentiment – that security could be found only through military co-operation in the Triple Entente with France and Russia, and not in *détente* with Germany. The Reich, at the head of the Triple Alliance, was coming to exactly the same conclusion and thus intensifying its own security dilemma. Almost unconditionally, the British and Germans decided to seek security by strengthening their alliances. This development increased the tendency of the international system to produce crises and war and created general insecurity – not because the alliance mechanisms were not sufficiently clear and calculable, but because they dangerously restricted the freedom of the participants to resolve emerging crises. In foreign as in domestic policy, the result was a loss of flexibility and control.[70]

Again and again in the vital years between 1905 and 1914, the great powers attempted to regain their lost freedom of manoeuvre and to break the ice of the 'cold war' to which Eduard Bernstein had already referred in 1893.[71] In this way a new national and international course might be charted and a genuine balance of power regained which would evade the automatic operation of the antagonistic alliance system. The difficulty lay in the fact that the statesmen were anxious to base their actions on reliable facts. In general, however, once all the facts are known the opportunity to act has already been missed.

None of the powers believed itself to be sufficiently strong on its own. Consequently, every effort by the powers to achieve security and *détente* was accompanied by an overwhelming anxiety 'to reduce as much as possible the significance of the intentions of the other side by means of their own actions'.[72] Britain and Germany, but also Russia, which despite its apparent strength felt threatened and humiliated by decades of failure, were unwilling to take the risk of *détente* as opposed to the apparent security of alliances. Instead, each wanted to ensure the 'absolute impotence' of the other side, 'in order to be absolutely secure that the other side cannot do any damage to themselves'.[73] The search for absolute security for one state inevitably brought with it the absolute insecurity of the others. Again and again, the whirlpool of the European security dilemma sucked in and destroyed any attempt to escape the deadly pull of the military alliance system and restore political freedom of action. All the great powers made some attempt to achieve this objective, at various times and in various ways. However, they did not act with the primary goal of restoring the Concert of Europe and securing peace. Instead, the powers manoeuvred in the hope of inflicting damage on the enemy alliance system and thus being better prepared for a coming war. This failure of statesmanship was in part a response to the charged emotions of the peoples of Europe, which were frequently even more narrow-minded and warlike than those of their rulers and were equally imprisoned by the concepts of alliance thinking. Statesmen lacked the time and opportunity – and also frequently the inclination – to lead their countries away from the rigid antagonism of the *Staatensystem*; this shirt of Nessus became ever more restrictive as each power sought to make an effective demonstration of its strength and resolution. It must remain an open question whether a policy of calculated *détente* from one power would have received a response from the other side and ultimately have provided the prospect of a new balance of forces. However, the attempt would certainly have been worthwhile.[74]

The German Reich adopted a very different mode of conduct. In fact, the apparent aggressiveness of German foreign policy in the two Morocco crises was primarily an attempt to break away from the defensive position it had done much to bring on itself and to escape the enemy 'ring'. These efforts were described by Hollstein in 1909;[75] 'We must, before the ring of great powers encircles us, attempt with all our energy and a resolution which does not flinch from the extreme, to break this ring.' Eventually, the policy adopted produced the opposite result. This German foreign policy, which prevailed until the crisis of July 1914, involved preventive measures to break apart the 'encirclement' of the Reich even at the risk of war. It had little chance of success. Equally futile were the simultaneous efforts of the Kaiser to establish a continental alliance of Russia, Germany and France against Britain and America. Moves of this kind were not merely reactions against the conduct of the other powers, but also had independent motives with political objectives. It was hoped that they would gradually eliminate Franco-German antagonism, taking as their starting-point the agreement between Wilhelm II and Tsar Nicholas II of Russia in Bjorkoe on 25 July 1905. The German leadership later attempted to detach the Russians from the opposing bloc by means of a settlement of mutual interests in Turkey and Persia; for example, within the framework of the meeting of the emperors in Potsdam on 4 and 5 November 1911. Attempts at Russo-German rapprochement were rejected by the Russian statesmen, partly as a result of the struggle between St Petersburg and Berlin for influence in Constantinople.

During his time in office between 1906 and 1911, the Russian Foreign Minister, Izvolski, was also making a vain attempt to gain greater freedom of manoeuvre for his country and to readjust the balance between France and Britain on one side and Germany and Austria-Hungary on the other.[76] In the Habsburg Empire, Berchtold succeeded Aehrenthal as Foreign Minister in 1912 and was anxious to reduce German dominance in the Triple Alliance. Moreover, the continuing contacts of members of the house of Habsburg with the western partners of the Triple Entente, especially France, were alarming to the German Reich, as was the persistent though unlikely possibility of a rapprochement between Vienna and St Petersburg.

In France, from 1912 at the latest once Poincaré had become 'overall master of foreign policy',[77] alternatives to the existing policy towards Germany and the alliance system had almost no chance of gaining ground despite the situation in parliament.[78] Poincaré, Prime Minister from 14 July 1912 and elected President a year later, was more anxious to maintain ties with Britain and Russia than to maintain peace, though he no longer espoused révanchist or offensive methods to satisfy French security needs. Jules Cambon constantly argued, from his position as ambassador in Berlin, that in this way Paris might become the 'victim of its alliance.[79]

It even seemed possible that the dialogue between Britain and Germany, the two powers at the head of their respective blocs, would lead to an improvement in relations. The potential for such a development was revealed by the successful co-operation between the two governments in the settlement of the Balkan and Adriatic crisis of 1912–13, which was comparable in many ways with the the crisis of July 1914. Furthermore, some progress had been made by London and Berlin towards solving the problems of Europe by means of a settlement overseas.[80] Unfortunately, these developments proceeded too slowly to permit the creation of an extensive agreement to solve the important territorial problems which emerged between Europe and overseas, between the crisis centre and a 'buffer zone' which was not as readily available as it had been in the nineteenth century. The progress made was not sufficient to halt the arms race, nor to destroy the blind mechanisms of the alliance systems and the disastrously automatic mobilization plans. Nor did the statesmen of Britain and Germany manage to defuse the time bomb which was ticking in south-east Europe.

The policy of *détente* was pursued by Bethmann Hollweg and Grey against strong, and ultimately overwhelming, domestic opposition. Its failure was revealed, for example, in the Haldane mission of February 1912. On the German side, attempts at rapprochement were wrecked by the stubborn determination with which the Kaiser and Tirpitz supported the expansion of the navy. On the British side, they failed because any tendency to regard a settlement with Germany as more important than the alliance with France was mistrusted and condemned by Paris and the Foreign Office, where the link with France had come to be seen as a partnership of destiny.

When analysing the problematic relationship between security and *détente*, it must be remembered that the British had regained their superiority in the Anglo-German naval rivalry well before 1914. However, British statesmen feared that a wedge might be driven between the country and its allies which would damage British credibility and the ability to make alliances in the future. The prospect of isolation in foreign affairs seemed a very real threat. The Germans were certainly asking far too much when they demanded British neutrality in the event of any European conflict in return for concessions in the field of naval armament. However, unconditional supporters of Anglo-French co-operation such as the British ambassador in Paris, Bertie, and France's new Prime Minister, Poincaré, resisted any form of rapprochement between the British and the Germans, even one based on a differentiated neutrality which would not violate either the letter or the spirit of the *entente* between Britain and France. The *entente* itself had originally been defensive but, partly as a consequence of the military agreements which had been made since December 1905, had undergone a fundamental change of character.

French pressure also had a considerable influence on British attitudes towards Russia. In the spirit of their long-term policy of withdrawal from Constantinople, British statesmen made repeated attempts to accommodate Russian objectives at the very time that Russo-German antagonism in that area was intensifying. Fear of the future, which plagued the British as well as the German ruling elite, persuaded British statesmen to move closer to Russia as France desired. Poincaré was aiming for a seamless alliance between Paris, London and St Petersburg. All the great powers became imprisoned in their respective blocs; all feared that any small step towards the opposing side would expose them to the danger of isolation; in order to avoid suspicion, all were forced to move even closer to their partners than before. As the blocs were cemented, the last vestiges of the political balance of power were lost. Treading on thin ice does not make it stronger.

The statesmen then became little more than accomplices of the system of bloc thinking. They wanted a balance of forces, but failed for a number of years to understand that the *Staatensystem* they had created actually destroyed genuine balance and reduced it solely to the level of military parity. When understanding dawned, they were incapable of restoring the necessary flexibility to the system. The inadequacies of the *Staatensystem* were intensified because the armed camps placed their trust in mobilization plans which were inspired by offensive thinking; during the crisis of July 1914 these plans finally had a more decisive effect than the arms race itself. The politicians therefore became, more and more, the servants of the military.

The apparent logic of the 'Schlieffen Plan' (1894–1905) actually contained disastrous consequences for Germany. Though there was a very real threat to the exposed central position of the Reich, the Schlieffen Plan left German statesmen scarcely any room to manoeuvre in the period between mobilization and the start of war. Schlieffen's 'dead hand automatically pulled the trigger',[81] though only as the consequence of a mistaken assumption that the threat of war would be sufficient to intimidate the enemy. In fact it had the opposite effect. The Russians revealed themselves ready to respond directly and aggressively, and even the French and British were prepared to demonstrate their military power and strength to the Germans and Austrians.

Long before, the normality which had been an integral part of the Concert of Europe during the Bismarck era had given way to the antagonism of military blocs; the multipolar balance of power had been lost. The primary issue was no longer how to keep the peace, but how to win a war which was regarded as unavoidable. Already, the great powers were concerned for their position *after* the coming struggle, and anxious that they would not have to fight alone for the future order of Europe and the world. Between 1905 and 1914 all the European great powers except Britain, which was territorially satisfied but still afflicted by the security dilemma, were influenced by revisionist and expansionist tendencies of the kind Bismarck and Salisbury had been able to restrain within Europe.

The two blocs now stood ready to move into action. Their military balance was such that the political balance of power had been lost, and they were so powerful that they had forfeited their room to manoeuvre. All the issues which separated the two rival alliance systems were now concentrated in the Balkans. This area lay between Europe and the rest of the world; in the period in question, it actually obstructed the process by which tensions had previously been diverted into the colonial sphere.[82] The Balkans 'formed the direct link between the continent and its periphery, and it was no accident that the growing tensions between the Powers which had developed from their imperial rivalry ... should surge into life here and that south-east Europe should become the starting-point of the great war'.[83]

From about 1911, a 'set of circumstances particularly likely to lead to war'[84] existed in the region. Previously there had been clear Austro-Hungarian hegemony over the west of the Balkans, a fact which had been conceded by the Russian Foreign Minister in that year with reference to Serbia; now, encouraged by the Russian ambassador in Belgrade, Hartwig, and with the support of Russia, Montenegro and Serbia had begun to challenge the Dual Monarchy. In contrast, in the eastern Balkans close to the straits which were so vital to Russia, 'Bulgaria was escaping from Russian claims to hegemony over this half of the Balkans and was relying on Austria-Hungary'.[85] Germany, tied to Austria-Hungary by the alliance mechanism, was beginning to involve itself directly in the Balkans as the opponent of Russia. The situation had thus changed since the Bismarck era, when the Reich had begun its policy in south-eastern Europe with the aim of relieving pressure at the centre. Since 1895, Britain had been withdrawing gradually from the region. However, the Periclean *Weltpolitik* of Wilhelmine Germany had led its statesmen to take the place of Britain as the rival of Russia in Constantinople, which had enormous and symbolic significance for the Russians.[86] The tension between St Petersburg and Berlin came into the open with the Liman von Sanders crisis at the end of 1913. It continued to reverberate through the Anglo-Russian naval talks of spring and summer 1914, which caused consternation in Germany and appeared to 'close the ring' of the hostile coalition, until the July crisis exploded into life.

Some European statesmen had been prepared to make the difficult attempt to escape the pressures leading to war, and to struggle to maintain the peace by retaining an 'element of free choice'.[87] These men, however, were no longer in office. In the Reich, the Secretary of State for Foreign Affairs, Kiderlen-Wächter, had died suddenly in 1912; and in Russia Kokovzov, the Prime Minister, was dismissed at the beginning of 1914.[88] The efforts of those who remained, Grey and Bethmann Hollweg, were simply too timid. Though aware that they had become prisoners of a security policy which had produced the opposite of what was intended, they were unable to break down the blocs and introduce fresh political movement. Ultimately, they resigned themselves to the outbreak of a war which had previously been avoided by the use of crisis management.

III

In earlier crises, in 1905–6, 1908–9, 1911 and 1912–13, the great powers had managed to avoid major war despite the growing security dilemma. Why did they finally fail in 1914? The course of the July crisis was disastrous because the factors tending towards war were concentrated in unparalleled numbers and intensity. Despite the similarities with previous crises since 1900, the decisions taken in July 1914 therefore had a uniquely significant effect.

In the first Morocco crisis of 1905–6, Austria-Hungary, though a steadfast ally of Germany, was not directly involved in the dispute. On the other side, Russia had temporarily ceased to feature as a powerful factor as a result of its military defeat in the war against Japan. Germany could therefore permit itself to draw back during the course of the confrontation even though it had not managed to disrupt the *entente*. In addition, the ring encircling the Reich was not yet as oppressive as it was to become after the convention between the 'whale' and the 'bear' was finalized in 1907. During the first Morocco crisis, German statesmen still regarded genuine and extensive co-operation between Britain and Russia as improbable.

During the annexation crisis of 1908–9, the German Reich responded to the Austro-Hungarian challenge to Russia by offering dangerously unconditional support. However, Russia was still not strong enough to react, especially as France failed to provide the tsar with any real assistance. The French *entente* with Great Britain had already been significantly extended as a result of agreements between the general staffs of the two countries; nevertheless, Britain's pledge of assistance to France, which was to regulate the sphere of responsibilities of the two nations, was provided only on 22–3 November 1912 in the form of an exchange of letters between Grey and

Cambon covering 'military alliance obligations'.[89] In any case, at this stage France was motivated more by a defensive desire for security than by the aggressive *révanchism* which developed later in response to the growing strength of the Triple Entente.

In the second Morocco crisis of 1911, Germany had drawn back when confronted by unexpected British pressure. This had been expressed in an *ad hoc* convention between Britain and France on 20 July 1911 which, though not formally ratified, included precise agreements on the deployment of a British expeditionary corps in France for 'opérations contre l'Allemagne'.[90] It was also given threatening voice in Lloyd George's Mansion House speech the following day. The resolute stance of the British caused great surprise. It seemed typical of the changed atmosphere in Britain that these sentiments were expressed by Lloyd George, a politician who had previously devoted his energies to domestic political issues in the struggle between 'social reform' and 'imperialism'. When bitter Russian memories of France's failure to provide support during the annexation crisis led them to stand aside in their turn, Britain sprang to the aid of France. The British conduct grew from several sources: fear of a continent dominated by Germany; anxiety that the French alliance might be lost if Britain failed to respond; and, ultimately, a fear of the latent threat of an agreement between St Petersburg and Berlin over the disposal of the collapsing Habsburg Empire, which might leave the British Empire completely isolated. The mood in both Russia and Germany was deteriorating following the Russian defeat by Japan in 1904–5 and Germany's political setbacks at the Morocco conferences. After the crises over Bosnia-Herzegovina and Morocco, it became doubtful whether Russia and Germany could permit themselves to draw back in a new crisis without suffering irreversible harm to their status as great powers and possibly sustaining grave domestic political damage.

The British and Germans were not directly involved in the conflict in south-east Europe in 1912–13; nor did their alliance partners subject them to the degree of pressure to which they were exposed a year later. Nevertheless, the British and German governments took the lead during the Balkan and Adriatic crisis and restored the peace in Europe. Did their conduct provide reliable evidence that European politics could be safely steered through future storms? British and German crisis management in 1912–13 remained in the public memory and even caused a certain optimism immediately after the assassination of 28 June 1914; it was not generally understood that the whole situation had changed and was now conspiring against attempts by the leaders of the Triple Alliance and the Triple Entente to maintain order and keep the peace. Neither imperialism nor the arms race *in themselves* provoked the outbreak of the First World War. The international situation had changed fundamentally since the turn of the century, with the loss of the political balance of power and the creation of a rigid set of military alliances. Against this background, a number of factors was increasing the danger of war. Individually or collectively, their cumulative effect made war seem not only probable, but even inevitable.

(1) On all sides, the feeling grew from crisis to crisis that war was inevitable and could not be delayed much longer. A 'fin de siècle' sentiment dominated Europe; almost instinctively, it sought fulfilment and salvation through war rather than through further attempts to organize the peace. Each nation therefore clung desperately to the alliance system which was thought to offer protection and security. The purpose of these alliances, however, was no longer to prevent war and maintain peace, but to achieve victory in the coming conflict by means of aggressive and carefully synchronized mobilization plans. Bismarck's own alliance system would have lost its meaning in the event of a *casus belli*, but the alliance systems of 1914 found their true fulfilment in war. The drift was comprehensible; at that stage war was regarded as an acceptable and even desirable alternative to peace by many statesmen and diplomats, was vaguely desired by broad classes of the population and was eventually greeted with hysterical enthusiasm by the masses.

(2) Against this background, British foreign policy during summer 1914 was motivated by the conviction that it would ultimately be better to wage major war rather than accept a German-dominated Europe and the prospective isolation of Britain. Anglo-Russian antagonism made less of an impact on this sentiment than Anglo-German hostility, which was based on the German naval challenge and the threat of continental hegemony. During the Anglo-Russian naval negotiations before the outbreak of the July crisis, Sasonov offered the British an agreement on mutual spheres of interest in Persia which would guarantee the 'security of India'.[91] The offer confirmed Grey in his policies, though from 6 July he must have been aware of the strength of the German reaction to the assassination of 28 June[92] and, unlike Poincaré, was no bloc fanatic.

Grey's timid search for alternatives and a return of flexibility, which bore some similarity to the equally futile efforts of Bethmann Hollweg, quickly faded as the crisis progressed. The Foreign Secretary's freedom of manoeuvre was further restricted because he feared not only that Britain would be isolated, but that its European and imperial position would be put in jeopardy by any Franco-Russian victory which was achieved without British help. Though Britain had successfully beaten off the German naval challenge, the country had not regained the autonomy it had sacrificed to the bloc thinking of the Triple Entente. Great Britain entered the war out of fear for the future and for the sake of its own continuing ability to forge alliances, both of which bound it to the Triple Entente with France and Russia. Its statesmen failed to recognize that the alliances had become an end in themselves and were doing more to damage than to serve 'British interests'. They placed excessive restrictions on the freedom of the country, which clearly continued to rest upon its own considerable power. Burdened by domestic anxieties and foreign policy alarm, British statesmen no longer regarded the future with the optimism they had felt in the time of Salisbury, when it seemed capable of being shaped as they saw fit. Instead the future seemed increasingly dark and negative. However, British leaders were convinced that the use of military means nevertheless offered an opportunity to exert a favourable influence on the course of history.

It is obviously difficult to recognize the point when an alliance ceases to be useful and tends to become harmful; when, instead of providing security, it begins to provoke insecurity; and when it allows immobility to take the place of stability. Grey led his country into the war through fear of an uncertain future over which Britain no longer seemed fully in control. Convinced that the existing structure of alliances and power politics would continue to determine the future of Europe and the world after a war, he preferred to run the risk of war rather than face the possible inability of Britain to make lasting alliances.

(3) In October 1912, Poincaré's France promised Izvolski that it would stand by Russia in the event of a conflict in south-east Europe caused by the conduct of Austria-Hungary. Since then, in contrast to the previous decades, France had largely reconciled itself to hostilities in Europe. After the second Morocco crisis, French military plans were altered to give them an offensive character.[93] Though the German Reich was facing difficulties in its own alliances after 1911 and was seeking *détente*, Poincaré became the greatest advocate of the primacy of a particular form of alliance politics; this did not have the maintenance of peace as its chief objective, but sought to demonstrate the superiority of the Triple Entente over the enemy coalition. Ambassador Jules Cambon, who supported the policy of a settlement with Germany, was deeply alarmed by the change of policy. On 1 November 1912 he wrote to his colleague Paléologue, a champion of the uncompromising line supported by Poincaré and the British Foreign Office:[94] 'You wanted war. We will have it.' Poincaré continued his harsh policy during the July crisis. Though the Austrian ultimatum was conveyed to the Serbs only after the departure of Poincaré and Viviani from Russia on 23 July 1914, he had already agreed with the Russian statesmen 'to take action at Vienna with a view to the prevention of a demand for explanations or any summons equivalent to an intervention in the affairs of Serbia which the latter would be justified in regarding as an attack on her sovereignty and independence'.[95] At this stage Poincaré was committed to an unremittingly harsh policy, whilst the Russian statesmen were ready for war.

(4) The conduct of Russia during the July crisis was very different to the attitude adopted in the preceding decade. Russia statesmen were influenced by the strengthened alliance between St Petersburg and Paris, by the close ties of both with Great Britain and by a feeling of renewed strength and aggressiveness. Britain was no longer the real leader of the Triple Entente, as it had been during the Balkan crisis of 1912–13; Russia was now pressing

impetuously forward, further encouraged by the fact that some time before, in 1912, France had promised to stand by the Russians in the Balkans.[96]

Tsarist Russia was anxious to make amends for the experiences of 1908–9. Particularly after Suchomlinov's disastrous and largely inaccurate assurances on 13 January 1914 that the country was militarily prepared for war, Russian statesmen believed themselves satisfactorily armed for the great conflict.[97] Kokovzov, who might have restrained these aggressive sentiments, was dismissed; Sasonov, who had previously taken a cautious approach to issues of peace and war, now supported the dangerous policy which was adopted. Russia had already revealed its determination when Germany provoked the Liman von Sanders crisis and was eventually forced to give way.[98] Throughout Europe men were urging that difficult foreign and domestic problems should now be solved by war, but in Russia they were more influential than elsewhere.[99]

Germany had now appeared alongside Austria-Hungary to replace Britain as Russia's traditional rival in the Balkans. In the July crisis, Russia attempted to triumph over the Dual Alliance of Germany and Austria-Hungary, and thus consciously ran the risk of major war. This conduct was applauded by Poincaré's France, no longer restrained by Britain and further encouraged by the belief that Russian strength had increased still further since the spring of 1914. Finally, with the militarily unnecessary general mobilization of 30 July 1914,[100] Russia set in motion the mechanism which was to trigger major war.

(5) As the Triple Entente gained the upper hand in the rivalry between the blocs after 1911, Austria-Hungary and Germany were forced on to the defensive. The foreign policy of the Habsburg monarchy was greatly influenced by these developments during the July crisis, when it followed different policies to those adopted in the Balkan crisis of 1912–13. The growth of Russian armaments, threateningly displayed in the Russian army manoeuvres of June 1914, created added pressure on Austria-Hungary. Foreign Minister Berchtold responded with a diplomatic offensive which was the product of a fear for the very existence of the Habsburg monarchy.[101] The creation of the Balkan League,[102] which Vienna regarded as a Russian weapon against Austria-Hungary, [103] provoked a strong and horrified reaction in Vienna.

Berchtold was afraid that a lack of harshness on the part of the Dual Monarchy during the July crisis would lead the German Reich to abandon Austria-Hungary. Against the will of Conrad von Hötzendorf, Chief of the General Staff, Berchtold therefore insisted on the bombardment of Belgrade by the Austrian artillery on 29 July 1914, an act which was militarily senseless. Yet his fears had some foundation. The Russians were speculating on the possibility of an agreement with Germany to the detriment of the Dual Monarchy; even Bethmann Hollweg considered this Bismarckian notion for a fleeting moment during the course of the July crisis.

The assassinated heir to the throne of the Dual Monarchy, Franz Ferdinand, had originally agreed with Conrad von Hötzendorf that war against Serbia was desirable, and had even recalled him to office. However, after the Adriatic crisis the archduke became a resolute advocate of a peaceful solution to the problems of the monarchy in south-east Europe. He had begun to work for von Hötzendorf's replacement, since he had no wish to become involved in a major war as a result of Serbia's links with Russia. Franz Ferdinand had come to see such a conflict as 'madness' which would only 'clear the way for revolution'[104] in domestic affairs. Yet even before his assassination, Austria-Hungary had decided on an aggressive Balkan policy which would inevitably make a peaceful solution to future crises in south-east Europe more difficult to achieve. The outlines of the policy can be seen, for example, in the memorandum drawn up by Councillor (*Sektionsrat*) Franz von Matschenko[105] before 24 June 1914. After the assassination, Vienna's decision to go on the political offensive in the Balkans was implemented by Foreign Minister Berchtold by means of Count Hoyos's mission to Berlin on 5–6 July. Austria-Hungary had been driven into a corner; urged on by Germany, it sought a solution in a '*Flucht nach vorn*' during the July crisis. Berchtold hoped that the Dual Monarchy could thereby retain its status as a great power, or at the very least go down fighting.

(6) Germany's conduct was comparable with that of the Dual Monarchy in many respects. The Triple Alliance had been pushed on to the defensive, and German gestures of arrogance were basically the product of a fear of defeat. The significance of the Anglo-Russian naval talks of spring and summer 1914 may have been exaggerated in Berlin, and they were partly the result of French pressure on the British; nevertheless, they helped to change the attitude and conduct of Germany, which was now very different to that which had been adopted during the great Balkan and Adriatic crisis of 1912–13.[106] Ironically, Britain and Germany had been reaching agreement on colonial issues in order to prepare the way for a settlement at the centre. But Britain was now firmly tied to the Triple Entente and was therefore not available as a mediator in the July crisis as far as the Germans were concerned. Just as the British were no longer able to restrain the Russians, as they had done in 1912–13, so Germany's policy towards Austria-Hungary had also changed dramatically. In 1913, the assistance provided to the Habsburg monarchy had been accompanied by pressure from Berlin to end the crisis peacefully by means of a compromise. In July 1914, in contrast, there was no such 'jet of cold water'[107] from Berlin. On the contrary, the Reich provided Austria-Hungary with *carte blanche* on 5–6 July. Thereafter, German statesmen constantly urged the Dual Monarchy not to draw back from a trial of strength, but to use offensive measures to destroy a defensive position which appeared to have become intolerable.

The attitude of Germany had changed considerably since the Balkan crisis of 1912–13. Its representatives feared a British 'landing in Pomerania'[108] in the coming war, and were expecting a Russian attack in 1916–17 at the latest. They had become determined to make fundamental changes to an international situation which they had come to regard as unacceptable, even at the cost of a major war which might involve British intervention on the side of the enemy. The German government embarked on a disastrous life-and-death experiment without offering any independent alternative plan in the event of the failure of its policy of calculated risk. In so doing, it pushed the decision on war and peace over to the enemy. The policy emerges clearly in a conversation between the historian Fritz Kern and Grand Admiral Tirpitz in January 1919:[109]

> I (Tirpitz agrees): Eventual preventive war. We say on 5 July: We must do something, otherwise in a few years Austria is no longer capable of alliance. By doing something, we pierce into the Entente at the same time. A trial of blood, see what it is actually thinking. If it makes war, then it wanted it, and then it is better in 1914 than 1916. Or it draws back, and then huge success. This is the wrong assumption.

Whatever the domestic political motives behind the German 'dual strategy',[110] linking foreign policy brinkmanship and internal preparations for war, the Reich felt compelled by the Schlieffen Plan to respond to the Russian general mobilization of 30 July 1914 and to declare war on Russia on 1 August.[111] Fear of Russia had led Britain to come to its side and join the alliance between Russia and France; precisely the same motive led Germany to adopt a very different policy, on a knife-edge between peace and war. Driven by fear of its powerful Russian neighbour and by the Triple Entente, it abandoned ultimate control of the outcome of its policy to the enemy coalition. Though the Reich did not desire war, it was ready to accept it rather than back down. In 1912–13 Britain and Germany had negotiated a compromise in the Balkan crisis. By July 1914 that possibility had disappeared; in their different ways, both sides felt almost compelled by Russian strength to act within the blocs which separated them rather than to overcome their differences. In a divided, antagonistic *Staatensystem* there was precious little freedom of manoeuvre. On 25 July, Sasonov expressed the fear of being 'snowed under in this affair',[112] and it was echoed five days later in Bethmann Hollweg's comment that 'direction has been lost and the stone has been set in motion'.[113] Because their assessments of the international situation had changed so profoundly between 1911 and 1914 and because all were committed to their own national strategies, all the powers had abandoned the possibility of a compromise as the political alternative to the risky experiments of July 1914.

Nevertheless, the July crisis can be understood only against the social and intellectual background of the period. Traditionally, even major war was still regarded as a legitimate element in international politics. In addition, the recent popularization of foreign policy had created new and unsuspected difficulties. The ability to observe restraint, which had been a feature of eighteenth-century cabinet government, had been threatened by the Napoleonic campaigns and the American Civil War and was lost in the twentieth-century 'age of the masses'. Statesmen appeared almost helpless, unable to maintain the balance of power and protect national sovereignty through bold diplomacy; finally, they proved incapable of avoiding the security dilemma.

More important than efforts to determine individual failure, it must be remembered that in 1914 major war was not regarded as a catastrophe which endangered humanity, but as a normal part of the politics and history of Europe. There was an obvious contradiction here. Whilst the coming war had long been seen on all sides as a final ideological struggle between races and cultures, the thinking of statesmen was still dominated by their expectation of a short war. Liberal thinkers (in the broadest sense of the term) were more aware of this paradox than the statesmen and diplomats of Europe. In view of economic and social developments, these thinkers believed that a great military conflict would be such folly that it seemed almost inconceivable. Some recognized that wars can benefit states, in victory and sometimes even in defeat, only until they reach a limited stage of economic development; thereafter, even when wars bring military victory, their consequences are frequently disastrous.[114] Unfortunately, insights of this kind were rare in 1914.

The generation of Bismarck was closer to the experiences of revolutionary France and the conservative restoration at the Congress of Vienna, so that its representatives were more easily convinced that war and revolution may appear in history as twins. This truth was less apparent to the Edwardian and Wilhelmine politicians who, after a long period of peace, had fatalistically come to accept the inevitability of a future war. The ability to imagine the consequences of a war, which Bismarck had associated with the certain destruction of the Reich and the revolutionary triumph of the anarchist forces which had been involved in the Paris Commune, was generally lost to European statesmen on the eve of the First World War.

Some of these statesmen did warn that war would not bring healing and consolidation to Europe, but destruction and anarchy to the existing order. They included Reich Chancellor Bethmann Hollweg in Germany at the beginning of June 1914, and Durnovo, the Russian Minister of the Interior, shortly before his departure in February 1914.[115] In an era of mass fervour, their attempts to pursue cabinet politics and calculate the risks of war were futile. They did not recognize that Napoleon I had done much to forfeit the ability of rulers to tolerate military defeats and political failures, since his own rule was bound up with the victory of arms. Full awareness of this loss of freedom seems to have dawned only as the politics of pressure, deterrence and bluff began to be caught up in the machinery of military mobilization plans which could not be restrained. Whether they wished it or not, the generals were pushed into the forefront of events.

The German response to the reckless Russian mobilizations of 29 and 30 July involved an almost automatic combination of mobilization and offensive. This fateful combination made the invasion of Belgium and the assault on Lüttich inevitable, and was tantamount to unleashing major war. France behaved differently. There, in accordance with the maxim that mobilization was not the same as war, Belgian neutrality was observed despite the demands of the Chief of the General Staff. Moreover, partly out of regard for British opinion, French troops were ordered to remain 10 kilometres from the German border on 31 July 1914.[116] The situation in Germany was the result of the disastrous victory of Moltke (denied him between 1871 and 1890), and of his dogmatic successor Schlieffen, over Bismarck. It was the victory of the trade of war over the art of diplomacy.

The operational plans of the combatants displayed a catastrophic immobility. For example, they allowed Russia to mobilize against Germany *and* Austria-Hungary, but not against the Dual Monarchy alone; on the other side, Germany was not in a position to go into battle against France without simultaneously moving against Russia. The plans reveal the extreme degree of rigidity which had overtaken policy and strategy, at least on the Russian and German sides. An automatic mechanism of this kind, designed to save critical time, was perhaps more understandable in the case of Germany, surrounded as it was in the centre of Europe; Russia, on the other hand, was much less vulnerable to attack.

Even outside Russia and Germany, there was no European statesman capable of reasserting his country's freedom of choice and manoeuvre in the face of overwhelming pressures. This failure was partly the consequence of the domestic conditions prevailing in all the nations involved. Existing authority was under threat everywhere, a fact which had a debilitating effect on foreign policy. Moreover, the liberal belief that parliamentary or democratic foreign policy is always peaceful was proving to be an illusion. Winston Churchill had already made a prophecy to this effect in the House of Commons on 13 May 1901. 'The war of peoples', he warned, 'will be more terrible than those of kings'.[117]

Throughout Europe, the general public was more belligerent than its governments. The unrestrained influence of the mass market obstructed genuine understanding of what was necessary. Prestige and fame had originally been associated with princes and their dynasties, but in an age of mass politics they were elevated into national issues. In national and international affairs, the prevailing tendency was loss of direction and the inability of statesmen to act freely. In his own era Salisbury had been able to control the tendency, but even he had noted it with some perplexity in the mid-1890s:[118] 'Governments can do so little and prevent so little nowadays. Power has passed from the hands of Statesmen, but I should be very much puzzled to say into whose hands it has passed. It is all pure drifting. As we go downstream, we can occasionally fend off a collision, but where are we going?'

The complex mechanisms of cabinet politics were no longer appropriate in the developing age of the masses. The arts of diplomacy were unable to withstand daily justifications before the shrill slogans of the *'terribles simplificateurs'*. It became increasingly difficult for statesmen to suggest retreat or accept defeats. War or peace, victory or defeat – these were the brazen slogans of the new age. Attempts to achieve the one and prevent the other by means of agreements gained by judicious policies became almost impossible. This was true even of a statesman such as Sir Edward Grey, who retained at least a degree of independence because he lived in a parliamentary system which had learned how to channel the demands of the masses more safely. The question of whether there was an excess or a lack of democratization in foreign policy during this period is a difficult one to answer. It must always be examined with the understanding that, though statesmen must win majorities in support of their foreign policy proposals, they require autonomy in order to implement them. Grey had this privilege to a much greater degree than Bethmann Hollweg, Berchtold, or Sasonov; he nevertheless decided, as a result of commitment to the alliance system, on the entry of Great Britain into the war.

Transcending forms of government and culture, though naturally connected with and dependent upon them, the political conceptions of the statesmen involved ultimately had a decisive effect. In the non-parliamentary states, their proposals were exposed to the unfiltered and unchannelled influences of society. In Russia, Nicholas II took the step into war with the comment that the people wanted it. Meanwhile in Germany, von Stumm, representative of the Political Department of the Foreign Office, explained the strategy of the Reich leadership to Theodor Wolff on 25 July 1914; this was to go on the offensive diplomatically, but to break off in good time should Russia mobilize against expectations: 'then it will of course be necessary to hold our military back'.[119] It did not happen. The freedom to retreat had by now been wrenched away from the diplomats and statesmen by the militarization and popularization of their craft. Perhaps James Joll is correct to invoke the authority of a bygone era, and the totalitarianism of an era yet to come, when he writes that only a Bismarck or a Lenin could have regained the necessary autonomy in politics at that stage.[120] It is not primarily

blindness, nor ignorance, that leads to the ruin of peoples and states. They do not long remain ignorant of where the road they have taken is leading them. But there is an instinct in them, encouraged by their nature, intensified by habit, and which they do not resist, which drags them further forwards so long as they have a vestige of strength left. That which exerts self-control is divine. Most peoples see their ruin before their eyes, but still go ahead.[121]

The war which broke out in 1914 had long been inwardly accepted as inevitable by almost all the parties – by governments and their peoples alike; it was even welcomed as a revolt against the rationalist and liberal ideas of the nineteenth century, as a way of breaking out from the uniformity of secure bourgeois existence, and as a desirable promoter of the spirit of the age, socialist revolution. War, even in its horrifying major form, was still the familiar alternative to peace. Today it is difficult to comprehend that such attitudes were once normal and led to the 'seminal catastrophe' (*Ur-Katastrophe*)[122] of our century. The First World War altered our world in a fundamental way, and also began to change our thinking about issues of peace and war.

NOTES

1 See Heinemann, U., *Die verdrängte Niederlage. Politische öffentlichkeit und Kriegsschuldfrage in der Weimarer Republik* (Göttingen: 1983).
2 On this subject see Jäger, W., *Historische Forschung und politische Kultur in Deutschland. Die Debatte 1914–1980 über den Ausbruch des Ersten Weltkrieges* (Göttingen: 1984), esp. p. 58 ff.
3 Lloyd George, D., *Mein Anteil am Weltkrieg. Kriegsmemoiren*, 3 vols (Berlin: 1933–6), Vol.I (1933), p. 41.
4 Fundamental here is Hildebrand, K., 'Staatskunst oder Systemzwang? Die "deutsche Frage" als Problem der Weltpolitik', *Historische Zeitschrift* 228 (1979), p. 624 ff.
5 Erdmann, K.D., *Die Zeit der Weltkriege (Gebhard. Handbuch der deutschen Geschichte)* (Stuttgart: 9th revised edn, 1976), pp. 53–4.
6 Fischer, F., *Griff nach der Weltmacht. Die Kriegszielpolitik des kaiserlichen Deutschlands 1914/18* (Düsseldorf: 1961).
7 Schöllgen, G., '"Fischer-Kontroverse" und Kontinuitätsproblem. Deutsche Kriegsziele im Zeitalter der Weltkriege', in *Ploetz. Geschichte der Weltkriege. Mächte, Ereignisse, Entwicklungen 1900–1945*, ed. A. Hillgruber and J. Dülffer (Würzburg: 1981), p. 163 ff.
8 On this subject see in particular the trail-blazing studies of Egmont Zechlin. Zechlin, E., *Krieg und Kriegsrisiko. Zur deutschen Politik im Ersten Weltkrieg* (Düsseldorf: 1979), esp. pp. 115 ff and 139 ff; also Zechlin, E., 'Juli 1914. Antwort auf eine Zeitschrift', *Geschichte in Wissenschaft und Unterricht* 34 (1983), p. 238 ff; Zechlin, E., 'Zum Kriegsausbruch 1914. Die Kontroverse', *Geschichte in Wissenschaft und Unterricht* 34 (1984), p. 211 ff.
9 See Farrar, L. L. jnr, *Arrogance and Anxiety. The Ambivalence of German Power, 1848–1918* (Iowa City, Iowa: 1981) and Farrar, L. L., *The Short-War Illusion. German Policy, Strategy and Domestic Affairs August-December 1914* (Santa Barbara, Calif. Oxford: 1973), p. 19 ff.
10 In this connection see Hölzle, E., *Die Selbstentmachtung Europas. Das Experiment des Friedens vor und im Ersten Weltkrieg* (Göttingen/Frankfurt/Zurich: 1975); and Joll, J., *The Origins of the First World War* (London/New York: 1984). See also Hildebrand, K., 'Imperialismus, Wettrüsten und Kriegsausbruch 1914. Zum Problem von Legitimität und Revolution im internationalen System', *Neue Politische Literatur* 20 (1975), pp. 160 ff and 339 ff.
11 See in general Mayer, A. A., *The Persistence of the Old Regime. Europe to the Great War* (New York: 1981).
12 Joll, *Origins*.

13 Above all see Berghahn, V. R., *Germany and the Approach of War in 1914* (London, 1973).

14 Watt, D. C., 'Part One 1898–1918', in D. C. Watt, F. Spencer and N. Brown, *A History of the World in the Twentieth Century* (London: 1967), p. 170.

15 Rohe, K., 'Zur Typologie politischer Kulturen in westlichen Demokratien. überlegungen am Beispiel Grossbritanniens und Deutschlands', in *Weltpolitik. Europagedanke. Regionalismus. Festschrift für Heinz Gollwitzer zum 65 Geburtstag am 30 Januar 1982*, ed. H. Dollinger, H. Gründer and A. Hanschmidt (Münster: 1982), p. 582.

16 Wilson, K. M., *The Policy of the Entente. Essays on the Determinants of British Foreign Policy, 1904–1914* (Cambridge: 1985), p. 2, looks at this problem from the British side.

17 See here Hildebrand, 'Imperialismus', p. 190.

18 Schroeder, P. W., 'World War I as Galloping Gertie: a reply to Joachim Remak', *Journal of Modern History* 44 (1972), p. 322.

19 Quoted in Keiger, J. F. V., *France and the Origins of the First World War* (London: 1983), p. 6.

20 Holbraad, C., *The Concert of Europe: A Study in German and British International Theory 1815–1914* (London: 1970), p. 117 ff.

21 Dehio, L., *Deutschland und die Weltpolitik im 20 Jahrhundert* (Munich: 1955), p. 89.

22 See the first chapter in this book, 'Great Britain and the foundation of the German Reich', p. 00.

23 Hillgruber, A., *Bismarcks Aussenpolitik* (Freiburg i.B.: 2nd edn, 1981), p. 198.

24 Kissinger, H. A., *Die weltpolitische Lage. Reden und Aufsätze* h(Munich, 1983), p. 125.

25 Kennan, G. F., *Bismarcks europäisches System in der Auflösung. Die französisch-russische Annäherung 1875 bis 1890* (undated), p. 86.

26 See the third chapter in this book, 'Between alliance and antagonism. The problem of bilateral normality in Anglo-German relations during the nineteenth century', p. 000.

27 Lutz, H., *Österreich-Ungarn und die Gründung des Deutschen Reiches. Europäische Entscheidungen 1867–1871* (Frankfurt-am-Main/Berlin/Vienna, 1979), p. 493.

28 'Aus dem Diktat des Reichskanzlers Fürsten von Bismarck, z.Z. in Kissingen vom 15.6.1877', in *Die Grosse Politik der europäischen Kabinette 1871–1914*, 2 vols (Berlin: 1922), p. 154.

29 Gillard, D., *The Struggle for Asia 1828–1914. A Study in British and Russian Imperialism* (London: 1977).

30 Bourne, K., *The Foreign Policy of Victorian England 1830–1902* (Oxford: 1970), p. 47 ff.

31 Herz, J. H., *Staatenwelt und Weltpolitik. Aufsätze zur internationalen Politik im Nuklearzeitalter* (Hamburg: 1974), p. 12.

32 Herz, *Staatenwelt und Weltpolitik*, p. 13.

33 Kennan, *Bismarcks europäisches System*, p. 407 ff.

34 Lutz, *Österreich-Ungarn und die Gründung des Deutschen Reiches*, p. 489.

35 Van Evera, S., 'The cult of the offensive and the origins of the First World War', *International Security* 9 (1984), p. 58 ff.

36 Dehio, *Deutschland und die Weltpolitik*, p. 15.

37 See in general Hildebrand, K., 'Deutscher Sonderweg und "Drittes Reich". Betrachtungen über ein Grundproblem der deutschen und europäischen Geschichte im 19. und 20. Jahrhundert', in W. Michalka (ed.), *Die nationalsozialistische Machtergreifung* (Paderborn: 1984), p. 389.

38 Berghahn, V. R., *Der Tirpitz-Plan. Genesis und Verfall einer innenpolitischer Krisenstrategie unter Wilhelm II* (Düsseldorf: 1971).

39 Kennedy, P. M., *The Rise of the Anglo-German Antagonism 1860–1914* (London/Boston, Mass./Sydney: 1980), p. 251.

40 Gillard, D. R., 'Salisbury and the Indian defence problem, 1885–1902', in K. Bourne and D. C. Watt (eds), *Studies in International History* (London: 1967), p. 242.

41 See here Hillgruber, A., 'Deutsche Russland-Politik 1871–1918: Grundlagen – Grundmuster – Grundprobleme', in A. Hillgruber (ed.), *Deutsche Grossmacht–und Weltpolitik im 19. und 20. Jahrhundert* (Düsseldorf: 1977), p. 79 ff.

42 'Minute' of Sir Arthur Nicolson on a report by Lord Granville to Sir Edward Grey of 18 July 1914, in *British Documents on the Origins of the War 1898–1914* (London: 1926), Vol. XI, no. 66, p. 53.

43 Schöllgen, G., *Imperialismus und Gleichgewicht. Deutschland, England und die orientalische Frage 1871–1914* (Munich: 1984), pp. 438–40.
44 Hillgruber, 'Deutsche Russland-Politik', pp. 76–7.
45 Delbrück, H., 'In Wehr und Waffen', *Preussische Jahrbücher* 142 (1910), p. 266.
46 Steiner, Z. S., *Britain and the Origins of the First World War* (London: 1977), p. 22.
47 Hildebrand, 'Great Britain and the foundation of the German Reich', p. 000.
48 Quoted in Wilson, K., 'British power in the European balance, 1906–14', in D. Dilks (ed.), *Retreat from Power. Studies in Britain's Foreign Policy of the Twentieth Century*, 2 vols (London: 1981), Vol. 1, p. 39.
49 Aron, R., *Frieden und Krieg. Eine Theorie der Staatenwelt* (Frankfurt-am-Main: 1963), p. 123.
50 Quoted in Beloff, M., *Imperial Sunset*. Volume I: *Britain's Liberal Empire 1897–1921* (London: 1969), p. 90, n. 4.
51 Joll, *Origins*, p. 63.
52 Joll, *Origins*, p. 109.
53 See the work currently being prepared by Förster, S., 'Die Eroberung Indiens 1783–1819' (London: forthcoming).
54 On this way of thinking of the historian Maz Lenz see Dehio, *Deutschland und die Weltpolitik*, p. 47.
55 Quoted in Craig, G. A. and L. George, *Zwischen Krieg und Frieden. Konfliktlösung in Geschichte und Gegenwart* (Munich: 1984), p. 58.
56 Löwenthal, R., 'Internationale Konstellation und innerstaatlicher Systemwandel', *Historische Zeitschrift* 212 (1971), p. 57.
57 Quoted in Schmitt, B. E., *England and Germany 1740–1914* (Princeton, NJ: 1916), p. 23.
58 Schmidt, G., 'Der deutsch-englische Gegensatz im Zeitalter des Imperialismus', in H. Köhler (ed.), *Deutschland und der Westen. Verträge und Diskussionsbeiträge des Symposions zu Ehren von Gordon A. Craig, veranstaltet von der Freien Universität Berlin vom 1–3 Dezember 1983* (Berlin: 1984), p. 76.
59 Schmidt, 'Der deutsch-englische Gegensatz', p. 76.
60 Fisch, J., *Die europäische Expansion und das Völkerrecht. Die Auseinandersetzungen um den Status der überseeischen Gebiete vom 15. Jahrhundert bis zur Gegenwart* (Stuttgart: 1984), p. 268.
61 Joll, *Origins*, p. 152 ff.
62 Schöllgen, *Imperialismus und Gleichgewicht*, p. 15 ff.
63 *British Documents on the Origins of the War 1898–1914* (London: 1928), Vol. III, pp. 397–431.
64 *British Documents* Vol. III, p. 408.
65 Kahler, M., 'Rumours of war: the 1914 analogy', *Foreign Affairs* 58 (1979/80), p. 377.
66 *British Documents*, Vol. III, p. 430.
67 *British Documents*, Vol. III, p. 429.
68 *British Documents*, Vol. III, p. 429.
69 *British Documents*, Vol. III, p. 431.
70 On this expression of Karl Rohe see Hildebrand, 'Between alliance and antagonism', p. 000.
71 Quoted in Joll, *Origins*, p. 67.
72 Kissinger, *Die weltpolitische Lage*, p. 121.
73 Kissinger, *Die weltpolitische Lage*, p. 121.
74 In this connection the difference between the relationship of Britain and Germany in the years before the First World War and that of America and Russia in our own time can clearly be seen, though simplistic parallels are often drawn. Whilst British foreign policy of the period neglected to make clear concessions in order to re-establish the balance of forces, at the beginning of the 1960s Henry Kissinger began the attempt, with generous accommodation from the American side, to establish a global balance of forces in the world to include all areas of international life and ultimately to involve five partners (USA, USSR, People's Republic of China, Japan, Western Europe). This proposal for a legitimate world order found early expression in the declaration of principle signed by the Americans and the Soviets to accompany SALT I. It failed. Wherever the responsibility for this failure lies, a quite different situation has been created from that of 1914; the differences are much greater than the similarities.

75 Freiherr von der Lancken Wakenitz, O., *Meine dreissig Dienstjahre 1888–1918* (Potsdam/Paris/Brussels: 1931), pp. 56–7.
76 Lieven, D. C. B., *Russia and the Origins of the First World War* (London: 1983), pp. 32–3.
77 Keiger, *France*, p. 54.
78 See Krumeich, G., *Aufrüstung und Innenpolitik in Frankreich vor dem Ersten Weltkrieg. Die Einführung der dreijährigen Dienstpflicht 1913–1914* (Wiesbaden: 1980), p. 246.
79 Quoted in Stengers, J., 'July 1914: some reflections', *Annuaire de l'Institut de Philologie et d'Histoire Orientales et Slaves*, Vol. XVII (Brussels: 1966), p. 120: Beyens to Davignon on 26 July 1914 about a conversation with Jules Cambon. See also n. 4 (pp. 120–1) of this article, giving details about the omission of this quote from the Belgian Grey Books and Beyen's memoirs.
80 Schöllgen, *Imperialismus und Gleichgewicht*, p. 329 ff.
81 Taylor, A. J. P., *A History of the First World War* (New York: 1976), p. 20; quoted in Farrar, *Arrogance and Anxiety*, p. 13.
82 Schöllgen, *Imperialismus und Gleichgewicht*, p. 291 ff.
83 Schöllgen, G., 'Das Zeitalter des Imperialismus' (manuscript undated), p. 118.
84 Schramm, G., 'Russland als Weltmacht', *Handbuch der Geschichte Russlands. Bd.3: 1856–1945. Von den autokratischen Reformen zum Sowjetstaat*, ed. G. Schramm (Stuttgart: 1983), p. 444.
85 Schramm, 'Russland als Weltmacht', p. 444.
86 Lieven, *Russia*, p. 5 ff.
87 Kissinger, H. A., *Memoiren 1968–1973* (Munich: 1979), p. 63.
88 See here Linke, H. G., *Das zarische Russland und der Erste Weltkrieg. Diplomatie und Kriegsziele 1914–1917* (Munich: 1982), pp. 21–2.
89 Schieder, T., 'Europa im Zeitalter der Nationalstaaten und europäische Weltpolitik bis zum Ersten Weltkrieg (1870–1914)', in *Handbuch der europäischen Geschichte*, ed. T. Schieder, Vol. VI: *Europa im Zeitalter der Nationalstaaten und europäische Weltpolitik bis zum Ersten Weltkrieg* (Stuttgart: 1968), p. 117.
90 Schieder, 'Europa im Zeitalter der Nationalstaaten', p. 117.
91 Zechlin, *Krieg und Kriegrisiko*, p. 161.
92 Steiner, *Britain*, p. 220.
93 Turner, L. C. F., 'The Russian mobilisation in 1914', in P. M. Kennedy (ed.), *The War Plans of the Great Powers, 1880–1914* (London/Boston, Mass./Sydney: 1979), p. 252.
94 Jules Cambon to Paléologue: 1 November 1912, in *Archives du Ministère des Affaires Etrangères. Papiers d'Agents Cote 43*. Jules Cambon Mss. 15. Also quoted in English in Keiger, *France*, p. 73.
95 *British Documents on the Origins of the War 1898–1914* (London: 1926), Vol. XI, no. 101, p. 80.
96 See Turner, 'The Russian mobilisation', p. 256.
97 Linke, *Das zarische Russland*, p. 21; see also Lieven, *Russia*, pp. 108–9.
98 Schramm, 'Russland als Weltmacht', p. 448.
99 Joll, *Origins*, p. 106.
100 Turner, 'The Russian mobilisation', p. 265.
101 Bridge, F., *From Sadowa to Sarajevo. The Foreign Policy of Austria-Hungary, 1866–1914* (London/Boston, Mass.: 1972), p. 367.
102 Bridge, *From Sadowa to Sarajevo*, p. 374.
103 Bridge, *From Sadowa to Sarajevo*, p. 446.
104 Quoted in Zechlin, *Krieg und Kriegrisiko*, p. 32.
105 Printed in Bridge, *From Sadowa to Sarajevo*, p. 443 ff.
106 Zechlin, 'Juli 1914', p. 238 ff.
107 Quoted in Zechlin, *Krieg und Kriegrisiko*, p. 32.
108 Riezler, Kurt, *Tagebücher, Aufsätze, Dokumente*, introduced and edited by K. D. Erdmann (Göttingen: 1972), p. 182. Entry 'Hohenfonow 7.7.1914': Bethmann Hollwegs Befurchtung. The Riezler diaries are used despite a controversy over their genuineness. The objections of Bernd Sösemann, who was especially doubtful about Kurt Riezler's memos for the period from 7 July until 14 August with reference to the originality of the text, have been answered by Karl Dietrich Erdmann. The genuineness of the source and the usefulness of the edition are beyond question. There is no need here for

consideration of Fritz Fischer and Bernd F. Schulte's contribution to the academic dispute over the correct text. See the article by Blänsdorf, A., 'Der Weg der Riezler-Tagebücher. Zur Kontroverse über die Echtheit der Tagebcher Kurt Riezlers', *Geschichte in Wissenschaft und Unterricht* 35 (1984), p. 651 ff.

109 Kern, F., *Skizzen zum Kriegsausbruch im Jahre 1914*, ed. and introduced by H. Hallmann (Darmstadt: 1968), p. 9.

110 Zechlin, 'Juli 1914', p. 242.

111 Vital here is Ritter, G., *Der Schlieffenplan. Kritik eines Mythos* (Munich: 1956); also Turner, L. C. F., 'The significance of the Schlieffen-Plan', in Kennedy, *War Plans*, p. 199 ff.

112 *Österreich-Ungarns Aussenpolitik von der Bosnischen Krise 1908 bis zum Kriegsausbruch 1914*, Vol. VIII (Vienna/Leipzig: 1930), no.10 688, p. 725.

113 *Die Deutschen Dokumente zum Kriegsausbruch 1914. Hrsg. im Auftrage des Auswärtigen Amtes*, new revised and extended edn, 2 vols (Berlin: 1927), no. 456, p. 164: 'Protokoll der Sitzung des k.preussischen Staatsministeriums am 30 Juli 1914'.

114 See here Toynbee, A. J., *Krieg und Kultur. Der Militarismus im Leben der Völker* (Frankfurt-am-Main/Hamburg: 1958), p. 8.

115 See Hildebrand, 'Imperialismus', p. 190.

116 Keiger, *France*, p. 161.

117 Quoted in Bartlett, C. J., *The Global Conflict. The International Rivalry of the Great Powers, 1880–1970* (London/New York: 1984), p. 88.

118 Salisbury to Cranbrook on 1 January 1895, published in Gathorne-Hardy, A. E. (ed.), *Gathorne-Hardy, First Earl of Cranbrook* (London: 1910), Vol. II, p. 345.

119 Wolff, T., *Tagebücher 1914–1919. Der Erste Weltkrieg und die Entstehung der Weimarer Republik in Tagebüchern, Leitsrtikeln und Briegen des Chefredakteurs am 'Berliner Tageblatt' and Mitbegründers der 'Deutschen Demokratischen Partei'. Erster Teil*, ed. and introduced by B.Sösemann (Boppard: 1984), p. 64 (no.3, 25 July 1914).

120 Joll, *Origins*, p. 204.

121 von Ranke, L., *Die Osmanen und die Spanische Monarchie im 16 und 17 Jahrhundert*, 4th extended edn: *'Fürsten und Völker von Süd-Europa. Leopold von Ranke's Sämmtliche Werke. Dritte Gesammtausgabe 35 und 36 Band* (Leipzig, 1877), p. 298. The quotation is at the end of the fourth chapter: 'Von den Auflagen und den Finanzen.3. Unter Philipp III' and closes the description of the financial hardships of the Spanish monarchy, its taxes in the various countries and their resistance. The oft-repeated comment of Ranke, separated in the text by a dash, has been used, for example, by Michael Stürmer in a general way: Stürmer, M., *Das ruhelose Reich. Deutschland 1866–1918* (undated), p. 365. I am grateful to my colleague Walther Peter Fuchs of Erlangen for arguing against too general an interpretation of the quote (letter to the author of 14 November 1984) and for his critical interpretation on this issue.

122 Kennan, *Bismarcks europäisches System*, p. 12.

*The Revolution in the
International Order in the
Twentieth Century*

5

Hitler's policy towards France until 1936

I
THE ISSUES

On 5 April 1940 the Reich Propaganda Minister, Joseph Goebbels, gave a selected group of German journalists an insight into the methods of Nazi domestic and foreign policy. He told them:[1]

> Until now we have succeeded in keeping our opponents in the dark about the actual objectives of Germany, just as our internal opponents until 1932 simply did not notice where we were heading, that our vow of legality was only a trick... If they had put a few of us in prison in 1925, it would have been all up with us and we would have been finished. No, they let us pass through the danger zone. It was exactly the same in foreign policy... In 1933 a French Prime Minister should have said (and if I had been French Prime Minister, I would have said it): The man who has become Reich Chancellor is the man who wrote the book *Mein Kampf*, in which it says this and that. The man cannot be tolerated in our vicinity. Either he goes, or we march. That would have been totally logical. It was not done. They let us alone, they allowed us through the danger zone unhindered and we were able to bypass every dangerous obstacle, and when we were ready, well armed, better than them, they started the war.

This description of the policy of the 'Third Reich' may be regarded with justifiable scepticism, particularly its outline of such a high level of advance planning, because we are now aware of the high level of improvisation which was an element of Nazi rule. Nevertheless, the comment raises questions which are still a matter for research today, and which have yet to be dealt with satisfactorily.

For example, we are better informed[2] about German policies towards Britain, Russia, the United States, Italy and Japan during the years of peace between 1933 and 1939 than we are about the German relationship with France. Yet there is no doubt that Germany's relations with France, widely regarded until the late 1930s as the strongest power on the continent, were extremely important to the Reich. Moreover, as the protector of the Paris peace treaties of 1919–20, France would be a major factor for a revisionist German Reich to deal with, whether as a partner or an opponent. One of the main reasons for this gap in research is certainly the inaccessibility of the relevant archives on the French side, particularly those of the Quai d'Orsay. But it is perhaps also due to an enigmatic, baffling element in Hitler's policy towards France, an almost contradictory quality; this lasted from the seizure of power until the dramatic remilitarization of the Rhineland on 7 March 1936, which marked a caesura in international relations during the interwar years. This feature of Hitler's foreign policy goes at least some way towards explaining the failure of historians to deal adequately with German policy towards France during the 1930s.

Returning to the quote with which this chapter began, it must be emphasized that the French assessment of the situation in the early years of Nazi foreign policy could scarcely have been as unequivocal as Goebbels was to suggest afterwards. Nor was Hitler's conduct at that stage as simple to analyse, in its strategy and tactics, its objectives and feints, as the Propaganda Minister later alleged. For example, though *Mein Kampf* is now regarded as written evidence of Hitler's programme, many contemporaries regarded it simply as a propaganda product of the 1920s which could be dismissed as little more than waste paper after the Nazi seizure of power.[3] In stark contrast to the sentiments expressed in *Mein Kampf*, during the first, revisionist phase of Nazi foreign policy the German government made a variety of friendly overtures towards the French. Undoubtedly, in the interwar years the prevailing mentality in the western democracies of France and Britain was dominated by the desire to maintain the peace even if a high price had to be paid; both the general public and the politicians were therefore inclined to pay attention to signals which appeared to promise peace and to ignore other, bellicose tones in political and diplomatic reports. In any case, the assessment of Hitler's foreign policy made by the weekly journal *L'Europe Nouvelle* on 26 November 1932 was very much the exception rather than the rule in France:[4] 'The aim of German policy according to M. Hitler is an operation in two stages: destruction of French power in order to assure expansion towards the east.' The experienced French ambassador in Berlin, François-Poncet, thus sent some reports to Paris which described the outlines of Hitler's foreign policy 'programme of action',[5] the apparent development of a planned 'Pax Germanica' for Europe and the associated threat to his own country; equally, however, he was obliged to inform his government of contrary indications, of friendly gestures and offers of co-operation from the German Reich Chancellor. In responsible positions in France, not least because of the unstable internal situation of the country, more faith was placed in reports of the desire for peace than in pessimistic accounts of developments in Germany. It was the goal of both French domestic and foreign policy between 1919–23 and 1939 to maintain external peace at almost any cost.

At the same time, it is also clear that during the 1930s, to a certain degree, Hitler was pursuing an ambivalent policy towards France. There was no obvious similarity between this policy and the sentiments he had expressed in *Mein Kampf*. Moreover, his conduct did not reveal the warlike and belligerent feelings which he expressed to his generals on 3 February 1933.[6] At that meeting Hitler claimed that the 'objective of his overall policy' was first of all to concentrate on 'regaining political power' in domestic affairs. Only then would he turn to the outside, with the following objectives: 'Perhaps the winning of new export possibilities, perhaps – and better – conquest of new *Lebensraum* in the east and its ruthless Germanization.' As regards the 'factor of France' in this analysis, Hitler feared a French preventive strike against the Third Reich whilst he was still consolidating his power. It was an attack of this kind to which Goebbels was to refer in 1940, and which Hitler regarded as possible during and even after 1933: 'Most dangerous time is that of the building up of the Wehrmacht. That will show whether France has statesmen; if yes, she will not allow us time but will attack us (probably with satellites in the east)' – by which he meant Poland and Czechoslovakia.

It is not the task of this chapter to investigate why the French government did not launch the preventive action which Hitler feared and which France's ally, Poland, contemplated for a time.[7] However, there were also many signs from the German dictator – though they did not predominate – which appeared to show that peace was the goal of his foreign policy. These were expressed in a number of ways: in his conversations with Ambassador François-Poncet, his public utterances, his press interviews and his speeches to war veterans of both countries; in von Ribbentrop's 'private' diplomacy; in the activity of the Comité France-Allemagne; and in the work of Ribbentrop's colleague, Otto Abetz, representative for France within the Hitler Youth. These signals reduced the impact of the perceptive warning sent at an early stage by Jean Dobler from the consulate general in Cologne:[8] 'In reality in Germany they have never spoken of peace in a more warlike tone . . . They will go as far as fighting in order to impose peace upon us, just like the famous duellist who maintained that he was killing his opponent in order to give him a lesson in life . . . Peace or war? In Germany today, everyone speaks of peace, but everything speaks of war.' It must also be remembered that whilst the domestic experiments of Nazi Germany and its ruthless anti-communist policies were rejected by the political left,[9] they actually enjoyed a certain popularity on the right at a time, as Jules Romains noted in November 1933,[10] 'when leaders have become extraordinarily significant again'.

Then as now, the issue centres on Hitler's intentions during the period. Were his attempts to achieve *entente* with France in the 1930s no more than tactical statements within a 'strategy of grandiose self-minimization', whilst he continued to pursue the policy towards France outlined in *Mein Kampf*? Or did the dictator actually seek, at least for a time and for whatever reason, some form of peaceful settlement with France?

II
PROBLEMS OF INTERPRETING HITLER

The question of Hitler's intentions is of central importance for the course of the inquiry. However, it also addresses a fundamental problem of 'interpreting' the dictator, which can be described as follows:[11] did Hitler follow a programme or was he a Machiavellian? In his foreign policy, did he follow maxims based on fixed and unalterable principle, or did he intervene wherever the moment seemed to offer a favourable opportunity? An investigation of Hitler's policy towards France may help to throw some light upon the apparently irreconcilable positions taken by historians on this issue.

A study of France as a factor in Hitler's thinking also involves another vital issue in contemporary historical research. There has been a recent tendency among historians, principally in West Germany, to question the significance of the personality and policies of Hitler in Nazi Germany in a more or less radical way. It is therefore appropriate to provide some reasons for devoting particular attention to the motives and objectives of Hitler within an investigation of Nazi foreign policy.

'Revisionist' assessments of Nazism and Hitler have not adopted the Marxist scheme of interpretation, in which the 'Führer' is regarded merely as the sword-arm of the economic requirements of capitalist society. Nevertheless, the representatives of the 'revisionist' school are convinced that Hitler should not be regarded primarily as a politician sustained by a high degree of intentionality and autonomy. They understand him much more as the exponent 'of the antagonistic forces of the unleashed society of the Third Reich'.[12] As an actor in the international system, the dictator appears to them to have been driven by irresistible social forces and circumstances immanent in the regime, rather than to have acted comparatively deliberately and with purpose. The attempt has been made, from a social imperialist perspective, to suggest that Hitler pursued his foreign policy in order to overcome internal crises; the foreign policy of the Führer is thus seen predominantly as a part of Nazi attempts to legitimize and consolidate power. This 'functionalist' view of Hitler's political objectives has led Hans Mommsen to reach a conclusion that I regard as a wholly erroneous, in which Hitler is described as 'in many ways' 'a weak dictator'.[13]

All these attempts at explanation undoubtedly contain an element of historical truth which must be recognized. Certainly, Hitler did not blindly follow a 'timetable of world conquest' independently of the society of the Third Reich and the international system. Yet the dynamics of his policy, which ultimately swept Hitler himself along, sprang from the fundamental programmatic concepts which he had developed earlier and had already begun to realize. So long as there are no reliable sources for the 'revisionist' thesis, we can continue to accept the assessment of Hitler's foreign policy objectives made by Norman Rich:[14] 'These were all the policies and decisions of Hitler, and the war aims . . . were predominantly, if not exclusively, the aims of Hitler.' The American historian is emphatic:[15] 'The point cannot be stressed too strongly: Hitler was master in the Third Reich.'

Functionalist attempts at interpretation understand Hitler primarily as an improviser who was dependent on social constraints. Even Nazi foreign policy as a whole is regarded as the product of the 'polycratic power structure of the so-called Führer state'.[16] The interpretation makes a fundamental error by confusing what was original with what was derived; that is, in regarding the indisputable consequences of Hitler's policy as its causes and motives. Though historians are only too easily inclined to explain historical accidents as conscious acts, the conviction that Hitler quickly became the decisive force behind German foreign policy is not the consequence of subsequent theorizing by historians. The sentiment was expressed at a very early stage by François-Poncet, a leading French diplomat. As an informed observer of the German scene, he was well aware of the rivalries and power struggles between the offices and agencies of the 'Nazi conqueror's state'. On 27 December 1933, however, he made an extremely perceptive report to his Foreign Minister, Paul-Boncour:[17] 'Adolf Hitler, today, is truly in control of his people. He exercises a complete hold over them . . . He maintains the balance between competing rivals; he judges over their quarrels; his authority is not in question.'

Contemporary comments of this kind only strengthen our doubts about the validity of attempts to subsume Hitler's Germany and Mussolini's Italy in a general concept of fascism, or even to speak of a 'fascist' foreign policy. It seems less than certain, in historical terms, that the term fascism can be separated from its political fighting function and applied to the academic terrain with any degree of accuracy. Such a move would tend to ignore the uniqueness of Nazism and Hitler as well as of Italian fascism and Mussolini. In fact, the French ambassador in Rome, de Chambrun, recognized the differences between Nazism in Germany and fascism in Italy very rapidly. He received support for his opinion from a prominent and competent witness, Benito Mussolini himself. De Chambrun commented on 15 August 1933:[18] 'The Duce told me more particularly, "Although our relations with Germany have a friendly appearance, this is strangely mistaken for the desire to establish a community of doctrine between fascism and Hitlerism. We agree only on the negative points, the struggle against communism for example, but our positive programmes are essentially different. I approve of neither their theories on race, nor their persecutions of the Jews.'"

In my opinion, the functionalist attempts to explain the foreign policy of Hitler are unsatisfactory, whilst the widespread use of the term fascism cannot provide an adequate explanation of the 'Hitler phenomenon'. Consequently, the dictator should continue to be judged as an object of investigation *sui generis*. The issue of his policy towards France is therefore a legitimate subject for academic inquiry, although other factors involved in Nazi and German foreign policy must also be taken into account.

From these observations on some basic problems of Hitler research, it should be apparent that Hitler's personality and policy were of decisive significance for the history of the foreign policy of the Third Reich. I intend now to summarize previous interpretations of Hitler's policy towards France and, in taking issue with them on certain points, to make the outline of my own position clear.

III
CURRENT POSITIONS IN RESEARCH

Three basic positions can be recognized in research at present. Typically, these offer a different assessment of Hitler's policy towards France in the period between the 1920s, when the future dictator wrote his programmatic material, and spring and summer 1940, when the German Reich won its military victory over France.

(1) In 1966 Eberhard Jäckel,[19] using the relevant passages in *Mein Kampf*, outlined the core of the foreign policy 'programme' to which Hitler's policies and war leadership were directed. In Jäckel's view, Hitler always planned to defeat France, but not merely as the 'hereditary enemy' of the German people whose conquest would enable him to realize the demands of the Reich for revision in central Europe. Jäckel argues that Hitler saw the elimination of the power of France – as the leading military factor connecting the forces of western, central and eastern Europe – as the crucial precondition for his planned war of *Lebensraum* against the Soviet Union. Once France was defeated, he would then be able to wage war in the east without the threat of a 'second front' at his rear. Jäckel's interpretation concludes with the argument that Hitler's 'programme'[20] is divided

into three major phases. In the first the concern is for rearmament at home and the conclusion of alliances with England and Italy. It will give 'Germany the possibility of calmly making those preparations which must be made one way or another for a reckoning with France'. In the second phase there will be war with France in some form. In this way, not only will the French attempt to achieve hegemony in Europe be eliminated, but also the threat to Germany on the flank during an expansion in the east. As a by-product, as it were, the German revisionist demands of 1918 would be fulfilled, but this was really only a second-ranking priority. After the destruction of France the great war of conquest against Russia can take place in the third and last phase, an easy task in military terms since there was nothing to stop it except the disorganized country of the Jewish Bolsheviks, but politically of epoch-making significance because the German sword is thereby providing material for 'the busy work of the German plough' for generations to come.

Jäckel then continues:[21] 'Today there is no more doubt that Hitler remained true to them [these ideas] through all the vicissitudes of his life until the end.' Following the theme of his Kiel habilitation thesis, Jäckel concentrates on the Franco-German relationship during the Second World War and not on the details of that relationship during the 1930s. Hitler's programme, in so far as it related to the 'factor of France', appeared to have been fulfilled. France, until then regarded as the strongest power on the European continent, had been defeated – not as an end in itself, not even with the primary aim of Germany's replacing France as the leading military power, but as the precondition for a war against Russia. In Jäckel's interpretation, it was the coming conflict with the Soviet Union which was preoccupying Hitler even during the campaign against France. He finally launched his attack on Russia on 22 June 1941, a year after the armistice with France.

At first sight, Jäckel's interpretation of Hitler's policy towards France, as part of his programme, appears convincing. However, it is not entirely satisfactory; the attempts of the Nazi regime to reach a settlement with the government in Paris, particularly in the period 1933–6 and again in December 1938, do not fit into this apparently simple, programmatic plan with its fixed approach to the 'factor of France'.

(2) An explanation for this fact was suggested by the journalist Wilhelm Ritter von Schramm, based on his own personal experiences. His argument is revealed in the title of his book: *Sprich vom Frieden, wenn du den Krieg willst* ('Speak of peace if you want war').[22] In fact, Schramm did not challenge the main thrust of Jäckel's interpretation. He described Hitler's overtures to France as a 'psychological offensive' by the dictator. Hitler's friendly gestures and protestations of his peaceful intentions were thus deliberately designed to lull the French people and their governments into a false sense of security, thereby distracting them from the real German intention to wage war. Von Schramm refers to a 'psychological war' conducted by Hitler against France during the 1930s; in it, the Führer shrewdly exploited political and diplomatic methods and appealed to public opinion in pursuit of his strategic goal of 'making the French unwilling to wage war'.[23]

Hans-Adolf Jacobsen, in his great work on Nazi foreign policy,[24] has made a convincing analysis of the main points of Hitler's peace policy as a 'strategy of grandiose self-minimization'. Nevertheless, von Schramm's one-sided interpretation of Hitler's policy towards France in the 1930s remains somewhat unsatisfactory. Should all the dictator's attempts to reach a settlement with his western neighbour between 1933 and 1939 be seen as merely camouflage to disguise the true intentions he had described in *Mein Kampf*? Did he really conceal these intentions until 1940, when they emerged as an intrinsic part of his foreign policy programme? How does such an interpretation, analysing the camouflage manoeuvres and true objectives in Hitler's policy towards France, square with his remarks to his generals and the Sturm-Abteilung (SA) and Schutzstaffel (SS) leaders, including Göring and Röhm, in the Reichswehr Ministry on 2 February 1934?[25] According to the testimony of the future Field Marshal von Weich, Hitler then suggested that 'short decisive strikes first to the west, then to the east' might 'become necessary' if the western powers refused to permit Germany's plans to conquer *Lebensraum* in eastern Europe. Clearly, his comments contained the threat of a preliminary strike against the west as a necessary prelude to the offensive in the east. But did they not also reveal an awareness of the possibility of an agreement with France as well as Great Britain? Though he remained sceptical about the prospect, did these comments not imply an actual preference on the part of Hitler for a settlement with the western powers concerning Germany's intention to wage a war of *Lebensraum* against the Soviet Union?[26]

(3) In his Bonn dissertation on the attitude of Britain towards secret German rearmament between 1933 and 1935, Norbert Wiggershaus[27] adopts a different approach to that of Jäckel and von Schramm. He points out that, particularly in the early years of his foreign policy, Hitler constantly contemplated co-operation with France. However, Wiggershaus bases his ideas on a source which was not made public until 1968 and has come to be regarded with suspicion by researchers. In Edouard Calic's version of two conversations between Hitler and Breiting, the editor-in-chief of the *Leipzige Neuesten Nachrichten*,[28] Hitler appears to have emphasized the necessity of a Franco-German agreement to combat the common threat to both countries posed by bolshevist Russia. Though the source now appears dubious, there is sufficient other evidence to make Wiggershaus's theory worthy of consideration. Hans-Adolf Jacobsen was therefore correct to put his pupil's findings into a wider perspective and to state:[29]

The high degree to which Hitler, in the first three years of his rule, courted the favour and agreement of the *two western powers* [my emphasis] is reflected in the fact that he spent almost 50% of his reception time on talks with the representatives of these two states . . . So far as we can judge today, the endeavours of Germany to reassure the western powers were meant sincerely. However, they were linked with the hope that the two states would place no significant obstacles in the path of German policy towards the Balkans and the east . . . Paris was to be persuaded to adopt a benevolent policy towards Germany by means of partial concessions. There was no more talk of a violent conflict between Germany and France, preliminary stage to a war of *Lebensraum* in the east.

These arguments were consolidated by Günter Wollstein's study on the early phase of Nazi foreign policy in the years 1933–4.[30] Though the author emphasizes the fact that Hitler always judged France to be a potential enemy, he nevertheless demonstrates that the dictator did much to deter France from launching a preventive strike during the critical phase when he was restoring the military capacity of the Reich (*Wiederwehrhaftmachung*). Wollstein stresses the tactical aspect of Hitler's policy towards France, but he also warns against the facile conclusion that Hitler's offers to Paris were no more than camouflage manoeuvres. He therefore writes:[31]

All the same, the first attempts of the Reich Chancellor to come to temporary agreement with a country which was classified as 'hostile' in his programmatic writings, should not be underestimated, particularly since at the start of 1934, when he was more intensively concerned with making common cause with England, he continued to regard hopes for bilateral agreements with France as a component part of his policy.

In his interpretation of German foreign policy towards the western powers, Wollstein even regards Hitler's endeavours to reach a settlement with France at this stage as more intensive than his efforts to gain the favour of Britain.[32] However, this particular argument depends on selective observations and is, in my opinion, incorrect; Hitler always wanted an alliance with Great Britain more than a Franco-German rapprochement.[33]

In two respects, Wollstein sees Hitler's overtures to France as a political function of a foreign policy which was fundamentally 'programmatic' in direction. First, he believes that the dictator was anxious to deter France from making a preventive strike against Germany in the short term; and secondly, he argues that in the longer term Hitler was attempting to reach an agreement with France which would allow him to realize his plans at the expense of the Soviet Union. Wollstein argues convincingly that such offers from Hitler, limited in time but nevertheless 'genuine', are quite compatible with the dictator's fixed concepts of *Lebensraum* war, the establishment of world power status and Nazi claims to global domination:[34] 'On the possibility of an alliance with France as with the Soviet Union, we must finally refer to Hitler's own thesis, expressed in *Mein Kampf*, that temporary alliances are always conceivable even with

Germany's enemies.' After a successful military operation against the Soviet Union, undertaken either with the toleration of France and Britain or in agreement with the two western powers,[35] France would in any case be restricted to the role of a European junior partner of Germany. To all intents and purposes, the great German world power would by then be master of continental Europe.

Obviously, further research in this field will lead to the emergence of new and different arguments. It is safe to conclude, however, that between 1933 and 1936 – and probably thereafter – Hitler adopted a thoroughly flexible foreign policy towards France in pursuit of several objectives. All of its possible options were designed to help him achieve his fundamental programmatic ideas. After a phase of domestic and external consolidation, he intended to lead Germany to supremacy in Europe, to win *Lebensraum* in the territory of the Soviet Union, to establish a world power position and, from a racial perspective, to establish global domination. Hitler's policy towards France in the first years of his rule therefore had the following objectives:

(1) Paris should be persuaded to tolerate rapid German rearmament;

(2) France should decide not to undertake preventive action against Germany;

(3) France was to be persuaded to adopt at least a neutral attitude towards Hitler's future plans for expansion in the east of Europe, and even perhaps to encourage them;

(4) the relative 'weakening' of French preparedness for defence thus appears to have been a secondary product of this policy and not its primary intention or an a priori motive of Hitler;

(5) nevertheless – and not untypically in bilateral power politics – attempts to court the favour of France were accompanied by political steps which were intended to weaken the French position in Europe in a way beneficial to Germany. Not least, such steps would improve the starting position of the Reich for its policy of 'equal rights', revision and expansion and thus make French statesmen more receptive to the offers of a settlement from the German Führer.

In the last analysis, Hitler was prepared to pursue the policy described in *Mein Kampf* and to make 'short decisive strikes to the west' before moving to the attack in the east. However, this was to be done only if France refused to come to an agreement with Germany which satisfied the short-term political needs of the Reich and the long-term plans of Nazi expansionism. It is clear that Hitler saw France primarily as a flexible factor in power politics within the overall framework of a programme rooted in his personal ideology.

At this point, it is necessary to describe Hitler's policy towards France in more detail. The survey will begin with an analysis of Hitler's ideas about and approach towards France in the years before the seizure of power. It will be followed by a description of the basic principles and outlines of Hitler's policy towards France between 1933 and 1936. In this way it will be easier to recognize Hitler's overtures to France, as well as his political manoeuvres against France, as aspects of a foreign policy which was directed towards certain programmatic expansionist goals. It will become clear that Hitler's policy towards France bore striking similarities to his relations with Great Britain in the same period. The system of alliances proposed by the Führer in the 1920s did not have the same ideological and programmatic quality that characterized his proposals for the conquest of the Soviet Union, his ideas for world power status and his ultimate global policy of racial domination.

IV
HITLER'S VIEWS OF FRANCE IN THE 1920S

In the first years of the Weimar Republic between 1919 and 1923, Hitler's ideas about France bore striking similarities to the belief in the 'hereditary enemy' across the Rhine which was widespread on the political right and in almost all nationalist circles in Germany.[36] France was regarded as the vital continental and military guarantor of the Treaty of Versailles and thus as the inevitable opponent of revisionist demands which were current at all levels of German society and in all political parties, including the Social Democrats. Until January 1923 Hitler regarded France, as well as Britain and the United States, as 'absolute enemies'.[37] He held Great Britain responsible for the 'theft' of Germany's former colonies and accused France of unjustly taking Alsace-Lorraine from the Reich. The objective behind his reproaches, accusations and claims was to revise the 'outrage of Versailles' and to restore the powerful Reich of the Hohenzollerns. Indeed, at this stage Hitler may even have contemplated a rapprochement between Germany and Soviet Russia, or between Germany and White Russia should there be a successful counter-revolution, in order to spike the guns of the western powers.

Hitler's ideas began to change after the Franco-Belgian occupation of the Ruhr in January 1923 and the growing – though exaggerated, by Hitler as well as Stresemann[38] – alienation between Britain and France. At the same time, his general concepts of foreign policy were being systematized. The Nazi Party leader then produced an outline of alliances which he thought would help him realize his fixed programmatic objective of a *Lebensraum* war against the Soviet Union.[39] He argued that it was both advisable and possible to create an alliance with Britain and Italy in order to defeat

France, and commented in *Mein Kampf* that 'the implacable mortal enemy of the German people is and remains France'.[40] Hitler's assessment of the 'factor of France' was decisively affected by his main ideological goal, which involved the destruction of the Soviet Union. He saw the elimination of France as a major political force largely as a precondition for subsequent German expansion in the east. War against France was not an end in itself; it was not even to be pursued with the main aim of destroying French supremacy on continental Europe to benefit the ambitions of Germany; instead, it would 'offer rear cover for an enlargement of the *Lebensraum* of our people in Europe'.[41] Hitler saw 'the destruction of France really only as a means ... of giving our people the expansion made possible elsewhere'.[42] A comparison with Britain is instructive here. The desired alliance with Britain was not an unalterable axiom of Hitler's programme[43] and did not possess the ideological quality attached to his fundamental programmatic objectives of *Lebensraum*, establishment of world power status and global racial domination. Similarly, the treatment of France in his proposals for alliance was primarily a function of his goals of expansion in eastern Europe. During the 1920s, when he was untroubled by the burdens of office and could follow his own military-strategic logic, Hitler concluded that France must be eliminated as a military factor threatening the western flank of the Reich before he could begin a campaign against Russia. In the 1930s, this military-strategic concept was replaced by a preference for political and diplomatic attempts to achieve a solution. However, it always remained latent as the *ultima ratio* of his policy and war leadership, as is revealed by his comments in the Reichswehr Ministry on 28 February 1934. This *ultima ratio* may also have been behind a surprising remark made by Hitler in October 1937. When Luftwaffe General Erhard Milch told Hitler about the many friendly gestures made to him by French military and political leaders during his visit to Paris, which made him hopeful of a Franco-German agreement, Hitler simply replied:[44] 'But one day I will thrash them.'

V
FRANCE AS A FACTOR IN HITLER'S FOREIGN POLICY, 1933–6.

After the seizure of power, Hitler was confronted by an international situation dominated by the threatened or actual isolation of the Third Reich. Nevertheless, the dictator had a series of short-term foreign policy objectives which were achieved in the period 1933–6. In pursuing them, he was not prepared to pay heed to powers such as Britain and Italy, which he saw as traditional allies of Germany. Nor would he allow himself to be dissuaded by France, though he had attempted to reach an agreement with that country since the seizure of power. He saw his early goals as essentially limited and as absolutely indispensable for the German Reich, so much so that he was unable to regard them as matters for negotiation. In addition, these early objectives were also supported by the overwhelming majority of leadership groups in Germany. The demands thus had a degree of moral and political authority and were regarded as long overdue by most Germans; to a certain extent, they received a sympathetic response from public opinion in Great Britain, which was already prepared for a policy of appeasement. There were a number of tasks and objectives which Hitler was not prepared to abandon or to negotiate with the western powers and Italy.[45]

(1) In insisting on the restoration of German military strength, Hitler was maintaining a degree of continuity with the foreign policy of the authoritarian cabinets of Brüning, von Papen and von Schleicher. Though his own conduct was more ruthless, at this stage it was supported by most of the conservative representatives of the Foreign Office and the Reichswehr. Hitler exploited Anglo-French tensions on this subject before destroying the armament negotiations which France had used in an attempt to protect its own, generally short-sighted, interests. He then proceeded with German rearmament, particularly on land and in the air. Apart from the exceptional case of the Anglo-German Naval Agreement of 18 June 1935, he was not prepared to reward approaches from the Italians or the western powers with German concessions in the armaments sector.

(2) In line with his remarks in *Mein Kampf* about the purpose and value of alliances, it became clear that Hitler preferred the principle of bilaterality instead of a multilateral order of the international system. Unlike Britain, France and Italy, he therefore attempted to devise bilateral alliances. However, faced with the threat of isolation for the Third Reich, he was forced to depart from the arguments of *Mein Kampf* and to approach Poland and France, as well as Britain and Italy, to this end. But the critical event in this period occurred on 14 October 1933, when Hitler's Germany left the League of Nations, which was supported by Britain and France as the major arena of international arbitration. There were clear parallels here with the conduct of Japan in East Asia. Nazi Germany had no respect for the principle of multilaterality and wanted to achieve an international order of a completely different quality; in place of multilaterality, the maintenance of the status quo and the peace, the new Reich Chancellor favoured bilaterality to assist him in his revisionist foreign policy and as preparation for eventual expansion to be achieved through war.

Hitler's attempts at rapprochement with France during the 1930s should also be understood within this framework. His search for bilateral alliances, with the aim of disturbing the existing order and ultimately overturning it, was diametrically opposed to the policies pursued – though with characteristic differences – by Britain and France. Throughout this period, the two western democracies were pursuing policies designed to maintain the status quo and the peace. Hitler was not prepared to abandon the fundamentals of his foreign policy and its objectives for the sake of an agreement with the western powers.

(3) Hitler ended the isolation of the German Reich on 26 January 1934, by concluding with Marshal Pilsudski a non-aggression pact between Germany and Poland. He thus provided a spectacular and surprising display of the flexibility and freedom of manoeuvre of the Third Reich in foreign affairs. In addition, he also managed to loosen the ring of French alliances around Germany for the first time since the 1920s. Hitler's step should not be regarded first and foremost as a deliberately anti-French act. It was not an attempt to isolate Paris in Europe in order to prepare the best possible conditions for a war against Germany's neighbour in the west. Instead, his conduct was part of a general reorientation of German foreign policy; where previously German foreign policy had been conducted alongside the Soviet Union against Poland, it was now, in the longer term, to be conducted alongside Poland against the Soviet Union. Hitler may also have hoped that the consequent weakening of France would also make Paris more receptive to the attempts of the German government to reach *entente*. In spite of the efforts of the French Foreign Minister Barthou for an 'Eastern Locarno' in June 1934 and despite the Stresa Front of April 1935, created by the European great powers against one-sided breaches of treaties by the German Reich, Hitler continued his efforts to achieve a political settlement with France. He remained anxious to prevent Germany from becoming isolated and to avoid German participation in a system of multilateral treaties.

(4) From a territorial point of view, Hitler does not seem to have considered making the Saar question into a matter for negotiation in Franco-German relations. The return of the Saar region to the German Reich appeared to him to be more or less certain after the plebiscite which was due in 1935. However, his approach to the future of Alsace-Lorraine, always an issue between Germany and France, was very different. Unlike other nationalists in the Reich, Hitler was prepared to abandon the German claim to Alsace-Lorraine in order to demonstrate to France his willingness to reach a settlement. There are obvious parallels here with his conduct towards other potential allies in the west: Hitler was also ready to do without colonial possessions and naval prestige for some time in order to win London over to his plans for an alliance; and he had already relinquished his claim to the South Tyrol in an effort to gain the support of Mussolini, despite the difficulties this policy caused him during the 1920s. Similarly, the dictator was attempting to convince France of his goodwill by abandoning revisionist demands over Alsace-Lorraine[46] and thus to make Paris receptive to his efforts at *entente*. Such concessions, it was hoped, would persuade the two western powers and Italy to give him a 'free hand' for his expansionist plans in eastern Europe.

Whatever these immediate concessions, Hitler's strategy had obvious hegemonic and even imperialist implications. His 'temporary'[47] alliances would have ensured that Germany acquired a dominant position over Italy, France and even Britain at the head of a central and eastern Europe which would be ruled from Berlin. In such a situation, the German Reich could then have made its demands for territorial revision and expansion almost at will.

(5) The reoccupation of the demilitarized Rhineland was also among the fixed goals of Hitler. It remains uncertain how much he might have been prepared to concede to France on this issue if Paris had agreed to his offer of an overall settlement. For the military action in the Rhineland occurred at a time when the dictator had already suffered the first failures in his attempts to reach a settlement with France, though these were not entirely abandoned in the following years. Nevertheless, military-strategic 'necessities' apparently played a considerable part in persuading Hitler to march into the Rhineland and consolidate the western flank of the German Reich.

Without doubt there were a number of foreign policy goals which Hitler saw as scarcely negotiable and which he was prepared to realize 'over the heads' of the western powers if necessary, or even against their will. Yet it is also beyond question that he made persistent overtures to France – though not as intensively as to Britain – in order to reach an *entente*.[48] To nations unaware of the fixed expansionist goals of the Third Reich, Hitler's foreign policy approach, in which adherence to non-negotiable 'essentials' coexisted with overtures to potential *entente* partners, must have seemed relatively normal and even justifiable within the framework of the existing system of power politics.

It is quite possible that Hitler's assessment of the factor of France in European politics changed after the seizure of power, under the influence of his foreign policy adviser, von Ribbentrop. As Wolfgang Michalka has convincingly demonstrated in his dissertation on 'Joachim von Ribbentrop and German policy towards England 1933–1940',[49] the existence of an independent von Ribbentrop foreign policy is beyond dispute. In the first phase of Nazi foreign policy, his advice helped to persuade Hitler to regard France as well as Britain as a potential partner in his anti-Soviet policy.[50] The dictator may have assumed that the western powers would be drawn by logic into becoming political partners in an *entente* with the Third Reich, compelled by the communist threat to the bourgeois democracies of the west and attracted by the hostility of Nazi Germany towards communism as an ideology and towards the Soviet Union within the international order. He overlooked the fact that, though the western European democracies had many disagreements with Stalin's Russia, their differences with Nazi Germany were almost irreconcilable. The policy of appeasement[51] pursued by the western powers during the 1930s did not make them inevitable accomplices in an alliance of capitalist nations, whether parliamentary or fascist, against Stalinist Russia. It was a development of this kind for which Hitler hoped and which the Soviet leaders continued to suspect.[52]

Hitler's overtures towards France were begun as early as 8 April 1933 in a discussion with Ambassador François-Poncet.[53] Admittedly, Hitler made no official offer to the French diplomat and did not hesitate to accuse France of bearing the chief responsibility for Germany's lack of equal rights in the international system. He also described Germany's eastern borders as unreasonable. Nevertheless, the conversations also contained other, much less aggressive elements, which François-Poncet reported to Paris:[54]

> 'I [Hitler] repeat that my government is sincerely and profoundly peaceable. We are convinced that a war, even if victorious, would cost more dearly in sacrifices of all kinds than it could yield. The problem, for Germany, is to escape from unemployment and economic crisis and to procure the nourishment for millions of beings who do not have enough to eat. The solution to such a problem does not lie in war. It lies only in a European effort at pacification and collaboration' . . . During the whole conversation, the Chancellor was courteous and amiable, not at all at a loss and certainly more open than a number of his predecessors.

These comments were by no means wholly unfavourable to France. In contrast, Hitler's remarks that same day during a rally of the SA in the Berlin Sportpalast were much harder to assess accurately; though these gave a clear insight into the law of motion of Nazi policy, they must have been scarcely comprehensible to the majority of people both inside and outside Germany. 'We want', said Hitler, 'to breed a new man.'[55] In French governmental circles at least, the official utterances and conduct of Hitler were accorded much more significance than the fanatical speeches of the Führer of the Nazi Party to the formations of his movement. In his great 'peace speech' of 17 May 1933,[56] Hitler decked himself out as a statesman for the benefit of world – including French – opinion. His remarks there were in harmony with the contents of the Four Power Pact which Germany signed on 15 July 1933, having initialled it on 7 June.[57] At this stage, the issue was not merely the possibility of a revision of the peace treaties and of German equality in the sphere of armaments. Even more important, there was recognition of the League of Nations as the arbitrating body in international politics – quite contrary to Hitler's principle of bilateral diplomacy – and acknowledgement of the Locarno treaty and the agreements of the Kellog-Briand Pact. The Reich goverment, so it appeared, was apparently interested in constructive co-operation within the European order. In a telegram to the Italian Duce on 16 July 1933, Hitler saluted the signing of the Four Power Pact proposed by Mussolini as a 'ray of hope in the life of the people of Europe'.[58] The French Premier, Daladier, then shared Hitler's interest in a personal meeting between the two leaders; between spring and summer 1933, he mentioned his readiness for discussions on a number of occasions.[59]

Hitler's policy of reconciliation was not greatly damaged among the 'inner circle' of European powers by speeches such as the one given on 27 August 1933 at the Niederwald monument in Rüdesheim, in which he confirmed the demand for the return of the Saarland to the Reich.[60] But only a few days later, in his speech to the Nuremberg party rally on 3 September 1933,[61] the motive behind his overtures to France and the other states of Europe became clear. In that speech he declared the struggle against bolshevism to be a European mission. Today we know that announcements of this kind did not possess a purely functional significance and were not designed solely as a gloss for other interests, such as the desire to secure domestic rule and to consolidate the position of the Reich in foreign affairs. Much more than this, and in a way contemporaries could scarcely understand, Hitler was revealing a goal of his long-term programme; it should be judged as a driving force behind his efforts to come to an agreement with Italy and the western powers so that he could pursue an offensive policy against the Soviet Union. Viewed from this perspective, Hitler's remarks to François-Poncet on 15 September 1933 are not surprising. The dictator expressly stated his desire to live in 'good understanding' with France and renounced Germany's claims to Alsace-Lorraine; furthermore, when taxed by François-Poncet about the the award to the SA of a standard bearing the inscription 'Strassburg' at the recent Nuremberg rally, Hitler described the 'deterioration of Franco-German relations' as not of Germany's making. The German Foreign Minister, von Neurath, produced a memorandum of Hitler's comments during the the discussions:[62]

> He [Hitler] could only repeat that he had no greater wish than to remove the differences which still exist between France and Germany . . . He could imagine no finer memorial to himself than if it should later be said of him that he had brought about the Franco-German rapprochement. He could state further that an Alsace-Lorraine question did not exist as far as we were concerned.

Hitler soon went beyond diplomatic channels in an attempt to overcome the temporary ill-feeling in Franco-German relations.[63] Thus, he turned directly to French public opinion in order to provide assurances of his friendly sentiments and to prove that he did not want a war of revenge in western Europe. On 16 November 1933 he received the editor-in-chief of the French economic journal *L'Information*, Comte Fernand de Brinon,[64] a representative of the moderate right in France who had shown steady interest in Germany. Hitler described himself as part of a consistent German policy towards France since the Stresemann era and argued that there were absolutely no controversial subjects between the two nations:[65]

> It is an insult for me when people always say of me that I want war! I would be a fool! For what would a war solve? It would only make the position of the world much worse. War would mean the end for both our races, which stand at the forefront of world development, and then it would not take long and Asia would entrench itself in our part of the earth and bolshevism would triumph.

When de Brinon mentioned the anti-French passages of *Mein Kampf*, which alarmed the French public, Hitler replied:[66]

> My book is a challenge which is full of violent invective and imprecations because it was written in prison. I wrote with the resentment of a persecuted apostle. But between the political programme of this book and that of the German Reich Chancellor there is a fundamental difference: changes and obligations have arisen, as always happens when an opposition comes to government. Am I to correct myself and remove from the book the points which have been repeated today? The politician does not correct himself through words, but by his conduct, by deeds. I can best correct *Mein Kampf* as regards France by advocating a Franco-German agreement with great vigour.

A good two years later, Hitler used almost identical language in response to another French journalist, Bertrand de Jouvenel. However, he was not telling either of them the truth. The important comments about France are actually in the second book of *Mein Kampf*, which he wrote when he was no longer in prison. Despite this fact, I am not convinced by Eberhard Jäckel's view[67] that the remarks in *Mein Kampf* remained part of Hitler's fixed and unchanged opinion of France.

Apart from the interview with de Brinon, which apparently made a positive impact on French opinion, Hitler's discussions with Ambassador François-Poncet on 24 November and 11 December 1933 reveal that he was still interested in a rapprochement with France. Thus, the French ambassador reported to Paris on his impressions of Hitler's goals in foreign policy: 'The hidden motive of an active policy directed over a short or long period against Soviet Russia does not seem to me to have left his mind.'[68] Then, on 13 December 1933, Hitler accepted the recommendation of the German ambassador in Paris, Köster, and held discussions with Jacques Chastenet,[69] the director of the newspaper *Le Temps* which was widely regarded as the mouthpiece of the Quai d'Orsay and the *classe dirigeante*.[70] Once again the dictator mentioned the communist threat to Europe which, in his view, made a Franco-German agreement necessary. That same day, he outlined the same objective to the Italian under secretary of state, Fulvio Suvich. On his return to Rome, Suvich made an extensive report to the French ambassador there, de Chambrun,[71] who dispatched a memorandum to his Foreign Minister:

> Hitler testified to his great desire to come to an understanding with France, adding that this result might easily be attained 'since Germany was prepared to renounce conclusively its claim to Alsace-Lorraine.' As for the Saar, he did not put in doubt the result of the plebiscite, which can be awaited with calm and patience by Germany.

Initially at least, Hitler's approaches to Germany's neighbour in the west did not seem to have been damaged by the plans for a rapprochement between France and the Soviet Union in the form of a military alliance, which the German embassy in Moscow discovered on 26 December 1933.[72] They also continued despite the differences between Germany and France in the field of military armaments as revealed, for example, in the conversation between François-Poncet and Hitler on 1 January 1934.[73] Attempts to establish friendly relations were demonstrated by the opening of the Franco-German youth rally in Berlin on 3 January 1934.[74] Nevertheless, despite all Hitler's efforts to gain the agreement of Britain and France for a foreign policy (and war) directed against the Soviet Union, the alternative *ultima ratio* of his foreign policy was always a possible option. It was this option he was describing to the generals and his SA and SS leaders on 28 February 1934, when he commented that in the event of a failure to reach agreement with France and Britain, which he considered quite probable, there would have to be a military conflict with the western powers before an offensive against the east of Europe.

For the time being, attempts to reach a settlement with France continued. They lay behind Ribbentrop's conversation with the French Foreign Minister, Barthou, during his visit to Paris in early March 1934, when Ribbentrop repeated the arguments for Franco-German co-operation.[75] Hitler was aware of Barthou's attempts to revive the ties between France and the states of east central Europe, so threatening to Germany, and particularly the alliance between Warsaw and Paris. However, he told Rosenberg that the plans of the Soviet Union and France for a pact were welcome to the German Reich, as France had now 'compromised' itself.[76] This comment again reveals Hitler's awareness of the alternative to his foreign policy of rapprochement with France. He had outlined it in February 1934 and was now calmly contemplating it once more. The alternative involved treating France, as an ally of bolshevist Russia, simply as an enemy of Germany. It was an approach which many contemporaries would find plausible.

At almost the same time, however, Ribbentrop was making a comparatively positive report of his impressions during his stay in Paris in June 1934 and of his conversation with Foreign Minister Barthou:[77] 'Nevertheless it seems to me ... to be probable that there is a certain desire in the French Foreign Minister for an agreement with Germany.' Rudolf Hess also advocated just such an understanding between the two nations in an exposition on foreign policy to the French paper *L'Intransigeant* on 20 September 1934.[78] Hitler himself, who favoured an understanding for very different reasons than Barthou, also proposed it in his conversation with the chairman of the Union National des Anciens Combattants, Jean Goy, in November 1934. He specifically assured Goy that he did not seek any 'transplanting of border posts' to the detriment of France.[79] Goy's association tended to represent the views of the political right in France, but in December 1934 Hitler also received representatives of the left-inclined Union Fédérale des Anciens Combattants et Victimes de la Guerre. His conduct at this stage was part of the attempt to win France over, as was the initiative undertaken through Joachim von Ribbentrop and Otto Abetz in the form of the Franco-German youth rally.[80]

On 13 January 1935, 90.67 per cent of eligible Saarlanders voted for the return of their region to the Reich. Three days later, Hitler told the American journalist Pierre Huss that, as he had assured French governments since 30 January 1933, 'Germany [has] no more territorial demands of France'[81] now that the Saar problem had been solved. In Hitler's view, there was now little to prevent Franco-German co-operation with an anti-Soviet emphasis, apart from the persistent Rhineland question. At the VII Congress on 28 January 1935, the Soviet head of government, Molotov, announced that the Nazi ideology of master race was not in itself an obstacle to good relations with Germany.[82] He was thereby demonstrating the abiding willingness of Stalin to co-operate with Hitler even during the western-oriented phase of the Soviet policy of 'collective security'.[83] Despite this conciliatory gesture, the German dictator did not change his anti-Soviet policy. As part of his efforts to win over the other great western power, Britain, he told Lord Lothian that Russia was the most unstable factor in the international system.[84] He also continued to campaign for a rapprochement with Paris for some time even after the signing of the Franco-Soviet Mutual Assistance Pact of 2 May 1935.[85] Even the protests of the European powers against the unilateral reintroduction of conscription by the German Reich on 16 May 1935 did not appear to make him abandon his efforts to win the French over; Franco-German veterans' gatherings and student rallies continued to take place in summer 1935[86] and on 12 October 1935 Hitler again had discussions with Fernand de Brinon.[87] At this stage, the Führer possibly thought that the French Foreign Minister Laval, who was temporarily following Barthou's political line, might agree to an anti-Soviet German

foreign policy under certain circumstances.[88] Hitler's attempts to court
the favour of France were summarized by Reich Foreign Minister von
Neurath on 19 November 1935:[89] 'On the part of the Führer there have
been repeated public and solemn expressions of the eagerness for
Franco-German discussions and the desire to improve Franco-German
relations.' However, all Hitler's offers for a Franco-German settlement
should be seen against the background of his anti-Soviet foreign policy.
Only two days later, he made it clear to the French ambassador that, in his
view, Franco-German co-operation was incompatible with the existence of
the Franco-Soviet Mutual Assistance Pact:[90] 'After more extensive remarks by
the Chancellor, he stated once more in conclusion that a rapprochement
of Germany and France was impossible on the basis of the Russian-French
Mutual Assistance Pact.'

These words were a warning to France that, if Paris continued to
co-operate with the Soviet Union, it could no longer expect to achieve a
political settlement with the German Reich. Was Hitler now contemplating
an anti-French alternative to his foreign policy, the *ultima ratio* he had
described in February 1934? Did he now envisage an initial military
strike against the west, if Britain and France refused to support – or
perhaps even to tolerate – his expansionist goals in the east? At any
event, the differences between Hitler's Germany and the French Republic
had become much more extensive; it was now increasingly probable that
Hitler would be forced to achieve his external objectives without French
support, and perhaps against France. Von Neurath reported the different
attitudes towards Russia which clearly separated Germany and France:[91]

When the ambassador then began to speak of the need for a European
solidarity, the Chancellor first of all asked whether he was counting Russia as part of Europe. After the ambassador answered in the affirmative,
the Chancellor declared that as far as he was concerned Asia began in
Russia and that the entry of Russia into European questions appeared
to him to be disastrous, as did the acceptance of the Soviet Republic
into the League of Nations on the initiative of France.

Despite the foundation of the Comité France-Allemagne in Paris in
November 1935,[92] Hitler's willingness to achieve rapprochement with
France was limited by the different ideological and political assessments
of the Soviet Union made by the two countries. His attempts to reach
agreement with France and Britain were designed to enable him to pursue an active anti-Soviet policy, and ultimately even military action against
Russia. Consequently, once France had allied itself with the Soviet Union,
the intended victim of his expansionist foreign policy, then his efforts to
reach *entente* with France were senseless. Hitler did not completely give
up hope that France would come round to his way of thinking, perhaps

because of the anti-Soviet attitude of the French Foreign Minister, Laval, and the anti-communist sentiments of French public opinion. Nevertheless, he was no longer prepared to have the same regard for French opinion as before. Despite the assurances of his peaceful intentions given to Madame Titayna of *Paris Soir* on 25 January 1936 and Bertrand de Jouvenel of *Paris Midi* on 21 February 1936,[93] he used the Franco-Soviet Mutual Assistance Pact as an opportunity to achieve an important objective – the reoccupation of the demilitarized Rhineland.[94] The plan, which he had already mentioned confidentially to his Wehrmacht adjutant, Hossbach, on 12 February 1936, was implemented on 7 March. The reactions of the western powers were fairly mild, since France could not bring itself to make a military intervention. Hitler had successfully consolidated his western flank even without a Franco-German agreement, in fact by direct action against the will of France. In this way he had helped to prepare the ground for an attack against the Soviet Union at some later date. Four months previously, he had revealed the motives behind his policy to the Japanese military attaché, Oshima, when he claimed that Russia must be carved up into its 'original parts'.[95]

Hitler refused to be diverted from this objective. Between 1933 and 1935–6 he had made considerable efforts to include France, as well as Britain and Italy, in a formation of European states led by the Third Reich and directed against the Soviet Union. At the same time, however, he made it clear that if Paris was allied with Moscow then it could not possibly be a partner for the Reich and that, if necessary, he would realize his foreign policy objectives without an *entente* with France. Indeed, even during these attempts to reach agreement with Paris, he mentioned the *ultima ratio* of his policy, which was not finally implemented until September 1939; this involved accepting the need to strike first against the western powers before he could launch a war against Russia. It would nevertheless be a mistake to dismiss Hitler's political and diplomatic initiatives during the 1930s as a mere tactical manoeuvre designed to disguise his real aggressive intentions towards France.

VI
RESULTS AND CONCLUSIONS

(1) A comparison of Hitler's attitude towards France in *Mein Kampf*, written during the 1920s, with the actual policy towards France he pursued as Führer and Reich Chancellor of Nazi Germany, makes it clear that his assessment of the factor of France had changed. This change is explained by the fact that Hitler always saw the

relationship of the German Reich with France as a political function of his programmatic objectives in the Soviet Union; depending on the international situation and national requirements, he was prepared to advocate an anti-Soviet German foreign policy in co-operation with France, without regard for France, or even against France. It is also possible[96] that Hitler's assessment of the political and military strength of France underwent a considerable change during this period. In the mid-1920s France appeared to be such a strong force within the European system that Hitler may have thought its defeat was absolutely essential before he could turn against the Soviet Union. In contrast, by the early 1930s the republic had been gravely weakened by a series of internal crises; the conquest of a nation in retreat, sheltering behind the Maginot Line, must have seemed less essential as a precondition for Germany's expansion to the east. Hitler may have come to believe that France would no longer prevent him from pushing through his anti-Soviet policies and military campaigns.

(2)   It would be premature and inappropriate to deduce from his conduct that improvisation was the decisive feature of Hitler's foreign policy and conduct of the war. Of course, the ability to improvise in matters of power politics was very apparent in his dealings with France during the period under investigation here. However, this quality was always applied in the service of the dictator's ideologically fixed objectives, which determined the foreign policy of the Third Reich.

(3)   Hitler's programmatic policy towards Russia marked the limits of the political flexibility of the Nazi Führer and demonstrated the primacy of ideological dogma over power political calculations, though these could sometimes be extensive. Hitler's fundamental objective in foreign affairs was to pursue an anti-Soviet policy, if possible in association with France, Italy and Britain, whilst Paris was attempting to include the Soviet Union in the political affairs of Europe. This conflicting approach was an barrier to all Hitler's efforts to achieve a Franco-German *entente*.

(4)   Political differences between the Third Reich and the French Republic on the subject of the Soviet Union were crucial. There were clear parallels in Anglo-German relations during the same period, when contrasting assessments of the factor of Russia helped keep the two countries apart. To a considerable extent, the disagreement determined the course of Franco-German relations. France could not be, and had no desire to be, the partner in a foreign policy which ran counter to its national interests of maintaining the status quo and the peace. Neither France nor Britain could see any advantage in a policy of supporting Hitler, nor of tolerating

143

his attempts to damage or eliminate the Soviet Union as a factor in the international order; it would scarcely be in the interests of the two western democracies if, after the eradication of the communist threat, an over-mighty Nazi continental empire rose to take its place.

(5) After 30 January 1933 there were three basic options open to French foreign policy in an effort to counter Nazi Germany:

(a) Paris could conceivably have conducted a war against Hitler's Germany in the first years after the seizure of power and thus removed the danger by means of preventive action. In fact, this policy was scarcely feasible. For one thing, the danger of Hitler's Germany, so glaringly obvious today, was not fully recognized at the time.

(b) Paris could have accepted Hitler's efforts to achieve rapprochement and pursued a resolute anti-Soviet policy. In effect, this would have meant the adoption by France of a policy of self-isolation, would have endangered the *entente* with Britain and would have been tantamount to France voluntarily becoming the junior partner of the German Reich.

(c) The only remaining possibility, which seemed most appropriate to French society and the nation, was in fact followed. For some time France did not pursue it as eagerly as Great Britain, which quickly became the driving force behind the western policy of appeasement; nevertheless, Paris had made the decision to protect its vital *entente* with London.[97] Quite apart from their moral objections, political convictions based on national interest led both western powers to refuse Hitler's proposals for partnership in his strategy against the Soviet Union. German attempts to reach *entente* with France failed because the western democracies could not share Hitler's assessment of the Russian issue. Among the consequences of this failure were growing political tensions between Hitler on one side and France and Britain on the other, which were a constant source of speculation for Stalin and made a major contribution to the outbreak of war between the German Reich and the western powers in 1939.

(6) Hitler's attempt to win France over should not be explained primarily as a tactical camouflage manoeuvre, nor as cunning psychological warfare to undermine French readiness to wage war. Instead, it reflected his subjectively genuine desire for an agreement with the parliamentary nations of Europe which would enable him to pursue an anti-Soviet foreign policy and even to wage war on Russia. Should the western powers refuse to co-operate or even to tolerate his policy, Hitler was ready to explore the possibility of achieving his ideological goals through political and military means either without France and Britain or 'over their heads'. That was not all. In the final analysis, he was always prepared to consider

as his *ultima ratio* the use of force against the west in order to secure his rear for the planned offensive in the east. Throughout, his policy towards France – even the contemplated alliance with Paris – was a function of his programmatic strategy.

(7) Between 1933 and 1936, Hitler repeatedly attempted to settle the differences between Berlin and Paris by diplomatic means, though he was not prepared to offer certain indispensable objectives of his foreign policy for negotiation. Apart from their attitudes towards Russia, the incompatibility between the two nations was rooted in the fact that France hoped to maintain the European peace at almost any cost, largely because of its own internal position, whilst Hitler's aims involved the destruction of the European status quo.

(8) His policy of courting the western powers continued even after the German entry into the demilitarized Rhineland, which had such a dramatic effect on the international situation.[98] At this stage, it was accompanied by the increasingly skilful threat of political sanctions against Paris and London and the latent possibility of military action against France and Britain. As Ernst von Weizsäcker, then envoy in Berne, had prophesied in November 1936, the dynamic foreign policy of the German Reich was leading France to 'link herself ever more closely to English policy'.[99] Hitler therefore tended to judge the western powers, Britain and France, more and more as a political unity.[100] This was the case when he again tried to win them over, when he threatened them, when he attempted to bypass them and, finally, when he made a direct challenge to them with reckless disregard of the risk of war. However, after the outbreak of war in 1939 he began to treat France and Britain separately once again. Reverting to the sentiments expressed in *Mein Kampf*, he became determined to drive Britain from the continent by military force and then to reach a settlement with Britain on the basis of a 'division of the world'. France, on the other hand, was now to be eliminated as a military factor and a European great power.[101]

NOTES

The lecture published here was given on 18 March 1977 during a conference, 'Colloque: La France et l'Allemagne (1932–1936)', organized by the French Comité d'histoire de la 2ᶜ Guerre Mondiale with the support of the German Historical Institute, Paris.

1 From the archive of the Forschungsstelle des Nationalsozialismus, Hamburg; also in the Bundesarchiv, Koblenz, Sammlung Jacobsen; published in part in Jacobsen, H.-A., *Der Zweite Weltkrieg. Grundzüge der Politik und Strategie in Dokumenten* (Frankfurt-am-Main/Hamburg: 1965), pp. 180–1; here quoted from Hillgruber, A., *Hitlers Strategie. Politik und Kriegführing 1940–1941* (Frankfurt-am-Main: 1965), p. 14. After the completion of this manuscript, an article appeared by Knipping, F., 'Frankreich

in Hitlers Aussenpolitik 1933–1939', in M. Funke (ed.), *Hitler, Deutschland und die Mächte. Materialen zur Aussenpolitik des Dritten Reiches* (Düsseldorf: 1976), p. 612 ff. Its conclusions are not at variance with my own.

2   This is revealed by the survey of the position of research in Hillgruber, A., 'Grundzüge der nationalsozialistischen Aussenpolitik 1933–1945', *Saeculum* XXIV (1973), p. 313 ff.

3   See Lange, K., *Hitlers unbeachtete Maximen. 'Mein Kampf' und die öffentlichkeit* (Stuttgart/Berlin/Cologne/Mainz: 1968).

4   Quoted in Kimmel, A., *Der Aufstieg des Nationalsozialismus im Spiegel der französischen Presse 1930–1933* (Bonn: 1969), p. 48.

5   François-Poncet, A., *Als Botschafter in Berlin 1931–1938* (Mainz: 2nd edn, 1949), pp. 264–5; see also, for example, the report of the French ambassador of 24 November 1933 in *Documents Diplomatiques Français 1932–1939, 1ʳᵉ Série (1932–1935)* (cited as DDF), Tome V, no. 52, esp. p. 107.

6   Vogelsang, T. (ed.), 'Dokumente zur Geschichte der Reichswehr 1930–1933', *Vierteljahrshefte für Zeitgeschichte* 2 (1954), pp. 434–5.

7   On the questions of French military strategy and diplomacy in the interwar years see Vaisse, M., 'La Ligne Stratégie du Rhin (1919–1930). De la Réalité au Mythe', *Problèmes de la Rhénanie 1919–1930. Die Rheinfrage nach dem Ersten Weltkrieg. Actes du Colloque d'Otzenhausen. 14–16 Octobre 1974* (Metz: 1975), p. 1 ff; see also Aron, R., *Frieden und Krieg. Eine Theorie der Staatenwelt* (Frankfurt-am-Main: 1963), pp. 56–7.

8   *DDF, 1932–1939*, 1, IV, no. 415, p. 737 ff.

9   See also d'Hoop, J. M., 'Frankreichs Reaktion auf Hitlers Aussenpolitik 1933–1939', *Geschichte in Wissenschaft und Unterricht* 15 (1964), p. 211 ff.

10 Romains, J., *Le couple France-Allemagne. Deutsche Bearbeitung* (Berlin: 1935), p. 20.

11 On the following remarks in this section, for more detail see Hildebrand, K., 'Innenpolitische Antriebskräfte der nationalsozialistischen Aussenpolitik', *Sozialgeschichte Heute. Festschrift für Hans Rosenberg zum 70. Geburtstag*, ed. H.-U. Wehler (Göttingen: 1974), p. 635 ff.

12 Broszat, M., 'Soziale Motivation und Führerbindung des Nationalsozialismus', *Vierteljahrshefte für Zeitgeschichte* 18 (1970), p. 409.

13 Mommsen, H., 'Nationalsozialismus', *Soujsystem und demokratische Gesellschaft. Eine vergleichende Enzyklopädie*, ed. C. D. Kernig, Vol. IV (Freiburg/Basle/Vienna: 1971), p. 702.

14 Rich, N., *Hitler's War Aims*. Vol. I: *Ideology, the Nazi State, and the Course of Expansion* (New York: 1973), p. xli.

15 Rich, *Hitler's War Aims*, Vol. I, p. 11.

16 Schieder, W., 'Spanischer Bürgerkrieg und Vierjahresplan. Zur Struktur nationalsozialistischer Aussenpolitik', in W. Schieder and C. Dipper (eds), *Der Spanische Bürgerkrieg in der internationalen Politik (1936–1939)* (Munich: 1976), p. 166.

17 *DDF, 1932–1939*, 1, V, no. 172, pp. 355, 357.

18 *DDF, 1932–1939*, 1, IV, no. 113, p. 197.

19 Jäckel, E., *Frankreich in Hitlers Europa. Die deutsche Frankreichpolitik im Zweiten Weltkrieg* (Stuttgart: 1966), esp. p. 13 ff.

20 Jäckel, *Frankreich*, pp. 20–1.

21 Jäckel, *Frankreich*, p. 27.

22 Schramm, W. Ritter von, *...sprich vom Frieden, wenn du den Krieg willst. Die psychologischen Offensiven Hitlers gegen die Franzosen 1933 bis 1939. Ein Bericht* (Mainz: 1973).

23 Schramm, Ritter von, *...sprich vom Frieden*, p. 17.

24 Jacobsen, H.-A., *Nationalsozialistische Aussenpolitik 1933–1938* (Frankfurt-am-Main/Berlin: 1968), p. 328.

25 Witness accounts from the Institute für Zeitgeschichte, Munich, no. 182, p. 8 ff, in K. D. Bracher, W. Sauer and G. Schultz, *Die nationalsozialistische Machtergreifung. Studien zur Errichtung des totalitären Herrschaftssystems in Deutschland 1933/34* (Cologne/Opladen: 1960), p. 749.

26 So Hitler's words are interpreted in Henke, J., *England in Hitlers politischem Kalkül 1935–1939* (Boppard: 1973), p. 156.

27 Wiggershaus, N. T., 'Der deutsch-englische Flottenvertrag vom 18 Juni 1935. England und die geheime deutsche Aufrüstung 1933–1935' (dissertation, Bonn: 1972).

28 Calic, E., *Ohne Maske. Hitler-Breiting Geheimgespräche 1931* (Frankfurt-am-Main: 1968). On the objections to the source see H. R. Trevor-Roper, *Sunday Times*, 7 March 1971.

29 Jacobsen, H.-A., 'Deutschland 1933–1935' in O. Hauser (ed.), *Weltpolitik 1933–1939. 13 Vorträge* (Göttingen/Frankfurt-Main/Zurich: 1973), p. 262.

30 Wollstein, G., *Vom Weimarer Revisionismus zu Hitler. Das Deutsche Reich und die Grossmächte in der Anfangsphase der nationalsozialistischen Herrschaft in Deutschland* (Bonn/Bad Godesberg: 1973). See also Weinberg, G. L., *The Foreign Policy of Hitler's Germany. Diplomatic Revolution in Europe 1933–1936* (Chicago/London: 1970).

31 Wollstein, *Weimarer Revisionismus zu Hitler*, p. 299.

32 Wollstein, *Weimarer Revisionismus zu Hitler*, p. 251.

33 Michalka, W., 'Joachim von Ribbentrop und die deutsche Englandpolitik 1933–1940. Studien zur aussenpolitischen Konzeption-Diskussion im Dritten Reich' (dissertation, Mannheim: 1976), esp. p. 109.

34 Wollstein, *Weimarer Revisionismus zu Hitler*, p. 12.

35 Wollstein, *Weimarer Revisionismus zu Hitler*, p. 13.

36 Here see Hildebrand, K., *Vom Reich zum Weltreich. Hitler, NSDAP und koloniale Frage 1919–1945* (Munich: 1969), p. 72 ff.

37 Hildebrand, *Vom Reich zum Weltreich*, p. 72.

38 Weidenfeld, W., *Die Englandpolitik Gustav Stresemanns. Theoretische und praktische Aspekte der Aussenpolitik* (Mainz: 1972), pp. 174–5.

39 Kuhn, A., *Hitlers aussenpolitisches Programme. Entstehung und Entwicklung 1919–1939* (Stuttgart: 1970), p. 96 ff.

40 Hitler, A., *Mein Kampf* (Munich: 1941), p. 699.

41 Hitler, *Mein Kampf*, p. 741.

42 Hitler, *Mein Kampf*, pp. 766–7.

43 For more detail here see Hildebrand, *Vom Reich zum Weltreich*, esp. p. 85.

44 Schramm, Ritter von, ...*sprich vom Frieden*, p. 103.

45 On the following comments see the vital studies of Wollstein, *Weimarer Revisionismus zu Hitler* and Weinberg, *Foreign Policy*.

46 On this subject see Kettenacker, L., *Nationalsozialistische Volkstumspolitik im Elsass* (Stuttgart: 1973), p. 32 ff.

47 François-Poncet, *Botschafter in Berlin*, pp. 170–1.

48 *DDF, 1932–1939*, 1, IV, no. 52, p. 107.

49 Michalka, 'Ribbentrop und die deutsche Englandpolitik'.

50 Michalka, 'Ribbentrop und die deutsche Englandpolitik', pp. 66–7.

51 On the appeasement policy of the two western powers see Schlenke, M., 'Die Westmächte und das nationalsozialistische Deutschland: Motive, Ziele und Illusionen der Appeasementpolitik', in G. Niedhart (ed.), *Kriegsbeginn 1939. Entfesselung oder Ausbruch des Zweiten Weltkrieges?* (Darmstadt: 1976), p. 285 ff.

52 Niedhart, G., *Grossbritannien und die Sowjetunion 1934–1939. Studien zur britischen Politik der Friedenssicherung zwischen den beiden Weltkriegen* (Munich: 1972), p. 14 ff.

53 *Akten zur deutschen auswärtigen Politik, 1918–1945* (cited as *ADAP*), Serie C: *1933–1937*, Vol. I, 1, no. 163, p. 297; *DDF, 1932–1939*, 1, III, no. 105, p. 189 ff.

54 *DDF, 1932–1939*, pp. 190–1.

55 Jacobsen, *Nationalsozialistische Aussenpolitik*, p. 768.

56 Domarus, M., *Hitler, Reden und Proklamationen 1932–1945*, Vol. 1 (Würzburg: 1962), p. 270 ff.

57 See Wollstein, *Weimarer Revisionismus zu Hitler*, p. 64 ff.

58 Jacobsen, *Nationalsozialistische Aussenpolitik*, p. 773.

59 For details see Michalka, 'Ribbentrop und die deutsche Englandpolitik', p. 68 ff.

60 Domarus, *Hitler*, pp. 295–6.

61 Domarus, *Hitler*, p. 299.

62 *ADAP, 1918–1945*, C, I, 2, no. 430, p. 794.
63 For more details of the fluctuations in Franco-German relations during the first months after the seizure of power, see Wollstein, *Weimarer Revisionismus zu Hitler*, esp. p. 147 ff.
64 Domarus, *Hitler*, p. 332 ff. On the meaning of the interview see also Schramm, Ritter von ... *sprich vom Frieden*, p. 39 ff. The text published on 22 November 1933 in '*Le Matin*' was, however, qualified by secret German documents published that same day in *Le Petit Parisien*, which dealt with the propaganda activity of the Reich in the western world and with Germany's departure from the League of Nations in October. For details see Weinberg, *Foreign Policy*, pp. 171–2.
65 Schramm, Ritter von ... *sprich vom Frieden*, pp. 40–1.
66 Schramm, Ritter von ... *sprich vom Frieden*, p. 43.
67 Jäckel, *Frankreich in Hitlers Europa*, p. 27.
68 *DDF, 1932–1939*, 1, V, no. 52, p. 107.
69 Jacobsen, *Nationalsozialistische Aussenpolitik*, p. 780.
70 Kimmel, *Aufstieg des Nationalsozialismus*, p. 206.
71 *DDF, 1932–1939*, 1, V, no. 165, p. 327.
72 Jacobsen, *Nationalsozialistische Aussenpolitik*, p. 781.
73 *ADAP, 1918–1945*, C, II, 1, no. 159, p. 287; *DDF, 1932–1939*, 1, V, no. 182, p. 383 ff (aide-mémoire of the French government).
74 Here see Schramm, Ritter von ... *sprich vom Frieden*, p. 50; Jacobsen, *Nationalsozialistische Aussenpolitik*, p. 782.
75 See Michalka, 'Ribbentrop und die deutsche Englandpolitik', p. 72.
76 Jacobsen, *Nationalsozialistische Aussenpolitik*, p. 790.
77 *ADAP, 1918–1945*, III, 1, No.31, p. 77.
78 Jacobsen, *Nationalsozialistische Aussenpolitik*, p. 794.
79 Jacobsen, *Nationalsozialistische Aussenpolitik*, p. 797.
80 Schramm, Ritter von ... *sprich vom Frieden*, p. 51 ff.
81 Domarus, *Hitler*, p. 474.
82 *Soviet Documents on Foreign Policy*, ed. J. Degras, Vol. III: *1933–1941* (London/New York/Toronto: 1953), p. 111.
83 This is the central thesis of Allard, S., *Stalin und Hitler. Die sowjetische Aussenpolitik 1930–1941* (Berne/Munich: 1974).
84 Butler, J. R. M., *Lord Lothian (Philip Kerr) 1882–1940* (London: 1960), p. 331.
85 A summary in Scott, W. E., *Alliance Against Hitler. The Origins of the Franco-Soviet Pact* (Durham, NC: 1962).
86 Schramm, Ritter von ... *sprich vom Frieden*, pp. 64–5.
87 Jacobsen, *Nationalsozialistische Aussenpolitik*, p. 808.
88 See, for example, Weinberg, *Foreign Policy*, p. 199, on Laval's rather 'pro-German' attitude.
89 *ADAP, 1918–1945*, C, IV, no. 418, p. 819.
90 *ADAP, 1918–1945*, C, IV, no. 425, p. 832.
91 *ADAP, 1918–1945*, C, IV, no. 425, pp. 832–3.
92 Schramm, Ritter von ... *sprich vom Frieden*, pp. 71–2.
93 Domarus, *Hitler*, p. 565 ff and 579 ff.
94 For the details of the affair see Braubach, M., *Der Einmarsch deutscher Truppen in die entmilitarisierte Zone am Rhein im März 1936. Ein Beitrag zur Vorgeschichte des zweiten Weltkrieges* (Cologne/Opladen: 1956); summary in Weinberg, *Foreign Policy*, p. 239 ff.
95 Jacobsen, *Nationalsozialistische Aussenpolitik*, p. 819.
96 For the reference to the possibility of such ideas in Hitler's assessment of the 'factor of France' I am grateful to my colleague A. Hillgruber (Cologne University), to whom I am also obliged for his critical inspection of the manuscript.
97 For Britain, as for France, the retention of the *entente* was a crucial factor in foreign policy. This is a central thesis of the study by Hauser, O., *England und das Dritte Reich. Eine dokumentierte Geschichte der englisch-deutschen Beziehungen von 1933 bis 1939 auf Grund unveröffentlichter Akten aus dem britischen Staatsarchiv*, Volume 1: 1933–1936 (Stuttgart: 1972), *passim*; see, for example, p. 35.

98 On one such occurrence see Bussmann, W., *Ein deutsch-französischer Verständ-igingsversuch vom 6 Dezember 1938* (Göttingen: 1953). See in general on the subject Scheler, E., 'Die politischen Beziehungen zwischen Deutschland und Frankreich zur Zeit der aktiven Aussenpolitik Hitlers, Ende 1937 bis zum Kriegsausbruch' (disserta-tion, Würzburg: 1962).

99 Hill, L. E. (ed.), *Die Weizsäcker-Papiere 1933–1950* (Frankfurt-am-Main/Berlin/Vienna: 1974), p. 103.

100 Henke, *England*, p. 156.

101 Hillgruber, *Hitlers Strategie*, pp. 27 ff and 144 ff.

6

War in peace and peace in war.
On the problem of legitimacy in the history of the international order, 1931–41

I

The atmosphere of the 1920s was profoundly influenced by the memory of the First World War and the hope of lasting peace. In contrast, expectations in the 1930s were dominated by fear of another major war and the certainty that it would come. In the previous decade, the fragile peace had only had to withstand military conflicts of a marginal nature,[1] but in the years between 1931 and 1941 the stability of the international system was shaken by a series of incidents. Within general peace there was regional war, for example in the Manchurian crisis of 1931–3. Throughout the period, elements of what Eduard Bernstein had already described as 'cold warfare'[2] could be observed. By the middle of the decade, in the martial words of Hermann Göring, there was a situation 'of mobilization, except that there is no shooting yet'.[3] The 1930s were marked by a whole series of separate military conflicts, sometimes declared and sometimes undeclared. By the middle of 1941, when Europe and East Asia were being ravaged by war, only two great powers were still at peace. Even here, the Soviet Union had already conducted aggressive operations against Poland and Finland before the German attack on its own territory and had been embroiled in incidents with Japan in 1938 and 1939; and the United States of America was already pursuing a 'policy short of war' against Germany and Japan.

The year 1931 marked the dividing point in the period between peace and war. Even at the time, the British universalist historian Arnold Toynbee regarded it as an *'annus terribilis'*.[4] With the world economic crisis at its height, it seemed to him that western civilization was in grave economic and cultural danger. The political threat to the international system was even more important, especially after the failure of disarmament proposals in 1931–3 and the subsequent intensification of the arms race. The crust of international morality, so closely linked in the public mind with phrases such as 'Locarno' and 'Kellog-Briand

Pact', was very thin. Raymond Aron had already described the Treaty of Versailles as 'artificial',[5] and the frailty of the Paris peace agreements and the new European order emerged with increasing clarity. The agreements for East Asia and the Pacific which had been concluded at the Washington Conference of 1921–2 also came under threat.

The legitimacy and normality of the new international order had not been universally recognized, but instead were subject to a variety of revisionist challenges. In this situation, the decisive question for many observers was whether the conduct of Japan in Manchuria from 18 September 1931 posed a fundamental threat to the legitimacy of that order. Was Japan's assault in East Asia designed to produce a genuinely revolutionary upheaval in the existing international order or only to revise it, though to a very great degree? Expansion with the aim of a revolutionary upheaval in the status quo was clearly incompatible with the established order; on the other hand, expansion with the aim of a revision in the status quo might actually help to develop and consolidate the traditional system. It was often difficult to determine the point where gradual alteration turned into abrupt change, or where revisions designed to alter the system turned into revolution which would destroy it.

From this point of view, legitimacy is understood 'as an international understanding about the nature of useful arrangements and about permitted goals and methods of foreign policy'. In the first instance, it is connected with stability rather than justice, though it also presupposes at least a minimum of the rule of law, of welfare and freedom. Legitimacy also means 'that all the great powers generally respect a certain international order, at least to the extent that no state is so dissatisfied with this order that it . . . expresses its dissatisfaction by means of a revolutionary foreign policy'. Furthermore, 'a legitimate order does not preclude conflicts, but it limits their objectives. There may still be wars, but they are fought out' within the framework and even 'in the name of the existing international structure, and the subsequent peace is justified as a better expression of the "legitimate" general conviction'.[6] Only when the system itself is endangered, for example when the existence and non-existence of the powers which are an integral part of it are at risk,[7] is legitimacy lost; then, revolution gains the upper hand. Normality, understood here as the possibility of limited change pursued mainly though not exclusively by peaceful means, is then destroyed. It is replaced by the exceptional circumstance, the outbreak of cataclysmic major war.

II

Contemporaries did not believe that such a change had occurred with the military operations and territorial readjustments which followed the

Mukden Incident and led on 18 February 1932 to the creation of the Manchukuo 'puppet regime' dependent on Japan.[8] On 10 September 1931 the president of the League of Nations, Lord Robert Cecil, had told the twelfth regular sitting of the Societé des Nations 'that there has scarcely ever been a period in the world's history when war seemed less likely than it does at present'.[9] The war in East Asia came as a surprise for the league but in general, especially against the background of Sino-Japanese conflicts in Shanghai in January 1932, it was regarded as a passing crisis.[10] The incident undeniably revealed a weakness in the League of Nations. However, the western powers actually hoped that the war would have a stabilizing effect, partly because they feared that communist liberation movements might undermine their own colonial territories in Asia. Even the United States was mollified after Japan cleverly declared the principle of the 'Open Door' in Manchuria to satisfy American interests. In contrast, the Soviet Union subsequently introduced a change of course in its own foreign policy, or pressed it home with more resolution. In Europe, the USSR was persuaded to draw closer to Poland and France against Germany, which it had now come to regard with mistrust, and to create security for itself in East Asia by means of calculated concessions to Japan. The non-aggression treaties which the USSR concluded with France and Poland in 1932 were also designed to neutralize any Franco-Japanese and Polish-Japanese rapprochement;[11] it was hoped that they would frustrate the anti-Soviet policy emanating from Poland and Rumania in association with France.[12]

In fact, there was a great deal of movement in the international situation. Japanese bellicosity and contempt for the League of Nations – which it left on 27 March 1933 – had an effect on the foreign policy of Germany[13] and Italy. Yet in general, the crisis in the Far East was not as profound in its effect as the conflicts in Africa and Europe in 1935–6, when the conduct of Mussolini and Hitler shook the international order in a much more fundamental way.[14]

The military conflict in East Asia actually seemed to be tolerable to the two guarantor powers of the Paris peace treaties, Britain and France. Britain was endeavouring to maintain the status quo in a relatively flexible and generous manner. British statesmen rejected war as a means of policy. But if the conflagration was kept within bounds and could be regarded as having a stabilizing effect, and if the British Empire's vital links in East Asia, the Mediterranean-African sphere and Europe[15] were not involved, it might be tolerated. Moreover, if insistence on the 'indivisibility of peace'[16] – a concept advocated in another context by the Soviet Foreign Minister Litvinov on 17 January 1935 – might lead to major war, then the divisibility of peace was to be preferred to such a risk. France, preoccupied with the German challenge in Europe and the nationalist revolutionary and communist threat in Indo-China, was also largely uninterested in the conduct of Japan. Admittedly, French conduct was different within Europe; from the end of the 1920s France had appeared increasingly inflexible and ungenerous in its support of the traditional European order which guaranteed its own predominant position.

In international affairs in the 1930s, the two status-quo powers were opposed by the group of revisionist states, which intended to alter parts of the system but not to destroy it entirely. In this category were Italy and Japan. Despite his demands for empire and '*Mare Nostrum*', and the Italian military intervention in Abyssinia, Spain and Albania, and even Greece and North Africa, Mussolini's claims appeared comparatively limited. They could even be regarded as compatible with the existence of the system, particularly as they were followed over a longer period as part of the classic diplomacy of the 'peso determinante': 'Mussolini affermava il revisionismo ma non voleva la revisione.'[17]

Japan was committed to expansion which was not merely economic. The Japanese army and navy were locked in struggle over whether the country should make its 'sword-thrust' against the Far Eastern mainland or against the peaceful possessions of the western powers; within the army, there was some argument as to whether Japan should adopt a neutral relationship with the Soviet Union to concentrate its attack on China, or should ally with China against the Soviet Union, here regarded as among the 'western' nations. Yet Japan was seeking expansion within the boundaries of the regional 'Great East Asian Co-Prosperity Sphere', as it was later called. Unlike Hitler's Germany, it did not intend to 'destroy'[18] either the Soviet Union or the United States, and recognized from 1938 that China could be conquered only with the greatest difficulty. The Amau Declaration of 18 April 1934 revealed that Japan was already considering a special Japanese role in East Asia and in China, but it linked its regional claims to hegemony with a strong anti-colonialist momentum. Japan was striving for regional domination in East Asia. However, it did not propose an ideologically motivated and universal concept of rule of the kind connected with German Nazism, Soviet communism,[19] or even with the liberal American vision of world civilization. In the global context, the *telos* of these latter states, consciously or unconsciously, aimed at direct or indirect rule which inevitably brought into question the existence, independence and identity of other (great) powers. In this sense, Hitler's Germany, Stalin's Soviet Union and Roosevelt's America[20] were not regional but global in their thinking; they were not gradualist and were based on revolution rather than compromise.

True to its origins and principles, the Soviet Union desired a ·comprehensive political, social and economic revolution in the existing international order. However, political circumstances had compelled it to defer the goal of world revolution and to accept the necessary breathing-space of 'socialism in one country'. Since the middle of the 1920s it had pursued the policy of 'peaceful coexistence', as defined by Stalin in the period 1925–7; this was designed to create calm in foreign affairs whilst still permitting agitation on hostile territory. Under pressure from both East Asia and Europe, from an increasingly anti-Soviet atmosphere in Germany and a political threat in Japan, the Soviet Union had changed from an 'anti-Versailles power' into a supporter of the League of Nations, which it joined on 18 September 1934. Even before that, it had opened diplomatic relations with the United States on 16 November 1933 in the hope that the Americans would provide a counterweight against Japan. In 1935, moreover, the Soviet Union introduced a change in the strategy of the Communist International. This ceased its accusations of 'social fascism' against social democratic and socialist parties and began to advocate the concept of a 'popular front'. Nevertheless, none of these moves signified that the goal of revolution had been abandoned; as Stalin himself recognized in 1925, it could also be achieved through war if the time seemed right. He explained his thinking on 19 January 1925 at the plenary gathering of the Central Committee of the Soviet Communist Party,[21] arguing that it was necessary to develop Soviet military power in order to cope with any situation arising from 'developments in the countries surrounding us'. 'War' might

> become unavoidable, of course not tomorrow or the day after, but certainly in a few years ... That does not mean that we would have to move against anyone in an unconditionally active way in such a situation ... But should war start, we will not be able to look on passively – we will have to enter, but we will be the last. And we will enter to bring the crucial weight to bear, a *weight* that ought to be decisive.

Despite the rapprochement with the west which was completed in the 1930s and in the Second World War, it was scarcely in Stalin's interests to fight for the international balance of power established by Britain and France in 1919–20. Nor did he intend to allow himself to be used as the tool of the 'non-revisionist capitalist powers' against 'fascism'. His comments to the British ambassador, Cripps, in Moscow on 1 July 1940 reveal something of his tactically flexible, long-term policy, which was superior to the strategies of western statesmen and the Nazi dictator alike. Stalin remarked that 'the foundation of the [Nazi-Soviet] non-aggression pact has been the common striving to set aside the old existing balance of power in Europe, which Great Britain and France were endeavouring to maintain intact before the war'.[22]

Like the Stalinist Soviet Union, Hitler's Germany also desired to over-turn the international order. The Nazi dictator intended to subject the international system to 'a master race seizing the world in the service of a higher culture'.[23] The defeat of France and the destruction of the Soviet Union were seen as necessary preconditions for a universal racial domination. Nazi aims thus differed profoundly from the revisionism of Stresemann, which was oriented towards Europe and bound by international law, and from the more aggressive and risky policy of the authoritarian cabinets of Brüning, von Papen and von Schleicher. However, the distinctions and dividing lines between revisionist great power claims and worldwide racial domination were far from clear to contemporaries, a situation which offered Hitler the opportunity to use the one as a foil for the other and to conceal the true nature of Nazi foreign policy for a considerable time. The totalitarian and universalist claims of Nazi foreign policy linked Hitler's Germany with the comparable methods and goals of the Stalinist Soviet Union and distinguished both from the expansionist revisionism of Italy and Japan.

In the interwar years the United States of America was dominated by the conflicts between isolationists and interventionists. Yet in this period it should not be counted among the status-quo powers such as Great Britain and France, nor among the powers such as Italy and Japan which were struggling for regional hegemony. Like the Soviet Union and Germany, the United States hoped to revolutionize the international system in the long term. Despite its long isolationism and obvious political eagerness to establish control in its own region, the country still remained true to its origins and principles in asserting a universalist concept. The principle of the indivisibility of world markets, of freedom and of peace was absolutely fundamental to US policy[24] and brought it into competition with Britain and France just as much as with Italy and Japan and with the Soviet Union and Germany. To put the issue in the simplest possible terms, the United States wanted either to rule the world or to escape it. Consequently, a policy of prudent gradualism was alien to the United States. As a result, its military isolationism endangered the world order as much as its selective interventionism. In the economic sphere US expansion was largely unconscious, but politically the United States was consciously offering its own vision to the world with an almost missionary zeal. It advocated the universal adoption of American institutions and the American 'way of life', founded in the secularized religion of individualism and the 'pursuit of happiness'. In the eyes of many Americans, this must inevitably lead to the liberal pre-eminence of the United States in the world. The sentiment was expressed with great clarity by an American senator from the Middle West:[25] 'With God's help, we will lift Shanghai up and up, ever up, until it is just like Kansas City.' It is scarcely surprising that the Conservative Prime Minister of Britain regarded this attitude, equally contemptuous of 'Nazis' and 'Bolshies', as very dangerous. Nevertheless, Britain felt compelled to conclude the Anglo-American Commercial Treaty of 17 November 1938 and to seek the assistance of the United States in the struggle for its existence. Despite all his reservations about the United States, Chamberlain recognized the lesser evil for his own country. In the same year, 'the mentality of Nazism which "comes from the devil"'[26] seemed to him to be the greatest and most acute danger to peace.

III

The international system collapsed because the upheavals in the existing order occurred on a worldwide scale and with increasing frequency. Though there were many attempts at 'crisis management', the underlying dynamism of the situation meant that none of these provided fundamental relief; war and anarchy in their many forms were encouraged. The developments in *Weltpolitik* placed the initiative in the hands of the revolutionary powers. For a short time, the main advantages were reaped by Hitler and then, at least until 22 June 1941, by Stalin. Ultimately the process was also of benefit to Roosevelt, though this fact was initially difficult to recognize in view of the fact that the situation between 1931 and 1941 had appeared so open. Room to manoeuvre is always at its greatest when challenges and threats cannot be recognized clearly. In contrast, once the nature of the problem is clearly recognizable, then room to manoeuvre is either very restricted or has ceased to exist altogether.

Great Britain faced a situation in which its resources were in danger of being overstretched. In particular, it was alarmed by the threat of co-operation between Germany and the Soviet Union or between Germany and Japan, as well as by Soviet 'appeasement' of Japan before 1936. Consequently, British statesmen were eager to make agreements to promote peace and stability. At first these were to be multilateral, generally in accordance with the policy of the League of Nations; later, however, Britain was also prepared to reach bilateral agreements without the participation of the league. British alliance policy was designed in the hope of preventing war and also obstructing the creation of antagonistic blocs which, with hindsight, were held largely responsible for the outbreak of the First World War in August 1914. Britain's treaties, pacts and alliances were intended to prevent the outbreak of war rather than to ensure that the country would be victorious if war broke out.

French powers of resistance were at times almost crippled by the strength of pacifist sentiments within the country. Nevertheless, France temporarily managed to create alliances which combined the intention to deter a potential enemy with the improvement of the country's defensive capability. It was therefore able to reach agreement with the Soviet Union,[27] though with limited results in practical politics. The Soviet Union, in a policy which had parallels with the foreign policy of the Third Reich, favoured the instrument of the non-aggression pact.[28] In general, in both Europe and East Asia, a truly Hobbesian condition of fear led the Soviet Union to seek security wherever it was offered.

At this stage in Europe, there were several options in the creation of alliances.

(1) The first was a solution which brought together the western powers and the Soviet Union, primarily against Germany. An option of this kind had been discussed by Foreign Ministers Barthou and Litvonov in Geneva in spring 1934, within an overall European framework which would actually include Germany ('Eastern Locarno'). On 2 May 1935 the solution was implemented in the limited form of a Mutual Assistance Pact between the Soviet Union and France, which Barthou intended to extend by means of military talks between the two countries. His successor Laval failed to pursue this objective, for reasons of anti-communism, out of fear of increasing the danger of war and revolution, and because he was convinced that the sheer existence of such an alliance would produce the required deterrence.

(2) The second option was co-operation between the western powers and Germany without the participation of the Soviet Union. This possibility constantly aroused Stalin's suspicion of a conspiracy between the 'capitalist-non revisionist' powers and the 'capitalist-revisionist' powers. It seemed to have been established with the creation of the Four Power Pact (Britain, France, Italy and Germany) on 15 July 1933, and re-emerged in the aftermath of the Munich Conference of 29–30 September 1938. On the bilateral level, this option emerged in the Anglo-German Naval Agreement of 18 June 1935. Stalin, deeply suspicious of attempts at rapprochement between Britain and Germany, was further alarmed by the 'Relief Mission' of summer 1939 and his fears were aroused once again by the flight to Britain of Rudolf Hess on 10 May 1941.[29]

(3) Co-operation between the totalitarian states of Germany and the Soviet Union remained a possibility. On the British side, it was feared from an early stage by the permanent under secretary of state in the Foreign Office, Vansittart.[30] This option was made a reality in the Nazi-Soviet pact between Hitler and Stalin, which lasted from 23 August 1939 until 22 June 1941. Its existence resulted in Molotov's condemnation of the western powers as the 'aggressors' on 31 October 1939, whilst he expressly exonerated Germany from the charge of 'aggression'.[31] The Nazi-Soviet agreement ultimately led to western plans in 1940, and British plans in 1941, for attacks directed simultaneously against the

Soviet Union and Germany in the form of the Russian oil centres of Baku and Batum.[32]

The various attempts to safeguard the peace in the 1930s by means of treaties collapsed in the great double crisis of 1935–6 (Abyssinia and the Rhineland). After these events it became clear that the western policy of appeasement had neither deterred nor mollified Mussolini and Hitler. At the same time, the League of Nations was being crippled, and went into its death throes in the course of the Spanish Civil War. In the 'world civil war' on the Iberian peninsula between 1936 and 1939, the policy of collective security failed completely and finally. Its collapse caused deep disappointment, particularly in the Soviet Union. But Great Britain had not been fully committed to collective security, because it could have led to the extension of military conflagration and it also stood in open opposition to the principle of non-intervention held to be necessary to maintain 'British interests'. In any case, war could bring no profit to Britain and could only cause the country great loss. Even Winston Churchill, already the strongest critic of the appeasement policy of Chamberlain, conceded in a conversation in March 1937:[33] 'Even if we won it would cost us so much that the victory would look like defeat.'

Anglo-Soviet hostility emerged clearly during the course of the Spanish Civil War. Consequently, British freedom of manoeuvre was extremely limited here as elsewhere. France, fearing that involvement in the Spanish Civil War might result in the country suffering the same fate,[34] withdrew its support for the Republican government in Madrid on 8 August 1936. The Soviet Union, threatened in the east by Japan and disappointed by the attitude of the western powers, was forced to choose between renewed attempts to reach agreement with the west and the bold alternative of rapprochement with Hitler's Germany. Hitler's own room to manoeuvre and powers of attraction were increased by the war in Spain. As mistrust between the western powers and the Soviet Union grew, Mussolini's Italy and Franco's Spain were both becoming increasingly dependent on the Reich. Hitler was ultimately able to abandon the defensive position which he had been forced to adopt after the seizure of power, a position which had first been alleviated by the conclusion of a non-aggression pact with Poland on 26 January 1934. The German move to the offensive was revealed in the change of policy towards Poland, which began in 1935, was intensified from 1937 and culminated in the offer of a comprehensive solution on 24 October 1938. The offer, repeated on 21 March 1939 more or less in the form of an ultimatum, was an attempt to bring Poland to the side of Germany as a 'junior partner'; it was designed either to neutralize the Soviet Union and begin the war in the west, or to encourage the continuation of western appeasement and enable Germany to attack the Soviet Union.[35]

During the Spanish Civil War, Roosevelt's United States made the first tentative attempts to consider the possible need for American intervention alongside the dominant policy of isolationism. The President denounced aggression in the Chicago 'quarantine' speech of 5 October 1937, and the strict Neutrality Laws were amended by the introduction of a 'cash and carry' clause in that year. Yet even these events did not at first appear to damage the dynamic position of the Third Reich. Hitler's Germany won a number of obvious foreign policy successes, which reached their climax with the *Anschluss* of Austria in March 1938. They included the creation of the 'Rome-Berlin Axis' on 25 October 1936, the Anti-Comintern Pact concluded between Germany and Japan on 25 November 1936 (joined by Italy on 6 November 1937) and the 'Pact of Steel' agreed between Germany and Italy on 22 May 1939. Nevertheless, the Third Reich did not succeed in creating a comprehensive and effective global network of alliances which could seriously have threatened the Soviet Union and/or the western powers, especially Britain. Nor did Hitler achieve his objective of destroying the political and military unity of the western powers and, in particular, of drawing Britain away from France.

In the Far East, the Soviet Union had abandoned its policy of concessions towards Japan in favour of more resolute conduct, even before the outbreak of the Spanish Civil War. With the signing of a Treaty of Defence with Outer Mongolia on 31 March 1936, the Soviet Union had now begun to offer determined opposition to the Japanese. The government in Tokyo rapidly developed some respect for the Soviet Union, and even began to fear the military strength assembling in the 'Soviet Far East'. Partly as a result of this trend, elements in the Japanese General Staff came to support the idea of a compromise with China and even an alliance with a dependent China so that the two could face Russia together. The outbreak of war between Japan and China on 7 July 1937 demonstrated the failure of this political-strategic concept in Tokyo. Instead, the confrontation between two highly armed nations led to a war which Japan could not finally win and which used up a large proportion of the country's resources. Under these circumstances, particularly after the border incidents of summer 1938 and 1939 with Soviet troops, Japan did not underestimate the military power of the Soviet Union. The western powers, on the other hand, were preoccupied by the great purges of the Red Army during 1937–8 and the difficulties encountered by Soviet troops during the Winter War between the Soviet Union and Finland (30 November 1939 to 12 March 1940). Consequently, western statesmen and diplomats in general underestimated the military potential of the Soviet Union. Partly as a consequence, until September 1939 their political and military planning relied on Poland as a 'third force' to hold the balance between the German Reich and the Soviet

Union; the strength of Poland was greatly exaggerated in Europe. Even in the second half of 1941, the west continued to underestimate Soviet powers or resistance until the battle for Moscow of 5–6 December 1941.

IV

During 1938–9 there was an increase in the number and intensity of conflicts. Initially, the Soviet Union appeared to be the main loser from these developments. The League of Nations policy it had pursued between 1934 and 1936 had ended in disappointment; Great Britain regarded the Soviet Union with grave suspicion, not least because of continuing British efforts to reach a 'general settlement' with Germany; relations with France had cooled considerably since 1936; and cautious Soviet attempts at rapprochement with the Third Reich were as yet unsuccessful.[36] Furthermore, there had been military incidents between the Soviet Union and Japan in spring and summer 1938 in the border area between Mongolia and Manchuria. These served to restrict Soviet freedom of action when Hitler provoked the Czechoslovakian crisis over the Sudeten issue, and were not resolved until August 1938. Only a month later, in September 1938, the Soviet Union felt that it had been excluded from the circle of great European powers, as Britain, France, Italy and Germany met at the Munich Conference to 'solve' the Czechoslovakian problem and – temporarily – keep the peace.

Japan was now waging war on the Far Eastern mainland and had not yet begun to achieve its ambitions in the Pacific, a fact which was of benefit to the United States but only increased the insecurity of the Soviet Union. In 1938 the Soviet Union had been withdrawing from involvement in the Spanish Civil War, but was now under great pressure to make a choice between its various policy options in Europe: understanding with the western powers; an arrangement with Nazi Germany; retreat into isolation. There were some parallels here with the situation faced by Great Britain, where there was some public support for the idea of concentrating on the empire, leaving the European continent to Hitler, and behaving generously towards Japan in the Far East. But just as British statesmen rejected the abandonment of *Weltpolitik* as dangerous, it seemed equally inadvisable for the Soviet Union to adopt such a policy. Stalin continued to fear that, in the event of co-operation with the western powers, the Soviet Union might be used as a battering ram against Hitler's Germany and be forced to 'pull the chestnuts out of the fire'[37] for Britain in particular. However, he still hoped to see the capitalist states in open hostility to one another and involved in a war which should last as long as possible. Stalin therefore made an alliance with Germany, which he regarded as weaker than the combined strength of Britain and France. In this way, he turned Hitler's drive for expansion from the east to the west – in his view for a long period, since the experiences of the First World War had led him to regard France as a strong military power. As *tertius gaudens*,[38] the Soviet dictator had gained a key position in the coming great war in Europe. Moreover, on the basis of the secret protocol to the Nazi-Soviet Non-Aggression Pact of 23 August 1939, he would also acquire significant territorial gains in east central Europe and the guarantee of a 'sphere of interest' stretching from Finland to Bessarabia. The position of the Soviet Union had already been eased by the British guarantee to Poland of 31 March 1939, which did much to place a decision on the date of peace and war in the hands of the Polish leadership.[39] The guarantee led Great Britain and Germany into a direct military confrontation, contrary to British expectations that this last signal to Berlin would deter Hitler from taking military action. Now, the conclusion of the Non-Aggression Pact with Hitler in summer 1939 demonstrated Stalin's desire not to prevent war 'but to unleash it indirectly, with Hitler as the actor who did the actual "unleashing"',[40] because he desired the war from a programmatic viewpoint.

Soon after the beginning of the blitzkrieg on 1 September 1939, Poland – result and symbol of the 'new system'[41] of the interwar years described by the British diplomat and historian Headlam-Morley – was defeated. It was occupied by the German Reich as far as a border line in east central Europe agreed with the Soviet Union in the secret protocol to the 'Hitler-Stalin Pact'. In his speech of 31 October 1939, Molotov described Poland as 'this ugly offspring of the Versailles treaty' and continued: 'Everybody realizes that there can be no question of restoring old Poland. It is therefore absurd to continue the present war under the flag of restoration of the Polish State'.[42]

After the defeat of Japan in the region round Nomonhan-Haruha, the imperial government grew ready to reach an armistice with the Soviet Union, especially as the Nazi-Soviet Pact had eased the threat to the European flank of the Soviet Union. The bitter Soviet-Japanese border battles following the Japanese invasion of the Mongolian People's Republic on 11 May 1939 came to an end on 19 September 1939, after fourteen days of talks in Moscow between Molotov and the Japanese ambassador, Shigenori Togo.[43] With the Japanese adopting an unmistakably conciliatory approach in the east, on 17 September 1939 there began the entry of the Red Army into eastern Poland, the part which had been secretly awarded to the Soviet Union. As a result of Britain's attempts to continue its policy of appeasement even after the outbreak of war, and the peace feelers put out to Britain by the German Reich,[44] Stalin continued to fear an Anglo-German agreement in Europe. His mistrust and suspicion were maintained by a number of other factors. A few weeks before the outbreak of war, the 'Far Eastern

161

Munich',[45] the solution of the Tientsin conflict between Japan and Great Britain in the Craigie-Arita Declaration of 24 July 1939, had finally buried Hitler's hopes of an alliance with Japan against the west and pushed him towards an agreement with the Soviet Union. An agreement in Moscow that same day between the British, the French and the Russians on the start of joint military consultations had had the same effect. Nevertheless, between autumn 1939 and summer 1940 the international situation in general developed more advantageously for the Soviet Union than ever before in its history. Admittedly, the situation became more dangerous once again when Hitler's Germany defeated France with surprising speed, thus confounding Stalin's speculation that the war would be a long one. Yet Stalin's Russia and Hitler's Gemany remained allies for the time being, despite the profound ideological and political hostility contained in their opposed but related standpoints.

V

In 1940–1, Britain alone held out against Nazi Germany. The British were fighting for the restoration and maintenance of a balance of power which had long ago been destroyed and lost. The situation was not due to the policies of the Third Reich alone. On 1 July 1940, Stalin gave Ambassador Cripps a blunt answer to the British argument that there must be some balance of power in Europe, even if not the old one, and not the hegemony of one power:[46] 'I am not so stupid as to believe the German assurances that they had no desire for hegemony, but I am convinced of the physical impossibility of such a hegemony, as Germany does not have the necessary naval power.' In fact Hitler's Germany was territorially exposed and would in time be vulnerable to the United States and the Soviet Union. These two great powers had not yet entered the war in Europe and the Far East, and would both be ready for war in 1942.

In comparison with the German Reich, the Soviet Union and the United States of America, the other powers played a subordinate role though remaining at the centre of events. In the desperate situation of 1940, Great Britain was forced to choose between the Pax Germanica of Hitler and the Pax Americana of Roosevelt, and opted for the role of junior partner at the side of the Americans. The American claim to a predominant position in the world emerged in the Atlantic Charter[47] of 14 August 1941, which was permeated with the political idea of freedom; the British, with an eye on their imperialist and associated economic interests, signed the document only with reservations. The Soviet Union played no part in it at all, since the Americans had ceased to regard Russia as an important political and military factor as it trembled under the military onslaught of the German Wehrmacht.

At this stage Roosevelt was largely preoccupied with the threat of Nazi Germany. He even hoped to make some use of Japan, aiming for the goal of regional domination in the Far East and parts of the Pacific, as an element in the political struggle against the Reich. Nevertheless, the oil embargo imposed on Japan by the American President on 1 August 1941, in response to the Japanese invasion of Indo-China on 25 July, was bound either to bring Japan to its knees or force it to a '*Flucht nach vorn*'. It was therefore a form of 'time bomb'[48] which would have been 'defused'[49] only if the German advance into Russia had not begun to falter at the end of July and the beginning of August 1941 in the battle for Smolensk. Against this background, imperial headquarters in Tokyo decided on 9 August 1941 to abandon the prospect of a co-ordinated war effort with the German Reich and a Japanese attack on the Soviet Union in 1941. Instead, it decided on 6 September 1941 to take the military initiative against the United States and the European colonial powers in the Pacific, if the secret negotiations with the United States had not resulted in a settlement by 10 October 1941, or a later deadline of the end of November. Roosevelt remained resolute, and Tokyo was driven to unleash war in the Pacific. As a result of the Japanese attack on Pearl Harbor (7 December 1941) and the German declaration of war on the United States of America (11 December 1941), the United States entered a truly 'world' war, uniting the eastern and European theatres of battle. Only the Soviet Union and Japan managed to maintain the neutrality they had agreed on 13 April 1941 and which remained balanced on a knife- edge until summer 1945.

The American President intended to wage the war first and foremost against Germany, which he regarded as the most dangerous threat to America's worldwide interests. This decision is understandable and, historically, was of great significance. The fact remains, however, that Hitler's Germany and Stalin's Soviet Union were both pursuing independent, autonomous objectives which were bound to lead to war in the long term. Stalin clearly recognized this fact on the eve of the German attack on the Soviet Union, though he did not foresee the date. On 5 May 1941, the dictator spoke before the graduates of sixteen Soviet military academies of the Red Army and nine military faculties of civilian universities. In the speech, also made to the 'heads of state, . . . of the party' and of the 'supreme leadership of army and navy', he commented that the Soviet Union was not yet in a position to wage war against Germany and was therefore forced to give way to Hitler in order to gain time. According to another text of the speech, he added:[50]

If he succeeds [in the attempt to avoid war in 1941] then war with Germany will almost inevitably take place in 1942, and under much more favourable conditions, since the Red Army will then be better trained and equipped. According to the international situation the Red Army will await a German attack or seize the initiative itself, as a lasting domination of Nazi Germany in Europe would 'not be normal'.

Stalin's own war aims were extensive and had a driving force of their own; from 1940 at the latest, they provided a hostile alternative to the Nazi programme of conquest.[51] From June 1941, the Soviet Union had resisted Nazi attack with its own resources and without any significant assistance from its western allies. Thereafter, the independent territorial demands of the Soviet Union,[52] which appeared, for example, in the conversations of Molotov with Hitler and Ribbentrop on 12–13 November 1940, became linked with the manifest security needs of the country. In this way, Soviet war gains achieved spurious legitimacy as reaction to the German invasion of 22 June 1941. Even as Stalin successfully extended the boundaries of his empire using traditional power politics, he was opposed – often vainly – by the aggressive ideas of liberal world civilization emanating from the United States with their economic and cultural background. In the aftermath, the United States and the Soviet Union alone emerged as true great powers.

VI

Europe in the 1930s was no longer the regulator of *Weltpolitik* as it had been in the nineteenth century. It had long ago lost the power to organize the earth according to its will and retained only the fatal capacity to throw the world into disorder. This fact helps to explain why so much of the destruction of the international order had its origin in Europe. Events in the Far East undoubtedly had an important effect, but not a decisive one; they helped to shake the international order but did not provide the *coup de grâce*.

Only two powers, Great Britain and France, spoke out for the retention of the Paris peace treaties and struggled for a balance of power which had already been lost before the outbreak of war. Yet Britain and France waged only a half-hearted struggle for a *Staatensystem* they had established. Particularly on the British side, the policies of 'appeasement' and of 'decadence'[53] were influenced for a certain time by the bad conscience of the victors about Germany, which had been humiliated at Versailles. Both Britain and France were also affected by a '*tornade pacifiste*'[54] in their countries. Thomas Mann wrote with bitter resignation in his diary on 22 September 1938:[55] 'What a trick to raise up a Great Reich by blackmailing the pacifist maturity of others! History will sing its

praises . . . men have come so far, their enlightenment lies in pacifism:
That is the great opportunity for the lowest level, its "historic" hour.'

The revolutionary powers of the period, Germany and the Soviet Union,
were helped and encouraged by the climate of revisionism in many states
in the interwar years. They were able to overthrow the existing system and
to pulverize its claims to legitimacy between the extremes of right and
left. The war aims of the two powers were very different, but also had a
family likeness in their ambitious and far-reaching claims. Stalin, however,
adopted – at least temporarily – a defensive position. In contrast, Hitler
set in motion a dynamic *'Flucht nach vorn'* which even he could then
scarcely keep under control and which led him to unleash war against
Poland, against France and against the Soviet Union, to name only the
most important stages of his strategy.

The United States of America, which eventually came to the side of Great
Britain and the Soviet Union in the struggle against Nazi Germany, was
fighting neither for the existence of the European balance of power it
regarded as obsolete, nor for Stalin's conception of communist class rule.
Instead it was fighting for the indivisibility of world trade, of freedom and
peace which were vital to American interests. The Americans too were
pursuing a revolutionary policy in comparison with the gradualism and
compromise of the old international system. The concepts of a communist
universal class domination, of a Nazi universal racial domination, and
an American universal liberal world civilization combined to bring an
overwhelming attack to bear to the old order represented by Britain and
France in the 1920s and 1930s. The attack ultimately destroyed the old
order even though two of the revolutionary powers actually allied with
the supporters of the traditional system to defeat Germany, the most
dangerous of the revolutionary powers.

In the face of this revolutionary challenge, the defenders of the international status quo faced a very difficult situation, though not necessarily
an impossible one. They did not take the necessary steps to protect their
interests in the order they represented and thus failed to gain time to
ensure its survival and development. However, the existing international
system collapsed largely because it proved impossible to practise a divisibility of peace in co-operation with revolutionary partners, and especially
with Hitler's Germany. The attempt to practise the art of compromise
with revolution was unsuccessful. A partly understandable, but ultimately
suicidal, fear of major war also deterred Great Britain and France from
making an adequate response to the first elementary challenges to their
order. After long hesitation and resistance, they were finally forced to
rely on friends and helpers to form an unnatural coalition with them;
these powers then endeavoured to replace the existing structure with
their own very different and even hostile proposals for the shape of the
international system.

The legitimacy of the system was also lost because its supporters spent too long debating whether the diverse crises and wars of the 1930s involved acts of limited revision or unlimited expansion. They ignored a valid historical rule that power, no matter for what end it is made available, will always be used at some stage, in some way, to apply political pressure or to wage war.

It was recognized too late that such power must be faced by a counterbalance, because balance is the only foundation for stability. No adequate counterbalance was created by the adherents of the traditional balance of power. A purely sectional or partial counterweight was ineffective, since only a comprehensive balance could have permitted an appropriate ideological, economic, political and military response to the threats to the international order. In the interwar years, partly out of impotence at the superior economic strength of the Anglo-Saxon powers, the economic 'have-nots' were driven to an apparently atavistic recourse to aggression. The response of the supporters of the status quo was no more than partial. On the British side, opinion about the methods of the German challenge led to a disproportionate reliance on the deterrent power of the air force, whilst the French faith in the invulnerability of the Maginot Line had fatal results.

Such failures in understanding eventually led to major catastrophe for Britain and France, the supporters of the international order in the interwar years. Among other factors, their failure was the result of a catastrophic tendency to ignore or underestimate the totalitarian challenge and concentrate on the undoubted horrors of war, in an effort to avoid preparing for the worst or facing up to the realities of the situation. The guarantors of the Paris peace treaties perpetually doubted themselves and their task and sacrificed the legitimacy of the *Staatengesellschaft* to an uncertain and dishonourable truce with force.[56] Despite their conduct, and even because of it, they finally lost the peace of the world.

NOTES

1 On this subject see Bartlett, C. J., *The Global Conflict. The International Rivalry, 1880–1970* (London/New York: 1984), p. 107 ff; also Ross, G., *The Great Powers and the Decline of the European States System 1914–1945* (London/New York: 1983), p. 37 ff; and Marks, S., *The Illusion of Peace. International Relations in Europe 1918–1933* (London: 1976).

2 Bernstein, E., 'Die internationale Bedeutung des Wahlkampfes in Deutschland', *Die Neue Zeit* Year XI, vol. II (1892–3), p. 294.

3 Quoted in Erdmann, K. D., *Die Zeit der Weltkriege (Gebhardt. Handbuch der deutschen Geschichte)*, 9 (Stuttgart: new revised edn, 1976), p. 407.

4 Toynbee, A. J. 'Part I. The world crisis', *Survey of International Affairs* (Oxford/London: 1932), p. 1 ff.

5   Aron, R., *Frieden und Krieg. Eine Theorie der Staatenwelt* (Frankfurt-am-Main: 1963), p. 58. The quotation runs: 'The Versailles Treaty was artificial in the sense that it did not express the real relationship of forces.'

6   Kissinger, H. A., *Grossmacht Diplomatie. Von der Staatskunst Castlereaghs und Metternichs* (Frankfurt-am-Main/Berlin/Vienna: 1973), pp. 7–8. In the passage omitted, Kissinger proposes the Weimar Republic as an example of a state which was pursuing a revolutionary foreign policy towards the Versailles peace treaty. This assessment is inaccurate, as shown by Hildebrand, K., *Das Deutsche Reich und die Sowjetunion im internationalen System 1918–1932. Legitimität oder Revolution?* (Wiesbaden: 1977), p. 3 and *passim*.

7   See also the comments of Kunisch, J., *Das Mirakel des Hauses Brandenburg. Studien zum Verhältnis von Kabinettspolitik und Kriegführung im Zeitalter des Siebenjährigen Krieges* (Munich/Vienna: 1978), pp. 22–3; also the provocative remarks on balance of power and hegemony in Schroeder, P. W., *Austria, Great Britain and the Crimean War. The Destruction of the European Concert* (Ithaca, NY/London: 1972), p. 402.

8   See Thorne, C., *The Limits of Foreign Policy. The West, the League and the Far Eastern Crisis of 1931–1933* (London: 1972).

9   Quoted in Toynbee, 'The world crisis', p. 1 ff.

10 Bartlett, *Global Conflict*, p. 156: 'a passing crisis'.

11 See Ahmann, R., 'Die operative Nutzung des Nichtangriffspaktes in den europäischen Beziehungen 1922–1939' (PhD dissertation, Münster: 1985), p. 262 ff.

12 Ahmann, 'Die operative Nutzung des Nichtangriffspaktes', p. 276 ff.

13 See Ratenhof, G., *Das Deutsche Reich und die internationale Krise um die Mandschurei 1931–1933* (Frankfurt-am-Main/Berne/New York/Nancy: 1984), esp. p. 300; on German foreign policy and Far Eastern issues in general see Fox, J. P., *Germany and the Far Eastern Crisis 1931–1938. A Study in Diplomacy and Ideology* (Oxford: 1982).

14 On this assessment of the facts and links see also Adamthwaite, A. P., *The Making of the Second World War* (London/Boston, Mass./Sydney: 1977), pp. 36–7.

15 Fundamental here is Pratt, L. R., *East of Malta, West of Suez* (Cambridge/London/New York/Melbourne: 1975), p. 1 ff.

16 Quoted in Jacobsen, H.-A., 'Primat der Sicherheit, 1928–1938', in *Osteuropa-Handbuch. Sowjetunion. Aussenpolitik 1917–1955*, ed. D. Geyer (Cologne/Vienna: 1972), p. 236.

17 di Nolfo, E., 'Il revisionismo nella politica estera di Mussolini', *Il Politico* 19 (1954), p. 91, quoted in J. Petersen, *Hitler-Mussolini. Die Entstehung der Achse Berlin – Rom 1933–1936* (Tübingen: 1973), p. 7.

18 *Staatsmänner und Diplomaten bei Hitler. Vertrauliche Aufzeichnungen über Unterredungen mit Vertretern des Auslandes 1939–1941*, ed. and introduced by A. Hillgruber (Frankfurt-am-Main: 1967), no. 83: 'Aufzeichnung über die Unterredung des Führers mit Graf Oshima im Führerhauptquartier am 15 Juli 1941 von 17 bis 19 Uhr', p. 606. On the fact that the conversation had already taken place on 14 July 1944 see Hillgruber, A., *Hitlers Strategie. Politik und Kriegführung 1940–1941* (Munich: 2nd edn, 1982), afterword, p. 731. An objective formed during the war must of course be assessed critically in the sense that the normal profile of a state is frequently distorted by the burdens of war, and extreme demands are made which deviate from the normality of peacetime foreign policy. Thus, for example, British war aims, developed in 1941–2 for a future reorganization of central and east central Europe, the radicalism of which has been described by Andreas Hillgruber (Hillgruber, A., *Der Zusammenbruch im Osten 1944/45 also Problem der deutschen Nationalgeschichte und der europäischen Geschichte* (Opladen: 1985), p. 23), need to be put into perspective. In contrast, Hitler's comment reveals continuity with his 'programmatic' foreign policy and warfare, though this had been compressed in time and intensified under the impact of military developments. See Hillgruber, A., 'Der Faktor Amerika in Hitlers Strategie 1938–1941', in A. Hillgruber, *Deutsche Grossmacht–und Weltpolitik im 19. und 20. Jahrhundert* (Düsseldorf: 1977), p. 197.

19 The horrors of Japanese conduct of the war (the massacre of Nanking, 1937; medical experiments in Manchurian prison camps; attacks by Japanese soldiers on the Chinese civilian population and western prisoners of war) were genuine war crimes, but –

so far as we know – did not reach the intensity and extent of deliberate Nazi and Stalinist annihilation.

20 This assessment is necessary for the theme under discussion here ('legitimacy or revolution of the *Staatensystem* in the *interwar years* of the twentieth century'). It is important to stress that what is not under discussion is the *fundamentally different quality* of the internal constitution of the United States and the 'American way of life' in comparison with the situation in the other revolutionary powers. On the 'Manichaean' elements of American foreign policy see Craig, G. A., 'Amerikanische Aussenpolitik und Deutschland, 1919–1983. Einige überlegungen', in *Deutschland und der Westen. Vorträge und Diskussionsbeiträge des Symposions zu Ehren von Gordon A. Craig veranstatltet von der Freien Universität Berlin vom 1–3 Dezember 1983*, ed. H. Köhler (Berlin: 1984), pp. 203–4.

21 Stalin, J. W., *Werke*, Vol. 7 (Berlin: 1952), p. 11.

22 *Stalin und Hitler. Pakt gegen Europa*, ed. and introduced by J. W. Brügel. (Vienna: 1973), p. 230.

23 Hitler, A., *Mein Kampf* (Munich: 1941), p. 438.

24 See also the work of Junker, D., *Der unteilbare Weltmarkt. Das ökonomische Interesse in der Aussenpolitik der USA 1933–1941* (Stuttgart: 1975).

25 Senator Kenneth Wherry of Nebraska in 1940, quoted in T. R. B. (Strout, R. L.), 'The tarnished age', *New Republic* (26 October 1974), p. 4.

26 *Foreign Relations of the United States. Diplomatic Papers 1938*, Vol. I: *General* (Washington, DC: 1955), p. 551. On this comment of Foreign Secretary Lord Halifax, Bartlett writes, probably mindful of the fact that the Prime Minister at that stage frequently stressed the predictability of Hitler: 'Chamberlain at times said much the same.' Bartlett, *Global Conflict*, p. 200.

27 On the consequences, which characterized Franco-Soviet relations in the 1930s, see Bartel, H. W., 'Frankreich und die Sowjetunion 1938–1940. Ein Beitrag zur französichen Ostpolitik zwischen dem Münchener Abkommen und dem Ende der Dritten Republik' (PhD dissertation, Bonn: 1983).

28 Ahmann, 'Die operative Nutzung des Nichtangriffspaktes', p. 37.

29 See a summary in Hillgruber, *Hitlers Strategie*, p. 513 ff.

30 See here Hildebrand, K., 'Der Hitler-Stalin-Pakt als ideologisches Problem. Zur Benutzbarkeit des Faschismus–und Totalitarismusbegriffs', in A. Hillgruber and K. Hildebrand, *Kalkül zwischen Macht und Ideologie. Der Hitler-Stalin-Pakt: Parellelen bis heute?* (Zurich: 1980), pp. 39–40.

31 *Soviet Documents on Foreign Policy*, selected and ed. by J. Degras, Vol. III: *1933–1941* (London/New York/Toronto: 1953), p. 388 ff, esp. p. 389.

32 See Kahle, G., *Das Kaukasusprojekt der Alliierten vom Jahre 1940* (Opladen: 1973); and Lorbeer, H.-J., *Westmächte gegen die Sowjetunion 1939–1941* (Freiburg i.B.: 1975).

33 Hagglof, G., *Diplomat* (Stockholm: 1971), p. 103, quoted in Bartlett, *Global Conflict*, p. 191.

34 Carlton, D., 'Eden, Blum and the origins of non-intervention', in W. Schieder and C. Dipper (eds), *Der Spanische Bürgerkrieg in der internationalen Politik (1936–1939)* (Munich: 1976), p. 290 ff, demonstrates that this domestic motive and not the pressure of Great Britain was critical for this decision of the French government.

35 On the Polish rejections of 19 November 1938 and 26 March 1939, their foreign policy motives and their consequences, see Hillgruber, A., 'Deutschland und Polen in der internationalen Politik 1933–1939. Vortrag, gehalten auf der XVIII. deutsch-polnisch Schulbuchkonferenz am 29.5.1985 in Naugard/Pommern', manuscript.

36 On Stalin's dual-track foreign policy towards the western powers and the German Reich, pursued even during the period 1934/5–8 (policy of collective security), see the work of Allard, S., *Stalin und Hitler. Die sowjetische Aussenpolitik 1930–1941* (Berne/Munich: 1974), with which there is no quarrel on this issue.

37 Stalin, J., 'Rechenschaftsbericht an den XVIII.Parteitag über die Arbeit des KZ der KPDSU (B) am 10 März 1939', in J. Stalin, *Fragen des Leninismus* (Moscow: 1946), p. 692.

38 See also Rhodes James, R. (ed.), *Chips. The Diaries of Sir Henry Channon* (London: 1967), p. 215, 3 September 1939: 'Everyone is smiling, the weather is glorious, but

I feel that our world or all that remains of it, is committing suicide, whilst Stalin laughs and the Kremlin triumphs.'

39   See Werner, K. F., 'Deutschland und Frankreich 1936–1939', in K. Hildebrand and K. F. Werner (eds), *Deutschland und Frankreich 1936–1939* (Munich: 1981), XIX, no. 16.

40   Hillgruber, A., 'Der Hitler-Stalin-Pakt und die Entfesselung des Zweiten Weltkrieges – Situationsanalyse und Machtkalkül der beiden Pakt-Partner', *Historische Zeitschrift* 230 (1980), p. 251.

41   Headlam-Morley, Sir James, *A Memoir of the Paris Peace Conference 1919*, ed. A. Headlam-Morley, R. Bryant, A. Cienciala (London: 1972), p. 163.

42   Degras, *Soviet Documents on Foreign Policy*, pp. 388–9.

43   Lupke, H., *Japans Russlandpolitik von 1939 bis 1941* (Frankfurt-am-Main/Berlin: 1962), p. 11 ff, esp. pp. 15 and 23.

44   See also Martin, B., *Friedensinitiativen und Machtpolitik im Zweiten Weltkrieg 1939–1942* (Düsseldorf: 1974), p. 52 ff.

45   Bartel, 'Frankreich und die Sowjetunion', p. 434.

46   Brügel, *Stalin und Hitler*, p. 231.

47   See here, not least for the important Anglo-American preliminary negotiations, Hillgruber, A., *Der Zenit des Zweiten Weltkrieges Juli 1941* (Wiesbaden: 1977), p. 32 ff.

48   Hillgruber, A., *Der 2.Weltkrieg 1939–1945. Kriegsziele und Strategie der grossen Mächte* (Stuttgart/Berlin/Cologne/Mainz: 2nd revised edn, 1983), p. 82.

49   Hillgruber, *Der 2.Weltkrieg 1939–1945*, p. 82.

50   For the paraphrase from Stalin's speech see *Akten zur deutschen auswärtigen Politik 1918–1945*, Serie D, Vol. XII, 2 (Göttingen: 1969), pp. 802–3; for the extended piece see Werth, A., *Russland im Krieg 1941–1945* (Munich/Zurich: 1965), p. 107.

51   The lack of resources for research into Soviet history does not allow us to determine to what extent – apart from the ideological quality of worldwide claims to Soviet dominance – extensive power political objectives emerged in Stalin's thinking *at an early stage*. Nor is it clear, for example, how far his conversations with Eden in Moscow between 16 and 20 December 1941 proposing (later modified) a division of Germany should simply be regarded as a wartime reaction or whether they revealed some long-term continuity in his thinking. The Soviet dictator's discussions with Ambassador Cripps on 1 July 1940 and with Foreign Secretary Eden in December 1941, plus the discussions of Molotov with Ribbentrop and Hitler on 12 and 13 November 1940 and with Ribbentrop on 13 November, clearly reveal the revolutionary and ambitious objectives of Stalin; they should be seen against the background of the annexation of the Baltic states in summer 1940 (on 21 July 1940 Estonia, Latvia and Lithuania were declared Soviet republics) and the unsuccessful attempt to subjugate Finland by military methods. See also n. 18.

52   See Hillgruber, *Hitlers Strategie*, pp. 305–6.

53   Duroselle, J. B., *La Décadence, 1932–1939* (Paris: 1979).

54   Duroselle, *La Décadence*, p. 272.

55   Mann, T., *Tagebücher 1937–1939*, ed. P. de Mendelssohn (Frankfurt-am-Main: 1980), p. 293.

56   This assessment places western appeasement policy in its context within the framework of global developments, in agreement with recent works such as Duroselle (n. 53) and Adamthwaite (n. 14). It is not meant to replace the understanding of British appeasement gained through the researches of Donald Cameron Watt, which is interpreted as a 'dual policy' of willingness to make concessions and firmness in the framework of domestic and foreign policy preconditions and conditions. This assessment has been summarized and appreciated in an essay by Niedhart, G., 'Appeasement: Die britische Antwort auf die Krise des Weltreichs und des internationalen Systems vor dem Zweiten Weltkrieg', *Historische Zeitschrift* 226 (1978), p. 67 ff.

7

The German Resistance and its proposals for the political future of Eastern Europe

I
ISSUE AND PROBLEMS

The following chapter is concerned with the German Resistance and its ideas for the future of eastern Europe. Throughout, the term 'German Resistance' refers to the members of two particular groups, the Goerdeler–Beck–Hassell group and the Kreisau Circle (or 'Kreisauer'). There were of course some obvious differences on domestic and constitutional issues between the 'high conservative' representatives such as Popitz and von Hassell and the other, liberal-conservative 'notables' round Beck and Goerdeler.[1] In the sphere of foreign policy thinking, however, there was a high degree of agreement between them. Not least, all of them held fast to the idea of the national state as the basis of their approach to foreign policy, though within the framework of a Europe which was moving closer together and recalling its common ground. It therefore seems appropriate to regard this group as one unit as regards its foreign policy ideas, and to treat it accordingly.

Significant differences can also be detected within the Kreisau Circle. For example, Adam von Trott zu Solz, a diplomat by profession, was much less willing to break with the idea of the national state[2] than was Count Moltke, the central figure of the group. By this stage, commitment to structures centred on the traditional form of the national state no longer played a part in Moltke's thinking.[3]

Faced by the overriding necessity of combining to overcome tyranny, these two branches of the German Resistance sought to come together in the period 1941–4 and therefore tried to reach suitable compromises in the sphere of foreign policy. For a number of reasons, the two groups are the main focus of this chapter. The foreign policy thinking of both groups, for example, has been better researched than has yet been the case for the Communist Resistance. To a certain extent, this is due to the fact that both the Beck–Goerdeler–Hassell group and the Kreisau Circle were able to make independent proposals for the future of Germany and Europe without being dependent on a foreign power and without being

170

committed to a comparatively rigid ideological orthodoxy. As they had no ideologically predetermined expectation of the future, there was a steady exchange of ideas and arguments within the groups and constant revision of their proposals and plans. Of course, this process took place against the background of certain traditional values; however, in the field of foreign policy as elsewhere, many of these values had been called into question by contemporary experiences with Nazism and its policies of war, occupation and racial domination. In addition, even the more conservative 'notables' did not intend to limit themselves to reaction pure and simple, or to return to the foreign policy measures of the Hohenzollern monarchy, since the virtues of at least some of these had become doubtful. Instead they were endeavouring to make an assessment of the 'political situation as a whole'[4] in Europe, in what they took to be the real legacy of Bismarck. This resolve brought them face to face with a serious problem, which they were unable to solve completely; it consisted of the fact that the resistance groups were never in a position to assess the practicality and acceptability of their proposals outside Germany. Their contacts with the west were difficult and meagre, whilst those with the Soviet Union were almost impossible and also seemed of very doubtful value.[5] Not least because of these enormous difficulties, the members of the German Resistance frequently resorted to written reports on the state of their thinking and opinions. For historians the advantages are obvious, since these sources clearly reflect the plans of the various groups for a foreign policy to be pursued after the removal of Hitler.

I have no wish to imply that an investigation of the foreign policy ideas of the Communist Resistance would not be of historical interest. However, for a number of reasons, the sources are much less favourable for such a study. This fact in itself is an indication that there were other political priorities in the resistance of German communists.[6] The communist groups in Germany which actively resisted Nazism concentrated much more, if not exclusively, on their daily work of conspiratorial activity.[7] Their ideas and plans for the future issued directly from a comprehensive ideology which explained and regulated all fundamental issues. Furthermore, the practical application of those plans, particularly in foreign policy, was also dictated by an unconditional recognition of the leading role of the Soviet Union. independent proposals were regarded as unnecessary, so that all available strength could be devoted to the anti-fascist struggle. For the members of the Communist Resistance, the meaning and justification of their struggle were never in doubt; they did not suffer the uncertainties which plagued the 'bourgeois' groups. Their attitude towards foreign policy has been described by Horst Duhnke:[8] 'For the German communists swimming in the current of Soviet foreign policy, questions were answered according to the actual or suspected attitude of the Soviet Union on the future of Germany.'

On the other hand, the foreign policy ideas of the Social Democratic Resistance were clearly articulated in the Kreisau Circle because of the membership of leading Social Democrats such as Leber, Reichwein and Mierendorf in the group. Their distinctive ideas for future foreign policy came to have a considerable influence on the thinking of Count Moltke and his colleagues. In the same way, concepts of foreign policy from both the Catholic and Protestant Churches and from the trade unions were also represented in the Kreisau Circle, though to a rather lesser degree.[9] In contrast, disaffected representatives of the military, the senior bureaucracy and industry made their own foreign policy ideas known in the Beck–Goerdeler–Hassell group. Thus, with the exception of the Communist Resistance, the foreign policy ideas of the politically and socially significant groups in the 'other Germany' during the 1930s and 1940s were reflected to some extent in the two groups studied here.

Secondly, it is important to remember that the ideas of the German Resistance for eastern Europe can be understood only within the overall framework of its foreign policy ideas. The temptation to concentrate solely on proposals for the east must be resisted. Such an approach would fail to give due weight to the broad, traditional conviction of both groups that the German Reich had a special and mediating role to play in world politics. Even Adam von Trott zu Solz had a vision of a 'Germany between West and East', for example; he demanded that its policy should include a reconciliation between the 'personal principle of the West' and the '*Realprinzip* of the East'.[10] The concepts of the German Resistance were influenced by the traditional thinking of the German ruling classes since the age of Bismarck. Many Germans had come to recognize – with varying degrees of clarity – the burdens which faced the new national state; some had realized that its continued existence might depend on its acceptance of the role of junior partner of the west or the east, of Great Britain or Russia. However, others hoped that the German Reich might rise to a strong independent position between these two world powers and become the third European force. Though Bismarck himself had contemplated this idea with the very greatest caution, it later became apparent in Caprivi's plans for the conduct of foreign policy. Thereafter, the sentiment frequently developed into a vague urge for expansion. During 1914–18, it was transformed into massive war aims which at times appeared almost unlimited and were quite unacceptable to the nations of Europe.[11] The German Reich had entered into the European system of states at a late stage and remained marked by its 'incompleteness'[12] in foreign policy. Not unnaturally, this situation also preoccupied the representatives of the German Resistance. It is therefore necessary to evaluate their ideas for the future of eastern

Europe within the context of a general understanding of their proposals for a future foreign policy.

Three methods of investigation will be adopted.

(1) First, the foreign policy ideas of the Beck–Goerdeler–Hassell group and the Kreisau Circle will be described. There will be no attempt to analyse every minute detail in the development of their proposals. Instead, the fundamental foreign policy problems of the German Resistance will be discussed and the main outline of their ideas delineated.

(2) A suitable method of assessing these proposals will be discussed and a number of myths dismissed. For example, the temptation to interpret the foreign policy ideas of the Resistance in the light of postwar developments in east and west must be avoided. It is not appropriate to explain the foreign policy proposals of Stauffenberg or the Kreisau Circle as the ideas of progressive patriots who hoped to achieve an 'eastern solution', marching side by side with the Soviet Union and the oppressed foreign workers in the German Reich towards a classless society.[13] Equally, it is one-sided to claim that the proposals of the group round Beck, Goerdeler and Hassell pointed the way to European unification[14] of the kind that has occurred in postwar Western Europe in the form of the EEC. The categories of assessment then in operation were different. The thinking of these resistance members, particularly as regards their idea of the national state and their commitment to European perspectives, must be assessed against the foreign policy traditions of the German Reich from Bismarck, through Caprivi, Bethmann Hollweg and Ludendorff, to Stresemann and Brüning. Moreover, an investigation of the reactions of other nations to these proposals will do much to reveal the degree of relevance and practicability they possessed. Finally, the plans of the German Resistance must be compared with Hitler's own programme in the field of foreign policy, war, occupation and race.

(3) Against this background, the ideas of the German Resistance for eastern Europe must be examined more closely. Their similarities to and differences from Nazi policy in east central and eastern Europe must be described and a careful comparison made with the 'principles' of Hitler's '*Ostpolitik*'. Finally there will be an examination of the proposals of the Resistance for a basic structure of international politics. It will become clear how much these plans differed from Nazi rule in Europe, in both its current and prospective form.

II

1 The ideas of the German Resistance for the future of foreign policy
Both groups in the German Resistance were deeply concerned with the problem of the national state and/or the European orientation of future

German foreign policy. Their responses to the problem, however, were different. By and large, the 'notables' remained committed to the traditional European national state and the accepted system of international politics. When contemplating the form of the German Reich in Europe, they therefore regarded the Little German national state created by Bismarck as the basis of future foreign policy. In the words of Ulrich von Hassell at a time when Germany was under increasing threat during the second half of the war, the notables were anxious 'to save at least the rudiments of the Bismarck Reich'.[15] The European dimension in the foreign policy of the circle round Beck, Goerdeler and von Hassell reflected their own view of power politics and was also a response to economic calculations. The notables believed that the best chance of survival for Germany and Europe lay in the creation of an economic and political *Grossraum* in which the Reich – as Herman Graml has pointed out[16] – would function as a force for European order. They continued to demand revision of the Versailles treaty by the great powers and to claim that the German Reich would become a force for order and stability as the leading power on the continent. Throughout the 1930s and even, with certain limitations, during the Second World War, the representatives of the Beck–Goerdeler–Hassell group maintained their demand for the re-establishment of the 'borders of 1914'[17] for the German national state. Indeed, they also clung to Greater German traditions and even took account of Hitler's territorial expansion by advocating the incorporation of Austria and the Sudetenland.

Apart from territorial demands and proposals, they hoped to establish continental Europe under German leadership as the 'third force' between Britain and the Soviet Union, the world powers on the periphery of the continent. Their ideas were based on the assumption that Britain and its empire had an excellent chance of survival. In fact, the notables believed that the change from empire into commonwealth would actually strengthen British power and saw the process as a model for the future of a continental Europe they wished to create.[18] They failed to recognize adequately the power shift within the western world, in which the United States was taking over the dominant role from a British Empire in retreat. Both Hitler and Stalin recognized this development, of historic significance in international politics, more clearly than the group round Beck, Goerdeler and von Hassell.[19]

The Soviet Union itself was regarded with the utmost mistrust and hostility by the notables on the grounds of its ideological orientation and domestic politics. Indeed, they were so alarmed by the potential power of the Soviet Union that they believed its very existence would require defence measures by a German-led Europe, which would include a Polish national state in the east of the continent.[20] However, the long-term goal remained 'to include Russia gradually in a European combination'.[21]

Goerdeler, co-author of these ideas in the document 'The goal' written in 1941–2, certainly did not advocate a military intervention against the Soviet Union. He had already warned urgently against military attacks on Russia, as these might 'call into action unsuspected national forces'.[22] Strongly influenced by economic considerations and his faith in a liberal-capitalist order, Goerdeler seems to have assumed that the communist economic system would collapse of its own accord because it was based on unnatural premises. In addition, he may have hoped to draw the Soviet Union gradually back into the capitalist system by means of its increasing ties and involvement with foreign economies. This notion, which was also at the root of Anglo-American offers of co-operation with the Soviet Union after both world wars, was doomed to failure because it did not recognize the primacy of political objectives for the Soviet Union. Apart from a number of territories which were to be ruled directly in line with revisionist and Greater German tradition, the notables intended that the German Reich, as the leading power in Europe between the two world powers, should influence the affairs of Europe in an informal way. They were thus adhering to an approach which had clear precedents in modern German history. The 'moderates' within the Wilhelmine elite and the group around Reich Chancellor Bethmann Hollweg had been committed to it; after his departure the tradition had been maintained by Secretary of State von Kühlmann and had then reappeared in the thinking of Stresemann, although in quite different historical circumstances. Unlike the Third Army High Command during the First World War, the notables were not planning to achieve their foreign policy ideas by military occupation.[23] On the contrary; Beck, Goerdeler and von Hassell were deeply hostile to thinking and conduct of this kind. The diplomat Ulrich von Hassell emphasized that Bismarck had thought in European terms and had always hoped to maintain political moderation.[24] They felt committed to this foreign policy tradition, and intended to follow it; and Goerdeler's positive judgements on Stresemann's national policy of revision, which he regarded as successful, should also be seen in this light.[25] Members of the group were determined to respect other national cultures, traditions and states. Nevertheless, they were convinced that the German Reich would still have a natural leadership role in Europe[26] – not as a right to brutal domination, but as a paternalistic role which would fall to the country as the first power within the European system of states. They defined the obligations of the Reich as follows:[27]

[Its] central position, numerical strength and great capacity *guarantee to the German people the leadership* of the European bloc, *if* it does not ruin this by unreasonableness or by a mania for power. It is stupid and arrogant to speak of a German master race. It is foolish to demand respect for one's own national honour and independence and to deny it to others. The nation will grow into the leadership of Europe that respects even the small nations and does not attempt to guide their destinies with brutal force. The impartial viewpoint must be decisive. Legitimate interests must be balanced skilfully and farsightedly.

There is a great difference between Hitler's contemptuous dismissal of the 'rubbish of small states' (*Kleinstaatengerümpel*)[28] in Europe and the comparatively moderate attitude of the notables. Indeed, if one accepts Hermann Heimpel's view that 'historically ... nation and Europe [are] not opposites'[29] and that the existence of nations is an intrinsic feature of European history, then it becomes clear that the notables were fundamentally determined to respect this European tradition whilst Hitler was attempting to destroy it.

The patriots in the German Resistance had been driven to take their stand by the exceptional situation of the Hitler dictatorship and the appalling pressures of the war. Yet, at root, the notables were actually addressing the old problem of the incompleteness of the German national state, a view first articulated by Max Weber in 1895.[30] According to this analysis, the *kleindeutsch* national state was doomed to discontent over its role as junior partner of one of the two world powers on the periphery of the continent. Prussia-Germany, as created by Bismarck, was thus fundamentally never satisfied; it was always both less and more than a national state.[31] From time to time, internal dynamics and foreign policy decisions led it to aim for the foreign policy leadership of Europe in an attempt to prevent the Reich from sinking to the position of a second-ranking power.[32] It was this vision of the future which the notables planned to achieve, in the interests of their nation and with a sense of responsibility towards the interests of Europe as they conceived them.

In May 1943 Goerdeler wrote a memorandum on these lines, the contents of which were intended for the British government. In his view, the new Europe should include a re-created Poland stretching as far as the eastern border of 1938, together with Finland and a 'completely free' and independent Czechoslovakia as part of a 'European community of interest and culture'. 'Among its members', argued Goerdeler, 'there must never again be war.'[33] The notables were scarcely aware how hostile the reaction to such plans would be. Opposition was inevitable, from the medium and smaller states of Europe as well as Britain and France, with whom the Reich hoped to co-operate as arbitrators. It was in fact very doubtful whether German leadership of Europe in any form was acceptable to the other European states, let alone the high level of leadership proposed by the notables. For example, the notables hoped earnestly for co-operation with Britain as part of a 'western solution' which would prevent a Soviet advance to central Europe in the course of the war. They failed to understand that the considerable differences between the foreign policy concepts of the liberal-conservative Resistance and the racial *Grossraum* plans of Hitler were not clearly recognized and appreciated in Britain.[34] The British leadership increasingly came to regard the plans of the notables, as well as the conduct of Hitler, as incompatible with the existence of the European order Great Britain hoped to re-establish. Thus Sir Robert Vansittart's assessment of Goerdeler's foreign policy ideas in 1938, initially controversial, was gradually accepted within the British government:[35] 'As you are probably both aware,' he informed his colleagues in the Foreign Office, Sir Alexander Cadogan and Sir Orme Sargent, following a conversation with Goerdeler in September 1938,

> I have known Dr Goerdeler personally and for some time. I have also for some time suspected that he was merely a stalking-horse for German *military* expansion, and by military expansion I mean the expansionist ideas of the German army as contrasted with those of the Nazi Party. There is really very little difference between them. The same sort of ambitions are sponsored by a different body of men, and that is about all...Do not trust Dr Goerdeler except as an occasional informant. He is quite untrustworthy, and he is in with the wrong kind of person and mind because his own mind is wrong...I do not count Dr Goerdeler as a German moderate.

Although the boundaries between the foreign policy objectives of the notables and the programme of Hitler are obvious today, they were much less apparent to the powers engaged in war with Germany. The British government, and then the United States government, became convinced that Hitler's plans for Europe and the European ideas of the liberal-conservative Resistance were both unacceptable. Yet the notables themselves never seem to have doubted the acceptability of their proposals. This failure was partly a consequence of the steady increase in the strength of the German Reich until 1941–2. It must be emphasized that Goerdeler never rejoiced at Hitler's successes in war, as other critics of the dictator did for a time after the defeat of France in 1940; moral imperatives ensured that he firmly rejected both Hitler's Reich and its foreign policy triumphs alike.[36] Nevertheless, it may have been an awareness of the massive increase in German power which made the notables regard German leadership as natural and even necessary in Europe, though it should be of a completely different quality to that of Nazi Germany.

Their belief in the need for German leadership in Europe explains the anxious desire of the Goerdeler–Beck–Hassell group to prevent the continuation of the war until the total defeat of Germany; in their view, the core of the Reich was to be maintained at all costs.[37] Here they were in fundamental disagreement with Moltke. He regarded a military defeat of the German Reich as a necessary prelude to a complete reorganization of international politics with the aim of transforming the traditional system of power politics into an order of 'European domestic politics'.[38]

For their part, the notables believed that the lasting antagonism between Great Britain and the Soviet Union was a vital precondition for the success of their concepts.[39] It is therefore understandable that the main outlines of their foreign policy ideas – despite alterations to individual details between the 1930s and 1944–5 – hardly changed at all. Their speculations and convictions on the Anglo-Russian or Anglo-Soviet hostility were rooted in the foreign policy tradition of Prussia-Germany and continued its errors. False assumptions about the strength of Anglo-Russian antagonism had misled the statesmen of Wilhelmine Germany[40] and had also been at the heart of Hitler's futile proposals for an alliance with Britain.[41] Certainly, political hostility between Britain and Russia, and then between Britain and the Soviet Union, was a vital factor in world politics in the nineteenth and twentieth centuries; since 1917, moreover, it had been heightened by an ideological dimension. However, the notables relied too heavily on the hope that antagonism towards the Soviet Union would persuade Britain to accept and welcome the Reich as a force for order on the European continent. They simply failed to take into account that, particularly after the fall of Chamberlain, the British government saw the German Reich as a greater danger than the Soviet Union.[42] British doubts about the intentions of Stalin in the second half of the war did not change this conviction. With hindsight, it is possible to detect errors of judgement in the British analysis[43] and to point out the differences between Hitler's European policies and the ideas of the notables. Nevertheless, it is important to remember that in the 1940s, the British and the Americans regarded the German Reich – even under the control of the 'other Germany' – as more of a threat than the Stalinist Soviet Union.[44]

Yet there is no disputing the moderation and deep sense of responsibility which characterized the thinking and proposed conduct of the group round Beck, Goerdeler and von Hassell, particularly in comparison with the policies of Hitler. The notables did not wish to evade the rules of international politics and did not demand fundamental changes in the international situation. Responsibility and moderation were to be the keynotes of their foreign policy. These facts become particularly clear on closer examination of their views on war and peace as the extreme values of political activity in the interplay of relationships in domestic and foreign policy.

Of course, the notables did not renounce war as the ultimate means of policy.[45] Unlike Hitler, however, they never regarded war as the law of motion of states. In their eyes, such a view seemed to endanger the existence of the Reich just as much as the revolutionary upheaval of the existing social order in Europe to which it could easily lead. Their assessment of the relationship between external war and internal revolution reveals further parallels with the thinking of Bethmann Hollweg, who did not totally reject war but warned against it at least partly because of its affinity with social revolution.[46] The assessment of war as a means of policy by the Goerdeler–Beck–Hassell group, and its awareness of the danger of internal revolution, contrasted strongly with a powerful foreign policy tradition in Wilhelmine Germany, whose adherents had hoped to conjure away internal conflicts by means of external war.[47]

An examination of the foreign policy concepts of the notables must be concluded with the admission that their horizons were fundamentally 'Eurocentric'. They were almost completely indifferent to colonial revolutionary liberation movements and attempts to achieve nationhood. They regarded the colonies in Africa and in East Asia from the perspective of their own membership of the 'white race' and its requirements for raw materials.[48] At that time, this attitude extended well beyond Germany and appeared in summer 1940, for example, in the peace initiative of Albert Plesman, the director of the Dutch airline KLM.[49]

The representatives of the Kreisau Circle had grave doubts about the purpose and desirability of the traditional system of European politics. They had little faith in the ideas of the notables, which the latter hoped to realize through a renaissance of the diplomacy of Bismarck. Moltke and his colleagues saw the existence of European nationalism as the fundamental evil which had repeatedly been responsible for driving Europe into war. Consequently, members of the Kreisau Circle had no interest in seeing German hegemony replaced by French hegemony, and then again by German.[50] Instead they hoped to replace the driving forces of nationalism, which they saw as fundamentally objectionable, once and for all. The political convictions of the Social Democrats in the Kreisau Circle did much to give direction to this advocacy of a radical future foreign policy and of international change. For example, Julius Leber had made the following diagnosis as early as 1928:[51] 'Europe suffers ... from a condition which is no longer suited to the world: from nationalism ... it is high time that politics begins to draw [proper] conclusions and throws the thing people call nationalism overboard.' Count Moltke optimistically believed that the end of nationalism was already in sight, since 'nationalism ... [had] proved itself to be a watchword which was no longer attractive' – 'as in France, so in Germany'.[52] Indeed, Moltke advocated the creation of a supranational European order. He had strong convictions about the relationship between the individual and the state and about the relationship between states:[53]

All solutions which followed the loss of faith as a unifying bond have proved to be so many distinguishing marks to set men against men. The subjects of a prince have become the natural enemies of the subjects of another prince, the members of one nation the natural enemies of the members of every other nation, the members of one national tradition [*Volkstum*] the natural enemies of members of every other national tradition. Under this development, Europe is breaking to pieces; it is the historic task of this war to overcome these conflicts and at least to re-establish a unified conception for Europe; the necessary consequence of this hope is the united sovereignty over Europe and the defeat of all individual claims to sovereignty.

Understandably, the proposal had not been worked out in all its details. Nevertheless, the plan for a Europe of equal rights, organized in small units in which border conflicts would become marginal, was aimed at achieving a European co-operation of equals. Unlike the notables, therefore, the members of the Kreisau Circle were not planning a world political condominium of the mighty. Within the circle, there were different assessments of the relationship between the national state and Europe. Thus Adam von Trott zu Solz, as a diplomat, was well aware of the strength and advantages of the European national state though he was never the remotest sort of hidebound nationalist; for instance, he was prepared to accept that it might be necessary for Germany to cede territory, such as 'East Prussia as compensation to Poland'.[54] Moltke, on the other hand, had distanced himself completely from the idea of the national state and was comparatively reconciled to territorial losses by Germany. His Silesian homeland, for example, would certainly be assigned to Poland.[55] In general, the members of the Kreisau Circle were committed to the vision of a European confederation, whose form has been described by the Dutch historian Ger van Roon in his book on the *New Order in the Resistance*:[56]

Moltke, constantly exchanging ideas with his colleagues, was deeply concerned with the issue. In his estate there are three versions of a memorandum 'Starting point, objectives and tasks' from the year 1941. According to this memorandum, the new Europe is to take the form of a confederation. Its borders are formed by the Atlantic, the Mediterranean and Black Seas, by the eastern border of Bessarabia, the old Poland, the former Balkan states and Finland. Alongside the creation of a united European sovereignty, the entire continent is to be divided into small non-sovereign structures, each with ties with others. As examples Moltke mentions the Scandinavian states, Baltic states, east European states, German states, Balkan states, west European states, Mediterranean states etc. Britain and Russia are not counted as part of the European confederation. In order to set up an effective counterweight to the great structure of the confederation, the individual states are to be built up as self-governing bodies with extensive responsibilities; there should thus be a development from below.

Without dealing with the details of this proposal, a number of points are apparent. It is not entirely fair to deny the members of the Kreisau Circle 'their own more or less definable foreign policy programme', as Gerhard Ritter has done.[57] Ritter was a representative of the 'realistic' school of international politics.[58] Consequently, he found it almost impossible to recognize the demands of the Kreisau Circle as genuine proposals for a future foreign policy. After all, their plans were based largely on ideas, faith and trust; they aimed for a fundamental transformation of the European tradition of nation states and power politics. As Raymond Aron concluded some years later in a general context, 'to condemn power politics means condemning the entire course of political history'.[59] Nevertheless, the proposals of the Kreisau Circle cannot be dismissed simply as part of the European tradition of radical protest against every form of foreign policy pursued by national states. Hostility of this kind had led the Cobdenites in nineteenth-century England to demand that foreign policy should be renounced altogether as it was nothing more than a sinecure of the idle nobility;[60] and in the twentieth century, the Russian revolutionaries had followed the example of Wilhelm Leibknecht and maintained that 'the best foreign policy' was 'none at all'.[61] The thoughts of the Kreisau Circle on the future international organization of the states were more sophisticated than that, even though they adhered to the 'idealistic' tradition of international politics,[62] assuming that the urge to power and competition could be left behind as features of European history and that a 'world commonwealth'[63] could eventually be established on earth. Members of the Kreisau Circle believed that their new social order would produce a new type of human being; as a Christian, this new man would be committed to the common good above all else and, as a member of a territorial unit without sovereignty, he would also be prepared to submit to the judgement of supranational arbitration.[64] Thus, their thinking was not concerned mainly with problems of foreign policy revision at all. Instead, they sought the salvation of Europe by means of fundamental internal reforms which would revolutionize the traditional foreign policy of Europe – indeed would abolish it. At the same time, their approach to a 'solution of the colonial question' remained conventional.[65]

The convictions of the Kreisau Circle were based on a philosophical and Christian outlook, which persuaded them to attempt to escape the empiricism of traditional history of the international order. Their opinions certainly come close to the 'idealistic' understanding of politics, whilst the plans of the notables round Goerdeler, Beck and von Hassell should be reckoned as part of the 'realistic' school.

When co-operation between the two groups commenced at the end of 1941, the foreign policy concepts of the notables and the Kreisau Circle began to influence each other. The two groups gradually reached a compromise position which held that, for the foreseeable future, Germany must remain a Reich. We can thus accept Hermann Graml's view that 'the intellectual world of the Kreisauer was virtually re-charged in the national sense'.[66] By and large, this co-operation helped to make the convictions of the Kreisauer appear more 'realistic' and the demands of the notables more 'European'. Nevertheless, the vision of the future of Europe proposed by the Kreisau Circle must have remained strangely alien to the rest of Europe. In contrast, the European concepts of the notables were never more remote from the rest of Europe than at the time 'they began to think in European thought'.[67] Whilst the Kreisauer were concentrating on a European future, the notables remained committed to the European past. Neither group appears to have assessed contemporary conditions in Europe from the vantage point of the embattled nations and their requirements. At this stage, therefore, we must consider what what standards and criteria we can use to assess the foreign policy ideas of the two groups.

2 Terms of assessment

The ideas of the group round Beck, Goerdeler and von Hassell should be regarded as part of a tradition of German foreign policy which had also been followed by Bethmann Hollweg and Stresemann *mutatis mutandis*. In particular, it influenced their acceptance of the principle of the national state. The notables characteristically intended Germany's leading role in Europe to be achieved largely informally, by economic means. As far as possible, they hoped to take into consideration 'the political situation as a whole' and to act in agreement with Europe rather than in hostility to it.

In general, the members of the Goerdeler–Beck–Hassell group were attempting to solve the problem which had accompanied the *kleindeutsch* national state since its foundation; in foreign policy, they hoped to put an end to its 'incompleteness' and to give it a secure future. As part of this process, adopting much the same principles as Stresemann,[68] they insisted on an independent role for Germany between east and west. As the statesmen of Prussia-Germany had done at the turn of the century, the notables overestimated the antagonism between the two world powers of Britain and the Soviet Union, which they regarded as almost irreconcilable. They failed to recognize that, whatever their political and ideological differences, these two powers were being drawn inexorably together by events on the continent, many of which had been set in train by Germany and concerned the problem of hegemony.[69] This same fatal miscalculation affected the thinking of the notables and considerably reduced their prospects of success. Certainly, the men round Goerdeler, Beck and von Hassell wanted to establish their vision of Europe by means of a comprehensive agreement with the other great powers and with full, universal acceptance of international law. Nevertheless, neither the major powers nor the smaller states of Europe could accept the Reich as leader of their continent, even under the control of the notables.

In the Europe of the 1930s and 1940s – even in the western parliamentary democracies – it was normal practice to think in terms of traditional power politics. Furthermore, considerable changes seemed possible within the existing system; for example, the British government of Neville Chamberlain had been prepared to accept substantial territorial gains by Hitler's Germany in the attempt to avoid war, which would threaten the international order and the social fabric. Thus far, the notables may actually have felt themselves in harmony with the British Conservatives; both were committed to the traditional system of national states, both were anxious to prevent social revolution at national and international level, neither wanted to unleash revolutionary upheaval in the international system in order to evade internal reforms. Nevertheless, it was these same categories of power politics which almost inevitably led to renewed misunderstandings and hostility between the notables and the British government. Whilst the Goerdeler–Beck–Hassell group thought their demands were in accordance with the interests of Britain and Europe, the government of Churchill regarded them as incompatible with British requirements and with those of the medium and small states of Europe. The notables believed that, in view of the Soviet threat, German leadership of the continent would be advantageous to Britain, especially as it would be established in agreement with Great Britain. However, at that time German domination was perceived by the British as an even greater danger than the Soviet Union. In consequence, British statesmen increasingly identified Hitler's *Grossraum* ideas with the foreign policy notions of the notables. The course of international politics was seriously affected by the failure of the notables to convince the British and Americans, on whose help they depended for the realization of their plans, that they were offering a genuine alternative to Hitler.

As regards the more 'idealistic' ideas of the Kreisau Circle, Hermann Graml has already indicated[70] that these fitted into a German foreign policy tradition that was first clearly expressed after Germany's defeat in the First World War. There is a connection with Bethmann Hollweg's criticism of the legacy of the European national state and imperialism,[71] which was extended in the 1920s by his colleague and adviser for many years, Kurt Riezler.[72] The Kreisauer thus revived Bethmann Hollweg's fundamental doubts about 'imperialism, nationalism and economic materialism'[73] in modern Europe; they emphasized the importance of impersonal and supranational forces as causes of the wretched conditions of international politics. However, it is justifiable to ask whether, in assuming a compulsion and an inevitability in the system, they were perhaps underestimating the degree of personal and national freedom of manoeuvre which continued to exist. The Kreisauer were condemning the basic principles of the international system, assuming that it would almost inevitably lead to war, revisionist demands and struggles for hegemony. Such beliefs had a great influence on Moltke's demand that there should no resistance to the military defeat of the German Reich. In this way, beginning with Germany, he felt that a general moral consciousness might emerge; ultimately, the intimate rules of international politics might be abolished – indeed, the history and conditions of the traditional system might finally be escaped.[74]

The 'idealistic' mentality of the Kreisau Circle must also be put into a wider European context and seen as part of a trend of radical attempts to reorient foreign policy. Such sentiments had been expressed at the Hague conferences during the Age of Imperialism and had survived in the thinking of European socialists and members of the various peace movements. Subsequently, in the changed atmosphere after the end of the First World War, they were rapidly overtaken and supplanted by *Realpolitik*. It is easy to believe that the 'idealistic' foreign policy concepts of the Kreisau Circle must have struck the British Tories as unworkable and alarming,[75] just as they rejected the demands of the notables as too extensive.

It was inevitable that the concepts of the two resistance groups would be compared with Hitler's programmatic policies on foreign affairs, war and racial issues. Though the proposals of the resistance groups were initially very different, each was offering a qualitative break with the policy of Hitler. This is obvious of the Kreisau Circle, but it is also true of the proposals of the notables. Whilst they considered war to be disastrous, it was the law of motion of Hitler's 'programme'. The notables saw themselves as the heirs to the foreign policy tradition of Bismarck, Bethmann Hollweg and Stresemann and aspired to the leadership of the Reich within the framework of Europe. In contrast, Hitler made only a show of following the traditions of German foreign policy whilst really breaking with them; in truth, he wanted to destroy the Europe of the nations and replace it by a Nazi *Grossraum*. Whilst the notables were anxious to avoid revolutionary upheavals in both domestic and foreign policy, Hitler's ultimate goal was a total, racial reorganization of Germany, Europe and the world. Though the foreign policy demands of the notables appeared unacceptably harsh to the nations of east central Europe, for example, and though they shared the traditional tendency of German foreign policy by advocating a different treament of west and east European issues,[76] they had nothing in common with Hitler's policies of occupation, resettlement and racial domination in eastern Europe. The notables were protected from such atrocity by the rationality in their plans and also because of their moral outlook, their (Christian) faith and their respect for the traditions of European culture and the European national state. It is in the light of these facts that the specific ideas of the German Resistance for the political future of eastern Europe must be examined.

3 The ideas of the German Resistance for the political future of Eastern Europe

For the members of the Kreisau Circle, the major priority was not to provide precise solutions to territorial problems, since they advocated the establishment of a Europe organized in supranational self-governing entities. However, as far as the relations of Germany with east central and eastern Europe were concerned, their attitude was dominated by a sentiment expressed by Moltke towards Poland – that is, by a willingness to 'make amends' ('*Wiedergutmachung*').[77] In 1930 Paulus von Husen, later to become a member of the circle, made a comment which must have sounded almost revolutionary to broad sections of the ruling classes and the population at large:[78] 'The existence of Poland and good relations between it and Germany are a European necessity.' The Kreisau Circle remained committed to this view, which was strengthened by the experiences of the Second World War. Moltke's own assessment of the Polish problem was further influenced by a strong feeling of contrition. For the members of the Kreisau Circle, there was never any doubt that a free Polish state would be re-established. Moreover, its representatives became convinced that it would be necessary for Germany to make considerable territorial concessions to Poland, though it would remain desirable that 'the eastern border ... of the old Poland' be re-established.[79] They were also certain that a free Czechoslovak state should be restored.[80] As far as Austria was concerned, the Kreisauer hoped that it would join the Reich voluntarily, thereby creating a counterbalance to the Prussian traditions of Germany.[81] Unlike the notables, who had certainly intended that border issues should be solved at least partly by the great powers, the Kreisauer were ready to demonstrate their contrition and generosity by means of reparations to the states damaged by Germany. During discussions among leading representatives of the German Resistance in June 1944, Julius Leber appears to have regarded the demand for the borders of 1914 as unrealistic; in contrast, he thought it appropriate to 'renounce [claims to] East Prussia, Alsace-Lorraine, the Sudetenland etc'.[82] With the exception of Moltke, sections of the Kreisau Circle – including its Social Democratic members – apparently believed for some time that Germany could obtain or retain the borders of 1933 or 1937. This demand, in view of military developments and an increasing sense of contrition among the Resistance, was then abandoned. Hermann Graml has investigated the willingness of the Kreisau Circle to make territorial concessions.[83] He argues that it derived from the sociopolitical stance of its members, which made them attach less importance to the development of power and strength in foreign policy. Whilst his assessment is basically correct as far as the Kreisau Circle is concerned, it also requires supplementing. Willingness to reform in domestic affairs and the development of strength in foreign policy are by no means mutually exclusive and can even be mutually supportive. Thus, it should not be argued that the notables were hoping to block domestic and social change by holding firm to traditional conventions and demands in foreign policy. This was not their intention, it did not reflect their view of themselves and it underestimates their willingness to adjust to changed domestic circumstances.[84]

As far as the attitude of the Kreisau Circle to the Soviet Union was concerned, its members were deeply suspicious of the Stalinist dictatorship. Like the Goerdeler–Beck–Hassell group, its members did not intend to include Russia in the European confederation. However, they were careful not to fall prey to phobias about the Soviet Union which might have obstructed the path to friendly co-operation. The Kreisau Circle never made the mistake of identifying regime and people in the Soviet Union.[85] Moreover, its members did not adopt hostility to that country as a basic principle, of the kind which was the measure and goal of the foreign policy of Hitler. They also did not support the idea of political co-operation between the Reich and Soviet Russia, of the sort adopted during the revisionist foreign policy of the Weimar Republic.[86]

When we consider the foreign policy proposals of the notables for eastern Europe, clear differences in the foreign policy thinking of Goerdeler and Hitler emerged at a very early stage. They were already visible in 1934, in a controversy over German policy towards the east, which also revealed much broader differences of principle in the assessment of the international situation.[87] Despite all the revisions which the notables demanded, they generally accepted the legitimacy of a Europe of various sovereign nations. In contrast, Hitler was attempting to destroy Europe and the international status quo.

Shortly before he became Reich Commissioner for Price Control on 5 November 1934, Goerdeler included a memorandum on the economic situation as part of a document 'to the German Reich Chancellor Adolf Hitler'.[88] His criticisms included Hitler's new policy towards Poland, which had been expressed in the Non-Aggression Pact of 26 January 1934.[89] With this pact, Hitler had abandoned the traditional line of German policy towards eastern Europe and introduced its 'abrupt reorientation'.[90] He had broken with the foreign policy of the Weimar Republic, aimed at an anti-Polish policy pursued together with the Soviet Union (and possibly also with France); instead he had decided – for the time being – to join Poland in an anti-Soviet (and possibly also an anti-French) policy. Goerdeler was bitterly critical of this change. He continued to demand a nationally acceptable solution to the border issues in east central Europe, since he regarded the Polish Corridor as a 'thorn in the flesh' of the German 'economy and honour' and believed that the problem must be solved in order to secure the existence of the Reich. He therefore advocated a 'struggle for liberation', for which the support of 'reliable peoples' – the western powers – would be required. Goerdeler's views were fully in line with the foreign policy tradition of the Weimar Republic, which he recommended should be pursued further. He rejected Hitler's change of course in foreign policy, though conceding that the agreement might be only a temporary expedient to provide freedom of manoeuvre to rearm.

At this early stage, Hitler's dramatic change of course and Goerdeler's reaction revealed fundamental differences in the ideas of the two protagonists about foreign policy and the east. Hitler hoped that his tactical move towards Poland would weaken and isolate France, thus giving him room to develop an expansionist foreign policy which would eventually be directed against the Soviet Union.[91] The manoeuvre caused great alarm in the German Foreign Office, but can be understood only against the background of his revolutionary foreign policy as a whole. Hitler was aiming to eliminate Russia/the Soviet Union, which had belonged to the European order of states since the eighteenth century, and to break it into its 'original historic parts' (or so he described it in a conversation with envoy Oshima two years later).[92] Hitler's temporary alliance with Poland went hand in hand with his resolute anti-Soviet policy and had as its eventual aim the overthrow of the international status quo, the elimination of the Soviet Union as a member of the European order and the destruction of the status of France as the leading military power in Europe.[93] In contrast, Goerdeler's nationalist, anti-Polish foreign policy was of a completely different quality. Despite or even because of his strongly anti-Polish attitude, and quite unlike Hitler, he never questioned the existence of France as a great power or of the Soviet Union as a power on the periphery of the continent. In effect, he continued to accept the traditional principles of Germany's negative Polish policy.[94] The tradition was a bitter one for Poland, but might at least have the function of maintaining the peace among the great powers and guaranteeing the European status quo. Goerdeler never questioned the existence of the international system itself. He always demanded gradual changes to the system in the form of revisions and never remotely called for the destruction of the traditional order of states.

The notables were generally committed to this approach in the east. They believed that revisions were compatible with the general situation in Europe, but were unable to recognize that the attitude of the Poles and the British would be very different to their own. Despite the vast difference between the political plans of Hitler for the east and those of the notables, Richard Breyer was correct to claim that 'Goerdeler could not under any circumstances bring himself to accept the abandonment of German claims for revision of the borders of Versailles';[95] it was his tragedy that it was Hitler who fulfilled the demands for revision of Germany's eastern borders. Breyer also commented perceptively on Goerdeler's proposals for the eastern borders and eastern policy of a future German Reich, which he hoped would function as a genuinely peaceful power at the head of a European federation of states:[96] 'Certainly, the heart of Goerdeler's plan must damage Polish interests, even though his "peaceful settlement" differed fundamentally from Hitler's method and he had long since left behind him the militant attitude he had adopted in the years shortly after Versailles.'

Of course, the notables intended to allow Poland and a Czech Republic to be re-established. Nevertheless, with some amendments, they continued to demand the eastern borders of 1914 for Germany and also believed that it would be necessary to keep Austria and the Sudetenland in the Reich. Though their willingness to compromise on western territories and border issues became clear in the course of the war, their attitude towards Poland remained constant[97]. Goerdeler thought that the defence of the eastern border of Poland would be worth every military effort by the German Reich, but his proposals took the status of Germany as a great power in east central and eastern Europe for granted and were inevitably regarded as unacceptable and inappropriate by the other states involved.

It is vital to emphasize that the notables never intended to continue the foreign policy thinking of the Third Army Command[98] and of Hitler; they had no wish to eliminate Russia/the Soviet Union as a partner in the European system and they firmly rejected Hitler's racial policies. Nevertheless, the course of events is clear: long before the First World War, the feeling had grown in Europe that the existence of the German Reich was incompatible with the needs and interests of the continent; in such a situation, the plans of the notables appeared closely linked with those of Hitler in the eyes of the world. In view of the vital differences between the ideas of the Goerdeler–Beck–Hassell group and the foreign, occupation and racial policies of Hitler, such a development is difficult to accept today. Nevertheless, the extensive territorial demands of the notables in east central Europe were quite unacceptable to the British. And for a nation like Poland which was suffering so greatly, there was little credibility in the attempt of the notables to advocate traditional power politics whilst claiming that they had nothing to do with the racial policies of Hitler. In east central Europe, traditional power politics and new racial policies were perceived as two sides of a coin.

Finally, the ideas of the two groups in the German Resistance for a postwar order must be investigated more closely. Both worked out their approach as part of their conflict with Hitler's dictatorship, but whilst the notables saw Nazism largely as a perversion of and a break with German and European traditions, the Kreisau Circle tended to condemn it as the almost inevitable result of the traditional structure of the European *Staatensystem*.

III

The American historian L. L. Farrar, in a stimulating book on the 'Short-War Illusion'[99] of the European Great Powers before and at the start of the First World War, argued that Europe had been in a condition of power-political deadlock since 1914. The *entente* was always capable of keeping the Reich within bounds, but was never able to deal with the German threat once and for all. For its part, the German Reich had enough power at its disposal to destroy the *Staatensystem* which had existed until 1914, but was not capable of dominating it or replacing it by a new order. This situation, it appeared to Farrar, would probably lead Europe into another conflict and destroy its dominance in the world once and for all. The deadlock of 1914, he concluded, was already pointing the way to the end of the traditional system in 1945.[100]

Such a conclusion is now possible, with the benefit of hindsight. Yet in the years between 1914 and 1945 there had been many attempts to restore the European system of states, to re-establish and revitalize it through change or revision, or to transform it through moral endeavour and give it an entirely new quality.[101] The foreign policy ideas of the Resistance can fairly be regarded as German contributions to these efforts.

The uncompromising demands of the Kreisauer were designed to escape the vicious circle of European power politics. They wanted to leave behind the system of stopgaps and the use of alliances and balance of power calculations to achieve national goals. In order to reach this goal they were ready to pay a high price; for example, in territory. 'Idealistic' conceptions of this kind must be understood primarily as a response to the monstrous experiences of the Second World War. However, even to contemporaries their ideas appeared unlikely to survive and to promise little for the future. How could a concept of foreign policy survive which advocated withdrawal from international politics because it promoted undesirable rivalry, or which simply denied the validity of the security dilemmas[102] of the various states? How could a credible foreign policy be based on the attempt to create a new type of human being, or rely on moral renewal and the protection of international law, particularly when the newly emerging major powers, the Soviet Union and the United States, were determined to extend the Pax Sovietica and the Pax Americana as far as possible?[103] It should also be remembered that the various European resistance movements[104] against Hitler were not generally inspired by European plans for the future. Quite understandably, it was patriotic commitment to the idea of the national state which spurred people on to fight against the Third Reich. The ideas which inspired the opponents of Nazism became mandatory in the shaping of the postwar world, which meant that the foreign policy ideas of the Kreisau Circle were even less likely to replace traditional power politics.

The proposals of the notables, on the other hand, were shaped by their view of the history of the European nations in general and the Prussian-German state created by Bismarck in particular. Any simple identification of their ideas with Hitler's foreign policy programme is untenable for obvious reasons. To equate the two would be tantamount to a failure to differentiate between peace and the desire for war, between the claim to leadership that goes with great power status and global racial domination, between respect and contempt for international law, between advocacy of the protection of national and racial minorities and the practice of genocide. As we have seen, these fundamental differences between the foreign policy of the dictator and the ideas of the liberal-conservative Resistance were not enough to persuade Europe to accept their idea of the Reich as a force for order (*Ordnungsmacht*) on the continent. The extensive demands of the notables in foreign policy meant that they were unable to escape the burdens of 'incompleteness' which had accompanied the Reich since its foundation and which had made the nations of Europe so fear the expansionist drives of the *kleindeutsch* national state. It would of course be totally unjust to ignore the differences of moral principle between Hitler and Goerdeler. Nevertheless, the reactions of Great Britain, fighting alone against Hitler, and of the states of Europe which had been occupied by the Third Reich, were understandable; at the critical moment, all of them recognized the old German danger in the plans of the notables and were bound to reject them.[105] The men round Beck, Goerdeler and von Hassell had hoped that these fears would disappear as the Reich assumed its political function as a force for order on the continent, assisting the world powers in the conflict with the Soviet Union. Their hopes proved to be an illusion. The problems and dangers which had surrounded the *kleindeutsch* national state since the end of the nineteenth century had assumed an enormous independent significance in the history of the world. These dangers were too great for them now to be assessed, either in Europe or the rest of the world, simply as a function in the Cold War between east and west.

NOTES

The following is an extended text, with enlarged footnotes, of a lecture given by the author on 2 June 1977 as part of a German-Polish historians' conference. It dealt with the theme 'The Resistance Movement against National Socialism in Germany and Poland' and took place in Lancut, 1–6 June 1977.

1   See the very pointed comments in Mommsen, H., 'Gesellschaftsbild und Verfassungspläne des deutschen Widerstandes', in W. Schmitthenner and H. Buchheim (eds), *Der deutsche Widerstand gegen Hitler* (Cologne/Berlin: 1966), pp. 116, 132.

2   Rothfels, H., 'Trott und die Aussenpolitik des Widerstandes. Dokumentation', *Viertel-jahrshefte für Zeitgeschichte* 12 (1964), p. 300 ff, esp. pp. 302–3;

3   Roon, G. van, *Neuordnung im Widerstand. Der Kreisauer Kreis innerhalb der deutschen Widerstandsbewegung* (Munich: 1967), p. 448 ff, esp. p. 452; Moltke, F. von, M. Balfour and J. Frisby, *Helmuth von Moltke 1907–1945. Anwalt der Zukunft* (Stuttgart: 1975), p. 245 f.

4   See Hassell, U. von, *Vom andern Deutschland. Aus den nachgelassenen Tagebüchern 1938–1944* (Freiburg.B.: 2nd edn, 1946), p. 356 (entry of 10 July 1944). On the term 'political situation as a whole' in Bismarck's thinking see especially the Kissinger Diktat of 15 June 1877, in *Die grosse Politik der europäischen Kabinette 1871–1914*, Vol. II (Berlin: 1922), p. 153 f.

5   See Ritter, G., 'Die aussenpolitische Hoffnungen der Verschwörer des 20. Juli 1944', *Merkur* 3 (1949), p. 1121 ff; Ritter, G., *Carl Goerdeler und die deutsche Widerstandsbewegung* (Stuttgart: 1954), p. 368 ff (new edn 1964); van Roon, *Neuordnung*, p. 295 ff; Rothfels, H., *Die deutsche Opposition gegen Hitler. Eine Würdigung* (Frankfurt-am-Main: new extended edn, 1969), p. 138 ff. See also Deutsch, H. C., *Verschwörung gegen den Krieg. Der Widerstand in Jahren 1939–1940* (Munich: 1969), esp. p. 107 ff; see also Young, A. P., *The 'X' Documents*, ed. S. Aster (London: 1974).

6   On the role of the KPD central office in Moscow see Fischer, A., *Sowjetische Deutschlandpolitik im Zweiten Weltkrieg 1941–1945* (Stuttgart: 1975) *passim*, for example p. 15; Duhnke, H., *Die KPD von 1933 bis 1945* (Cologne: 1972), p. 365 ff.

7   Different from this is the situation of the communists held in concentration camps who, through co-operation and arguments with Social Democrats and other imprisoned opponents of the Third Reich, were more concerned with ideas for the shaping of a new Germany. See, for example, the 'Buchenwald Manifesto' in Duhnke, *KPD*, p. 520.

8   Duhnke, *KPD*, p. 433.

9   The ideas of the two Churches on foreign policy, as well as those of the trade unions, require deeper investigation before they can be fully assessed.

10   See Rothfels, *Opposition*, pp. 166–7.

11   Very important here is Schieder, T., 'Das Deutsche Reich in seinen nationalen und universalen Beziehungen 1871 bis 1945', in T. Schieder and E. Deuerlein (eds), *Reichsgründung 1870/71. Tatsachen. Kontroversen. Interpretationen* (Stuttgart: 1970), p. 422 ff; Hillgruber, A., 'Kontinuität und Diskontinuität in der deutschen Aussenpolitik von Bismarck bis Hitler', in A. Hillgruber, *Grossmachtpolitik und Militarismus im 20. Jahrhundert. 3 Beiträge zum Kontinuitätsproblem* (Düsseldorf: 1974), p. 11 ff; on the Age of Bismarck, see Hillgruber, A., *Bismarcks Aussenpolitik* (Freiburg i.B.: 1972), pp. 156–7; on the 'Caprivi Era', see Leibenguth, P., 'Modernisierungskrisis des Kaiserreichs an der Schwelle zum wilhelminischen Imperialismus. Politische Probleme derära Caprivi (1890–1894)' (dissertation, Cologne: 1975), p. 188 ff, pp. 215–16 and 308–9; on the Wilhelmine period, see Dehio, L., *Gleichgewicht oder Hegemonie. Betrachtungen über ein Grundproblem der neueren Staatengeschichte* (Krefeld: 3rd unrevised edn, undated), p. 200 ff, and Dehio, L., *Deutschland und die Weltpolitik im 20. Jahrhundert* (Munich: 1955) ('Deutschland und die Epoche der Weltkriege'; 'Ranke und der deutsche Imperialismus'; 'Gedanken über die deutsche Sendung 1900–1918'); Fischer, F., *Krieg der Illusionen. Die deutsche Politik von 1911 bis 1914* (Düsseldorf: 1969) and Fischer, F., *Griff nach der Weltmacht. Die Kriegszielpolitik des kaiserlichen Deutschlands 1914/18* (Düsseldorf: 3rd revised edn, 1964). On common points and differences in the two 'revisionist' positions of Dehio and Fischer see Pistone, S., *Ludwig Dehio* (Naples: 1977), esp. p. 173 ff.

12   On the problem of the 'incomplete' national state see Schieder, T., 'Grundfragen der neueren deutschen Geschichte. Zum Problem der historischen Urteilsbildung', in H. Böhme (ed.), *Probleme der Reichsgründungszeit 1848–1879* (Cologne/Berlin: 1968), p. 21 ff. In this connection, the category 'incomplete' is not used to refer to domestic affairs, to the question of the constitutional and parliamentary issues of the Bismarck state. In the sphere of foreign policy, moreover, it does not refer exclusively to the irredentist (and, after the First World War, revisionist) dimension in public opinion

and policy of the Little German national state. Beyond the customary usage of the term, it also refers to the fact that the German Reich was unable, within the status quo created in 1870–1, to conduct itself as a fully independent state and great power towards the two world powers of Great Britain and the Soviet Union. Prussia-Germany thus saw itself faced by two alternatives: first, it could seek support from one or other of these two powers, thus putting at risk its own independence; or secondly, it could make irredentist (or revisionist) demands, which would provoke problems of hegemony, in an attempt to achieve full sovereignty as a national state and a great power by means of direct or indirect expansion.

13 On the assessment of Stauffenberg by communist historians in the Soviet Union and East Germany see Müller, C., *Oberst i.G.Stauffenberg. Eine Biographie* (Düsseldorf: undated [1971]), p. 18 ff.

14 Schramm, W. Ritter von, 'Erhebung 1944. Vom "Widerstand" zu den "Vereinigten Staaten von Europa"', *Politische Studien* (1954), p. 170 ff; Schramm, W. Ritter von, 'Das andere Deutschland und der Wirtschaftsraum Europa', *Wehr und Wirtschaft* (1964), p. 294 ff.

15 Hassell, *Vom andern Deutschland*, p. 324 (entry of 19 August 1943).

16 Graml, H., 'Die aussenpolitischen Vorstellungen des deutschen Widerstandes', in Schmitthenner and Buchheim, *Der deutsche Widerstand*, p. 30 ff., esp. p. 39.

17 For more details of Goerdeler's assessment of border questions in the east during 1943 see Ritter, *Goerdeler*, p. 329.

18 Ritter, *Goerdeler*, pp. 279 and 319; Schramm, W. Ritter von, *Beck und Goerdeler. Gemeinschaftsdokumente für den Frieden 1941–1944* (Munich: 1965), pp. 90–1 ('The goal').

19 On this subject see Hillgruber, A., *Hitlers Strategie. Politik und Kriegführung 1940–1941* (Frankfurt-am-Main: 1965), pp. 199 ff, 217–18, 300 ff, 533 and 572; Hillgruber, A., 'Eine Bilanz des Zweiten Weltkrieges aus der Sicht der kriegführenden Mächte', in Hillgruber, *Grossmachtpolitik und Militarismus*, p. 53 ff; Hillgruber, A., *Der Zenit des Zweiten Weltkrieges Juli 1941* (Wiesbaden: 1977).

20 Ritter, *Goerdeler*, p. 312 ff; Breyer, R., 'Carl Goerdeler und die deutsche Ostgrenze', in *Zeitschrift für Ostforschung* (1964), p. 198 ff; Graml, 'Aussenpolitische Vorstellungen', pp. 30, 33 ff, 60 ff.

21 Schramm, Ritter von, *Beck und Goerdeler*, p. 100 ('The goal').

22 Schramm, Ritter von, *Beck und Goerdeler*, p. 100. Wilhelm Ritter von Schramm (p. 34 ff) and Gerhard Ritter (p. 274 and p. 319) date authorship of the major points in the manuscript between the end of 1940 and spring 1941. However, Hans Mommsen has argued convincingly that the document was written at the turn of 1941–2. Mommsen, H., 'Gesellschaftsbild und Verfassungspläne', pp. 269–70 (n. 109). Rothfels, *Opposition*, p. 205 (n. 44), supports Hans Mommsen's suggested date.

23 Fischer, *Griff*, p. 654, admittedly identifies the different political conceptions of the Third Army High Command and the Foreign Office too closely. See in contrast another view, which perhaps exaggerates the freedom of manoeuvre of the diplomats, in Baumgart, W., *Deutsche Ostpolitik 1918. Von Brest-Litousk bis zum Ende des Ersten Weltkrieges* (Munich: 1966). On the qualitative alterations in foreign policy objectives and methods during the First World War see Hillgruber, A., *Deutschlands Rolle in der Vorgeschichte der beiden Weltkriege* (Göttingen: 1967), p. 58 ff.

24 See n. 4.

25 Schramm, Ritter von, *Beck und Goerdeler*, p. 195 f ('The way').

26 Schramm, Ritter von, *Beck und Goerdeler*, p. 98–9 ('The goal'). With reference to the relationship of the national state and the European idea in Goerdeler's political thought, Walter Lipgens claims that Goerdeler made the journey 'by means of an extraordinary route . . . in the period 1942–1944 from an initially solely utilitarian conception of Europe to one based on principle'. Lipgens, W., *Die Anfänge der europäischen Einigungspolitik 1945–1950. Erster Teil: 1945–1947* (Stuttgart: 1977), p. 50 (n. 75). He bases this belief mainly on Goerdeler's convictions about 'Practical measures for the rearrangement of Europe', apparently written at the beginning of 1944. Published in Lipgens, W., *Europa-Föderationspläne der Widerstandsbewegungen 1940–1945. Eine Dokumentation* (Munich: 1968), document 53, p. 165 ff. Lipgens regards the changes in Goerdeler's proposals as 'progress' towards the political goal

of a united Europe; he thus sees in Goerdeler a development from a representative of the national state and advocate of German hegemony over Europe to a protagonist of the European idea in a supranational sense. See Lipgens, W., 'L'idea dell'unità europea nella resistenza in Germania e in Francia', in S. Pistone (ed.), *L'idea dell'unificazione europea dall Prima alla Seconda Guerra Mondiale* (Turin: 1975), pp. 107–8, esp. n. 29.

27 Schramm, Ritter von, *Beck und Goerdeler*, pp. 98–9 ('The goal'). In connection with the leadership claim of the German Reich mentioned here, see the traditional idea of hegemony, which Heinrich Triepel understands partly as a means to 'integration'; he also defines 'leadership as leadership of another to a specific goal' (pp. 134–5) which is binding on both the hegemonic power and the group of states it organizes and leads: Triepel, H., *Die Hegemonie. Ein Buch von führenden Staaten* (Stuttgart: 2nd edn, 1943), p. 134 ff.

28 Goebbels, J., *Tagebücher aus den Jahren 1942–1943*, ed. L. P. Lochner (Zurich: 1948), p. 322 ff. Quoted by Jacobsen, H.-A., *Grundzüge der Politik und Strategie in Dokumenten* (Frankfurt-am-Main/Hamburg: 1965), p. 198.

29 Heimpel, H., *Der Mensch in seiner Gegenwart* (Göttingen: 1954), p. 173. See also p. 68: 'The idea of the nation is itself a European idea... Europe exists with nations.' On 'national multiplicity as a problem of the unification of Europe' see also Wittram, R., *Das Nationale als europäisches Problem. Beiträge zur Geschichte des Nationalitätsprinzips, vornehmlich im 19 Jahrhundert* (Göttingen: 1954), p. 9 ff.

30 Weber, M., *Gesammelte politische Schriften* (Tübingen: 2nd edn. 1958), p. 23.

31 On this problem see Rothfels, H., 'Der geschichtliche Standort der Reichsgründung', in H. Rothfels, *Bismarck. Vorträge und Abhandlungen* (Stuttgart/Berlin/Cologne/Mainz: 1970), p. 130; also Schieder, 'Das Deutsche Reich', p. 440f; on this thinking see Zernack, K., 'Historische Bildung – Geschichtsbewusstsein – Nationsbewusstsein und die deutsch-polnischen Beziehungen', *Politik und Kultur* (1976), p. 43.

32 The issue of the mixture of defensive and offensive motives and objectives must also be more closely investigated than has previously been the case in the history of German foreign policy from Bismarck to Hitler. This concerns the 'security dilemma' of the states, which John Herz has recognized as a central issue of international politics. Herz, J. H., 'Idealistischer Internationalismus und das Sicherheitsdilemma', in J. Herz, *Staatenwelt und Weltpolitik* (Hamburg: 1974), p. 39 ff.

33 Ritter, *Goerdeler*, p. 329. As regards the extent of the territorial and border demands of the notables, there was a certain degree of change dependent on the military situation which Ritter, *Goerdeler, passim*, describes; see also a summary in Graml, 'Aussenpolitische Vorstellungen', *passim*. The group round Beck, Goerdeler and von Hassell kept with some constancy to their demands for 'the Reich border of 1914 in the east. See the Goerdeler Peace Plan, apparently meant for British readers and probably written in late summer or autumn 1943, in Ritter, *Goerdeler*, appendix VI, p. 570 ff, here p. 571.

34 Kettenacker, L., 'Die britische Haltung zum deutschen Widerstand während des Zweiten Weltkriegs', in L. Kettenacker (ed.), *Das "Andere Deutschland" im Zweiten Weltkieg. Emigration und Widerstand in internationaler Perspektive* (Stuttgart: 1977), p. 49 ff, esp. p. 54 and pp. 64–5.

35 Public Record Office, London, Foreign Office 371/21659.7999.C 15084/G of 7 December 1938. Published in part in Young, *'X' Documents*, p. 234. For British assessment of the foreign policy plans of the conservative opposition in Germany see Young, *'X' Documents*, p. 235. I am grateful to Dr Wolfgang Michalka (Frankfurt University) for making available the original of the document quoted above.

36 Ritter, *Goerdeler*, p. 266 ff.

37 See n. 14.

38 Memorandum on the plans of Moltke in December 1943, published in van Roon, *Neuordnung*, documentary appendix, p. 582 ff, here p. 584.

39 See, for example, Goerdeler's peace plan of late summer or autumn 1943, published in Ritter, *Goerdeler*, appendix VI, p. 570, esp. points 1–7.

40 See the study by Hölzle, E., *Die Selbstentmachtung Europas. Das Experiment des Friedens vor und im Ersten Weltkrieg* (Göttingen/Frankfurt-am-Main/Zurich: 1975).

This investigates the consequences of German misjudgement of the 'dogma' of Anglo-Russian antagonism and the effects of German *Weltpolitik* on Anglo-Russian rapprochement after the turn of the century; it attempts to place these in perspective by referring to (and probably overestimating) the innate compulsions of the international system and its tendency to arrangements between the world powers; see p. 105 ff. In contrast, Peter Winzen in his Cologne dissertation on 'Bülows und Holsteins Politik der freien Hand 1895–1901' (dissertation, Cologne: 1973) emphasizes the important desire of the two men (though it sprang from different motives and aimed at different objectives) for Germany to emerge as the 'third power' from the 'expected collision between the two rival world powers'. Winzen, P., *Die Englandpolitik Friedrich von Holsteins 1895–1901. Zweiter Teil der Inaugural-Dissertation* (Cologne: 1975), p. 392. On the plethora of motives ('"social", "European" and "imperial interests"', p. 200) which persuaded the British to accept rapprochement with Russia between 1905 and 1907, see Wormer, K., 'Russland, Deutschland und das Empire. Studien zur englischen Aussenpolitik vor dem Ersten Weltkrieg' (dissertation, Mannheim: 1975), p. 198 ff.

41 Hillgruber, *Deutschlands Rolle*, p. 75.
42 Kettenacker, 'Die britische Haltung', pp. 59, 64, 74. See also Jäckel, E., 'Wenn der Anschlag gelungen wäre', in H. J. Schultz (ed.), *Der Zwanzigste Juli. Alternative zur Hitler?* (Stuttgart/Berlin: 1974), p. 75. On the factor of the Soviet Union, so decisive for the course of the war and in the postwar order, in the British debate about the fate of Germany in the 'Cold War' which began before the Second World War was over, see Fromm, H., 'Kriegszieldiskussion in England 1939 bis 1945' (dissertation., Frankfurt-am-Main: 1974); on the attitude of the British government on this question see chapter II/3 on 'The beginnings of British appeasement policy towards Moscow' in the habilitation thesis of Lothar Kettenacker on the development of British war aims towards Nazi Germany in the Second World War.
43 For example, Richard Löwenthal does this in a contribution published in Kettenacker, *Das 'Andere Deutschland'*, p. 92 f.
44 On the American attitude see Nicholls, A. J., 'American views of Germany's future during World War II', in Kettenacker, *Das 'Andere Deutschland'*, pp. 81, 84–5.
45 See Müller, K.-J., 'Ludwig Beck – Ein General zwischen Wilhelminismus und National-sozialismus', in J. Geiss and B. J. Wendt (eds), *Deutschland in der Weltpolitik des 19. und 20. Jahrhunderts* (Düsseldorf: 1973), p. 522.
46 Dirr, P. (ed.), *Bayerische Dokumente zum Kriegsausbruch und zum Versailler Schuldspruch* (Munich: 3rd extended edn, 1925), p. 113 (report of Lerchenfeld of 4 June 1914). See also Hildebrand, K., 'Wettrüsten und Kriegsausbruch 1914 (I). Zum Problem von Legitimität und Revolution im internationalen System', *Neue Politische Literatur* XX (1975), pp. 170, 190.
47 On this subject see Berghahn, V. R., *Germany and the Approach of War in 1914* (London: 1973), p. 165 ff, esp. p. 185.
48 Schramm, Ritter von, *Beck und Goerdeler*, pp. 100–1 f. and p. 104 ('The goal').
49 Martin, B., *Friedensinitiativen und Machtpolitik im Zweiten Weltkrieg 1939–1942* (Düsseldorf: 1974), pp. 324–5. Plesman's 'late imperialistic' concept of peace proposed a partition of the rest of the world dependent on the great industrialized nations; it included the Soviet Union and Japan in its peace plans, which were to find their best field of supranational co-operation in Africa.
50 Graml, 'Aussenpolitische Vorstellungen', p. 46.
51 Graml, 'Aussenpolitische Vorstellungen', p. 46.
52 Moltke's memorandum; first draft of 24 April 1941, 'Starting Point, Objectives and Tasks', published in van Roon, *Neuordnung*, documentary appendix, p. 511.
53 Quoted in van Roon, *Neuordnung*, p. 452.
54 See Graml, 'Aussenpolitische Vorstellungen', p. 52 ff; Rothfels, *Opposition*, pp. 153–4; the quotation in *Spiegelbild einer Verschwörung. Die Kaltenbrunner-Berichte an Bormann und Hitler über das Attentat vom 20.Juli 1944. Geheime Dokumente aus dem ehemaligen Reichssicherheitshauptamt*, Archiv Peter für historische und zeitgeschichtliche Dokumentation (Stuttgart: 1961), p. 34. It should not be forgotten that in principle Trott thought that the 'only possibility' for ending the war lay in granting the Reich, 'still ... the second strongest power' in 'Europe between east

and west', 'an honourable peace without occupation, without cession of territory, war contributions, without political encirclement and economic shackles'. See also Kramarz, J., *Claus Graf von Stauffenberg. 15. November 1907 – 20. Juli 1944. Das Leben eines Offiziers* (Frankfurt-am-Main: 1965), p. 178. Trott's ideas reveal some parallels with the foreign policy plans of the notables.

55 Van Roon, *Neuordnung*, p. 457.
56 Van Roon, *Neuordnung*, pp. 454–5.
57 Ritter, *Goerdeler*, p. 334.
58 See Meyers, R., *Die Lehre von den Internationalen Beziehungen. Ein Entwicklungs- geschichtliches überblick* (Düsseldorf: 1977), p. 55 ff.
59 Aron, R., *Frieden und Krieg. Eine Theorie der Staatenwelt* (Frankfurt-am-Main: 1963), p. 693.
60 Bourne, K., *The Foreign Policy of Victorian England 1830–1902* (Oxford: 1970), p. 83.
61 Geyer, D., 'Voraussetzungen sowjetischer Aussenpolitik in der Zwischenkriegszeit', in D. Geyer (ed.), *Osteuropa-Handbuch. Sowjetunion. Aussenpolitik 1917–1955* (Cologne/Vienna: 1972), p. 31.
62 See Meyers, *Internationale Beziehungen*, p. 44 ff.
63 Van Roon, *Neuordnung*, p. 467.
64 Van Roon, *Neuordnung*, p. 467.
65 Van Roon, *Neuordnung*, pp. 465–6.
66 Graml, 'Aussenpolitische Vorstellungen', p. 65.
67 Graml, 'Aussenpolitische Vorstellungen', p. 41. On the idea of European unification in the various resistance movements see Lipgens, *Anfänge der europäischen Einigungspolitik*, esp. p. 43 ff.
68 See Turner, H. A. jr, 'Stresemann und das Problem der Kontinuität in der deutschen Aussenpolitik', in G. Ziebura (ed.), *Grundfragen der deutschen Aussenpolitik seit 1871* (Darmstadt: 1975), p. 284 ff, esp. p. 287.
69 Very important here is Dehio, *Gleichgewicht oder Hegemonie*, for example, pp. 197, 201, 204 ff and 227.
70 Graml, 'Aussenpolitische Vorstellungen', p. 48.
71 See Bethmann Hollweg's letter to Prince Max of Baden on 17 January 1918, published in Vietsch, E. von, *Bethmann Hollweg. Staatsmann zwischen Macht und Ethos* (Boppard: 1969), p. 327 ff. Apart from occasional, fundamental criticism of traditional European power politics, Bethmann Hollweg continued, after the defeat of Germany, to view the problem of the outbreak, course and end of the war from the traditional standpoint of the national state.
72 Erdmann, K. D., 'Kurt Riezler – ein politisches Profil (1882–1955)', in K. D. Erdmann (ed.), *Kurt Riezler. Tagebücher. Aufsätze. Dokumente* (Göttingen: 1972), p. 134 ff.
73 Vietsch, *Bethmann Hollweg*, p. 328.
74 See n. 37 and n. 51.
75 The extent of British awareness of and reaction to the political ideas of the Kreisau Circle would be worth further investigation.
76 See also Nolte, E., *Der Faschismus in seiner Epoche. Action francaise. Italiener Faschismus. Nationalsozialismus* (Munich: 1963), pp. 434–5 (term 'European normal war', etc.).
77 Van Roon, *Neuordnung*, p. 458.
78 Van Roon, *Neuordnung*, p. 458.
79 Moltke's memorandum, third draft of 20 June 1941. Published in Van Roon, *Neuordnung*, documentary appendix, p. 518.
80 Rothfels, H. (ed.), 'Zwei aussenpolitische Memoranden der deutschen Opposition (Frühjahr 1942)', *Vierteljahrshefte für Zeitgeschichte* 5 (1957), pp. 394 and 387; reprinted in van Roon, *Neuordnung*, documentary appendix, p. 572 ff. See also van Roon, *Neuordnung*, p. 459. On the plan to re-establish free Polish and Czechoslovakian states 'in the framework of the ethnographic borders' and the resulting claims to the Sudetenland and parts of West Prussia, see Graml, 'Aussenpolitische Vorstellungen', p. 67.
81 Van Roon, *Neuordnung*, documentary appendix, p. 572 ff; Rothfels, 'Zwei aussen- politische Memoranden', pp. 394, 387.

82 Kaltenbrunner Berichte, p. 118.

83 Graml, 'Aussenpolitische Vorstellungen', p. 69.

84 Hans Mommsen's somewhat critical judgement of the political ideas and proposals of the German Resistance (Mommsen, 'Gesellschaftsbild und Verfassungspläne', esp. p. 162 ff) perhaps takes insuffient account of the situation and conditions under which members of the Resistance were operating. For example, he underestimates the willingness of various resistance members to accept political and social change. See also Hildebrand, K., 'Weltmacht oder Untergang: Hitlers Deutschland 1941–1945', in O. Hauser (ed.), *Weltpolitik II 1939–1945. 14 Vorträge* (Göttingen/Frankfurt-am-Main/Zurich: 1975), pp. 317–18.

85 Van Roon, *Neuordnung*, p. 461.

86 On these two possibilities of German *Ostpolitik* in the interwar years see also the work by K. Hildebrand, *Das Deutsche Reich und die Sowjetunion im internationalen System 1918–1932. Legitimität oder Revolution?* (Wiesbaden: 1977).

87 Ritter, *Goerdeler*, p. 68 ff.

88 I was unfortunately unable to see the original of the document, which is in the 'Nachlass Goerdeler' of the Bundesarchiv Koblenz.

89 See Wojciechowski, M., *Die polnisch-deutschen Beziehungen 1933–1938* (Leiden: 1971; first published in Polish in 1965), p. 70 ff, esp. p. 102 ff; also Wollstein, G., *Vom Weimarer Revisionismus zu Hitler. Das Deutsche Reich und die Grossmächte in der Anfangsphase der nationalsozialistischen Herrschaft in Deutschland* (Bonn/Bad Godesberg: 1973), p. 217 ff; and especially, Wollstein, G., 'Hitlers Nichtangriffspakt mit Pilsudski von 1934', *Begegnung mit Polen. Zeitschrift für deutsch-polnische Verständigung* 12 (1974), p. 82 ff.

90 Bracher, K. D., *Die Krise Europas 1917–1945* (Frankfurt-am-Main/Berlin/Vienna: 1976), p. 167.

91 Wollstein, *Weimarer Revisionismus zu Hitler*; Wollstein, 'Hitlers Nichtangriffspakt'.

92 Jacobsen, H.-A., *Nationalsozialistische Aussenpolitik 1933–1938* (Frankfurt-am-Main/Berlin: 1968), p. 819.

93 On the revolutionary quality of Nazism and the foreign policy of the Third Reich in general, see Bracher, K. D., 'Tradition und Nationalsozialismus', in K. D. Bracher, *Zeitgeschichtliche Kontroversen. Um Faschismus, Totalitarismus, Demokratie* (Munich: 1976), p. 62 ff.

94 Zernack, K., 'Das Zeitalter der nordischen Kriege von 1558 bis 1809 als frühneuzeitliche Geschichtsepoche', *Zeitschrift für Historische Forschung* 1 (1974), p. 56 and *passim*.

95 Breyer, 'Goerdeler und die Ostgrenze', p. 201.

96 Breyer, 'Goerdeler und die Ostgrenze', p. 202.

97 Breyer, 'Goerdeler und die Ostgrenze', p. 205.

98 Hillgruber, *Deutschlands Rolle*, p. 58 ff, esp. pp. 61–2.

99 Farrar, L. L. jr, *The Short-War Illusion. German Policy, Strategy, and Domestic Affairs. August–December 1914* (Santa Barbara, Calif./Oxford: 1973).

100 Farrar, *Short-War Illusion*, p. 151.

101 See Baumont, M., *La faillité de la paix (1918–1939)*, 2 vols (Paris: 4th edn, 1960 [Vol. 1] and 5th edn, 1968 [Vol. 2]); Carr, E. H., *International Relations between the Two World Wars 1919–1939* (New York: 1966); Graml, H., *Europa zwischen den Kriegen* (Munich: 1969); for the 1920s, Marks, S., *The Illusion of Peace – International Relations in Europe 1918–1933* (London: 1976).

102 Herz, *Staatenwelt und Weltpolitik*, p. 39 ff.

103 Hillgruber, *Bilanz des Zweiten Weltkrieges*, p. 57 ff.

104 Henri Michel has defined the role of the national state as the motive and goal of the European resistance movements against Hitler's Germany: 'The Resistance movement is a patriotic struggle for the liberation of the Fatherland' (in *Internationale Hefte der Widerstandsbewegung*, nos. 8–10, (1963), p. 78, quoted in Plum, G., 'Widerstandsbewegungen', in C. D. Kernig (ed.), *Sowjetsystem und demokratische Gesellschaft. Eine vergleichende Enzyklopädie*, Vol. VI (Freiburg i.B./Basle/Vienna: 1972), p. 962. See also the demand from a French Association of Resistance Fighters for a clear definition of resistance and resistance movement 'which maintains the *national* legitimacy of the R[esistance movement] (with regard to France, drawing

on the source of *traditional and emotional patriotism*'). *Internationale Hefte*, pp. 961–2; author's emphases.

The historical strength of the national state tradition of Europe within the resistance movements and its effects on the shaping of postwar Europe was not fully assessed by Walter Lipgens in his major work on the beginnings of European unification policy, though he does refer to the problem (Lipgens, 'Anfänge der europäischen Einigungspolitik', for example, p. 57 ff). The author assumes that, under the impact of the Second World War at the latest, the principle of a supranationally organized Europe had come to be regarded as a superior idea and an achievable goal. He thus regards the existence of national state traditions as regrettable deviations (for example, p. 193 ff, when he describes 'the attempt to maintain nationalist policy by de Gaulle'); on other occasions, Lipgens judges such relapses as functions of the European policy of the two 'victorious world powers . . . who had decreed the restoration of the European national states' (p. 639). Lipgens seems to have underestimated the continuity and durability of the idea of the national state in Europe and perhaps lost sight of the fact that the major characteristic of Europe has been pluralism. The tradition has contributed to the contemporary situation, in which there is an unparalleled growth in the number of sovereign national states in the world. On this subject see Schieder, T., *Zum Problem des Staatenpluralismus in der modernen Welt* (Cologne/Opladen: 1969), p. 7 ff. On the dialectics of European unity and the multiplicity of national states in modern European history, on the problem of European unification 'on the basis of the equal rights of all states . . . with the goal of integration, not domination' as 'a third way' in European history, and therefore on a 'decision . . . against the tradition of hegemonic unification policy and against a relapse into the tradition of multi-state power politics', see Bracher, *Krise*, p. 290 ff, here p. 394.

105   On the contemporary British attitude see n. 41; on the assessment of the proposals of the German Resistance by strongly nationalist communist historians in Poland, see Kozensky, J., 'Polnische Stimmen zum deutschen Widerstand', in J. Hütter, R. Meyers and D. Papenfuss (eds), *Tradition und Neubeginn. Internationale Forschung zur deutschen Geschichte im 20. Jahrhundert* (Cologne/Berlin/Bonn/Munich: 1975), p. 377 ff; on the assessment of the foreign policy proposals of the German Resistance in Soviet historical writing see, for example, Melnikow, D., *Der 20. Juli 1944. Legende und Wirklichkeit* (2nd extended edn [Hamburg: 1968]), pp. 66–7, 148–9, 151–3, 164, 171ff and 224.

*The Federal Republic
and its Policies towards
East and West*

8

The provisional state and 'eternal France'.
Franco-German relations, 1963–9

I

'ATLANTICISTS' AGAINST 'GAULLISTS'

In the first half of the 1960s, international politics entered a period of considerable change. The Cold War, which had favoured the establishment and continued existence of the Bonn state and had reduced France to the status of a middle-ranking power dependent on the United States, was moving towards its close. The course of international relations began to be influenced by the development of *détente* and polycentrism. In such a situation, the role of the *'Grande Nation'* once again became increasingly important. By contrast, the foundations of West German foreign policy came under pressure. Between 1955 and 1958 at least, German foreign policy had been assisted by the compatibility of its political alliance with the United States, its inclination towards integration in Europe and the national striving for reunification. In the 1960s, this fortunate congruence was clearly disintegrating. At the beginning of the Erhard era, the incomplete and provisional nature of the Federal Republic was again apparent. The hope of the Adenauer period that Germany would find a place in an integrated Europe – typical of the 1950s – vanished both practically and as an ideal. Precisely 'in the years from 1963 to 1969',[1] the President of France resolutely opposed the concept of such an amalgamation, which the Germans in particular had advocated with understandable intensity. De Gaulle regarded the traditional national state as a *'finalité de l'histoire'*[2] and visualized the objective of a 'Europe of fatherlands', in which 'the European countries would remain what they are';[3] in his view, such a situation would also accommodate the French claim to leadership of the western part of the continent. The Federal Republic was thus faced with a choice in foreign policy, of a kind which had played a tempting and dangerous part in German history since the nineteenth century. At this stage, the enormous economic strength of West Germany gave it considerable attractions as a prospective partner. The French and Americans were constant rivals during these years, making

201

efforts to win the support of the Federal Republic and to put pressure on it when support was not forthcoming. Consequently, the Federal Republic also faced an 'important task within the European and Atlantic Alliance',[4] based on the importance of balancing the needs of the partners and bringing them together. A number of dangers also arose from the West German 'diplomatic splits'[5] between Paris and Washington. The Federal Republic was placed in a difficult position which frequently threatened to overstretch its resources and shake its very foundations. It might reasonably be wondered how the Bonn republic could manage such a policy at all since, though its national, military and economic sovereignty was protected, the country was also directly restricted by the imposition of supranational controls.

Prudently, the governments of Erhard and Kiesinger chose not to overstep the limits imposed upon them by the western victors of the Second World War. West German politicians were well aware that France could assert its own position much more vigorously against the United States, without actually losing American support, than could Germany. Without a reconciliation with France, therefore, there could be no trouble-free relationship with the United States of America either. The situation was further complicated when a historical threat dating from 1944–6 became a live issue again after 1964; the danger was that disappointment over his unsuccessful German policy would persuade de Gaulle to turn towards the Soviet Union. The French President did not see the Soviet Union primarily as the embodiment of communist world revolution, but tended to regard Russia as a historic partner of France in the European and global concert. The visit of Gromyko to Paris in April 1965, the subject of much anxious speculation in Bonn despite the duty of consultation between France and Germany, was – in Erich Mendes' contemporary description – a 'shock'[6] far beyond the confines of the Christian Democratic Union (CDU). De Gaulle's comment in September 1965 to 'a highly placed visitor from the western camp',[7] when he said that 'the German danger ... [was] more acute than the Soviet', had a similar effect. In view of this situation, complicated by a temporary British-Soviet rapprochement and by the continuing 'special relationship' of the two Anglo-Saxon powers, it was extremely difficult for West German politicians to establish a balance.

At least in the Erhard years, French and Americans demands on the Federal Republic were excessive. De Gaulle in particular pressed impatiently for West Germany to accept an exclusive association (*Zweierverbindung*) between Paris and Bonn; in this way, he was also demanding that Bonn should join the proposal for a 'French hegemony'[8] in western Europe and provide the material basis for France's global political claims. In fact, the excessive display of French self-confidence only increased the extreme insecurity of the West Germans, persuading them to seek the protection of the Americans even more than before. De Gaulle was infuriated by such behaviour, which he regarded as fit only for a satellite state. Nevertheless, it was clear to his critics that his own conduct had done much to drive Bonn more closely into the arms of Washington. As well as attacking the United States like some national Don Quixote, had he not also halted the advance of the European movement, and even set it back?

As often before in German history, the foreign policy options of the Federal Republic had an important influence on the domestic situation. The German longing for a national idyll, the inclination to choose the 'Switzerland' option which had contributed to the popularity of Ludwig Erhard, was shown by the requirements of international politics to be wholly illusory. Once before, in the nineteenth century, the contemporaries of the 'poets and thinkers' had been drawn into the mainstream of Grand Policy by the sheer force of political events; now their successors, the consumers and tourists of the Federal Republic, were equally unable to escape the conditions of international politics. Bonn was compelled to grapple with the problem which had been forced upon it, the choice between Washington and Paris. There was no longer a united western world under the leadership of the United States; the French President was engaging in political and monetary provocation of the USA; and finally, in the tours of Germany by de Gaulle and Kennedy (1962–3), the *grande vision* of French leadership had clashed with the 'grand design' of the United States, just as the French and American strategies had clashed in the Franco-German Friendship Treaty (22 January 1963) and its preamble (16 May 1963).

After Erhard became chancellor, the French President continued his efforts to bring the Germans to his side. However, the United States had no desire to lose a loyal and reliable ally, especially at a time when Paris had become an adversary of Washington and was condemning the American war in Vietnam. The camps of 'Atlanticists' and 'Gaullists', which engaged in bitter and public feuds throughout the summer and autumn of 1964, had therefore evolved as a result of an international political conflict, though their conduct also had significant domestic motives. Among the most prominent 'Atlanticists', who were not hostile to France but opposed too exclusive a relationship with Paris to the detriment of the tie with America, were Federal Chancellor Erhard, Foreign Minister Schröder and Defence Minister von Hassel. The leading 'Gaullists' included Konrad Adenauer, Freiherr zu Guttenberg, Franz Josef Strauss and Josef-Hermann Dufhues. In both groups, the leading representatives were themselves separated by different interpretations of 'Atlanticism' and 'Gaullism'; this fact was made glaringly obvious by their numerous private and public comments in speeches and interviews as well as in internal meetings of the CDU. It was entirely typical of the period that the argument raged across party lines. The 'Atlanticist' camp was able to count on large sections of the Christian Social Union (CSU), the Free Democratic Party (FDP) and the opposition Social Democratic Party (SPD) as well as on representatives from the employers' associations, the trade unions and the academic world; it also received journalistic support from *Stern* and from *Zeit*. Behind the 'Gaullists' stood sections of the CDU and almost all the CSU, which concentrated on the fight against Foreign Minister Schröder and used powerful and sometimes highly unorthodox methods. Their arguments were supported, among other newspapers, by the *Rheinischer Merkur*.

Now that the smoke which surrounded the embattled positions of the Atlanticists and Gaullists in the first half of the 1960s has cleared, it is reasonable to ask what de Gaulle was really offering the Federal Republic of Germany. Something capable of useful development, according to Konrad Adenauer, who advocated the French option; not enough, in the pragmatic judgement of Gerhard Schröder, who was opposed to this experiment in foreign policy. In the last analysis, the Foreign Minister regarded American protection as more certain. He held to this opinion despite the fact that de Gaulle sometimes appeared to be more resolute in Europe than the Americans, who were heavily engaged in South East Asia. The French President created the impression that in the event of a conflict he would be ready to respond quickly with the nuclear weapons at his disposal. In contrast, the USA was taken up with the new doctrine created by General Taylor and McNamara, the Secretary of State for Defense; the proposal to introduce a 'cease-fire' before resorting to the major use of nuclear weapons was a move that could threaten the very existence of the Federal Republic of Germany. Nevertheless, Schröder remained convinced that the German Question could only be kept open, or eventually solved, with the support of the United States rather than through a privileged association with de Gaulle's France. Exactly the opposite assumption lay behind the conduct of Konrad Adenauer, who was revealing an astonishing degree of flexibility for a man of his age. Adenauer hoped to continue the policy he had begun in the Franco-German treaty and to pursue his long-standing foreign policy objectives with a new protecting partner. He did not trust the Americans, fighting in Vietnam and concentrating on nuclear *détente* with the Soviet Union. Like Franz Josef Strauss, Adenauer wanted to accept de Gaulle's offer of a *Zweierverbindung* without delay and make it the core of a new Europe, in order to create security for the Federal Republic of Germany and to construct a great power bloc in continental Europe. A bloc of this kind would not oppose the United States in any respect; outside the territorially limited *'force de frappe'*, the USA would still be responsible for providing a nuclear umbrella over much of Europe. Consequently, the new alliance would stand staunchly by the USA in the event of a crisis for the western superpower in the region. However, Adenauer hoped that

Franco-German co-operation would create a position of strength, which America no longer guaranteed with any certainty. From such a position, there could be negotiations on the German Question with Soviet Russia, if Moscow was driven by economic difficulties and political problems with China and its satellite states to adopt a more accommodating attitude.

General de Gaulle repeatedly emphasized that France would concede the reunification of Germany if the Germans would accept certain conditions, such as renunciation of the eastern territories and of nuclear weapons. Did he suggest the fulfilment of this national longing only because he knew it was more or less out of the question for many years?[9] At any rate, he could safely assume that reunification, held out to the Federal Republic as the reward for its agreement to the *Zweierverbindung* between Paris and Bonn, would not take place until the distant future. For the rest, Franco-German friendship was actually based on the foundation of the division of Germany. De Gaulle was determined to extricate the Federal Republic from the American embrace, since the Federal Republic was economically potent as well as strategically vital for France, and to bring it over to the French side. His conversation with Konrad Adenauer in the Elysée Palace on 9 November 1964 reveals how far he was prepared to go in the attempt, though without ever making a binding commitment. If Germany should choose, as he saw it, to opt for France and for Europe, the general did not completely rule out an examination of the issue of joint control of nuclear weapons. However, he obviously preferred that, in such circumstances, France and its *force de frappe* would also take responsibility for the security of the Bonn state. In Franco-German consultations as well as in private conversations, the President urged the Federal Republic to choose between Paris and Washington. His policy was clearly revealed when he visited Bonn in July 1964. However, he did not obtain the desired response to his demand, since the Federal government still preferred to seek its main protection and security at the side of the United States. It was not prepared to cut free from the guardianship of a powerful patron in order to entrust itself to a much weaker hegemonic power and to follow it on what appeared to be a journey 'into the inopportune'.[10] De Gaulle repeatedly told Erhard: 'You must decide'. But the decision was not a simple one. Apart from the complex problem of German security requirements and reunification policy, de Gaulle could not give a satisfactory response to German anxieties about control over the *force de frappe*. When de Gaulle spoke about the advantage of a European defensive capability independent of America, Erhard refused to be fobbed off:[11]

Is it actually, if I just consider your conception as a map exercise, is your French *force de frappe* a French *force de frappe* in such a case, or is it a European? To that he said, it is of course a French [one], but of course it then stands ready, if we have a European Europe, for the protection of Europe. I said, the answer does not satisfy me; I would like to know if you have sole control of the French *force de frappe* in such a case, or is it a European *force de frappe* in which others have a right of co-determination. The answer was quite clear, it is a French *force de frappe*, but which would automatically be used for the protection of Europe, to which I was naturally able to reply, then we only have to choose whether to be dependent on the American nuclear weapon or to be dependent on the French nuclear weapon.

De Gaulle was highly irritated by the Bonn summit and by Erhard's answer to French pressure:[12] 'We cannot come to a decision on this question' [i.e. between Washington and Paris]. He complained to Konrad Adenauer that the Franco-German treaty had not come to life and the marriage had not been consummated. 'I have remained a virgin,'[13] remarked the President.

Federal Chancellor Erhard, despite his critical approach to France's European and Atlantic policy, nevertheless remained anxious to reach a settlement with France. Many of the reasons for this attitude are to be found in the domestic and party political arena. Under the influence of his advisers,[14] the Chancellor, without entertaining any illusions about actual successes which might be achieved, wanted to stress the friendly nature of the relationship with France in order to hold his ground in the election struggle which had already begun. At German request, the summit meeting between Erhard and the French President in January 1965 was therefore given an exclusive setting. It took place not in Paris but at Castle Rambouillet, a location which Erhard believed gave it a 'symbolic value'.[15] The Chancellor was determined to produce a convincing success from the summit. To this end, he had taken an important decision at the end of 1964. At the last minute, after German resistance lasting a year, the Federal Chancellor declared on 1 December 1964 that West Germany was prepared to agree to the French demand for a common price for grain within the EEC. Apart from domestic calculations and election tactics, Ludwig Erhard (like Konrad Adenauer) believed that this concession, financially costly for the Federal Republic, might persuade General de Gaulle to adopt a more friendly attitude towards European integration.

This assumption rapidly proved to be completely mistaken. De Gaulle's policies were a severe disappointment to Erhard, whose hopes had been raised prematurely after the summit at Rambouillet. On 30 June 1965, de Gaulle allowed negotiations in the Council of Ministers over the financing of the Common Agricultural Policy to fail and plunged the EEC into a new crisis. France boycotted the meeting of the Council of Ministers for some time afterwards. De Gaulle's 'policy of the empty chair' underlined his determination to put the national interest before the treaties of Rome. After the crisis caused by French rejection of the British application to

join the EEC on 14 January 1963, Paris had once again put the existence
of the EEC in question.

II
IN THE SHADOW OF THE NATO CRISIS OF 1966

Previously, the relationship of Bonn with Washington and Paris had
remained largely within the framework of a relatively normal set of
foreign policy options, offering possibilities as well as dangers. After
the federal election of 1965, however, the issue flared up again with
increasing intensity, especially in 1966. At this stage, there was a real threat
of damaging consequences for the Federal Republic. The French ambassador in Bonn described the difficult situation facing the Erhard government
in autumn 1965:[16] 'The Germans . . . suddenly felt themselves left alone.'
This was also an accurate summary of feeling in Germany at the time. The
conflict between Paris and Washington was increasing. French criticism of
American policy in Vietnam was constant and extremely sharp. The old
'fool in Paris', as Dean Acheson once called the French President,[17] and
his country had already discovered the difficulties of winning a military
victory in the swamps of South-East Asia. De Gaulle, in attacking America's
military conduct in South-East Asia, was now seeking recognition from the
Third World and fanning the flames of anti-Americanism everywhere. He
was also discovering the sweetness of revenge, since the United States
was labouring under a burden that France had carried until the 1950s
without adequate American support. The West German policy of loyal
support for the United States was criticized mercilessly by the Gaullist
leadership. Thus Hervé Alphand, the French ambassador in Washington,
noted in his diary on 4 February 1966:[18]

> Another source of disagreement between us . . . In reality, Germany
> has no interest there. They have never been interested there, even
> under Hitler. As Bismarck said: 'These are the rats of the earth.'
> They have never left, as we have, the centre of Europe. They have
> never been, as we have, a global power. Thus the position of France
> vis-à-vis the Third World is much more progressive than theirs. One
> can clearly see this on the subject of the affairs of Vietnam.

At the same time, however, the Federal Republic's relations with the
United States of America came under strain as NATO entered a period of
crisis. The instability in the alliance could not be attributed solely to
de Gaulle's departure from the military organization of NATO in March
1966, though this offended America and its partners. There were much
wider issues involved, concerning the national interest of the United States

in *détente* with the Soviet Union. In pursuit of this objective Washington was prepared to accept some relaxation of NATO, which had particularly unfortunate consequences for the Federal Republic. Moreover, the Soviet Union did not respond by adopting a more cordial attitude towards Bonn. NATO continued to fulfil its tasks and was not wantonly sacrificed by the Americans. Nevertheless, in view of American global, nuclear and East Asian requirements, Washington was attaching less importance to NATO than before at least until 1968, when events in Czechoslovakia prompted it to provide more resolute support for a time. So were politicians like Konrad Adenauer and Franz Josef Strauss correct to advocate close co-operation with France?

The issue was complicated by the growing 'American challenge'[19] to Europe in other fields, such as the American investment offensives in certain vital areas, and the alarming advantage of the United States over the European nations in the field of space technology. These developments provoked the CSU leader Franz Josef Strauss to issue a serious warning:[20] 'If the creative spirit in Europe were to fail, our trade policy with the United States would be thrown out of balance and we would very soon endanger our economic position. With a long period of production in the framework of licences, we would be able to offer little more than services in return.' He argued that the welfare of both the Europeans and the Americans in the western community required attempts to prevent 'Europe ... from a political and military point of view, intensified by the economic dislocation of forces, [from sinking to the level of] a total satellite of the United States of America'.[21] Strauss recommended in his 'Proposal for Europe' that European independence in the western alliance should be protected by close co-operation between the Federal Republic of Germany and France.

Federal Chancellor Erhard was forced to deal with these arguments at a time when his government was already under severe pressure. In addition to its domestic problems, relations between the Federal Republic and the United States were troubled by the problem of foreign exchange stabilization payments and differences of opinion about the concept of defence. Even during his successful visit to the United States in September 1966, the Federal Chancellor raised a large number of questions concerning the strategy of 'flexible response'; Secretary of State Rusk eventually felt compelled to respond vehemently that 'the Americans [had] never abandoned an ally'.[22] In view of Soviet-American attempts to reach *détente*, the German delegation was not convinced. Numerous questions remained to be answered.

On the issue of 'offset' payments, McNamara and Johnson did not move an inch towards Erhard. His failure to gain concessions was a contributory factor in the fall of the Chancellor, who had long been isolated at home. Circumstances were conspiring to reopen discussion about the proper direction of German foreign policy. Had not the arguments of the Gaullists become even more convincing? Was President de Gaulle now a better guardian of German security interests, and a more credible ally in any attempt to end the division of Germany? The Gaullists argued that close co-operation with France offered a real chance to bring western integration and the prospect of reunification into harmony, along similar lines though on a smaller scale than in the 1950s. A new impetus could thus be given to German foreign policy. If the Federal Republic was to decide against the French offer, now that American protection no longer seemed so certain as before, then it could easily be plunged into a dangerous isolation in foreign affairs.

Partly because of this fear of isolation, Bonn reacted with suspicion to de Gaulle's dramatic visit to the Soviet Union in June and July 1966. There was also a mixed response to his greeting on that occasion, 'Eternal France salutes eternal Russia', attempting to play down the historical significance of the October Revolution and to accentuate the traditional importance of the nation. On the positive side, de Gaulle's commitment to the national state as the characteristic and definitive category of European history and politics made him inclined to support Bonn's view of the German Question, even in the USSR. On the other hand, West German politicians, including the Gaullists, did not share de Gaulle's attitude towards Russia, particularly his tendency to underestimate what they saw as the revolutionary force of communist ideology. The Atlanticists for their part regarded the President's proposals, which had emerged once again during his eight-day journey through the Soviet Union, as 'unacceptable in two ways'. Secretary of State Lahr of the Foreign Office briefly summarized the official view of the government in a private letter of 6 July:[23] 'We do not desire a Franco-Soviet condominium over Europe, in which we and the other European countries would have little say, and, above all, we do not wish to put our freedom (guaranteed by the USA alone) at risk.' However, the Gaullists were no longer certain that the American guarantee was secure. Strauss was aware of the fact that de Gaulle was personally driven by the need for prestige,[24] and he had no desire to destroy West German ties with the United States; nevertheless, he was already arguing in February 1966, even before Erhard's visit to de Gaulle in Paris, 'for an agreement with de Gaulle at almost any cost'.[25] Yet it remained doubtful whether France was really in a position to replace the United States in the nuclear and conventional relationship, even to a limited extent. A majority in all three big parties in parliament thought not, an attitude for which there was wide support in the country. This belief explains why the Atlanticists continued to hold the upper hand despite the deterioration in German-American relations in 1966, and why the Gaullist alternative was not adopted. It must remain an open question whether a historic opportunity in Franco-German relations had already been let slip two years before, in summer 1964. In any event, the option had been a genuine, if risky, alternative. Ex-Chancellor Adenauer had continued to weigh the situation carefully without committing himself body and soul to de Gaulle. For example, he disagreed fundamentally with the French President's judgement of Soviet policy. Shortly after an exchange of views with the general in Paris, Adenauer explained his attitude to the CDU's federal executive committee on 21 March 1966:[26] 'I would like to say to you that I do not agree with the view of Herr de Gaulle that a stabilization has occurred in the east. I would not like there to be any doubt about that. There is not the slightest evidence for it.' His speech that same day to the CDU Party Conference in Bonn, in which he said that the Soviet Union had 'joined the ranks of peoples ... who desire peace',[27] does not detract from the force of this opinion. Remarks of this kind had a very different meaning for Adenauer[28] than for de Gaulle. The President's own view of 'eternal Russia' was based on wishful thinking and frequently concealed a core of *Realpolitik*; he saw it as a nation which would join peacefully and unthreateningly in a 'Europe from the Atlantic to the Urals', in a relationship proceeding from *détente* through *entente* to co-operation. In contrast, Adenauer never underestimated the ideological dynamism of the Soviet Union. In the 1960s, however, he believed that the USSR did not intend to wage war since it could realize its goals in Europe more satisfactorily through a policy of *détente*. But should war break out, Adenauer believed that the US nuclear umbrella had become inadequate and might no longer provide the degree of protection which de Gaulle could make available, on grounds of national interest, for Frenchmen and Germans alike. In limited European conflicts France would probably react more swiftly and resolutely; it would therefore provide a greater deterrent than the United States, which was more prepared to accept setbacks. There could be some defeats which were relatively small and acceptable for the Americans, but would be major and disastrous for the Federal Republic of Germany.

There is no need here for detailed arguments for and against these alternative concepts of foreign policy. Ultimately, the Gaullist approach was not adopted, for reasons which are both numerous and plausible. The overbearing conduct of General de Gaulle made it obvious that France would generally have been a weaker though not a more benevolent patron than the Americans. Was the Federal Republic ever likely to entrust its security to a latent Nietzschean whose horror at the quiet life drove him to seek out danger? De Gaulle was decribed by André Malraux as a 'man of the day before yesterday and for the day after tomorrow';[29] he had little interest in everyday challenges and could only feel contempt for many aspects of the modern western way of life, including the domestic and foreign policy gradualism of the Bonn republic. To oversimplify the issue: the representatives of West Germany's gradualist culture and strategy seemed bound to reject a policy which placed de Gaulle's own country at the centre of world events and revealed the strength of his conviction that 'without greatness, France could not be France'.[30]

De Gaulle's provocation of the United States and his European partners continued. It sometimes appeared as though the visible weakness of his country was goading him to make a series of heroic gestures. If so, he had remained faithful to the principle he had followed during the Second World War, when the Anglo-Saxon powers had frequently complained about the obstinacy of the man who regarded them with such antagonism. He had commented then: 'I am too brittle to bend.' The 'policy of the empty chair', adopted from summer 1965 in the EEC Council of Ministers, gave the Germans dramatic and concrete evidence that Paris had little regard for the 1950s concept of European integration. During the community's constitutional crisis, which was settled only by a fragile compromise formula in January 1966, the French believed that the Federal Republic had not mediated between the two positions but had led the other members against France.

The relationship between Paris and Bonn had not greatly improved when the great NATO crisis shook the Western world and led to another clash between the interests of France and Germany. Compromise formulas – 'as much NATO and as much with France as possible'[31] – could not disguise the conflict, though these were undoubtedly important for the CDU in domestic politics. The unspoken dialogue between Bonn and Paris, between Erhard and de Gaulle, and even between his successor Kiesinger and the French President, continued as follows:[32] 'I do not understand you. You want Europe to be able to speak with a loud voice, but you don't want it to have a body.' – 'I do not understand you. You want Europe to have a body, but you permit its soul to be American!'

As a result of de Gaulle's resolute anti-Americanism, it was expected that France would not renew the NATO treaty which was due to expire in 1969, at least not in its existing form. In May 1965, the American Defense Secretary McNamara had told his German colleague von Hassel that he was expecting 'the departure of France from NATO next spring'.[33] But there was still widespread surprise when de Gaulle announced in March 1966 that France would withdraw from the militarily integrated organization of NATO on 1 July 1966, though without leaving the alliance itself. The President intended to use the advantages of the alliance in the event of war, but was unwilling to relinquish the traditional freedom of a country in an alliance to make a sovereign decision over the *casus belli* and the *casus foederis*. He was no longer prepared to accept integration under the patronage of the United States, which he regarded as hegemonic, disadvantageous and humiliating. His decision to cease military co-operation within the framework of NATO reflected his most profound beliefs about the value and sovereignty of France, as well as his response to serious political considerations. France was unwilling to allow itself to be drawn into a European conflagration by events in Asia. De Gaulle therefore claimed that peace was divisible; he distinguished between Europe, pacified by the policy of *détente*, and an Asia ravaged by tensions and military conflicts. The crisis in Asia should not be allowed to disturb the peace of Europe. Soviet-American disagreements should be confined to that distant part of the world and not transferred to Europe. He therefore insisted that for France to preserve the peace, in the event of a war in Europe France must be able to decide whether there had been an unprovoked attack from the Soviet Union or whether the Russians had been provoked. If, in the French view, the USSR was taking limited revenge for conduct connected with American actions in Vietnam, France would wish to stand aside.

Was it possible for the Federal Republic to go along with a policy of this kind? Undoubtedly not, unless it adopted the plan of a Franco-German *Zweierverbindung* without reservation. With his latest spectacular act, de Gaulle was once again indicating to the Germans that the decision was urgent. The French departure from NATO created much greater difficulties for the West German state, vulnerably placed in the centre of Europe, than for the other partners in the alliance. For a whole variety of reasons, Bonn did not have the luxury of the calm response of the American President, who was prepared to wait for the end of de Gaulle's rule even though he had been re-elected only in December 1965. In fact, Washington seemed ready to adopt an indulgent attitude towards its traditional French ally. In contrast, it appeared thoroughly intransigent towards its 'model pupil', Bonn, which had remained obliging and had never rejected the principle of integration even during the NATO crisis. In sombre mood, the Federal Chancellor had indicated the possibility West Germany had rejected, 'if we had the ambition, of creating our own position now between the fronts'.[34] Bonn had to decide what should be done with the French troops stationed on German territory after they had been removed from integrated NATO control. The problem led to an exchange of notes between Paris and Bonn, and to increasingly sharp exchanges until summer 1966. During this period, Foreign Minister Schröder – determined to protect German interests – assessed de Gaulle as the 'hardest, most clear-headed and coldest politician in the world'.[35] However, Chancellor Erhard soon demonstrated considerable generosity towards France on this issue. Negotiations began on the basis of a transition arrangement and a calmer atmosphere prevailed. On 21 December 1966, when the Grand Coalition had already taken office, the negotiations led to a Franco-German agreement on the status of the French troops in Germany.

It had nevertheless become clear to Bonn that France was just as implacable in the pursuit of its objectives as the Americans had been in the controversial foreign exchange question. The outcome was disillusioning for the Federal Republic, but it seemed that the Federal Republic's own foreign policy and its military security would still be better protected at the side of the United States of America. Consequently, despite German-American differences, Bonn kept closer to Washington than to Paris. De Gaulle had predicted, threateningly, that the Federal Republic could now find itself on the risky path 'into isolation' as the 'stand-in of an extra-European power in Europe'.[36] In any event, the 'country in danger'[37] was now thrown back on its own resources more than ever before and was forced to redefine its own *raison d'état*. Not least, it was forced to consider the division of Germany as an unresolved central issue which was beginning to emerge once again. In this situation, external developments could easily lead to domestic consequences against which Henry Kissinger had warned so urgently:[38]

> Should the Federal Republic become the focal point of European tensions, disappointment could cause the Germans to turn to the question that they regard as the cause of their isolation. Their irritation would then be directed against those they regard as the authors of their isolation. In this lies the German 'problem'... The most exposed western ally, sixteen million of whose people find themselves as hostages in the hands of the Communists, stands in the centre of every dispute. It could be that the internal structure of the Federal Republic is not equal to this demand.

III
THE POLICY OF LOYAL MEDIATION

As in many other fields, the Grand Coalition which succeeded the Erhard government worked as a 'repair shop' to remove German-American conflict over the foreign exchange stabilization payments and the Nuclear Weapons Non-Proliferation Treaty.[39] German-American relations improved and Bonn regained some of its room to manoeuvre in foreign affairs. However, this advantage was not gained by attempts to reduce the role of de Gaulle's France in Bonn's *Westpolitik*. On the contrary, Kiesinger and his Foreign Minister were careful to pay particular attention to France. 'Paris is the second most important partner that we need', commented the leader of the Social Democratic parliamentary delegation to the SPD party council:[40]

> Whether we like it or not. One has only to imagine the most extreme theoretical case, that the French say to the Poles or to others in eastern Europe, yes, you are quite right, these Germans are really *révanchists*.

If that should happen, I say, it is an extreme theoretical case, German foreign policy would be finished. No one can damage us so terribly as the French, they know it too, they don't threaten us with it, they know that it is an implied threat. Therefore . . . considerable regard for France is unavoidable, we are in a strait-jacket here.

This approach remained valid despite the difficulties which the general continued to create for German and European statesmen. Thus, Foreign Minister Brandt warned the parliamentary delegation of his party that it was necessary 'to consider . . . beyond actual points of conflict, whether we bring the Franco-German relationship safely through a difficult period'.[41] Yet, like his chancellor, Brandt realistically assumed that European unity could make no real headway whilst President de Gaulle continued in office. The situation in Europe was therefore very difficult, since de Gaulle used every conversation to try to persuade Chancellor Kiesinger of the virtues of his idea of a political *Zweierverbindung*.

In contrast to what has been described as the 'polemical Gallophobia of the Erhard/Schröder era',[42] relations between Paris and Bonn began to improve. Admittedly, the 'friendly realism of the Kiesinger/Brandt government'[43] had very little in common with the eager exclusiveness of the Adenauer period. The new government repeatedly evaded de Gaulle's invitations to close political co-operation. With perhaps even more clarity and frankness than he had shown to Erhard, de Gaulle told the new chancellor that the Anglo-Saxons were pursuing a policy of the status quo in Europe; France, on the other hand, had fundamentally different military and political conditions to deal with. He claimed that France was interested in German reunification so long as this process, as Kiesinger expressed it, took place according to de Gaulle's 'beautiful formula' and 'without too much ambition in border and armaments questions'.[44] Thus, during his state visit to Poland in September 1967, de Gaulle made an unmistakable reference to the legitimacy of the postwar frontiers of Europe, which Bonn could accept only with difficulty. In contrast, he regarded the German Democratic Republic as an 'artificial state',[45] as he told the Soviet leader plainly during his visit to the USSR in June–July 1966. In fact, he tended to view it – and therefore with dislike – as the successor to Prussia. And just as the artificial Prussian *Rationalstaat* had been in constant danger of total destruction in the early modern period, de Gaulle thought that East Germany could also be disposed of. Here he was guided by the idea that Russia and Poland could be persuaded to concede the existence of a reunited Germany whilst, in return, the Germans could be made to abandon their claim to the former eastern territories and to renounce nuclear weapons. His own position had clearly changed a great deal since 1945.[46] He told Chancellor Kiesinger in January 1967:[47]

214

France is for German unity. It knows that, if it wants peace and wants to co-operate to that end with Germany for a long time and on a large scale, it cannot oppose German unity. Naturally there are certain limits. France does not wish to see Germany re-emerge in the form of Hitler's Reich, with excessive frontiers and ambitions or equipped with weapons which can be wrongly used. But it wants to see Germany united.

Faced with the choice between Anglo-Saxon hegemony and the 'German danger', de Gaulle judged the Anglo-American threat to be far more serious. Indeed, he even regarded a reunited Germany, dependent on France for its political security, as a counterbalance against American and British claims to supremacy. Fundamentally, President de Gaulle thought that the American threat was more dangerous than the Soviet – a view summarized in his famous remark that 'whisky is stronger . . . than vodka'.[48] He thought that Russia was 'alone' and 'not belligerent'; in contrast, America saw it 'as natural to rule, and in fact everywhere. France cannot agree to that'.[49]

According to de Gaulle's ceaseless argument, the precondition for a long-term policy leading towards German unification lay in an exclusive co-operation between Paris and Bonn. It would permit both partners, against the background of a linked sovereignty in economic, techno-logical and military affairs, to deal on an independent footing even with the world powers. With a glance at the history of the twentieth century, de Gaulle left no doubt as to who would take the lead in such a union. In fact, both Konrad Adenauer and Kurt Georg Kiesinger were convinced that, because of the immediate past, Germany could not assume such a role. De Gaulle's visions of a Franco-German connection no longer aroused the bitter disagreements between Atlanticists and Gaullists which had characterized foreign and domestic affairs in the first years after the resignation of Adenauer as chancellor. Economics Minister Schiller described this happy state of affairs during a trip to the United States in summer 1967:[50] 'We are living at the moment in a loyal triangular relationship with America and France and are attempting in many respects to mediate, loyally to mediate.' Kiesinger certainly recognized that de Gaulle's sympathy for German reunification, born out of his conception of French interests, offered certain prospects which Americans and British policies no longer contained during the 1960s. However, partly for domestic political reasons, the Chancellor considered that it would be premature and even dangerous to recognize the Oder-Neisse line with this prospect in mind. The emergence of strong nationalist sentiment in the Federal Republic encouraged his belief that it was not a suitable moment to announce the abandonment of German claims; West German politicians were also anxious to avoid the danger of neutralism in foreign affairs which could easily flow from such a tendency, encouraged by the political right or left. In general, the limits of any co-operation between the Federal Republic and France which was aimed at political union rapidly became apparent in the years between 1967 and 1969.

Despite this difficult situation, the Federal government would not be cajoled into creating a front against Paris because of French stubbornness in obstructing the progress of European unity. Instead, Bonn began to act as mediator, with a degree of success. In German eyes, the main requirement was for Europe to survive the anachronistic era of de Gaulle without too much damage to European unification in its traditional sense. The Germans had to stand the test when, on 10 May 1967, Great Britain made its second application to join the EEC to the President of the Council of Ministers in Brussels. De Gaulle firmly rejected the British application. His economic reasons for opposing the entry of Britain into the EEC were ultimately only a pretext. The French President would certainly have made a stand against an economically healthy Great Britain; at bottom he wanted Europe to be led by France, not by Britain. In his eyes, even the British were part of the Atlantic danger which he was endeavouring to remove from the Old World. 'England belongs to the Americans', he told Federal Chancellor Kiesinger on 13 March 1969, thus revealing the central, historical motive for his refusal to allow Britain to join the EEC. He continued:[51]

> Perhaps the English regret it, but they started it during the war, he saw it himself, it was there when Churchill subordinated himself to the Americans. Since then they have been under the Americans. They would have their 'special relationship' and they thought this would be an advantage for them. Perhaps it is, but it is not possible to build a European Europe with the English as long as the English are as they are.

The period of European euphoria over supranational integration was long over. Indeed, the insight that the European quality in Europe actually consists of its nations made even the German Chancellor unhappy with the prospect of 'a European hot pot . . . which would be controlled . . . by a Commission'.[52] The foreign policy of Kiesinger and Brandt was committed to a particular approach. It sought to avoid the anonymity of the supranational entity as well as to prevent a relapse into the nationalism of the nineteenth century; it aimed to give the European region real shape and weight in the world, though without removing national identities. At first, though, difficulties had to be faced in Europe. The British, supported for a time by the Italians and the Dutch, continued to press for entry to the EEC despite the French veto. In the Chancellor's own party, a considerable number of deputies wanted Kiesinger and his Foreign Minister to go ahead and construct Europe without de Gaulle. The Federal government was convinced that such conduct was impractical and utopian. In fact, there were paradoxes in the vehement support of some Germans for British entry into the EEC, since the British had the same objective as de Gaulle – they wanted to assume the leadership of Europe. The leader of the Social Democratic parliamentary delegation was careful to explain to the SPD council about the 'power political conflict between London and Paris.'[53] And the British Foreign Minister George Brown, who never made any secret of his thoughts, urged Willy Brandt in December 1967:[54] 'Willy, you must get us in, so we can take the lead.'

Franco-British antagonism was a fundamental obstacle to the unity of Europe. The Federal government often had to make great efforts to prevent the collapse of achievements already gained in this field. Historians often underestimate the value of successful efforts to prevent worse things from happening, and weigh achievements too lightly by comparing them with the many desires that remain unfulfilled. There was wide agreement amongst European politicians that the British would eventually be successful in their application to join the EEC. They were not merely looking forward to the end of the de Gaulle era, even after his government had shown serious weaknesses during the events of May 1968 and had been irrevocably damaged. For example, Kurt Birrenbach advocated the entry of Britain into the EEC at least partly to maintain the West German policy of voluntary self-imposed moderation. Since the days of Adenauer, German foreign policy had attempted to weave together the sovereignty and the integration of the Federal Republic into an inseparable whole. In the Anglo-French conflict, Bonn was anxious 'that an equilibrium of power within the West is achieved'.[55] Indeed, Helmut Schmidt believed that, in many ways, 'our interest in the balance of power . . . speaks for the inclusion of England'.[56]

In fact, at precisely this time the economic strength of the West German partial state was growing to such an extent that Britain's co-operation in the EEC was absolutely necessary to maintain the required balance in Europe. By the beginning of 1969, therefore, a corresponding change in French policy towards Europe had begun to emerge. Admittedly, during the WEU crisis of February and March 1969, there were further fierce exchanges between the British and the French.[57] But shortly before, in a conversation of 4 February with the British ambassador in Paris, Christopher Soames, the President had adopted a very different and conciliatory tone towards the British. As a result of indiscretions and misunderstandings, this conversation later made headline news. De Gaulle had been depressed by the Bonn Currency Conference of November 1968, which had plainly revealed the economic strength of the Federal Republic of Germany and the impotence of France. The French President seems to have offered to work more closely with the British in the field of weapons technology and to create a great free trade zone in Europe. In part, he intended to make British entry into the EEC superfluous. Yet it is also certain that de Gaulle's offer was prompted by a desire to create a counterweight against the Germans, who had become the dominant economic force in Europe and had continued to resist his idea of an exclusive union with France. The British informed the states of the EEC of their lack of interest in this proposal rather than the government in Paris. De Gaulle, under pressure in domestic affairs and exposed on the currency issue, was thereafter even more resentful of London. However, his fury did not alter the trend in historical developments, which was beyond his personal control. The re-examination of French foreign policy begun by de Gaulle was continued by his successor, Pompidou. Under his leadership, Paris again moved closer to the United States and to NATO and signalled its willingness to cease opposition to British entry into the EEC. This new flexibility was connected with the growing fear of German economic strength felt by the *Grande Nation*. During the 1960s, the Germans had served more or less successfully as 'honest brokers'.[58] At the Bonn Currency Conference of November 1968, however, German politicians had enforced their national interest against the combined resistance of the deficit nations who were also their allies and protectors. It was the first occasion in the history of the West German state that such an assertive line had been taken and, for a moment, the latent threat of isolation which had always hovered over the Germans became overt.

There were major, historically based differences in the positions adopted by 'eternal France', economically weak but politically respected, and the economically powerful but politically vulnerable West German provisional state – however well established it had become in the mean time. Other states, whose past appeared normal, could safely follow their own *Sonderwege* and even disregard the rules of the Western states. Latitude of this kind was not permitted to the Federal Republic, limited as it was by history and by its dependent status in security matters. 'As long as the rest of the world has the impression that for the sake of our own special problems we are making a policy which could drag others into a crisis, it is bad': these words, spoken by Chancellor Kiesinger to a meeting of CDU parliamentary delegates on 30 September 1968, aptly described a general maxim of Federal German foreign policy in the years between 1963 and 1969.[59] Yet there were advantages in the cautious gradualism in domestic and foreign affairs to which the Federal Republic was committed. In particular, in its dealings with a French President who insisted on his special role in Europe, Bonn was able to avoid the danger of isolation within the Western world. The Federal Republic generally succeeded in establishing a loyal relationship with both the United States and France. The hard-won normality of West German foreign policy, in which its representatives sought to secure Bonn's interests within the West whilst also accommodating the needs of the West as regards reunification and *Ostpolitik*, was not endangered. De Gaulle's bold proposal for a joint Franco-German *Sonderweg* in world history was not compatible with a restrained and austere policy of this kind. In principle, West German politicians were anxious to avoid extremes in foreign policy and to maintain a central position, an approach which the general was bound to regard as mean-spirited and pessimistic. After the honeymoon of the Adenauer period, the Franco-German relationship was beset by difficulties during the 1960s. Nevertheless, these problems did not endanger the 'marriage of convenience'[60] between Paris and Bonn, which continued to reflect the interests of both states.

NOTES

There are a number of points to be made in preface to this survey of Franco-German relations between 1963 and 1969.

(1) The chapter deals with relations between France and Germany during the chancellorships of Ludwig Erhard and Kurt Georg Kiesinger.
(2) It rests largely on unpublished material from the archives of the Konrad-Adenauer-Stiftung, the Ludwig-Erhard-Stiftung and the archive of the 'Büro Kiesinger'.
(3) The use of these archives explains why the theme is investigated from the German point of view and concerns the 'factor of France' in the network of Bonn's foreign policy during these years.

1 Lipgens, W., 'Europäische Integration', in R. Löwenthal and H.-P. Schwarz (eds), *Die zweite Republik. 25 Jahre Bundesrepublik Deutschland – Eine Bilanz* (Stuttgart: 1974), p. 50. In the following chapter, only direct quotations will usually be given footnotes. For the rest, see the appropriate chapter in my book *Von Erhard zur grossen Koalition* (Stuttgart/Wiesbaden: 1984).
2 Schmid, C., *Erinnerungen* (Berne/Munich/Vienna: 1979), p. 751.
3 Social Democracy archive, Friedrich-Ebert-Stiftung (cited as FES), SPD-Präsidium, 11 June 1965: Brandt contribution (report on a conversation with de Gaulle).
4 Blankenhorn, H., *Verständnis und Verständigung. Blätter eines politischen Tagebuchs 1949 bis 1979* (Frankfurt-am-Main/Berlin/Vienna: 1980), p. 448.
5 Lojewski, W. von, *Bonn am Wendepunkt. Die Krise der deutschen Aussenpolitik. Analyse und Bilanz* (Munich/Esslingen: 1965), p. 24.
6 Political archive, Friedrich-Naumann-Stiftung, FDP Bundeshauptausschuss, 30 April 1965.
7 Grewe, W. G., *Rückblenden 1976–1951* (Frankfurt-am-Main/Berlin/Vienna: 1979), p. 644.
8 Archive of Ludwig-Erhard-Stiftung (cited as LES), Nachlass Erhard I.2.24: Strauss to Erhard, 5 February 1966. Handwritten marginal note by the Chancellor.
9 See, for example, Bohlen, C. E., *Witness to History 1929–1969* (London: 1973), p. 514.
10 Schmid, *Erinnerungen*, p. 751.
11 LES, Nachlass Erhard 739: 'Bundeskanzler Erhard vor dem Fraktionsvorstand (Aussenpolitik) 28.7.1964'.
12 LES, Nachlass Erhard 739: 'Bundeskanzler Erhard vor dem Fraktionsvorstand (Aussenpolitik) 28.7.1964'.
13 Lahr, R., *Zeuge von Fall und Aufstieg. Private Briefe 1934–1974* (Hamburg: 1981), p. 403.

14 LES, Nachlass Erhard 751: 'Der Sonderkreis'.
15 *Neue Zürcher Zeitung*, 11 January 1965: 'Die neue Begegnung de Gaulles mit Erhard'.
16 Seydoux, F., *Botschafter in Deutschland. Meine zweite Mission 1965–1970* (Frankfurt-am-Main: 1978), p. 90.
17 Guttenberg, K. T. Freiherr zu, *Fussnoten* (Stuttgart: 1971), p. 138: entry of 'summer 1967' on a comment made to him by Dean Acheson.
18 Alphand, H., *L'étonnement d'être. Journal (1939–1973)* (Paris: 1977), p. 472.
19 Servan Schreiber, J.-J., *Die amerikanische Herausforderung* (Hamburg: 3rd edn, 1968).
20 LES, Nachlass Erhard II.1.39: Strauss to Erhard, 5 July 1966.
21 LES, Nachlass Erhard II.1.39: Strauss to Erhard, 5 July 1966.
22 Christian Democratic archive, Konrad-Adenauer-Stiftung (cited as KAS), diary of Kai-Uwe von Hassel (cited as Hassel diary), 26 September 1966.
23 Lahr, *Zeuge*, p. 445.
24 Lahr, *Zeuge*, p. 445.
25 LES, Nachlass Erhard I.2.24: Strauss to Erhard, 5 February 1966.
26 KAS, CDU Bundesparteivorstand, 21 March 1966.
27 Speech to the CDU party conference in Bonn, in *Konrad Adenauer, Reden, 1917–1967. Eine Auswahl*, ed. H.-P. Schwarz (Stuttgart: 1975), p. 482.
28 See in more detail in the following chapter in this book, 'Adenauer and Soviet Russia, 1963–1967: the foreign policy ideas of the retired Federal Chancellor', p [/].
29 Quoted in Baring, A. and C. Tautil, *Charles de Gaulle. Grösse und Grenzen* (Cologne/Berlin: 1963), p. 97
30 De Gaulle, C., *Memoiren. Der Ruf 1940–1942* (Frankfurt-am-Main: 1955), p. 7.
31 KAS, CDU/CSU parliamentary delegation, 19 April 1966: contribution of Barzel.
32 Grosser, A., *Das Bündnis. Die westeuropäischen Länder und die USA seit dem Krieg* (Munich: 1978), p. 267.
33 KAS, Hassel diary, 31 May 1965.
34 KAS, Hassel diary, 15 March 1966.
35 KAS, Hassel diary, 4 April 1966.
36 KAS, Hassel diary, 15 May 1966: report of a comment by de Gaulle.
37 Krone, H., 'Deutschland – Frankreich – Amerika. Unsere Sicherheit im Bündnis', *Politische Meinung* 11 (1966), p. 25.
38 Kissinger, H., 'Die deutsche Frage als Problem der europäischen und der internationalen Sicherheit', *Europa-Archiv* 23 (1966), pp. 832, 834.
39 Archive in 'Büro Kiesinger' (cited as ABK). Vertrauliche Hintergrundsgespräche mit Journalisten 008: 'Informationsgespräch B.K.Kiesinger mit Journalisten der Landespressekonferenz Baden-Württemberg', 21 March 1968: contribution of Kiesinger.
40 FES, SPD-Parteirat, 30 June 1967.
41 FES, SPD-Fraktion, 6 February 1968.
42 Hänsch, K., 'Die Entwicklung der europäischen Gemeinschaften', in *Die Internationale Politik 1966–1967*, ed. K. Carstens, D. Mende, C. Rajewsky, W. Wagner (Munich/Vienna: 1973), p. 200.
43 Hänsch, 'Die Entwicklung der europäischen Gemeinschaften', p. 200.
44 ABK, Protokolle. D. Gesprächsaufzeichnungen. Ausland. 24.4.1967–28.2.1968. 288: Aufzeichnung Kiesinger – Seydoux, 30 June 1967: contribution of Kiesinger.
45 Quoted by Salis, J. R. von, 'Der Fortgang der Entspannung zwischen West und Ost', in *Die Internationale Politik 1966–1967*, p. 137.
46 On this subject in general see Ménudier, H., 'Frankreich und das deutsche Problem', *Deutschland-Archiv* 10 (1977), p. 1034 ff.
47 ABK, Dokumentation. D. Aussenpolitik. Verhältnis zu Frankreich. 312: 'Analyse der Aussenpolitik in den beiden ersten Vier-Augen-Gesprächen zwischen Bundeskanzler Dr. Kiesinger und Präsident de Gaulle am 13. und 14. Januar 1967 (Zusammenfassung der wesentlichen Ausführungen)'.
48 ABK, Dokumentation. D. Aussenpolitik. Verhältnis zu Frankreich. 312: 'Aufstellung der Gesprächsthemen bzw. Kurzfassung des Gesprächsinhalts zwischen Bundeskanzler Kiesinger und Präsident de Gaulle beim Konsultationstreffen in Bonn 12./13. Juli 1967 lt. Dolmetscherprotokollen: Vier-Augen-Gespräch (13. Juli morgens, Spaziergang im Park)': actual comment by de Gaulle.

49 ABK, Dokumentation. D. Aussenpolitik. Verhältnis zu Frankreich. 312: 'Analyse der Aussenpolitik in den beiden ersten Vier-Augen-Gesprächen zwischen Bundeskanzler Dr. Kiesinger und Präsident de Gaulle am 13. und 14. Januar 1967 (Zusammenfassung der wesentlichen Ausführungen)'.
50 FES, SPD-Parteirat, 30 June 1967.
51 ABK, Protokolle. D. Gesprächsaufzeichnungen. BK. Ausland mit de Gaulle 1967–1969. 292: Aufzeichnung Kiesinger – de Gaulle, 13 March 1969.
52 ABK, Protokolle. D. Gesprächsaufzeichnungen. BK. Ausland mit de Gaulle 1967–1969. 292: Aufzeichnung Kiesinger – de Gaulle, 14 March 1969.
53 FES, SPD-Parteirat, 30 June 1967.
54 Brandt, W., *Begegnungen und Einsichten. Die Jahre 1960–1975* (Hamburg: 1976), p. 202.
55 FES, SPD-Parteirat, 30 June 1967.
56 FES, SPD-Parteirat, 30 June 1967.
57 Schmoeckel, R., 'WEU-Krise und "Soames-Affaire" Februar 1969', unpublished manuscript in ABK.
58 Brandt, *Begegnungen*, p. 205.
59 KAS, CDU/CSU-Fraktion, 30 September 1968.
60 Poidevin, R. and J. Bariéty, *Frankreich und Deutschland. Die Geschichte ihrer Beziehungen 1815–1975* (Munich: 1982), p. 421.

9

Adenauer and Soviet Russia, 1963–7.
The foreign policy ideas
of the retired Federal Chancellor

I

Konrad Adenauer resigned from the office of Federal Chancellor on 15 October 1963. Both inside and outside Germany, he was regarded as the embodiment of the 'policy of strength' which saw the Soviet Union as the main adversary of the Western world and its most advanced post, the Federal Republic of Germany. Even after his departure as head of government, the patriarch continued to be chairman of the CDU; as such, he was one of a number of power centres in the structure of Bonn politics during the brief Erhard era. Adenauer used this position, as well as his international role as an 'elder statesman' of the West, to issue a series of warnings about the Soviet danger. His activities continued, in public and in private, until his last great speech in the Madrid Ateneo on 16 February 1967. Against this background, Adenauer's speech to the CDU conference in Bonn on 21 March 1966 caused something of a sensation. Towards the end of his speech to a gathering which had relieved him of the office of chairman of the Christian Democratic Union and nominated him as honorary chairman for life with a seat and vote on every party committee, he made the following remarks:[1]

Recently something has happened in world history which in my opinion should have been very much emphasized by all the newspapers. But, my friends, our newspapers apparently have not understood it. It was the peace mediations of the Soviet Union between India and Pakistan. I must say quite openly, that was a surprising development for each of us who has previously been aware of the relations between Pakistan and India . . . [The fact] that the Soviet Union helped to find peace between these two peoples, *for me that is evidence that the Soviet Union has joined the ranks of peoples who desire peace.* (Applause and movement) – I know that I am making a bold statement here. But, ladies and gentlemen, the fact remains that the Soviet Union has produced peace between these two peoples who were under arms and facing each other.

Among the delegates, there was a great deal of speculation about the motives and objectives of Adenauer and the function and meaning of his words. His interpretation of Soviet policy aroused equal astonishment and interest in the press and public of the Federal Republic of Germany. Had the former Chancellor, now 90 years old, turned from a 'Cold Warrior' into a modern *détente* politician?

In retrospect, one thing seems certain: the CDU party conference, which had promised to be a turgid and boring affair after the great election victory of Ludwig Erhard in September 1965, had been given a new lease of life by Adenauer's speech. However, this does not adequately explain his intentions, since it was not his main aim to open a debate for any secondary purposes. Adenauer shared Bismarck's view that 'external things were an end in themselves' and were 'more important than the rest'.[2] Any preoccupation with the tactical implication of Adenauer's comments would result in a failure to do justice to their actual contents. The old Chancellor's remarks were rooted in his ideas about the 'country in danger',[3] to use the phrase with which Adenauer's confidant Heinrich Krone described Germany and its traditional legacy of an exposed central position.

Taking into account his policies and attitude in the 1950s and 1960s, it is most unlikely that Adenauer had responded to the restless atmosphere of the Federal Republic and to western demands for *détente* by joining those politicians who were advocating a 'new *Ostpolitik*' – the *Vordenker*, to use a phrase then in vogue. In fact, he adopted a sceptical attitude to this 'policy of movement', which was regarded almost as an end in itself by many of its representatives whilst others supported it as a step towards their long-term objectives. Konrad Adenauer cannot be compared to a Metternich, suddenly advocating reconciliation with revolutionary France. Instead, his words suggest an almost Bismarckian, multifaceted view of foreign policy. Russia always occupied an important place in this scheme; however, specific policies towards that country would be influenced by awareness of the prevailing trends in world politics at any given moment. Adenauer's remarks did not signify any painful metamorphosis in his attitudes. He had not been converted from the Saul of his 'policy of strength' into the Paul of an advocate of *détente*. His views and conduct actually revealed a continuity of approach towards foreign policy, though this was naturally adjusted to take account of changing times.

The idea that mistaken or inadequate information about the military strength of the Soviet Union lay at the root of his comments also fails to offer a *comprehensive* explanation of his controversial remarks. Directly after the speech, Defence Minister von Hassel went to Adenauer with details of the offensive capability of the Soviet forces, which was in stark contrast to the apparent peaceableness of the USSR. Shortly afterwards, von Hassel arranged for the honorary chairman of the CDU to meet a group of military experts, who provided him with a graphic analysis of the relationship of forces in Europe and the possibilities these offered the Soviets. Adenauer was impressed by the information he was given. The expert references to the ability of the Russians to overrun Europe almost from a standing start actually confirmed his own beliefs, which had been expressed on many occasions. What they did *not* do was disprove Adenauer's assessment of the nature of Soviet policy.

The former Chancellor doubted that the Soviets were really planning to use military force to attack Europe at that time, or indeed in the foreseeable future. Konrad Adenauer had been an important figure during the two great crises over Berlin and Cuba between 1958 and 1962, when there had been an imminent threat of war. He had since become convinced that the Soviets would not attack Western Europe for the time being, but were banking on the success of *détente* politics to help them achieve their objectives. The former Chancellor himself continued to regard *détente* with grave suspicion. In his opinion, expressed a month before his speech in Bonn, such policies would lead to what he described as '*Kottfreundschaft*' between the Soviet Union and the United States. The phraseology was vivid, as well as apt:[4] 'America has a curious relationship to Soviet Russia. They are half friends, they are half enemies. We are by the Rhine near Cologne and there is a good word for such a relationship, namely *Kott-Freund*. *Kott* means bad and *Freund* means friend. So *Kott-Freund*, that is the Americans and Soviet Russia.' He feared that *détente* between the superpowers would be applied, successfully and ruthlessly, over the heads of the West Germans. Adenauer considered that the involvement of the United States in South-East Asia – which he rejected as highly dangerous – was resulting in a disastrous American neglect of the European 'cockpit' of world politics, to the ultimate detriment of American interests as well as those of the Europeans. On the basis of this and other arguments, he no longer believed that the Russians intended to wage war directly.

In the course of his long life, Adenauer had learned to recognize the ebb and flow of tension and détente as the natural rhythm of power politics, which had also applied during the Cold War between the United States and the Soviet Union. Between 1962 and 1968, there was indeed a comparatively long period in which Europe did not seem to be threatened by war. Despite his constant concern for the direction of foreign policy which was so critical for his country, there was some justification for his conviction that the Soviet Union had 'joined the ranks' of the nations 'who desire peace' – 'because Soviet Russia itself needs peace'.[5] It is an open question whether this important phrase, as Adenauer noted[6] on 23 March 1966 in a version which was otherwise identical, had been left out of his speech because of the poor lighting or whether he had some other motives for not mentioning it. In any event, the phrase illuminated an important aspect of his thinking. Moreover, it was not an unusual remark for an experienced observer of international politics, accustomed to thinking in categories of power politics, to have made. This element of his thinking throws more light on Adenauer's interpretation of Soviet foreign policy, which was inevitably greatly compressed in the Bonn speech. The analysis was closely connected with his conception of foreign policy and policy towards the East. The framework of his convictions had been developed long before, but was now being adjusted to meet the demands of a new international situation.

On 25 March 1966, the political commentator of the *Frankfurter Allgemeine Zeitung* attempted to make a balanced assessment of the affair. He was not satisfied by arguments which traced the comments on 'Adenauer's peaceable Soviet Union'[7] solely to the powerful influence of de Gaulle, with whom the old Chancellor had held a meeting in Paris shortly before. The *Frankfurter Allgemeine Zeitung* reminded its readers, on the day the 'peace note' of the Federal Republic of Germany was handed over, 'that Adenauer, despite his harsh tone against Moscow, had made surprising gestures revealing friendliness to the Soviet Union at an earlier stage. Moreover, his anti-communism never detracted from his awareness that the German state under Hitler had perpetrated appalling outrages against the Soviet Union and its population.'[8] Adenauer's relationship with de Gaulle, and the French President's assessment of international politics, admittedly had a significant influence on the opinions of the former Chancellor about the realities of international politics. However, Adenauer did not always share de Gaulle's views *en bloc*. Thus, on 21 March 1966, he informed the federal executive committee of the CDU about his differences with de Gaulle:[9] 'I would like to say to you that I do not agree with the view of Herr de Gaulle that a stabilization has occurred in the east. I would not like there to be any doubt about that. There is not the slightest evidence for it.'

As before, he remained mistrustful of the ideologically motivated power politics of the Soviet Union. Adenauer rejected East–West *détente* because, as a result of inadequate prospects of intervention and veto, he regarded it as detrimental to the interests of his own country. Despite the foundations of his foreign policy, however, Adenauer was convinced even during the 1950s that it would be necessary to establish contacts with the Soviet Union if the German Question was to be settled and the relationship between the two states improved. In his view, such policies could best be achieved by West German integration within the West and in close co-operation with the protecting powers of the Federal Republic of Germany. This conviction was not then the central strand of his policy, which was recognizably directed to the West. Nevertheless, a determination to pursue an *Ostpolitik* lay not far behind it; as a future task which was never forgotten, it occupied the position of a distant goal.

In Adenauer's view, it was both historically unavoidable and therefore politically necessary for West Germany to reach a settlement with the Soviet Union. The precondition for such a move, however, was to ensure defensive preparedness in the Western alliance and even, in the event of the failure of deterrence, to be prepared to use force. He hoped to pursue a moderate and flexible 'policy of strength', for which careful concern for a strong defensive position was necessary. This goal had nothing to do with the chimera of the roll-back concept, which had been announced for propaganda purposes, always had pejorative overtones and was obviously unsuccessful. Instead Adenauer hoped to establish a position of defensive strength in power politics which would enable the country to take the offensive in the ideological struggle; thereafter, it would be necessary to wait, with vigilance and staying power, until events provided a favourable opportunity for a new initiative.

Adenauer was well aware that, in a parliamentary democracy, the virtues associated with the long-term and tenacious pursuit of political concepts may be lacking. Particularly at the beginning of the 1960s, when the television age began to exert a dominating influence on the Federal Republic of Germany, there was a strong public desire for rapid successes. Adenauer was also alarmed to observe a return of the notorious 'German unrest' among his countrymen in the Federal Republic, whose political freedom of manoeuvre was greatly restricted by the priority given to reunification politics and by the stagnation of the European movement since 1962.

Konrad Adenauer continued to place security above all other objectives in Federal German foreign policy. He never lost his interest in the national question, but it had a 'subordinate, though important rating . . . in the overall design of Adenauer *Ostpolitik*'.[10] This organizing of goals was entirely characteristic of his policy. It was fully in harmony with an idea to which West Germany had been committed since the 1950s, and which involved making the goal of disarmament causally dependent on progress in the reunification issue and vice versa. This element of continuity in foreign affairs and *Ostpolitik* lasted until Adenauer's 'truce proposals' to the Soviets at the end of his chancellorship. However, he was no longer in a position to negotiate on the subject. When Moscow finally agreed to negotiations on equal terms in May 1963, Adenauer's resignation had already been set for the following October. In any event, Konrad Adenauer was always certain that *Ostpolitik* had to be based on two conditions, among others. First, it must be the direct policy of the Chancellor's office and must not be delegated to the Foreign Office. He suspected that the Foreign Office continued to be influenced by the 'Rapallo tradition', which Adenauer regarded as a threat to the existence of the Federal Republic; consequently, *Ostpolitik* must be kept under the direct control of the Chancellor. Secondly – and linked with his first conviction – he thought that a sucessful *Ostpolitik* was possible and meaningful only if it was achieved through direct contact with Moscow, supported by consultations in the Western alliance.

After the experiments of the years between 1963 and 1969, this assessment exerted renewed influence on the government of Willy Brandt, although in a very different way. Adenauer was bound to regard Foreign Minister Schröder's policy of 'bypassing' Moscow, pursued with the recommendation and support of the United States government, as inappropriate. The policy involved determined efforts to develop contacts with those members of the eastern bloc who were striving for greater independence from the Soviet hegemonic power; the Kremlin was to be made to realize that the Soviet Zone (as the German Democratic Republic was then commonly called) was an anachronism which was isolated on all sides. Moreover, Adenauer was not convinced by the new Chancellor's demand, at the beginning of the liberal Erhard era, that the question of German reunification should become a central theme of world politics again. He was far from certain that such conduct was appropriate to the needs of the changed international situation. Erhard's 'sense of mission',[11] his commitment to a 'Europe of free and equal peoples' and to a formula which also kept open Atlantic (trade) options, was not supported by Adenauer. His own proposals for foreign policy were based on a very different view of man and understanding of politics, which made the differences between the old and new chancellors very obvious. In these two men 'Machiavelli' and 'Cobden' came face to face, the tradition of continental *raison d'état* versus the legacy of the Anglo-Saxon idea of civilization, a realistic versus an idealistic view of foreign and international politics. The positions adopted by Adenauer and Erhard could be reconciled only with great difficulty.

When younger West Germans began to take renewed interest in German reunification during the 1960s, the situation offered serious risks as well as welcome opportunities. On 17 July 1965, Franz Josef Strauss was moved to issue a warning:[12] 'Anyone who steals a glance to the right in the direction of restoration of the national state inevitably ends up slipping to the left.' Nevertheless, there was considerable pressure on the CDU to raise the issue again, in order to combat the danger of an emergent 'rightist' and/or 'leftist' nationalism and to keep pace with the renaissance of nationalism throughout Europe during the 1960s. Adenauer never underestimated the significance of the difficulties faced by the Germans, but he favoured the pursuit of other options in an effort to solve them.

His comments in Bonn, which caused a sensation that has become difficult to understand with the passage of time, should be judged against the background of his constant preoccupations in foreign policy. Germany had been a focal point for the pressures of European and world politics for 300 years and, in Adenauer's view, could not be expected simply to relinquish all claims to foreign policy even during a liberal era when domestic concerns had been of primary importance. He believed that it was essential for West German politicians to respond with particular care to events in international politics which would have important consequences for Germany and the Federal Republic.[13]

II

As we have seen, from a *military perspective* Adenauer assumed that the Soviet Union currently had no plans to provoke war; the maintenance of peace, associated with the attractive magical formulas of disarmament and *détente*, were now more helpful to their unchanged political and military objectives in Germany and Europe. Admittedly, the attitude of Moscow might change comparatively quickly. In the event of a European or German conflagration, the old Chancellor had become convinced that American protection would no longer be adequate if there was a need for an immediate and unhesitating response. He still wanted to remain under the global American nuclear umbrella, though he believed that it could no longer provide full protection for the Federal Republic of Germany. The strategic planning of the McNamara period had led the Americans to propose a cease-fire in the event of conflict; although such conduct might indeed serve to prevent the escalation of conflict on a worldwide scale, in certain circumstances it might threaten the very existence of the Bonn republic. Consequently, Adenauer considered it necessary for the Federal Republic to move closer to France. He believed that the French national interest would force de Gaulle to resort to arms in such circumstances, to prevent France from losing its West German *glacis* and to stop the Russians reaching the French border.

This calculation was one of the reasons which drove Adenauer to choose the bilateral option of close association (*Zweierverbindung*) with France. However, he had no desire to reject or offend the Americans. Like other leading politicians in Bonn, he was aware that the final, definitive choice between Washington and Paris must be avoided in view of the great tradition of Franco-American relations. In fact, he did not even regard it as a matter for debate. For Adenauer, whose major preoccupation remained security, the chief problem concerned the protection of the Federal Republic by the French *force de frappe* and German participation in the production of the most modern means of deterrence. He was anxious to raise this question, carefully but firmly, in discussions with de Gaulle. But as the President told Adenauer in the Elysée Palace in November 1964,[14] the precondition for French help and accommodation in this field was that West Germany should decide on the closest co-operation with France; the Federal Republic must loosen its ties with the United States in favour of a 'western political organization' in Europe which would *de facto* be led by France.

There were other fundamental differences in the political outlook of the two statesmen. Unlike de Gaulle during the 1960s, Adenauer did not consider the United States to be more dangerous than Russia. The French President believed that the United States was the more powerful force and was moving towards expansion by indirect means. To use his own *bon mot*, 'whisky' would ultimately prove to be stronger than 'vodka'. However, it was precisely because Adenauer judged the Russian danger to be so great that he wanted to use French strength to counteract the instability in Europe which was the result of American policy. To a certain degree, de Gaulle was to take the place of Dulles. There was a major problem in Adenauer's desired solution, concerning the need for West Germany to have an influence on French policy and some kind of share in the *force de frappe*. Despite his proposals for a political union, de Gaulle treated this issue with great reserve. It must remain an open question what would have happened if the option demanded by the French President as a precondition for the solution of this problem had been adopted by the Federal Republic.

From an *ideological perspective*, Adenauer did not share de Gaulle's view of the Soviet Union as 'eternal Russia', as an historic great power and as a traditional member of the European Concert. Instead, he saw the USSR as the combination of the traditional expansionism of Russia with the new, revolutionary idea of communism. He frequently described the Soviet Union as Soviet Russia, probably out of familiarity with the terminology in use after the end of the First World War; the wording encapsulated the two tendencies – ideology and power politics – which in his view determined the conduct of Moscow in foreign policy. Adenauer was convinced of the need for resolute and even aggressive opposition to the communist ideology behind *détente* and peaceful coexistence. In this respect the spirit of the times was against him; public opinion was fascinated by the formula of 'change through rapprochement', largely convinced by the theory of convergence and swayed by euphoric expectations of *détente*. Of course, there were reactions against all these prevailing tendencies of the age, but Konrad Adenauer generally appeared to be swimming against the tide in international politics. For a time, the hope was simply to avoid being swept away altogether by the powerful waves of the new era. For the rest, Adenauer's comments in Bonn may even have intensified the tendency towards détente politics although he was not among its adherents. In any event, his repeated calls for a watchful ideological opposition to the communist challenge were not as successful as he had hoped. The '*limes* of the West'[15] had obviously become fragile. The old statesman always feared that the Soviet Union would try to gain influence over Western Europe using peaceful and ideological methods and was convinced that resolute efforts must be made to counteract the danger. The trend of the times did not support such views.

From the *political and diplomatic perspective*, in contrast, Adenauer believed that the Soviet Union faced crises in domestic and external affairs which would present certain possibilities for the Federal Republic of Germany. There might well be an opportunity to open direct discussions with Moscow, although not of course in the form of a German solo effort. In November 1966, in a conversation with the president of the *Bundestag*, Gerstenmaier, Adenauer spoke of the need for a new, major West German effort to reach gradual agreement with the Soviet Union. Since the Soviet Union was caught in a pincer grip between the United States and Red China, an attempt to reach agreement must sooner or later have some prospects of success. In his view, de Gaulle was the Western statesman who could provide most help to Bonn;[16] the French President's high standing in Moscow, and his attitude to the German Question, made him eminently suitable for the task.

Adenauer was thus convinced that the Federal Republic must make common cause with France as the precondition for a new West German initiative towards the Soviet Union. Such a union also seemed desirable in order to prevent the four victorious powers of the Second World War from drawing too close together as a result of *détente*. In particular, a Franco-Russian rapprochement might have disastrous consequences for the Federal Republic. Nevertheless, the historic phase of *détente*, which did not succeed the Cold War but constituted another element of it, appeared to him to offer a better chance to negotiate with the Russians, since Moscow was more convinced of the need to achieve peace and stability on its western flank in view of the threats it was facing elsewhere. Signs of Soviet willingness to adopt this approach had been visible since the 1950s. It had now been greatly increased by Sino-Soviet border disputes, by the demands for national independence from the European satellites of the Soviet Union (though Adenauer was less impressed by these than other Western statesmen) and by the evidence of the economic difficulties faced by the Soviet Union in providing supplies for its people. At the end of 1963, for example, Adenauer had suggested that these factors should be used in a very different way from that currently adopted by the West.

Since Moscow was facing a number of dangers and threats, Adenauer thought it feasible to negotiate with the Soviets from a position of relative strength based on a strong defensive military position and an aggressive ideological stance. However, at that time the United States was pursuing a different approach to foreign policy; following Soviet restraint in South-East Asia and Central Europe, the USA was attempting to reach agreement with the Soviet Union on nuclear issues. In Adenauer's opinion, this course was against the interests of Germany and Europe. He therefore opted for Franco-German bilateralism, though remaining aware of the differences between his own conception of foreign policy and that of de Gaulle. According to his analysis, the necessary strength which was a precondition for his *Ostpolitik* could only be acquired by forging closer links between the two states on either side of the Rhine. Furthermore, such a *Zweierunion* was desirable because it would make an arrangement between Russia and France impossible. Adenauer never ceased to fear this particular variation in European politics; following the unsuccessful Bonn summit between de Gaulle and Erhard in July 1964, after which the French President complained to Adenauer that he had 'remained a virgin',[17] he saw it as a distinct possibility for a time. Moreover, an *entente* between Paris and Bonn would also prevent a new 'Rapallo'. Though no one in a responsible position in the Federal Republic officially had any desire for such an outcome, the prospect continued to alarm Adenauer as a potential policy as well as an historical memory.

In conclusion, it should be emphasized that Adenauer's eccentric comments about the Soviet Union at the Bonn party conference should not be taken at face value, but placed in the context of an overall analysis of his thinking. His ideas continued to be based on a firm determination to guard the security and freedom of the Federal Republic and, in the long term, to secure a solution of the national question. Yet Adenauer was prepared to adjust the policies which were designed to achieve these ends, in order to meet the changing conditions of international politics. The former Chancellor believed that the situation in the 1960s offered the possibility of negotiations with the USSR about the problems which divided the two states. An initiative of this kind should be linked to certain conditions, based on military, ideological and political-diplomatic factors. In this sense, Adenauer's concern with questions of *Ostpolitik* and policy towards the USSR was of long standing. Since the Soviet Union now seemed prepared to make some concessions to keep the peace, it could be regarded as peace-loving and an attempt could be made to open discussions with it.

Even after his resignation as chancellor, Konrad Adenauer followed the proposals outlined here. In the prevailing polycentrism of the Federal Republic, his was one of a number of foreign policy concepts under discussion. Adenauer was constantly plagued by doubts about the stability of his fellow countrymen as a result of the desperate upheavals of recent German history. His anxieties persuaded him to contemplate a close alliance between the Federal Republic and de Gaulle's France; thus ideologically immunized, West Germany could then take the calculated risk of negotiating with the Kremlin.

Events did not develop as Adenauer would have wished. On the domestic scene, the Atlanticists were stronger than their Gaullist opponents; and in the sphere of foreign policy, de Gaulle's insistent demands for a decision actually had a negative effect for a time, leading the Federal Republic to move closer to the United States. Moreover, as soon as Adenauer had issued his central demands for an aggressive ideological approach to communism as the condition for a normalization of relations between Bonn and Moscow, he observed signs of a re-emergence of the old *horror immobilitatis* in Germany. This historic intellectual burden of the Germans, adding to the geopolitical problems of their country's exposed central position, undermined much of his argument that the Federal Republic should negotiate with the Soviets from a position of strength. For Adenauer, willingness to accept the Soviet desire for peace was linked with the ability to oppose Moscow resolutely, and even uncompromisingly, wherever necessary.

For a time, policies other than those Adenauer had proposed were adopted, though the fundamental convictions which underlay his foreign policy concept were not disproved. However, the remarks on the 'peaceable Soviet Union' made by the former Chancellor in his famous Bonn speech certainly worked to the advantage of the 'peace note' issued by the Federal Republic of Germany on 25 March 1966, some four days later. All in all, an analysis of Adenauer's foreign policy ideas and of his suggestions for *Ostpolitik* in the period 1963–7 tends to confirm the comment made by Heinrich Krone in his diary about 'the sensation of the party conference: the Soviets are peaceable':[18]

I really believe that the Old Man sees world politics in this way and that we Germans should take notice of it; but equally true is his thesis, and he regards it as equally true, that the Soviets, communism, is the enemy, the world enemy.

NOTES

1 Speech to the 14th CDU Party Conference in Bonn, in *Konrad Adenauer, Reden 1917–1967. Eine Auswahl*, ed. H.-P. Schwarz (Stuttgart: 1975), p. 482. The emphases in the quotation are the author's. The article here was written as part of an investigation of the history of the Federal Republic of Germany, 'Von Erhard zur Grossen Koalition 1963–1969'. The author has therefore restricted himself largely to providing the sources for direct quotations. Beyond the relevant literature on the subject, the article is based on materials available for study in the Konrad-Adenauer-Stiftung, the Ludwig-Erhard-Stiftung, the 'Archiv Kurt Georg Kiesinger' and the Friedrich-Naumann-Stiftung, to which institutions the author is deeply grateful.

2 *Die politischen Reden des Fürsten Bismarck. Historisch-kritische Gesamtausgabe*, Vol. 3: *1866–1868*, H. Kohl (Stuttgart: 1892), p. 27 (speech of 3 February 1866 in the Prussian Chamber of Deputies).

3 Krone, H., 'Deutschland – Frankreich – Amerika. Unsere Sicherheit im Bündnis', *Politische Meinung* 11 (1966), p. 25.

4 Minutes of proceedings of the CDU executive committee, 16 February 1966.

5 '23 März 1966: Aus der Rede des Vorsitzenden der CDU, Adenauer, auf dem 14 Bundesparteitag der CDU in Bonn', *Dokumente der Deutschlandpolitik*, IV, Vol. 12:

1 Januar bis 30 November 1966, Erster Halbband (1.1.-31.5.1966), ed. G. Oberländer, published by the Bundesministerium fir innerdeutsche Beziehungen. Academic advisers: K. D. Bracher and H.-A. Jacobsen (Frankfurt-am-Main: 1981), p. 380.

6   '23 März 1966', *Dokumente der Deutschlandpolitik*, p. 380.

7   Tern, J., 'Adenauers friedfertige Sowjetunion', *Frankfurter Allgemeine Zeitung*, 25 March 1966, in: *Frankfurter Allgemeine Zeitung für Deutschland. Die Erste Seite. Das politische Weltgeschehen auf der Titelseite der Frankfurter Allgemeinen Zeitung vom 1 November 1949 bis zum 17 November 1980*, Vol. I: *1949–1967* (Frankfurt-am-Main: 1981).

8   Tern, 'Adenauers friedfertige Sowjetunion'.

9   Minutes of proceedings in the CDU federal executive committee, 21 March 1966.

10   Schwarz, H.-P., 'Adenauers Ostpolitik', in W. F. Hanrieder and H. Rühle (eds), *Im Spannungsfeld der Weltpolitik: 30 Jahre deutsche Aussenpolitik (1949–1979)* (Stuttgart: 1981), p. 217. See also Schwarz, H.-P., 'Adenauer und Russland', in *Im Dienste Deutschlands und des Rechts. Festschrift für Wilhelm G.Grewe zum 70 Geburtstag am 16 Oktober 1981*, ed. F. J. Kroneck and T. Opperman (Baden-Baden: 1981), p. 365 ff.

11   Lahr, R., *Zeuge von Fall und Aufstieg. Private Briefe 1934–1974* (Hamburg: 1981), p. 385.

12   Mimeographed manuscript (seen in 'Nachlass Erhard') of the paper given by the chairman of the CSU at the party conference of the Christian Social Union in Nuremberg on 17 July 1965.

13   Very important here is Hildebrand, K., 'Staatskunst oder Systemzwang? Die "deutsche Frage" als Problem der Weltpolitik', *Historische Zeitschrift* 228 (1979), p. 644.

14   Memorandum of the Adenauer–de Gaulle discussion of 1 November 1964 in the 'Archiv Kurt Georg Kiesinger'. See also Adenauer's comment to the newspaper *Die Welt* of 3 January 1966, quoted in *Archiv der Gegenwart* of 2–3 January 1966, p. 12271: 'Q.: "Will you recommend to Charles de Gaulle the *European atomic force* advocated by Franz Josef Strauss?" A[denauer]: "But of course! I have already asked de Gaulle whether other powers might be able to take part. He said then: As soon as we have a political union and a political leadership suitable for making decisions."'

15   Röpke, W., *Die deutsche Frage* (Erlenbach: 1945), pp. 248–9.

16   Memorandum of Gerstenmaier on his conversation with Adenauer on 25 November 1966 in the 'Archiv Kurt Georg Kiesinger'.

17   Lahr, *Zeuge*, p. 403.

18   'Neue Dokumente zur Deutschland–und Ostpolitik Adenauers', ed. and introduced by Klaus Gotto, in R. Morsey and K. Repgen (eds), *Adenauerstudien III* (Mainz: 1974), pp. 188–9.

10

The German Eigenweg:

On the problem of normality in the modern history of Germany and Europe

I

Any attempt to investigate the exceptional and the normal features in the history of nations, and to analyse the details of each by means of historical comparison, is difficult. Nevertheless, the results can be fruitful.[1] Even a cursory examination of European history reveals that non-academic and non-scientific interests have always accompanied the search for specific national characteristics and influenced their assessment as normal, exemplary, or undesirable. In English Whig historiography, for example, the history of England itself became the obligatory yardstick by which all history was to be judged, from the starting-point of the year 1215. A similar drive for recognition can be observed in writings on tsarist Russia, the global rival of Great Britain during the nineteenth century; its claims for universal significance dated from the days of Ivan IV in the sixteenth century and the claim to the direct legacy of Rome. A different but related vision was the missionary idea of the 'American way of life', fed by an uncompromising internal drive for felicity (the 'pursuit of happiness'), which issued from 'God's own country' and influenced its attempt 'to make the world safe for democracy'. In the twentieth century, this vision has been opposed chiefly by the communist ideology of the USSR with its proposals for a classless society and total obedience to Soviet dictatorship.

The existence of these and other exceptional features of peoples and nations is itself an element of historical normality. Many other nations have had their own vision. Hence, the Spaniards in the Age of Catholicity and Counter-Reformation, and the French in the name of civilization and revolution, have both attempted to provide the justification for their own hegemonic demands and their own special role. In this way, they have tried to follow their unique national *Sonderwege* (lit.: 'special paths') through history, and have often left a trail of bloodshed behind them in the process.

234

Visions of this kind initially involved the belief of a people that they were different from and better than their neighbours in some way. Time and time again, these positive self-images have been subjected to bitter attack. First, criticisms have come from other states. For example, for centuries the Spaniards were impugned by the '*leyenda negra*' and isolated from the rest of Europe. Then the nations which followed the Spaniards as hegemonic powers, particularly the French and Germans, were attacked with a barrage of almost interchangeable terms of abuse; thus, they were accused of being power-crazed, immoral, avaricious and loose-living. These accusations came mainly from England/Britain, the world power which was anxious to maintain the balance of power in Europe. In all of them, unfavourable comparisons were drawn with the ostensibly exemplary normality of Britain itself.

Secondly, negative self-images arose within national frontiers, encouraged by feelings of national incompleteness, backwardness, or defectiveness of some kind. Until the middle of the nineteenth century, some Englishmen were deeply critical of the insular path the country had chosen in the modern era; in particular, they attacked the free trade system, the British *Sonderweg*. Even in France, there was no universal conviction that the country stood 'à la tête de la civilisation'. French philosophers of the Enlightenment such as Voltaire and Diderot had an obvious 'feeling of inferiority towards England and Prussia..., which continued through the entire nineteenth century and finally reached its peak at the end of the century'; at that time, 'inside and outside France there was a widespread feeling that France and the Latin peoples as a whole were sunk in deep decadence and could no longer stand their ground against the competition of the "modern" and "Germanic" nations, namely the USA, Britain and, especially, Germany'.[2]

The idea of the *Sonderweg* has thus existed throughout European history, whether in a positive or a negative sense, whether as a verdict from abroad or as a self-reproach from within. As a phenomenon observed throughout Western Europe, it is associated with the simple fact that peoples, states and nations are wont to seek their own, individual and special route through history.

All these comments also relate to the course of German development. Moreover, since the Second World War the concept of the *Sonderweg* has been indissolubly linked with a historic catastrophe of almost unimaginable proportions. Investigation of the German *Sonderweg* has thus been inseparable from the impact of the Third Reich and has been particularly concerned with the causes, emergence and development of the Hitler dictatorship. Until 1945, the *Sonderweg* formula had actually possessed a distinctly positive meaning in Germany, though it was used in a negative and critical way in the Anglo-Saxon world. Since that date, however, the term has constantly been used to refer to the totalitarian rule of Hitler. At the heart of the matter, to simplify the issue as much as possible, lies the following question: was there a German *Sonderweg* which led – more or less directly – to the Third Reich?

For a long period, German history was understandably dominated by the question of how the terrible experience of the Third Reich *came about*. Yet, gradually, German and international history is moving out of the long shadows of the Third Reich; it is thus able to observe the details of that period in a comparative perspective and take account of recent experience and knowledge. Consequently, another question is gradually acquiring the importance it deserves – one which is concerned with 'how it actually *was*'. The epochs of German history *before* Hitler are gradually being freed from the stigma that they were only, or mainly, a prelude to the 'German catastrophe'. Alongside this development, there is a growing understanding that it is intellectually unsatisfactory to measure and judge German development against either French or British history when these are accorded exemplary or model status. There is an increasing awareness that the quality of a period should be judged at least in part by what it contains, rather than by what has developed from it in the past, or may develop in the future.

The German *Sonderweg* formula, in its positive and negative sense, can valuably be examined against this historical background. In the following article, important periods of the German *Eigenweg* (lit.: 'own path') in modern European history will be examined and its special characteristics described. Particular attention will be paid to the phenomenon that Karl Dietrich Bracher once described as the *Sonderbewusstsein* (lit.: 'special consciousness')[3] of the Germans concerning their existence between the worlds of west and east. To a certain extent, these factors in German history created a precondition for 'enabling' the Nazi seizure of power to take place, without necessarily or even probably being causally involved with the development and the consequences of the *Sonderfall Hitler*. An investigation of the normal and the exceptional elements in German history requires study of the emergence of German nationalism, which appeared in a European setting only in the nineteenth century. This nationalism, permanently dissatisfied with its achievements and attempting to obtain more, provides an important insight into specific characteristics of German development.

The nationalism of the Germans was kindled into fervent life by the challenge of Napoleon, but restrained again, at least temporarily, by the Congress of Vienna at the end of the Napoleonic Wars. The establishment of the German Confederation did much to satisfy the European interests of the great powers. A small-scale balance of forces in central Europe, its solution to the German problem, served to encourage the larger balance of the powers which guaranteed external peace to the continent and the world. Germany was to exist as it had since the Peace of Westphalia, 'formless by nature, [lying]... on the point of intersection of the pressure lines of great continental politics'.[4] However strong its territories were individually, the whole was weak; this very weakness promoted the desired stability of Europe and helped to guarantee the peace. In short: the disorganization of Germany was closely linked with the orderliness of the *Staatensystem*.

However, the French Revolution had introduced a new era. Where the Age of Absolutism had been characterized by a mechanistic *Staatensystem* and dominated by the dynastic principle, the national state movement (together with the struggle for a constitutional state) became the dominant feature of the modern age. National movements emerged everywhere in Europe except Britain and France, where their goals had long been achieved, and the shock waves of nationalism crashed powerfully against the barriers erected by the Congress of Vienna. Like the east and south, the German centre of Europe was deeply affected by this profound historical trend. The route from cosmopolitanism to the nation-state, to use Meinecke's formula, was already beginning to emerge. From their limited territorial existence, the Germans were to awake into the national, totalitarian state of the modern age. As yet, however, Grillparzer's sombre prophecy that humanity would be followed first by nationality and then by bestiality lay only in the distant future.

During the revolution of 1848, it became clear that the demands of the Germans were exceptionally ambitious – and were to remain so for the next century. German patriots in 1848 wanted to achieve internal freedom and external power at one and the same time; they ignored the fact that the two demands could not easily be brought into harmony and could even be mutually exclusive – as had been the case in Britain, which tended to be regarded as a model by German liberals. The demands of the men of 1848 for the fulfilment of all their desires reveal something of the vision which has always accompanied the national history of the Germans. For genuine and serious reasons, the liberals tried to avoid having to decide between their two great demands; instead, they hoped to achieve *'la synthèse du disparate'*.[5]

In the 1848 revolution, the Germans who advocated the introduction of a parliamentary system and in some cases a measure of democratization were also demanding a Reich and a navy of a size unacceptable to Europe. In this single fact lie many of the reasons why the German endeavours of 1848–9 ended in failure. The acute difficulties faced by the Germans at a decisive moment in their history are only partly comparable with the problems faced in the creation of the Italian national state at the time. The Germans were forced to make the attempt to solve their national, imperial, constitutional and social questions *simultaneously*, since these had been raised together and with dangerous abruptness. In contrast, the English and the French had faced these problems consecutively, over a much longer and more manageable period of time. This peculiarity of German development has with justice been described as a 'tragic concurrence of the fundamental problems of recent history',[6] which has been decisive for its course.

In contrast, there was no 'French Question' on the other side of the Rhine because – to exaggerate – it had already been answered by Hugo Capet by the end of the tenth century. By the end of the Hundred Years War at the latest, despite its appalling internal condition, France had discovered a national feeling of solidarity, a sense of 'belonging together'. The work of Henri IV and of the great cardinals ultimately ensured that the French revolutionaries of the eighteenth and nineteenth centuries had no need to aim for the unity of the nation, which was already a fact in the form of 'eternal France'. The situation for the men of 1848 in Germany was very different.

The revolution of 1848 failed more because of this historical context than as a result of the attitude of Germany's European neighbours. The great powers did not oppose German strivings for national unity from the outset; indeed, they even regarded them as in tune with the spirit of the times, and therefore as normal. Britain and Russia, the two powers in control of the *Staatensystem*, grew hostile only when German demands for the future borders of the emerging nation became too ambitious. Public opinion in Britain was only dimly aware that the forces in Germany which were agitating for a parliamentary system and a measure of democratization were also responsible for making the most extensive and unreasonable territorial demands. This was a considerable factor in German and European history, which had significant influence in the future. Yet it remained difficult for the British, and later the Americans, to comprehend, until well into the twentieth century. British and American political culture was permeated by rationalist sentiments about the peaceful nature of democratic and republican governments. We have since learned only too well how questionable this liberal belief is, and what a decisive effect the Anglo-Saxon–German misunderstanding has had.

In 1870–1 the foundation of the *kleindeutsch* national state was accepted for very different reasons by Russia, France and Austria-Hungary, and was even welcomed by Great Britain. By the 1860s at the latest it had become obvious that the German Confederation was no longer capable of fulfilling its role of securing the peace and maintaining the political balance in Europe. It was therefore hardly surprising that the British, for example, were quickly persuaded of the merits of German national unity in Bismarck's state; such a development could be seen as of benefit to Britain's position as a world power, to 'British interests'. These would be enhanced by the stabilization of the insecure and brittle balance of power, and by the possibility of an end to the polarization of forces on the continent which had been visible since 1867, after the Luxemburg Crisis.

Disraeli's famous remark that the creation of the Reich was a 'German Revolution' of greater significance than the French Revolution of a hundred years before, and that England would be the real victim of it, should be seen mainly as the foreign policy onslaught of an opposition leader intent on replacing Gladstone's 'Great Ministry'. German unification had taken *kleindeutsch* form, and the new Reich did not construct a great navy nor assert any imperial ambitions overseas. Its creation could therefore be seen in a positive light in Britain and was at least not directly opposed by the rest of Europe. It remained to be seen whether the Reich Chancellor would maintain the policy of moderation he had surprisingly but convincingly demonstrated in 1866 and 1871.

Bismarck's achievement was that he established as much unity as was compatible with the international situation. The price was that parliamentarization in the British sense, though not in constitutional terms, was postponed. As a result of a policy of moderation and self-limitation, Bismarck gave the new Reich a function and a role in the European *Staatensystem*. Yet it remained doubtful whether Germany could survive in the future, since it was so dependent on the status quo. Its unique fate lay in the fact that it could not safely adopt the policies pursued by the other European states; it could not appear to be expansionist and imperialist. The new Reich had to be established 'against the spirit of the age'[7] in international affairs and foreign policy as well as in domestic and constitutional terms.

Despite the growing burden of these restrictions, Bismarck succeeded in establishing a high degree of normality in the relations of the Reich with foreign countries, in bilateral and multilateral relationships alike. In this way, he provided constant evidence of the function and importance of Germany in the European *Staatensystem*. His success was reflected in Germany's attitude to the great powers of Britain and Russia, but also in relations with Austria-Hungary and even with France, which improved significantly between 1880 and the middle of the decade.

In this historical sense, 'normality' means that the status quo of the *Staatensystem* was not truly threatened from any side – no more, but no less. It does not mean that there could be no wars or confrontations, but simply that no great power should be faced with a situation in which its very existence was placed in jeopardy. War remained quite compatible with the normality of the system as it was then understood; and in the Reich, fears that it would inevitably lead to a reversal of the process of national unification were never silenced. When the 'War in Sight' crisis of 1875 was ended by Britain and Russia in favour of France and against the interests of Germany, the indirect guarantees given for the new Reich tended to be overlooked, although it was clear that Europe had rejected further expansion by Germany rather than the continued existence of the Reich itself.

In a complex international situation, some Germans came to understand that the Reich was to be allowed to exist, but not to grow. The insight caused many difficulties for the Germans and made many fear for the survival of the Reich. The situation fostered the German *Sonderbewusstsein*, which was rooted in the country's endangered central position. Indeed, it even strengthened German conviction that the particular form of constitutionalism created as the result of foreign policy pressures was the correct and necessary solution for the Reich. Nevertheless, these widespread beliefs did not destroy the normality with which Bismarck's Germany, despite acute conflicts, lived with its neighbours.

The Germans never lost the feeling that they were living with the threat of total destruction. Yet from the vantage point of Britain and Russia, Germany belonged to the European *Staatensystem* as a great power and even as an arbitrating factor. The British attitude was based on a fundamental illusion which sprang from the special character of British development and culture and from the country's own *Sonderweg* in European history; it held that the economic and social modernization of Germany would gradually lead to reasonable political conditions – that is, to a genuine parliamentary system on the British model. The fact that progress may lead to ends which are far from parliamentary or peaceful dawned on the British, and then the Americans, only dimly and belatedly.

In the 1890s, the Reich finally prepared to pursue *Weltpolitik*, to do what the other nations of Europe had long been doing. The decision was the prelude to its downfall, since it overtaxed the country's domestic and its external resources alike. In some ways, Germany was to suffer the fate which had befallen every land power which had striven for hegemony, from the Spaniards to the French, from Charles V through Philip II and Ludwig XIV to Napoleon I. However, the situation also reflected the specifically Prussian legacy. As a result of its unique geographical and intellectual traditions since 1756, the 'country in the middle' had become accustomed to living with the threat of destruction (*'Gift in der Tasche'*[8]). Nevertheless, during the prelude to the First World War, German policy remained largely within the confines of what was recognizable and familiar in European history. From the turn of the century, as a result of German efforts to establish a *Weltpolitik*, a powerful navy and a hegemonic position, tolerable bilateral relations between the states were replaced by the antagonism of conflicting power groups. The situation was by no means irreversible; the development of Anglo-German relations after 1909, though ultimately ending in failure, makes this clear. The situation was exacerbated by the development of an ideological element in a hostility based initially on power politics. The growth of ideology had a corrosive effect on relations between states, as political 'foe images' were constructed throughout Europe. Even this development was not a new departure in European history, though in this case it had profound consequences for the political climate.

In all the great states of Europe in 1914, the existing *Staatensystem* continued to be largely accepted. None of the great powers went to war in August 1914 for the sake of ambitious territorial conquests and offensive political objectives. Instead, the 'European security dilemma'9 had a greater effect on the disastrous outcome of the July crisis, because it transfixed every state involved and paralysed the conduct of the statesmen. The danger was fatally intensified by underlying social and cultural phenomena; these included a visible weariness with peace and a fateful desire for the resolution of problems through adventure and war.

The course of the First World War demonstrated that the Reich was too powerful to be compatible with the balance of forces in Europe. But it was also not strong enough and – especially as regards the Wilhelmine leadership – not capable enough to assert itself as the hegemonic power of Europe and organize the continent accordingly. This was a German dilemma which can be detected from the nineteenth century until the present day. As far as the competing models of international politics are concerned, the establishment of hegemony or the balance of power, the First World War failed to produce any definitive solution.

The survival of the Reich as a national state after 1918 can be regarded as an almost miraculous feature of German history. As often before in Prussian and German history, its survival was closely connected to the constraints of the international situation. Despite the armed conflict of states and peoples, the British at least remained generally convinced that Germany should be retained as a factor in the European balance of power after the war. They were determined to smash Prussian militarism ruthlessly, but not to dismember or entirely disarm the German national state. Many plans were forged against Germany as the war progressed, and many agreements were made against it by the superior enemy coalition. However, the October Revolution of 1917 in Russia made an enormous impact on the thinking of the western powers, and especially on Britain. British statesmen in particular were eager to sustain the existence of a Germany which was ideologically immune to bolshevism; the Reich should be economically able to make a contribution to the reconstruction of Europe and politically able to act as a balancing force against revolutionary Russia and even perhaps against France, which still had some hegemonic ambitions of its own.

In the British view, the German national state was to be punished severely but also treated justly. Its future function in Europe should be to act as a balancing factor among the powers; indeed, it might even find a genuine role in a new order of the peoples as the task of reconstruction of the Old World got under way. After the war, the Political Intelligence Department of the Foreign Office, mockingly described as the 'Ministry of all the Talents', was strongly influenced by men such as Edwyn Bevan, George Sanders and Alfred Zimmern. Deeply concerned with the German problem and the peace issue, they accepted the destruction of Prussian militarism as a fact and were convinced 'that in Germany there has been a genuine change of heart and a sincere response to democracy'.[10] In view of such expectations, British support for the continued existence of the German national state is understandable. Admittedly, the struggle to win the soul of Germany for the west, of which Austen Chamberlain spoke in the 1920s, was not yet decided. The war had helped to strengthen the German *Sonderbewusstsein*, the conviction that Germany occupied a unique and precarious position in the middle which was combined with the intellectual legacy of the German *Eigenweg*. Moreover, all the German political parties echoed the demand for a revision of the frontiers of the Reich after Versailles. They nevertheless sought to achieve this objective in very different ways, reflecting considerable differences in outlook and in approach to practical politics.

Revisionist goals offered a starting-point for Nazi agitation, behind which lay expansionism and racism of a wholly different quality. A historically critical development then began to emerge. The development had a decisive effect on the path taken by Germany from parliamentary democracy, which guaranteed the constitutional state and freedom, through authoritarian cabinets which placed restrictions on freedom and remained committed to the constitutional state, to totalitarian dictatorship which utterly destroyed both freedom and the constitutional state. What was conventional provided the foil for what was entirely abnormal; almost imperceptibly, the *Eigenweg* led to the *Sonderfall Hitler*; general elements in German history ended in the singular atrocity of Nazi dictatorship in a process simultaneously seamless and abrupt, so that the change was not rapidly recognized or adequately opposed.

The situation in the international sphere was very similar. For various reasons, the Vatican and Moscow established contacts with the Third Reich. Britain and France adopted a policy of appeasement, attempting to avoid the inhumanity of war by means of a policy of 'normality'. In fact, normality was not possible; the western democracies failed to recognize that such a policy could not be achieved with totalitarian opponents, or even to admit it to themselves. When the danger posed by Nazi dictatorship could no longer be ignored, past omissions and mistakes could be rectified only with the greatest difficulty. At the outset, it had been difficult to separate the traditions of German history from the uniqueness of Hitler; after a certain time, the attempt itself seemed largely irrelevant.

Viewed from this perspective, the failure of the conservative German Resistance round Beck, Goerdeler and von Hassell becomes easy to understand. Towards the end of the Second World War the western nations, like the peoples of the occupied territories, were not prepared to distinguish between conventional hegemony and Nazi racial domination. The fate of Nazi Germany fulfilled Schiller's dictum, based on the conviction of an identity between world history and the Last Judgement, that there was 'for despotically ruled states... no salvation except in destruction'.[11]

Before the outbreak of war in 1939, the British longing for a lost normality had prevented a true understanding of the objectives of Hitler. At the international and national level alike, extremes can succeed only when the established powers promote, permit, or fail to prevent them. From 1933 the quality of normality, in the sense of what was compatible with and customary in European history, was lost in Hitler's Germany. It was the *Sonderfall Hitler* which destroyed it, and with it the German national state.

II

If 'the European thing about Europe'[12] lies in the existence of its nations, then the pursuit of its *Eigenweg* by each nation and state is part of the normality of Europe. The observation was true in the Middle Ages, when every little *patria* struggled to set itself apart from its neighbours, and it has continued to be true until the present day. The conviction can be seen, for example, in Charles de Gaulle's advocacy of '*la France éternelle*'; for the general, and for others as well, France's special role in Europe was absolutely beyond question. The pursuit of the national *Eigenweg* has been a persistent feature of European history.

However, there have also been specific and unique features of German development which have been described in outline in this chapter. From a very early stage, these features separated the country with uncertain borders from the developing 'European prototype of national monarchy'.[13] The specifically German characteristics produced both assets and adversity, both power and impotence, both grandeur and misery in German history; they were so intermingled and interrelated that they could be distinguished and separated only with the greatest difficulty. The establishment of an earlier Reich under the Carolingians had actually obstructed the development of a unified national state on the territory of the empire, a task achieved by Germany's western neighbours, England and France, since the thirteenth century. During the Middle Ages, then, a dynamic particularism in internal affairs began to develop in response to the sheer external size of the Reich. In this respect the Hohenstaufen period, 'only an epoch of restoration despite all its splendour... in adhering to the old royal and imperial thinking, [established] that alienation in Europe, that German non-conformity with the ideas valid at the time, which have burdened German history until today'.[14] From the beginning of the thirteenth century Germany was an object of European politics, a focus for the other powers as they developed as national states and began their long struggle for dominance. The inhabitants of the German territories, however, began to realize the significance of their position only in the course of the seventeenth century.

There were some features of German history which accelerated the tendency to a German *Sonderweg*, whilst others had an opposite or entirely different effect. The tendencies encouraging the *Sonderweg* were intensified at the close of the fifteenth century and the beginning of the sixteenth, as the German Middle Ages came to an end and a new era began. There was no national dynasty at the head of Germany of the kind which had become customary elsewhere in Europe. Though the Habsburgs had ruled continuously since 1483, they were based at the periphery of the German lands and, in comparison with other European states, were scarcely able to exert a centralizing and national influence. Even the outwardly impressive supranational traditions of the Reich and its constitution, as well as the European and global interests of the Habsburgs, had their disadvantages. These ensured that the Germans simultaneously possessed both more and less than their neighbours: they had a universal and supranational imperial house, but no national and integrating monarchy; a comprehensive claim to empire, but no kind of German foreign policy and army organization.

Beyond state and politics, though inseparably linked with them, the Reformation and its aftermath had major consequences for Germany. First, confessional conflicts caused a violent and implacable struggle in which the adherents of the Pope and of Luther waged religious wars in a divided Germany. Partly because they remained fundamentally unresolved, these conflicts left behind deep traces of confessional and ideological passion. With characteristic changes and fractures, these passions continued through to influence German party politics in modern times.

There was a second unique feature of German development which became apparent after the Religious Peace of Augsburg in 1555. Once again, it produced both benefits and disadvantages, making an accurate assessment of its significance extremely difficult to achieve. Within the numerous territories of the Reich there was religious unity, 'confessional "purity"'; but in the Reich as a whole, there was a 'juxtaposition of Catholic and Evangelical enjoying equal rights, therefore confessional parity'.[15] There was no national religion of the kind which had developed in England, France, or Spain, historically bloody but politically definitive. To a certain extent the Old Reich could act as bulwark of freedom, simultaneously keeping apart and uniting the confessions. This synthesis of irreconcilable elements can even be regarded as a typical feature of the Old Reich and a historic peculiarity of the Germans; one of its characteristic features was that it allowed the avoidance of any binding decision of principle.

Particularly in the Lutheran territorial states, there developed a close connection between church and politics which greatly affected German history. Here, too, there were differences from the development of the western theory and practice of the state. The effect on the theory of German public administration and policing was considerable, and came to be seen as a disadvantage only comparatively recently. In modern England and France, the aim of the state was restricted more and more to 'civil government', which was regarded as the essential framework and precondition for civic and private life. In Germany, by contrast, the administration retained the tasks of religious policing which had been transferred to it through the Reformation. The sovereign princes protected the spiritual rule, a fact which greatly influenced all state activities as well as the development of 'good policy'. The state government and administration in Germany gained 'a quasi-religious dignity'.[16] In western Europe, the theory of the state was directed predominantly 'outward', towards secular maxims of power politics and *'raison d'être'*. At the centre of German thinking, in contrast, were 'inward' concepts, developed from the symbiosis of church and politics, of Lutheranism and princely state, of the welfare and education of the subjects. Germany was dominated by thinking of this kind until the nineteenth century.

The obligation of the authorities to care for their subjects encouraged the specific German tradition of successful reform. Long seen as a model, it was in direct contrast to the experiences of other states and peoples. Successful reforms did much to cut the ground from beneath revolution. The controversial question of whether seventeenth-century Germany was open to the influence of the Enlightenment or was isolated from this western development is difficult to answer, though it may tell us a great deal about the development of early modern Germany between the poles of the normal and the exceptional. However, in the following century German development was clearly different from that of western Europe. The revolution that Whigs and Tories introduced in England in 1688–9, and which Turgot in France sought to forestall by means of reforms from above during the last thirty years of the eighteenth century, appeared superfluous in Germany. There, enlightened absolutism was a 'sufferable evil';[17] it was a special feature, a 'special form of Enlightenment',[18] which continued as a historical force from the time of Frederick the Great and Joseph II into the nineteenth century. The 'German theory of the state' contained both advantages and disadvantages, progress and submissiveness together. It received perhaps its most illuminating commentary in 1824, in Goethe's remark to Eckermann:[19] 'Revolutions are quite impossible the moment governments are constantly just and constantly alert, so that they meet them halfway with appropriate improvements and do not resist for such a long time that necessary changes are forced through from below.'

Despite these features of German intellectual and political development, certain facts should not be forgotten. They are valid irrespective of whether Germany had blossomed economically and culturally in the sixteenth century before 1616–48, or whether it remained 'backward'[20] in the seventeenth and even eighteenth centuries after the Thirty Years War; they apply irrespective of whether the population was affected by the western European Enlightenment or was moulded by the reforms imposed by the authorities. Whatever the truth of these arguments, the Reich was not a state with natural and fixed frontiers like its European neighbours. It can be regarded as a 'monster' which was both imposing and provincial. As Samuel Pufendorf has commented, the Reich was an anarchy in the form of a monarchy, a political structure composed of parts which did not make a whole. Compared with France or England, it seemed entirely without inner logic.

The insecurity of its borders and the exposed central position of the country encouraged a special German unrest (*deutsche Unruhe*). Intellectually, this was manifested in the great upheavals of the Reformation, particularly in their Lutheran form, and in the influential and rigorous Idealist philosophy which rejected all sympathy with western notions of 'common sense'. However, the intermediate intellectual and geographical position of the Germans, between the religious positions of the confessions and the power political goals of the European states, made their avoidance of a final decision almost inevitable and encouraged their tendency to choose the neutrality of the 'third way' as necessary for their survival. This intermediate position between the fronts was given concrete political form in the shape of the Prussian state.

At the beginning of the Swedish War in 1630, after King Gustavus Adolphus had landed in Pomerania, Elector Georg Wilhelm of Brandenburg applied to the Swedish king to be allowed to remain neutral in the conflict between Protestants and Catholics. In response, he discovered that:[21] 'Such a thing is nothing more than noisy *Quisquiliae* which the wind picks up and blows away.' *'Tertium non datur'* was the abrupt answer of Gustavus Adolphus to his brother-in-law, anxious for neutrality in unfortified Berlin. But the elector's successors remained loyal to the goal of neutrality, in principle, until the era of Bismarck and often pursued it in problematic and critical situations, such as the Crimean War. Neutrality, it was believed, made possible the existence of Prussia between the fronts. To sustain it required disproportionate military 'strength'; according to the 'paternal exhortation' of the Great Elector to his son in the Political Testament of 19 May 1667, such strength was better than all 'alliances'.[22] A ruthless and unscrupulous readiness to switch allies, described by Richelieu as a 'political malaria',[23] might also be necessary for the survival of small states. In addition there was a desire to maintain the internal stability of society, which was assisted by Prussia's policy of toleration in an attempt to conciliate religious tensions. The development of pietism and the growth of an intense spiritual religious belief were a response to this policy and also encouraged its implementation. Within the spiritual framework which had been established, the neutral authoritarian state also concerned itself with social justice.

The Prussian *'Rationalstaat'* was an experiment. To protect its independence and survive as a state, it must avoid conflicts wherever possible and evade unequivocal decisions. However, these principles left a legacy which Prussia's European neighbours, observing the diplomatic and belligerent conduct of Prussia, could easily regard as a fraud. It must have appeared to outsiders that, instead of making clear decisions on a large scale and cultivating 'conventional wisdom' in everyday affairs, Prussia and Germany had adopted the opposite policy. Alongside the principle of neutrality and the refusal to take up unequivocal positions, there developed an unpredictable quality of decisiveness which occasionally led the Germans to break out of their restricted situation and seek new borders. The tradition of the German yearning for neutrality embraced a desire to choose neither north nor south, neither Luther nor the Pope, neither Habsburg nor France, neither Russia nor England, neither capitalism nor communism, neither America nor the Soviet Union; the yearning, which is deeply rooted in history, was regarded by the Prussians and later by the Germans as necessary in order to maintain their autonomy. From time to time the Germans became aware that their overstretched, constricted state in the middle of Europe could achieve its chosen 'third way' and its political neutrality only by developing an adequate level of strength. But as time passed, efforts to protect the Prussian-German state and to safeguard its existence as a great power appeared increasingly artificial as it sought to hold the balance between the powerful empires of west and east, between the British Empire, the United States and Russian *imperium*. Bismarck struggled in masterly fashion to prevent the loss of this position, but without conclusive success. In contrast, Wilhelmine statesmen attempted to protect Germany with offensive and warlike means, and in this way came within a hair's breadth of destroying it altogether. Stresemann then fought for its existence with the economic strength still at the disposal of the Reich. At the same time, calls were made from very different points on the political spectrum for an end to the tightrope walk between two spheres in favour of dependence on either the west or the east. The German struggle for autonomy ultimately abandoned the *Eigenweg* and culminated in the *Sonderfall Hitler*. The dictator's policies can even be regarded as an utterly unjustified attempt to secure the independence of the Germans against capitalist democracy and communist dictatorship, by means of global and racial domination whose biological foundation transcended the historical dimension. In the process Hitler gambled with the existence of the German national state and, probably for the foreseeable future, destroyed it.

It is time to return to the special features which have marked the course of German history. The characteristic desire to avoid definitive decision lives on today, in the demand for the withdrawal of both parts of Germany from the confrontation between East and West. Moreover, like the 'German unrest' which continued to alarm Konrad Adenauer until his death, it is connected with the history of the Germans, with the upheavals in their intellectual development, with the lack of natural frontiers and the existence of their traditional middle position. Since 1648, the obvious danger to the Germans themselves has repeatedly led them to threaten others. Yet it must be said that none of the factors mentioned here, no special features or idiosyncrasies of the Germans, created a German *Sonderweg* which inevitably led either indirectly or directly to Hitler. The true special case in German history, however, was the dictator.

Hitler's seizure of power and his policies were, of course, only possible against the background of German and European history. But in the interwar years of our century, all the parliamentary states of Europe came under pressure from the 'totalitarian temptation' (J.-F. Revel) from left and right. At that time, the political tide was moving powerfully to the right. The states of Europe faced the problem, each according to its own political traditions and special features; some remained committed to parliamentary government whilst others became authoritarian or fascist. The Weimar Republic inclined towards the second category, towards an authoritarian or fascist solution of its crises. Here it was affected by its historical development, by the anti-parliamentarianism which had become associated with the foreign policy *Sonderbewusstsein* of the Germans, and by sociohistorical factors connected with the dominance of certain groups in society. Weimar Germany thus tended towards the solution adopted in Salazar's Portugal, the Greece of Metaxas, Franco's Spain and, some years before, the Italy of Mussolini.

The role of the East Elbian 'military-agrarian'[24] complex in this process remains an open question. There remains a controversy about whether the conduct of its representatives was comparable with that of other pre-industrial classes in Europe, or whether they had long maintained an excessive degree of power. Nevertheless, it is clear that the representatives of the older ruling classes made a considerable contribution to 'enabling' the establishment of Nazi dictatorship in 1933, though without being able to foresee the consequences for themselves, for Germany, for Europe and for the world. The emergence of the *Sonderfall Hitler* and of Auschwitz were not foreseeably or compellingly connected with the enabling of the Nazi dictatorship. Instead, they had comparable European and non-European parallels; they were, *horribile dictu*, an element of the political normality of the time and exerted a clear though transient attraction even in the western democracies. The totalitarian development of the Hitler dictatorship, despite its German and European forerunners, was more firmly rooted in the ground of the twentieth century, which contemporaries were already describing as the 'age of tyrants'.[25] The 'crisis'[26] of the epoch has been comprehensively and forcefully described by Karl Dietrich Bracher.

As time passes and the historical context becomes more clearly visible, even the *Sonderfall Hitler* seems increasingly to be a more 'general' phenomenon. Khrushchev's secret speech to the twentieth congress of the Communist Party of the Soviet Union in 1956 revealed, so far as one can judge, that the perpetration of atrocities comparable with those of Hitler need not end in punishment but may result in success. This does not alter the important historical fact that Stalin's great victory in the Second World War, which cannot be separated from his crimes, saved the peoples of the Soviet Union from *foreign* slavery and enabled the USSR to become a world power, whilst Hitler's defeat – also inseparable from his crimes – ended in the *de facto* destruction of the German nation and delivered its population over to foreign rule of varying quality and duration.

It is important to emphasize that the fundamental difference between authoritarian or even fascist regimes on one side, and Hitler's Nazism on the other, lay in the racial policy of the Third Reich. The policy was manifested in the murder of between 4 and 6 million Jews, in the destruction of 'life unworthy of life' (translator's note: the murder of mentally sick and handicapped Germans) and in the attempts at racial breeding conducted by the Nazi dictatorship. This was the dreadful reality of the *Sonderfall Hitler* as it developed between 1933 and 1945. There was no causal relationship, at least no seamless link, between these atrocities and the German *Eigenweg* in European history or the foreign policy *Sonderbewusstsein* which had developed since 1648 and been intensified in the nineteenth century. The normality of European history is defined and determined by the differences in its nations. The act of tracing the German *Eigenweg*, therefore, may improve the ability of the historian to recognize the great historical exception of German history, to locate the links which bound it to the past in domestic and foreign policy, but also to understand and describe the 'fracture' of 1933 with reference to the totalitarianism of Nazi rule and racial policy.

The racial policies of the Third Reich have rightly been regarded as its unique outrage and atrocity. This fact explains – or has been used to explain – the consequences of the war as they were applied to Germany. With the passage of time, however, we have learned that Hitler's Reich was not defeated with the sole aim of liberating, controlling and educating the Germans. Soviet war aims, and to an extent those of the

British and Americans, were much more ambitious. Independently of German conduct, Stalin in particular pursued his own wide-ranging goals in foreign policy; with the toleration of the United States, he was able to shape postwar developments very much to his advantage. The former allies persistently deferred their ideological differences and conducted and shaped their conduct to take account of the 'brown' past of the Germans, which they regarded as unique. Behaviour of this kind was influenced by the fact that Hitler had already broken abruptly with all measures of principle and of practical utility. Moreover, Stalin, who was pursuing similar goals and using comparable methods, had beaten back the assault of the Nazis in the 'Great Patriotic War' and was one of the victors of the conflict. He ordained silence. The Germans, however, continued to be burdened with the legacy of the *Sonderfall Hitler*. As Joachim von Merkatz, summing up the bitter experiences German conservatives had suffered in an age of totalitarian dictatorship, remarked on 6 May 1969 during a debate on the statute of limitations: 'The rest remains unresolved, for ourselves and for the next two or three hundred years.'

The comparison with the destructive quality of Soviet communism and the recognition of the hostile kinship between Hitler and Stalin, between Nazism and communism, leads to other insights. In ways Ranke never imagined, ideas which come to rule possess a compelling power which can help to explain the 'unexpected baseness of human nature'[27] revealed in racial and class dictatorships. Totalitarianism, genocide and mass expulsions belong to the signature of the twentieth century,[28] though they are also, thank God, not its norm and not its normality.

In summary, a number of points should be made.

There can be no question of a German *Sonderweg* into the Third Reich in the sense of any historic necessity or inevitability in German development.

National *Eigenwege* are the European element in the history of the continent. In this sense the German *Eigenweg*, despite its damaging exceptional features such as the anti-parliamentarianism of the Imperial Reich and the Weimar Republic, remains part of the many facets of the normality of European history.

Further research is required to explain the Hitler dictatorship. There may be fruitful comparisons with Stalinist Russia and with aspects of contemporary history, such as the emergence of 'Stone Age' communism in Cambodia. Work of this kind will certainly produce shocking academic findings and evidence of appalling human experiences. Yet the investigation and description of these matters must not be shirked, for 'appalling truths lose their power as soon as they are recognized'.[29]

It must be emphasized that the author has no intention of minimizing the horrors of the Nazi past. Though the totalitarianism of the twentieth century could easily be regarded as a dreadful symbol of the futility of human existence, it need not be accepted blindly as destiny. The Sisyphean labours of the historian can help to liberate us from such fatalism: the historian's search for truthfulness combats the rule of terror; the historian's awareness of the transitory and unfree nature of man is a precondition for transcendence and freedom; and the historian's academic approach, even in the certainty of failure, provides a sense of individual and general purpose. Unlike the men of antiquity, today we can even 'imagine Sisyphus as a happy man'.[30] To put the matter in a more liberal and less existential way, more practically and less philosophically: *comprehensive* diagnosis is the precondition for successful therapy.

Between 1955 and 1963 the integration of the Federal Republic into the West was achieved with apparent success, though today it appears somewhat more fragile. The situation, which is rooted in history, was reflected, for example, in the political antagonism between Konrad Adenauer and Gustav Heinemann. It remains to be seen whether such developments will reduce the meaning of the German *Eigenweg* to its historical significance and strip it of its political topicality.

NOTES

1 Parts of this essay are based on my ten theses on the theme: 'Deutscher Sonderweg und "Drittes Reich". Betrachtungen über ein Grundproblem der deutschen und europäischen Geschichte im 19. und 20. Jahrhundert', published in *Die national-sozialistische Machtergreifung*, ed. W. Michalka (Paderborn/Munich/Vienna/Zurich: 1984), pp. 386–94.

2 Nolte, E., in *Deutscher Sonderweg – Mythos oder Realität?* (Kolloquien des Instituts für Zeitgeschichte) (Munich/Vienna: 1982), p. 36.

3 Bracher, K. D., in *Deutscher Sonderweg*, p. 46.

4 Dehio, L., *Gleichgewicht oder Hegemonie. Betrachtungen über ein Grundproblem der neueren Staatengeschichte* (Krefeld: 1948), p. 189.

5 Rivière, J., *L'Allemand. Souvenirs et Réflexions d'un Prisonnier de Guerre* (Paris: 1918), p. 189.

6 Nipperdey, T., in *Deutscher Sonderweg*, p. 24.

7 Ziekursch, J., *Politische Geschichte des neuen deutschen Kaiserreiches*, Vol. I: *Die Reichsgründung* (Frankfurt-am-Main: 1925), p. 3.

8 Mehring, F., *Zur preussischen Geschichte vom Mittelalter bis Jena* (Berlin: 1930), p. 201.

9 Hildebrand, K., 'The crisis of July 1914', see p. [/] in this book.

10 Headlam-Morley, Sir James, *A Memoir of the Paris Peace Conference 1919*, ed. A. Headlam-Morley, R. Bryant, A. Cienciala (London: 1972), p. XXVII (introduction by Agnes Headlam-Morley).

11 Schiller, F. von, 'Universalhistorische übersicht der vornehmsten an den Kreuzzügen teilnehmenden Nationen, ihrer Staatsverfassung, Religionsbegriffe, Sitten, Beschäftigungen, Meinungen und Gebräuche', in F. von Schiller, *Erzählungen und Kleine Historische Schriften. Schillers Sämtliche Werke (Tempel-Klassiker)*, Vol. 9 (Leipzig: undated), p. 348.

12 Heimpel, H., 'Entwurf einer deutschen Geschichte. Eine Rektoratsrede', in H. Heimpel,

Der Mensch in seiner Gegenwart. Acht Historische Essais (Göttingen: 2nd extended edn), p. 173.

13   Lutz, H., *Die deutsche Nation zu Beginn der Neuzeit. Fragen nach dem Gelingen und Scheitern deutscher Einheit im 16. Jahrhundert* (Munich: 1982) (Schriften des Historischen Kollegs. Herausgegeben von der Stiftung Historisches Kolleg. Vorträge 1), p. 5.

14   Heimpel, 'Entwurf', p. 189.

15   Maier, H., 'Die Konfessionen', in H. Maier, *Die Deutschen und die Freiheit. Perspektiven der Nachkriegszeit* (Stuttgart: 1985), p. 91.

16   Maier, H., 'Wohlfahrtsstaat und Sozialstaat', in Maier, *Die Deutschen und die Freiheit*, p. 88.

17   'The Declaration of Independence, 4 July 1776', in *Documents of American History*, ed. H. S. Commager (New York: 3rd edn, 1947), p. 100: 'Prudence, indeed, will dictate that Governments long established should not be changed for light and transient causes; and accordingly all experience has shown, that mankind are more disposed to suffer, while *evils* are *sufferable*, than to right themselves by abolishing the forms to which they are accustomed' (author's emphases).

18   Stadelmann, R., 'Deutschland und die westeuropäischen Revolutionen', in R. Stadelmann, *Deutschland und Westeuropa. Drei Aufsätze* (Schloss Laupheim: 1948), p. 26.

19   *Gespräche mit Goethe in den letzten Jahren seines Lebens. Von Johann Peter Eckermann*. Mit einer Einleitung, erläuternden Anmerkungen und Register herausgegeben von Ludwig Geiger (Lepizig: undated), p. 441.

20   Vierhaus, R., 'Die Ideologie eines deutschen Weges der politischen und sozialen Entwicklung', in *Die Krise des Liberalismus zwischen den Weltkriegen*. Mit Beiträgen von Y. Arieli, H.-P. Bahrdt *et al.*, ed. R. von Thadden (Göttingen: 1978), p. 104.

21   Mann, G., *Wallenstein* (Frankfurt-am-Main: 1971), p. 740.

22   'Politisches Testament des Grossen Kurfürsten (1667)', in *Politische Testamente der Hohenzollern*, ed. R. Dietrich (Munich: 1981), p. 66.

23   Netzer, J., 'Des Heiligen Römischen Reiches Streusandbüchse', in *Preussen. Porträt einer politischen Kultur*, ed. H.-J. Netzer (Munich: 1968), p. 31.

24   Stern, F., 'Prussia', in D. Spring (ed.), *European Landed Elites in the Nineteenth Century* (Baltimore, Md/London: 1977), p. 46.

25   Halévy, E., *L'ère des Tyrannies* (Paris: 1938).

26   Bracher, K. D., *Europa in der Krise. Innengeschichte und Weltpolitik seit 1917* (Frankfurt-am-Main/Berlin/Vienna: 1979).

27   Röpke, W., *Die Deutsche Frage* (Erlenbach-Zurich: 3rd revised and extended edn, 1948), p. 72.

28   Hillgruber, A., *Der Zusammenbruch im Osten 1944/45 als Problem der deutschen Nationalgeschichte und der europäischen Geschichte* (Opladen: 1985), *passim*, esp. p. 30.

29   Camus, A., 'Der Mythos von Sisyphus', in A. Camus, *Das Frühwerk* (Düsseldorf: 1967), p. 517.

30   Camus, 'Der Mythos von Sisyphus', p. 519.

Index

DATE DUE

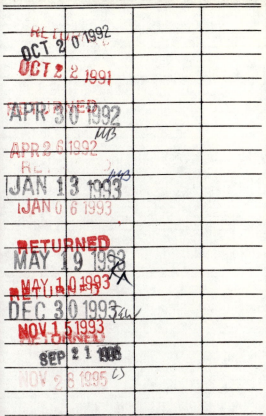